CCNP Implementing Secured Converged WANs (ISCW 642-825) Lab Portfolio

BI 3496250 6

David Kotfila

Joshua Moorhouse

Ross Wolfson, CCIE No. 16696

LFAAM

BIRMINGHAM CITY
UNIVERSITY
DISCARDED

Cisco Press

800 East 96th Street

Indianapolis, Indiana 46240 USA

T.I.C.
MILLENNIUM
POINT
LEARNING CENTRE

CCNP Implementing Secured Converged WANs (ISCW 642-825) Lab Portfolio

David Kotfila · Joshua Moorhouse · Ross Wolfson

Copyright© 2008 Cisco Systems, Inc.

Published by:
Cisco Press
800 East 96th Street
Indianapolis, IN 46240 USA

All rights reserved. No part of this book may be reproduced or transmitted in any form or by any means, electronic or mechanical, including photocopying, recording, or by any information storage and retrieval system, without written permission from the publisher, except for the inclusion of brief quotations in a review.

Printed in the United States of America

First Printing March 2008

Library of Congress Cataloging-in-Publication Data

Kotfila, David A.

  CCNP implementing secured converged WANs (ISCW 642-825) lab portfolio / David Kotfila, Joshua Moorhouse, Ross Wolfson.

   p. cm.

  ISBN 978-1-58713-215-5 (pbk.)

  1. Extranets (Computer networks) 2. Wide area networks (Computer networks) I. Moorhouse, Joshua D. II. Wolfson, Ross G. III. Title.

  TK5105.875.E87K64 2008

  005.8—dc22

2008006745

ISBN-13: 978-158713-215-5

ISBN-10: 1-58713-215-X

Warning and Disclaimer

This book provides labs consistent with the Cisco Networking Academy CCNP Implementing Secured Converged WANs (ISCW 642-825) curriculum. Every effort has been made to make this book as complete and as accurate as possible, but no warranty or fitness is implied.

The information is provided on an "as is" basis. The authors, Cisco Press, and Cisco Systems, Inc., shall have neither liability nor responsibility to any person or entity with respect to any loss or damages arising from the information contained in this book or from the use of the discs or programs that may accompany it.

The opinions expressed in this book belong to the authors and are not necessarily those of Cisco Systems, Inc.

Publisher
Paul Boger

Associate Publisher
Dave Dusthimer

Cisco Representative
Anthony Wolfenden

Cisco Press Program Manager
Jeff Brady

Executive Editor
Mary Beth Ray

Managing Editor
Patrick Kanouse

Senior Development Editor
Christopher Cleveland

Senior Project Editor
Tonya Simpson

Copy Editor
Sheri Cain

Technical Editors
Tommy Crawford,
Geovany González

Editorial Assistant
Vanessa Evans

Book Designer
Louisa Adair

Proofreader
Paula Lowell

Trademark Acknowledgments

All terms mentioned in this book that are known to be trademarks or service marks have been appropriately capitalized. Cisco Press or Cisco Systems, Inc., cannot attest to the accuracy of this information. Use of a term in this book should not be regarded as affecting the validity of any trademark or service mark.

Corporate and Government Sales

The publisher offers excellent discounts on this book when ordered in quantity for bulk purchases or special sales, which may include electronic versions and/or custom covers and content particular to your business, training goals, marketing focus, and branding interests. For more information, please contact: **U.S. Corporate and Government Sales**   1-800-382-3419
corpsales@pearsontechgroup.com

For sales outside the United States, please contact: **International Sales**
international@pearsoned.com

Feedback Information

At Cisco Press, our goal is to create in-depth technical books of the highest quality and value. Each book is crafted with care and precision, undergoing rigorous development that involves the unique expertise of members from the professional technical community.

Readers' feedback is a natural continuation of this process. If you have any comments regarding how we could improve the quality of this book, or otherwise alter it to better suit your needs, you can contact us through e-mail at feedback@ciscopress.com. Please make sure to include the book title and ISBN in your message.

We greatly appreciate your assistance.

This book is part of the Cisco Networking Academy® series from Cisco Press. The products in this series support and complement the Cisco Networking Academy curriculum. If you are using this book outside the Networking Academy, then you are not preparing with a Cisco trained and authorized Networking Academy provider.

For more information on the Cisco Networking Academy or to locate a Networking Academy, please visit www.cisco.com/edu.

Americas Headquarters
Cisco Systems, Inc.
170 West Tasman Drive
San Jose, CA 95134-1706
USA
www.cisco.com
Tel: 408 526-4000
800 553-NETS (6387)
Fax: 408 527-0883

Asia Pacific Headquarters
Cisco Systems, Inc.
168 Robinson Road
#28-01 Capital Tower
Singapore 068912
www.cisco.com
Tel: +65 6317 7777
Fax: +65 6317 7799

Europe Headquarters
Cisco Systems International BV
Haarlerbergpark
Haarlerbergweg 13-19
1101 CH Amsterdam
The Netherlands
www-europe.cisco.com
Tel: +31 0 800 020 0791
Fax: +31 0 20 357 1100

Cisco has more than 200 offices worldwide. Addresses, phone numbers, and fax numbers are listed on the Cisco Website at **www.cisco.com/go/offices**.

©2007 Cisco Systems, Inc. All rights reserved. CCVP, the Cisco logo, and the Cisco Square Bridge logo are trademarks of Cisco Systems, Inc.; Changing the Way We Work, Live, Play, and Learn is a service mark of Cisco Systems, Inc.; and Access Registrar, Aironet, BPX, Catalyst, CCDA, CCDP, CCIE, CCIP, CCNA, CCNP, CCSP, Cisco, the Cisco Certified Internetwork Expert logo, Cisco IOS, Cisco Press, Cisco Systems, Cisco Systems Capital, the Cisco Systems logo, Cisco Unity, Enterprise/Solver, EtherChannel, EtherFast, EtherSwitch, Fast Step, Follow Me Browsing, FormShare, GigaDrive, GigaStack, HomeLink, Internet Quotient, IOS, IP/TV, iQ Expertise, the iQ logo, iQ Net Readiness Scorecard, iQuick Study, LightStream, Linksys, MeetingPlace, MGX, Networking Academy, Network Registrar, Packet, PIX, ProConnect, RateMUX, ScriptShare, SlideCast, SMARTnet, StackWise, The Fastest Way to Increase Your Internet Quotient, and TransPath are registered trademarks of Cisco Systems, Inc. and/or its affiliates in the United States and certain other countries.

All other trademarks mentioned in this document or Website are the property of their respective owners. The use of the word partner does not imply a partnership relationship between Cisco and any other company. (0609R)

About the Authors

David Kotfila, CCNP, CCAI, is the director of the Cisco Academy at Rensselaer Polytechnic Institute (RPI) in Troy, New York. Under his direction, 350 students have received their CCNA, 150 students have received their CCNP, and 8 students have obtained their CCIE. David is a consultant for Cisco, working as a member of the CCNP assessment group. His team at RPI has authored the four new CCNP lab books for the Academy program. David has served on the National Advisory Council for the Academy program for four years. Previously, he was the senior training manager at PSINet, a Tier 1 global ISP. When David is not staring at his beautiful wife, Kate, or talking with his two wonderful children, Chris and Charis, he likes to kayak, hike in the mountains, and lift weights.

Joshua Moorhouse, CCNP, recently graduated from Rensselaer Polytechnic Institute (RPI) with a B.S. in computer science, where he also worked as a teaching assistant in the Cisco Academy. He currently works as a network engineer at Factset Research Systems in Norwalk, Connecticut. Josh enjoys spending time with his wife Laura, his family, and friends.

Ross Wolfson, CCIE No. 16696, recently graduated from Rensselaer Polytechnic Institute (RPI) with a B.S. in computer science. He currently works as a network engineer at Factset Research Systems. Ross enjoys spending time with his friends, running, and biking.

About the Technical Reviewers

Tommy Crawford is the manager of network engineering and architecture for a publicly traded company within the entertainment industry. Prior to his current position, Tommy consulted as a lead network engineer in charge of designing, implementing, and troubleshooting complex IP network infrastructures for many Fortune 500 companies and Internet service providers (ISP). Tommy holds his CCAI certification, and he has developed course work and taught CCNA, CCNP, and network security courses for Westwood College, Denver North Campus, in Denver, Colorado.

Geovany González is an electrical engineer with a B.S. from the National University of Colombia in Medellín, Colombia, South America. He obtained networking certifications in different areas, such as quality of service; routing and switching; LAN and WAN design; network security; operational systems, such as Linux and Windows; and voice and telephony over IP. Geovany is a Cisco IP telephony specialist and the author of a technical course used for several service providers to train their engineers. Geovany's professional experience has focused on education and consulting, including working as an instructor at the National University in Colombia and as an academic manager at Cisco Networking Academy Program for Colombia and Ecuador, South America. Geovany has also worked as an international Cisco Systems instructor working for a Cisco Learning Solutions Partner. Currently, Geovany is the Latin American representative for the Network Development Group. His enthusiasm for education and technical expertise have enabled him to play a key role in the promotion of NetLab+, which is a remote lab appliance for information-technology training, both in Latin American and throughout the world.

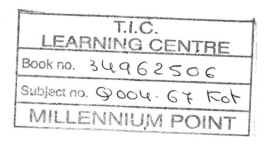

T.I.C.
LEARNING CENTRE
Book no. 34962506
Subject no. 004.6ϟ Kot
MILLENNIUM POINT

Dedications

To my wife, Kate—my love, my life. For 33 years, you have been my very heart and soul. I love you, honey.

—David Kotfila

To my parents, who taught me focus and dedication and showed me faith, hope, and love. To my siblings, Sandra and Peter, with whom I have found camaraderie, fun, and laughter for many years.

—Joshua Moorhouse

I dedicate this book to my mom Joanne, my dad George, and my brother Todd.

—Ross Wolfson

Acknowledgments

David Kotfila: Every teacher lives for highly motivated students who love a challenge. It has been both a privilege and FUN to work with Josh Moorhouse and Ross Wolfson, my coauthors. Their tireless efforts to produce these labs deserve high praise.

Many, many thanks to Mary Beth Ray and Chris Cleveland of Cisco Press. I had some health issues and some overcommitment issues that made me a difficult author to work with. Both Mary Beth and Chris deserve sainthood status for their patience.

Jeremy Creech was the manager of the lab-authoring process. Jeremy brought years of classroom experience and an encyclopedic knowledge of the technology to this project. Jeremy's hands-on approach is the model for what a technical manager should be.

Many thanks to Geovany González of NDG, NetLab+. Geovany was tireless in his efforts to make these labs technically more accurate. Thanks also to Tommy Crawford for his careful reading and editing of the text.

Joshua Moorhouse: David Kotfila and Chris Price deserve high praise for their tireless work in pushing our Cisco Networking Academy to reach for the stars. Ross Wolfson has been fantastic to work with in developing practical ways to teach networking concepts.

It was a pleasure to work with the production teams at Cisco Press, as well as in the Cisco Networking Academy Program, on this project. Finally, many thanks to the folks at NDG for helping us make these labs accessible to the broader Academy audience.

Ross Wolfson: I would like to thank David and Josh for being a great team to work with and write these labs. I would especially like to thank David, because without him, this book would have never happened.

Contents at a Glance

Contents

Icons Used in This Book

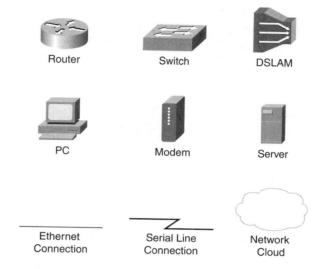

Router   Switch   DSLAM

PC   Modem   Server

Ethernet Connection   Serial Line Connection   Network Cloud

Command Syntax Conventions

The conventions used to present command syntax in this book are the same conventions used in the IOS Command Reference. The Command Reference describes these conventions as follows:

- **Boldface** indicates commands and keywords that are entered literally as shown. In actual configuration examples and output (not general command syntax), boldface indicates commands that are manually input by the user (such as a **show** command).

- *Italics* indicate arguments for which you supply actual values.

- Vertical bars (I) separate alternative, mutually exclusive elements.

- Square brackets [ ] indicate optional elements.

- Braces { } indicate a required choice.

- Braces within brackets [{ }] indicate a required choice within an optional element.

Introduction

My first motivation for writing this book was to serve the needs of CCNP instructors and students in the Cisco Networking Academy Program. For the past four years, I (David) have had the privilege of serving on the National Advisory Council for the Cisco Networking Academy, representing four-year colleges and universities. Also on the council are numerous two-year community colleges. Inevitably, at council meetings, we discussed both CCNP curriculum and labs. As I spoke with a number of my CCNP instructor peers, a common theme emerged. Instructors felt that the labs needed to be rewritten to be more comprehensive. In the past, labs have lacked complexity. When I realized that I was rewriting the Networking Academy CCNP labs, and that my peers were rewriting the same labs, the thought occurred to me that perhaps an engineering school, like RPI, was up to the task of writing these labs in a way that would better serve the needs of the community. It is not that the previous labs were inappropriate; rather, it's just that the Cisco Networking Academy has grown up. Having just celebrated its tenth birthday, folks in the Academy are ready for bigger challenges. I believe that these labs fill that role.

My second motivation for writing these labs was to help networking professionals who are trying to upgrade their skill set to the CCNP level. As a former hiring manager at a Tier 1 ISP, I have a strong sense of what an industry is looking for when it hires someone with CCNP credentials. Each year, numerous hiring managers from Fortune 500 companies contact me about hiring my students. I know the level of expertise they expect from a CCNP. These labs reflect the convictions those managers shared with me.

My third motivation for writing these labs was to see how much of a challenge university undergraduates could rise to if they were asked to do a big job. My coauthors, Josh Moorhouse and Ross Wolfson, were both undergraduates when they authored these labs. I gave them a huge task, and they responded with skill and grace. I firmly believe that we frequently do not ask enough of our students. If we ask for greatness, we will sometimes get it. If we settle for the normal, we are more assured of success, but we might miss the opportunity to see our students soar to new heights. With these labs, whether you are an instructor or student, I hope that your technical knowledge soars to new heights.

Goals and Methods

The most important goal of this book is to help you master the technologies necessary to configure secure WANs in a production environment. After all, what is the point of getting certified and getting that dream job or promotion if you cannot perform after you are there? Although it is impossible to simulate a network of 300 routers, we have added loopback interfaces to simulate additional networks and increase complexity.

This book's secondary goal is to help people pass the ISCW certification exam. For two years, I was on the CCNP Assessment authoring team. After all of those years of complaining, "What were they thinking when they put *that* question on the exam?," suddenly, the questions I was writing were the subject of someone else's complaint. I know how important it is, both to students and networking professionals, to pass certifications. Frequently, prestige, promotion, and money are all at stake. Although all the core configurations on the certification exam are covered in this book, no static document, like a book, can keep up with the dynamic way in which the certification exam is constantly upgraded.

Who Should Read This Book?

Cisco Networking Academy instructors and students who want a written copy of the electronic labs will find this book greatly useful. In addition to all the official labs that are part of the Networking Academy curriculum, additional Challenge and Troubleshooting labs have been added to test your mastery.

Networking professionals, either in formal classes or studying alone, will also find great value in this book. Knowing how expensive it can be to purchase your own lab equipment, as many labs as possible were written with only three routers. (To adequately cover some topics, four routers were necessary.) Final configurations were included with each lab so that even if you do not have all the equipment, you can walk through the configurations in your head.

What You Need to Configure the Labs

These labs were written on four Cisco 2811 routers using the IOS image c2800nm-advipservicesk9-mz.124-10.bin.

You should be able to configure the labs on any Cisco router that uses a 12.4 advanced IP services image of the IOS.

Classes and individuals using older Cisco devices (or less robust versions of the IOS) might find that some of the commands are different or not supported.

Example: It is not possible to run the 12.4 release of the advanced IP services IOS image on a Cisco 2600 Series router. It is possible to run this image on a Cisco 2600XM router if you upgrade the Flash and RAM and can obtain the new IOS image.

How This Book Is Organized

People preparing for the ISCW certification exam should work through this book cover-to-cover. Networking professionals needing help or a refresher on a particular topic can skip right to the area in which they need assistance.

The chapters cover the following topics:

- **Chapter 1, "Remote Network Connectivity Requirements"**—This chapter covers design concepts associated with remote-network connectivity. No labs are associated with it. However, there is a walk-through of the lab setup that is used throughout this book.

- **Chapter 2, "Teleworker Connectivity"**—The equipment necessary for configuring Point-to-Point Protocol over Ethernet (PPPoE) is physically different than the hardware necessary for the labs in the rest of this curriculum. Networking Academy students can simulate configuring this equipment using a Flash application, dsl_standalone. (Networking professionals can use a sample configuration if they do not have access to this application.)

- **Chapter 3, "IPsec VPNs"**—Cisco, in recognition of how difficult it is to stay current in all the protocols that a network engineer needs to stay current in, advocates the use of their GUI configuration tool, Security Device Manager (SDM). Like any GUI tool that creates configurations for you, it's easy to use. Also, like any GUI tool, times arise when the GUI produces unexpected configurations and/or side effects. Therefore, it is necessary to know how to use the GUI (to save time) and how to edit the command-line interface (CLI) for the times when the GUI produces problematic results. This chapter's labs teach you both skills.

- **Chapter 4, "Frame Mode MPLS Implementation"**—Multiprotocol Label Switching (MPLS) is a technology that is growing in its deployment. The basic lab for this chapter is possible using only three routers. MPLS virtual private networks (VPN) are also common. Although the certification requirement is only that you be able to describe (not configure) MPLS VPNs, we have included an optional lab on how MPLS VPNs are configured. Unfortunately, it is necessary to have five routers to really see what is occurring on the Internet servirce provider's (ISP) side of the configuration. If you do not have this much hardware, you can still get a reasonable understanding of how MPLS VPNs work by merely reading this lab.

- **Chapter 5, "Cisco Device Hardening"**—When the first routers rolled off the production line, the burning issue wasn't security. It was how we could get these devices to easily talk to each other using a variety of different protocols. Therefore, by default, many protocols and services were automatically turned on. As the Internet has matured, security has become a primary concern. Therefore, it is now necessary to turn off these services unless they are being used. Two tools help you accomplish this: One-Step Lockdown and AutoSecure. However, if you have a network situation that is somewhat unique—and who doesn't?—you also need to know the CLI commands so that you can edit the generic configurations that these tools generate. These labs teach you both.

- **Chapter 6, "Cisco IOS Threat Defense Features"**—The labs demonstrate how to configure Cisco IOS Firewall and Intrusion Prevention System (IPS). As with previous chapters, you see how to configure them using SDM and how to configure and edit them by using CLI.

- **Chapter 7, "Case Studies"**—The first case study requires you to configure IPsec and Frame-Mode MPLS using CLI. The second case study requires you to configure Cisco IOS Firewall and IPS. As in previous chapters, you are asked to do some of this using SDM and do other tasks using CLI.

NETLAB+ Compatibility

NDG has worked closely with the Cisco Networking Academy CCNP lab team to develop ISCW labs that are compatible with the installed base of NETLAB AE router pods. For current information on labs compatible with NETLAB+ go to http://www.netdevgroup.com/ae/labs.htm.

CHAPTER 1

Remote Network Connectivity Requirements

Lab 1-1: Lab Configuration Guide

Figure 1-1 and Figure 1-2 describe Ethernet and serial connectivity between the routers of your pod. These 13 connections (8 Ethernet and 5 serial) are used as the master template for most labs in the Implementing Secure Converged Wide-Area Networks (ISCW), Building Scalable Cisco Internetworks (BSCI), and Optimizing Converged Cisco Networks (ONT) curricula. These other courses are mentioned because some Academies use remote labs with fixed physical topologies.

Figure 1-1   Ethernet Connectivity Diagram

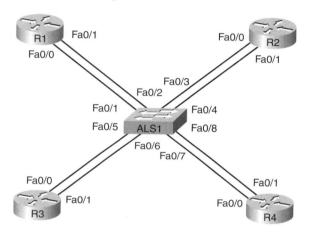

Figure 1-2   Serial Connectivity Diagram

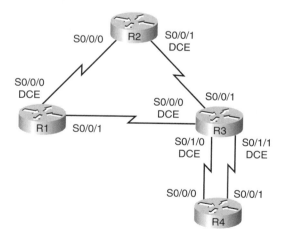

Notable exceptions to these diagrams do occur because of content covered in some of the courses, namely:

- ISCW Lab 4-2: Implementing MPLS VPNs, Challenge Lab
- BSCI Case Study 3: OSPF Five Routers
- BSCI Case Study 4: BGP
- ONT Lab 6-1: Configuring a WLAN Controller
- ONT Lab 6-2: Configuring a WLAN Controller via the Web Interface
- ONT Lab 6-3: Configuring a Wireless Client
- ONT Lab 6-4: Configuring WPA Security with Preshared Keys
- ONT Lab 6-5: Configuring LEAP

All labs assume that you have complete control over each of the devices in your pod, including access to the switch to configure VLANs and assign switchports as access ports on a VLAN or as trunk ports.

Although most labs do not make use of every single link, you should cable your pod according to the diagrams shown in Figure 1-1 and Figure 1-2 to avoid recabling your pod for each lab.

Teleworker Connectivity

The configuration of Point-to-Point Protocol over Ethernet (PPPoE) requires different hardware than any other lab in the ISCW curriculum. Because the configuration is relatively straightforward, it is not deemed worth the financial investment to purchase equipment simply for one lab. Students in the Academy program have access to an e-lab that runs in Flash. Network professionals can examine the sample configurations in this chapter. Both sets of individuals should be able to describe the following concepts:

- Remote connection topologies for teleworkers

- Cable technology

- How cable system technology is deployed

- DSL technology

- How ADSL is deployed

- How to configure the CPE as the PPPoE or PPPoA client

- How to troubleshoot broadband ADSL configurations

For further research on these topics, consult the following websites:

- **Enterprise Architectures.** http://www.cisco.com/en/US/netsol/ns517/networking_solutions_market_segment_solutions_home.html.

- **Security and VPN.** http://cisco.com/en/US/products/hw/vpndevc/index.html.

- **CableLabs.** http://www.cablelabs.com/.

- **Long Reach Ethernet & Digital Subscriber Line (xDSL).** http://www.cisco.com/web/psa/technologies/index.html.

- **RFC 2516, "A Method for Transmitting PPP over Ethernet (PPPoE)."** http://www.faqs.org/rfcs/rfc2516.html.

- **RFC 1483, "Multiprotocol Encapsulation over ATM Adaptation Layer 5."** http://www.faqs.org/rfcs/rfc1483.html.

Scenario: Configuring the CPE as the PPPoE Client

Figure 2-1 shows the topology for this scenario.

Figure 2-1   Customer PPPoE Network Diagram

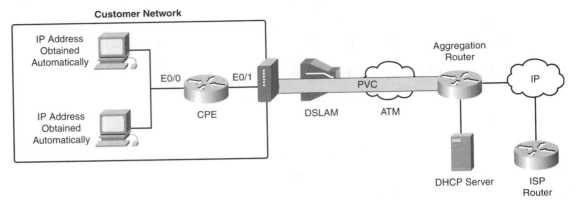

Step 1. Configure the Ethernet 0/1 interface of the Cisco router with a PPPoE client configuration, as follows:

```
interface Ethernet0/1
  no ip address
  pppoe enable
  pppoe-client dial-pool-number 1
```

Step 2. Create and configure the dialer interface of the Cisco router for PPPoE with a negotiated IP address and a maximum transmission unit (MTU) size of 1492, as follows:

```
interface Dialer0
  ip address negotiated
  ip mtu 1492
  encapsulation ppp
  dial pool 1
```

Step 3. Configure the Ethernet 0/0 interface of the router with port address translation (PAT) to allow the sharing of the dynamic public IP address of the dialer interface, as Figure 2-2 shows. Use the **ip tcp mss-adjust** command on this interface to limit TCP maximum segment size because of PPPoE overhead.

Figure 2-2   Additional PPPoE Configurations

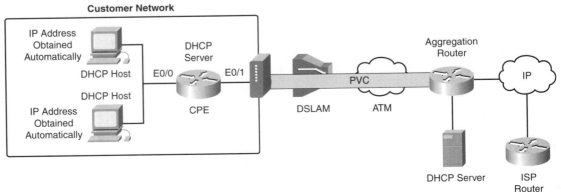

```
interface Ethernet0/0
  ip nat inside
  ip tcp mss-adjust 1452
!
interface Dialer0
  ip nat outside
!
ip nat inside source list for interface Dialer0 overload
access-list 101 permit ip 10.0.0.0 255.255.255.0 any
```

Step 4.   Configure the router to be the DHCP server for the end-user PCs that are behind the router:

```
ip dhcp pool MyPool
  network 10.0.0.0 255.255.255.0
  default router 10.0.0.1
```

Step 5.   Configure a static default route on the router:

```
ip route 0.0.0.0 0.0.0.0 Dialer0
```

Scenario: Configuring the CPE as the PPPoE Client over the ATM Interface

Figure 2-3 shows the topology for this scenario.

Figure 2-3   Customer PPPoE over ATM Interface Network Diagram

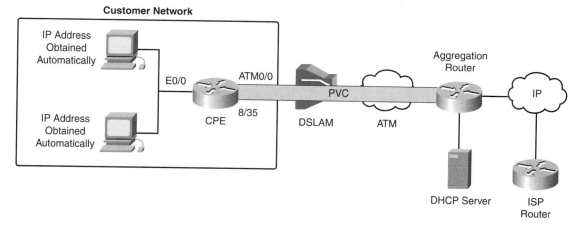

Step 1.   Configure the ATM interface (ADSL interface) of the router with an ATM permanent virtual circuit (PVC):

```
interface ATM0/0
  no ip address
  dsl operating-mode auto
  pvc 8/35
  pppoe-client dial-pool-number 1
```

The **pvc** command establishes the settings for the virtual circuit—virtual path identifier/virtual channel identifier (VPI/VCI)—on the router and must match the configuration by the service provider. ATM uses the VPI/VCI to identify an ATM virtual circuit.

Step 2.   Create and configure the dialer interface of the router for PPPoE with a negotiated IP address and an MTU size of 1492:

```
interface Dialer0
  ip address negotiated
  ip mtu 1492
  encapsulation ppp
  dialer pool 1
```

Step 3.   Configure the Ethernet 0/0 interface of the router with PAT to allow the sharing of the dynamic public IP address of the dialer interface, as shown in Figure 2-4. Also, configure the TCP maximum segment size.

Figure 2-4   Additional PPPoE over ATM Interface Configurations

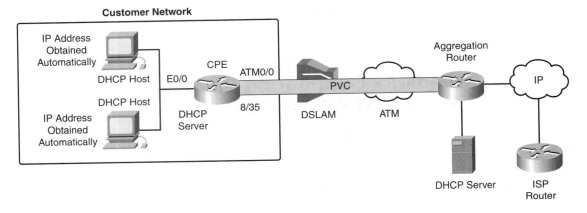

```
interface Ethernet0/0
  ip nat inside
  ip tcp mss-adjust 1452
!
interface Dialer0
  ip nat outside
!
ip nat inside source list 101 interface Dialer0 overload
access-list 101 permit ip 10.0.0.0 255.255.255.0 any
```

Step 4.   Configure the router to allow it to be the DHCP server for the end-user PCs behind it:

```
ip dhcp pool MyPool
  network 10.0.0.0 255.255.255.0
  default router 10.0.0.1
```

Step 5.   Configure a static default route on the router:

```
ip route 0.0.0.0 0.0.0.0 Dialer0
```

Lab 3-1: Configuring SDM on a Router (3.10.1)

The objectives of this lab are as follows:

- Prepare a router for access with Cisco Security Device Manager.

- Install SDM onto a PC.

- Install SDM onto a router through a Windows host.

Figure 3-1 illustrates the topology that is used for this lab.

Figure 3-1   Topology Diagram

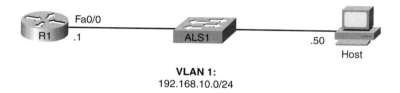

VLAN 1:
192.168.10.0/24

Scenario

In this lab, you use some basic commands to prepare a router for access via the Cisco Security Device Manager (SDM) to allow connectivity from the SDM to the router. You then install the SDM application locally on a host computer. Finally, you install SDM onto the flash memory of a router.

Step 1: Lab Preparation

Start this lab by erasing any previous configurations and reloading your devices. After your devices reload, set the appropriate hostnames. Ensure that the switch is set up so that both the router and host are in the same VLAN. By default, all ports on the switch are assigned to VLAN 1.

Step 2: Prepare the Router for SDM

The Cisco SDM application uses the virtual terminal lines and HTTP server to manipulate the configuration of the device. Because a user must log in to access or change the configuration, some basic commands must be issued to allow remote access.

These basic IOS commands are not SDM-specific. However, without these commands, SDM cannot access the router, and it will not work properly.

First, create a username and password on the router for SDM to use. This login needs to have a privilege level of 15 so that SDM can change the configuration settings on the router. Make the password argument of this command the last argument on the line, because everything after the password argument becomes part of the password. The username and password combination is used later when accessing the router:

```
R1(config)# username ciscosdm privilege 15 password 0 ciscosdm
```

HTTP access to the router must be configured for SDM to work. If your image supports it (you need to have an IOS image that supports crypto functionality), enable secure HTTPS access using the **ip http secure-server** command. Enabling HTTPS generates some output about RSA encryption keys. This is normal. Also, make sure the HTTP server uses the local database for authentication purposes:

```
R1(config)# ip http server
R1(config)# ip http secure-server
% Generating 1024 bit RSA keys, keys will be non-exportable...[OK]
*Jan 14 20:19:45.310: %SSH-5-ENABLED: SSH 1.99 has been enabled
*Jan 14 20:19:46.406: %PKI-4-NOAUTOSAVE: Configuration was modified.  Issue "write
  memory" to save new certificate
R1(config)# ip http authentication local
```

Finally, configure the virtual terminal lines of the router to authenticate using the local authentication database. Allow virtual terminal input through both Telnet and Secure Shell (SSH):

```
R1(config)# line vty 0 4
R1(config-line)# login local
R1(config-line)# transport input telnet ssh
```

Based on your knowledge of SDM, why do you think that the router needs to have these nonSDM-specific commands entered?

_____

_____

_____

_____

Step 3: Configure Addressing

Now that the router has all the commands necessary for remote access, connectivity must be established between the PC and the router. The first thing you need to do is configure the Fast Ethernet interface on the router with the IP address shown in Figure 3-1. If you have already configured the correct IP address, skip this step.

```
R1(config)# interface fastethernet0/0
R1(config-if)# ip address 192.168.10.1 255.255.255.0
R1(config-if)# no shutdown
```

Next, assign an IP address to the PC. If the PC already has an IP address in the same subnet as the router, you can skip this step. These steps might vary depending on your Windows version and theme.

First, access the PC Control Panel window and open the Network Connections management interface, as shown in Figure 3-2.

Figure 3-2   Microsoft Windows Control Panel

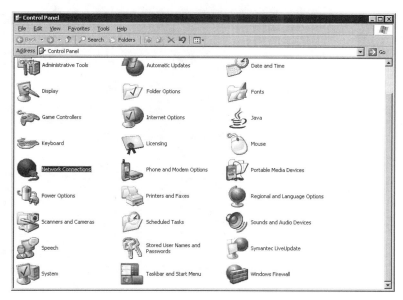

Right-click the LAN interface that connects to the Catalyst switch and click **Properties**. From the window shown in Figure 3-3, choose **Internet Protocol (TCP/IP)**, and then click the **Properties** button.

Figure 3-3   Network Connection Properties

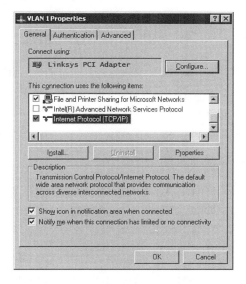

Finally, configure the IP address on the interface, as shown in Figure 3-4.

Figure 3-4   IP Properties

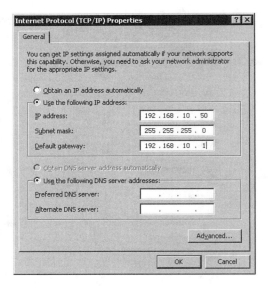

Click **OK** once to apply the TCP/IP settings. Click **OK** again to exit the configuration dialog box for the LAN interface. Open the Start Menu and click **Run**. Issue the **cmd** command and press the **Return** key. At the Windows command-line prompt, ping the R1 Ethernet interface. You should receive responses. If you do not receive any responses, troubleshoot by verifying the VLAN of the switchports and the IP address and subnet mask on each device attached to the switch:

```
C:\Documents and Settings\Administrator> ping 192.168.10.1

Pinging 192.168.10.1 with 32 bytes of data:

Reply from 192.168.10.1: bytes=32 time=1ms TTL=255
Reply from 192.168.10.1: bytes=32 time<1ms TTL=255
Reply from 192.168.10.1: bytes=32 time<1ms TTL=255
Reply from 192.168.10.1: bytes=32 time<1ms TTL=255

Ping statistics for 192.168.10.1:
    Packets: Sent = 4, Received = 4, Lost = 0 (0% loss),
Approximate round trip times in milli-seconds:
    Minimum = 0ms, Maximum = 1ms, Average = 0ms
```

Step 4: Extract SDM on the Host

Now that the router is ready to be accessed from SDM and connectivity exists between the router and the PC, you can use SDM to configure the router.

Start by extracting the SDM zip file to a directory on your hard drive, as shown in Figure 3-5. In this example, the directory used is C:\sdm\, although you can use any path you want. If your version of Windows has a built-in zip utility, use that to extract it, or if you don't have it built in, you can use a third-party tool, such as WinZip. To get to the built-in Windows Extraction Wizard, right-click the SDM zip file and click **Extract All**. If you decide to use a third-party tool, extract the file to the directory of your choice and go to the next step.

Figure 3-5   Zip File Menu

After the extraction wizard opens, from the screen shown in Figure 3-6, click **Next** to get to the destination selection screen.

Figure 3-6   Windows Extraction Wizard

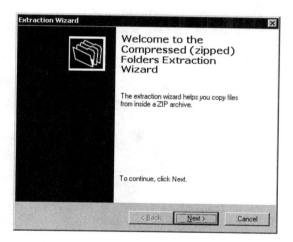

Select the folder you want to use as the destination directory, and then click **Next**, as shown in Figure 3-7.

Figure 3-7   Destination Selection Dialog

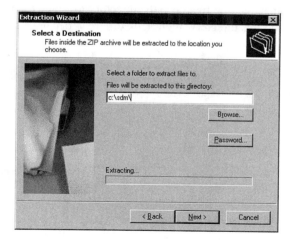

The files are extracted. It might take a few seconds for the extraction to finish, as Figure 3-8 shows.

Figure 3-8   Windows Extraction Wizard

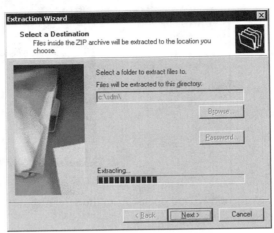

Afterward, you are prompted to decide whether you want to show the extracted files. Check this option if it is not already checked, and then click **Finish**, as shown in Figure 3-9.

Figure 3-9   Final Extraction Wizard Dialog

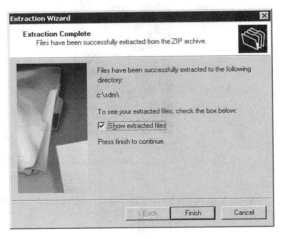

After you extract the file, open the directory to which the file was extracted, as shown in Figure 3-10. The files in this directory might look different, depending on the version of SDM you have.

Figure 3-10   Directory of SDM Extraction

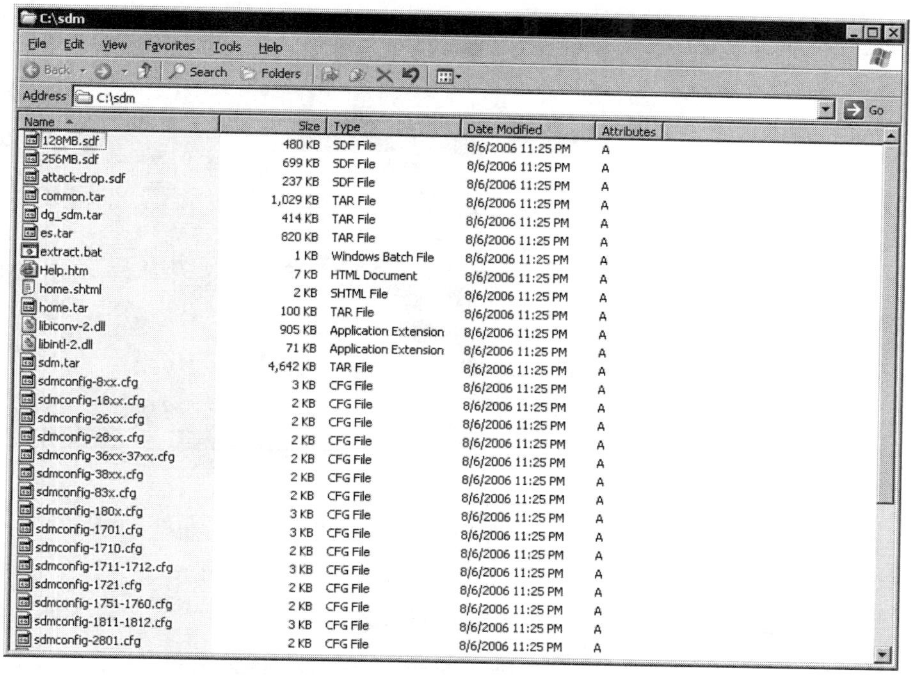

You are almost ready to use SDM to configure the router. The final step is installing the SDM application on the PC.

Step 5: Install SDM on the PC

Double-click the **setup.exe** executable program to open the Installation Wizard. After the Installation Wizard screen opens, as Figure 3-11 shows, click **Next**.

Figure 3-11   Welcome Screen for SDM Installation Wizard

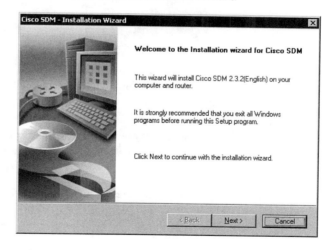

Accept the terms of the license agreement and click **Next**, as shown in Figure 3-12.

Figure 3-12   SDM License Agreement

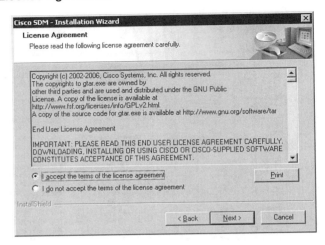

The next screen, shown in Figure 3-13, prompts you to choose from three options where you want to install SDM.

Figure 3-13   Installation Location Options

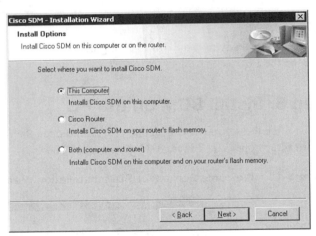

When installing SDM, you can install the application on the computer and not place it on the router's flash memory, you can install it on the router without affecting the computer, or you can install it to both. Both installation types are similar. This lab explains how to install SDM on your computer and on the Cisco router. It is not necessary to explain how to install it on both because that is self-evident after you learn how to install to one or the other. If you do not want to install SDM to your computer, go to Step 7.

What are the advantages and disadvantages of installing SDM on the computer only?

_____

_____

_____

_____

What are the advantages and disadvantages of installing SDM on the router only?

_____

_____

_____

_____

What are the advantages and disadvantages of installing SDM on both the router and PC?

_____

_____

_____

_____

For now, click **This computer**, and then click **Next**. Use the default destination folder and click **Next** again, as shown in Figure 3-14.

Figure 3-14   Local Installation Location Dialog

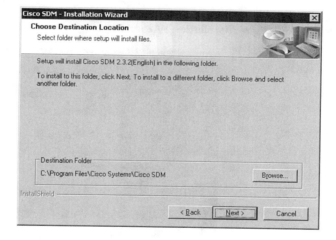

From the screen shown in Figure 3-15, click **Install** to begin the installation. Figure 3-16 shows the progress of the installation.

Figure 3-15   Installation Prompt

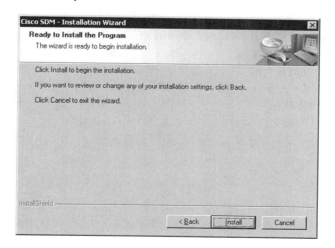

Figure 3-16   Installation Progress Information

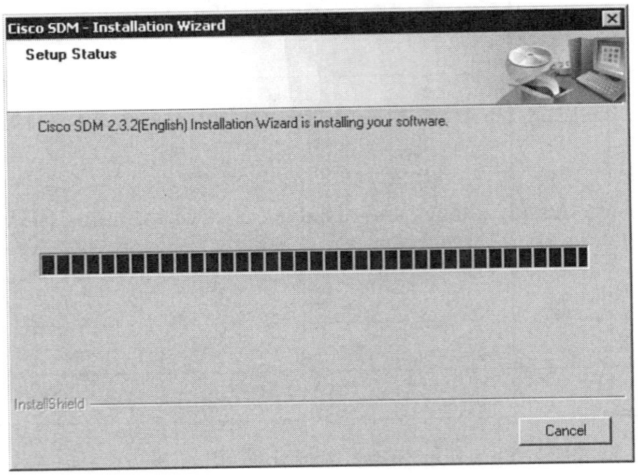

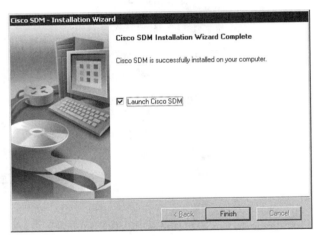

The software installs, and you are prompted with a final dialog box to launch SDM. Check the **Launch Cisco SDM** box, and then click **Finish**, as shown in Figure 3-17.

Figure 3-17   Final Installation Wizard Report

Step 6: Run SDM from the PC

SDM should start up from the installer when you complete Step 5, if you checked the Launch Cisco SDM option. If you did not, or you are running SDM without just installing it, click the icon on the desktop labeled **Cisco SDM**. The SDM Launcher dialog box opens. Enter the IP address of the router shown in Figure 3-18 as a device IP address. Check **This device has HTTPS enabled and I want to use it** if you enabled the HTTP secure server in Step 2. Then, click the **Launch** button, as shown in Figure 3-18.

Figure 3-18   SDM Launcher Window

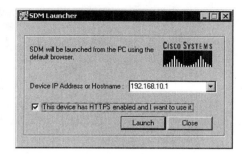

Click **Yes** when the security warning appears. Note that Internet Explorer might block SDM at first, and you need to allow it or adjust your Internet Explorer security settings accordingly to use it. Depending on the version of Internet Explorer you run, one of these settings is especially important for locally running SDM, and it is in the Tools menu, under Internet Options. Click the **Advanced** tab, and under the Security heading, check **Allow active content to be run in files on My Computer** if it is not already checked.

From the screen shown in Figure 3-19, enter the username and password that you created in Step 2.

Figure 3-19   HTTP Authentication Screen

You might be prompted to accept a certificate from this router, as shown in Figure 3-20. Accept the certificate to proceed. Then, give the username and password for the router and click **Yes**, as shown in Figure 3-21.

Figure 3-20   Internet Explorer Security Alert Prompt

Figure 3-21 SDM Authentication Dialog

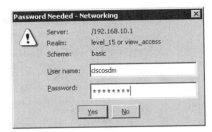

SDM reads the configuration off the router, as shown in Figure 3-22.

Figure 3-22 SDM Load Progress Indicator

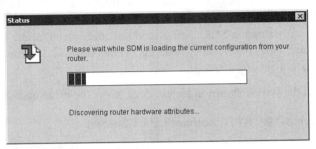

If everything was configured correctly in Step 2, you are able to access the SDM dashboard, as shown in Figure 3-23. If your configuration here looks correct, it means you successfully configured and connected to SDM. Your information might vary depending on which version of SDM you run.

Figure 3-23 SDM Dashboard

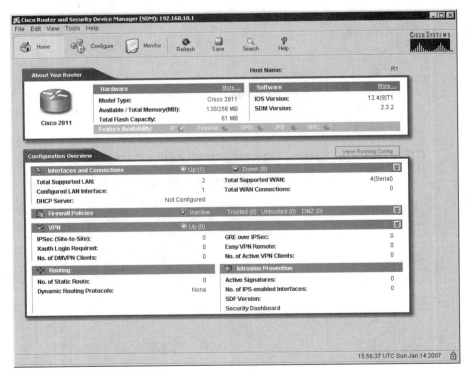

Step 7: Install SDM to the Router

Follow Step 6 until the prompt shown in Figure 3-24 appears. When this window appears, click **Cisco Router** to install SDM to your router's flash memory. If you don't want to install SDM to your router's flash memory or do not have the available space on the flash drive, do not attempt to install SDM to the router.

Figure 3-24   Installation Location Options

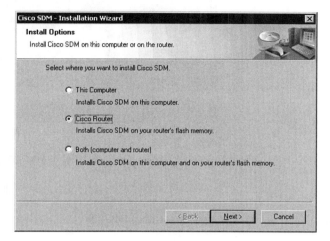

Enter your router's information so that the installer can remotely access and install SDM to the router, as shown in Figure 3-25.

Figure 3-25   Router Authentication Dialog

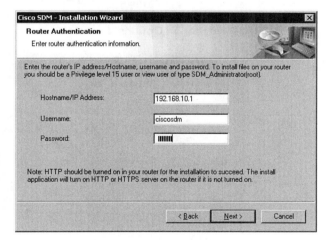

Cisco SDM connects to the router, as shown in Figure 3-26. You might notice some messages being logged to the console. This is normal.

Figure 3-26   Router Connection Indicator

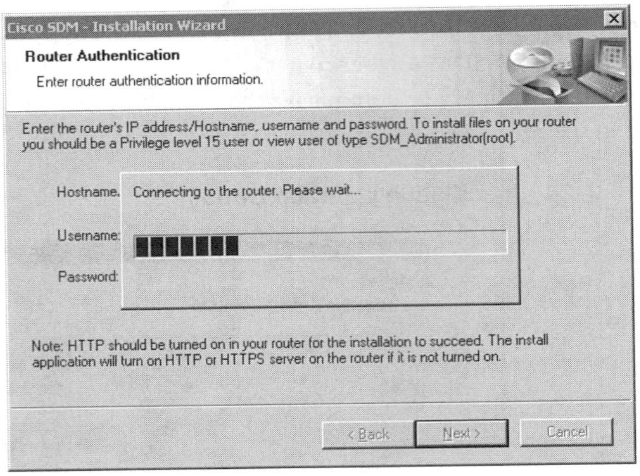

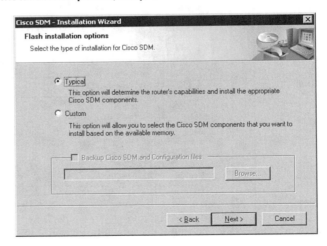

```
Jan 14 16:15:26.367: %SYS-5-CONFIG_I: Configured from console by ciscosdm on vty0
   (192.168.10.50)

Jan 14 16:15:30.943: %SYS-5-CONFIG_I: Configured from console by ciscosdm on vty0
   (192.168.10.50)

Jan 14 16:15:36.227: %SYS-5-CONFIG_I: Configured from console by ciscosdm on vty0
   (192.168.10.50)

Jan 14 16:15:39.211: %SYS-5-CONFIG_I: Configured from console by ciscosdm on vty0
   (192.168.10.50)

Jan 14 16:15:44.583: %SYS-5-CONFIG_I: Configured from console by ciscosdm on vty0
   (192.168.10.50)
```

As shown in Figure 3-27, choose **Typical** as your installation type and click **Next**.

Figure 3-27   SDM Installation Options, Step 1

Leave the default installation options checked in Figure 3-28, and click **Next**.

Figure 3-28   SDM Installation Options, Step 2

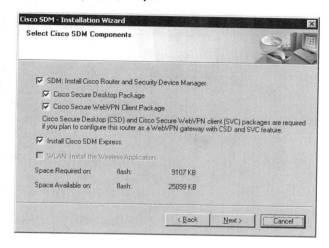

Finally, from the screen shown in Figure 3-29, click **Install** for the installation process to begin, as shown in Figure 3-30. During the installation, more messages might be logged to the console. This installation process takes a while. (Look at the timestamps in the console output to estimate the duration on a Cisco 2811.) The time varies by router model.

Figure 3-29   Confirmation Prompt

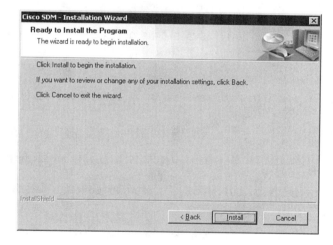

Figure 3-30   Installation Progress Indicator

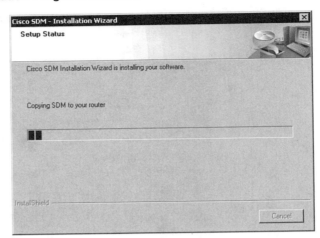

```
Jan 14 16:19:40.795: %SYS-5-CONFIG_I: Configured from console by ciscosdm on vty0
  (192.168.10.50)

Jan 14 16:19:43.855: %SYS-5-CONFIG_I: Configured from console by ciscosdm on vty0
  (192.168.10.50)

Jan 14 16:19:49.483: %SYS-5-CONFIG_I: Configured from console by ciscosdm on vty0
  (192.168.10.50)

Jan 14 16:25:57.823: %SYS-5-CONFIG_I: Configured from console by ciscosdm on vty0
  (192.168.10.50)

Jan 14 16:26:02.331: %SYS-5-CONFIG_I: Configured from console by ciscosdm on vty0
  (192.168.10.50)

Jan 14 16:27:42.279: %SYS-5-CONFIG_I: Configured from console by ciscosdm on vty0
  (192.168.10.50)

Jan 14 16:27:46.767: %SYS-5-CONFIG_I: Configured from console by ciscosdm on vty0
  (192.168.10.50)

Jan 14 16:28:11.403: %SYS-5-CONFIG_I: Configured from console by ciscosdm on vty0
  (192.168.10.50)

Jan 14 16:28:15.795: %SYS-5-CONFIG_I: Configured from console by ciscosdm on vty0
  (192.168.10.50)

Jan 14 16:29:04.391: %SYS-5-CONFIG_I: Configured from console by ciscosdm on vty0
  (192.168.10.50)
```

At the end of the installation, you are prompted to launch SDM on the router. Before you do this, go to the console and issue the **show flash:** command. Notice all the files that SDM installed to flash. Before the installation, the only file listed was the first file, the IOS image:

```
R1# show flash:

CompactFlash directory:
File  Length     Name/status
   1  38523272   c2800nm-advipservicesk9-mz.124-9.T1.bin
   2  1038       home.shtml
   3  1823       sdmconfig-2811.cfg
   4  102400     home.tar
   5  491213     128MB.sdf
   6  1053184    common.tar
```

```
  7    4753408   sdm.tar
  8    1684577   securedesktop-ios-3.1.1.27-k9.pkg
  9    398305    sslclient-win-1.1.0.154.pkg
 10    839680    es.tar
[47849552 bytes used, 16375724 available, 64225276 total]
62720K bytes of ATA CompactFlash (Read/Write)
```

As shown in Figure 3-31, make sure that the **Launch Cisco SDM** option is checked, and then click **Finish** to launch SDM.

Figure 3-31   Final SDM Installation Dialog

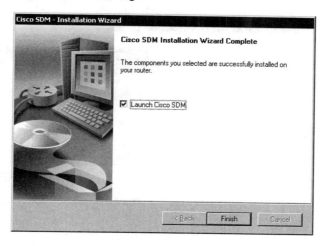

Step 8: Run SDM from the Router

SDM starts up from the installer when you complete the previous step, if you checked the **Launch Cisco SDM** option. If you did not, or you are running SDM without just installing it, open Internet Explorer and navigate to the URL https://<IP address>/ or http://<IP address>/, depending on whether you enabled the HTTP secure server in Step 2. When you are prompted to accept the certificate, as shown in Figure 3-32, click **Yes**.

Figure 3-32   Internet Explorer Certificate Confirmation

Ignore the security warnings shown in Figure 3-33 and click **Run**.

Figure 3-33   Internet Explorer Security Confirmation

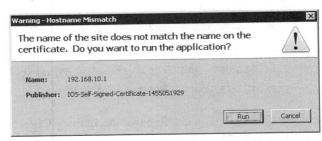

From the screen shown in Figure 3-34, enter the username and password you configured in Step 2.

Figure 3-34   SDM Authentication Dialog

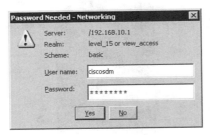

SDM reads the configuration off the router, as shown in Figure 3-35.

Figure 3-35   SDM Load Progress Indicator

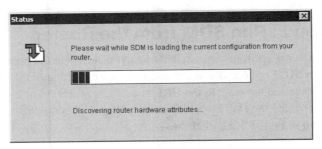

After SDM finishes loading your router's current configuration, the SDM homepage appears. If your configuration here looks correct, it means you successfully configured and connected to SDM. What you see might differ from what appears in Figure 3-36, depending on the router model number, IOS version, and so forth.

Step 9: Monitor an Interface in SDM

In SDM, you can look at an interface to verify that SDM is properly working and communicating with the router. To do this, click the **Monitor** tab at the top, and then click **Interface Status** on the left sidebar. You should see the graphs start to populate when FastEthernet0/0 is selected, as Figure 3-37 illustrates.

Figure 3-36   SDM Dashboard

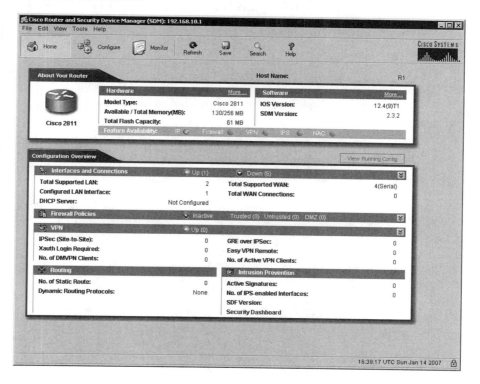

Figure 3-37   SDM Monitor Interface Status

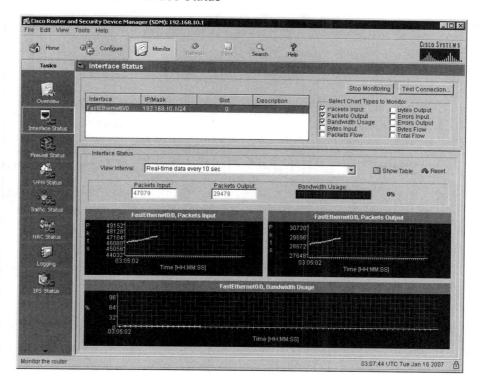

Lab 3-2: Configuring a Basic GRE Tunnel (3.10.2)

The objectives of this lab are as follows:

- Configure a GRE tunnel.

- Configure EIGRP on a router.

- Configure and test routing over the tunnel interfaces.

Figure 3-38 illustrates the topology that is used for this lab.

Figure 3-38 Topology Diagram

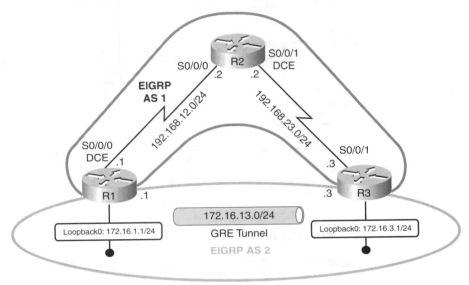

Scenario

This lab introduces tunnels. In later labs, you configure more advanced tunnels using encryption, but this lab shows the basic mechanics of generic routing encapsulation (GRE) tunnels.

Step 1: Configure Loopbacks and Physical Interfaces

Configure the loopback interfaces with the addresses shown Figure 3-38. Also, configure the serial interfaces shown in the figure. Do not forget to set the clock rates on the appropriate interfaces and issue the **no shutdown** command on all serial connections. Verify that you have connectivity across the local subnet by using the **ping** command. Do not set up the tunnel interface until the next step:

```
R1(config)# interface loopback 0
R1(config-if)# ip address 172.16.1.1 255.255.255.0
R1(config-if)# interface serial 0/0/0
R1(config-if)# ip address 192.168.12.1 255.255.255.0
R1(config-if)# clockrate 64000
R1(config-if)# no shutdown
```

```
R2(config)# interface serial 0/0/0
R2(config-if)# ip address 192.168.12.2 255.255.255.0
R2(config-if)# no shutdown
```

```
R2(config-if)# interface serial 0/0/1
R2(config-if)# ip address 192.168.23.2 255.255.255.0
R2(config-if)# clockrate 64000
R2(config-if)# no shutdown
R3(config)# interface loopback 0
R3(config-if)# ip address 172.16.3.1 255.255.255.0
R3(config-if)# interface serial 0/0/1
R3(config-if)# ip address 192.168.23.3 255.255.255.0
R3(config-if)# no shutdown
```

Step 2: Configure EIGRP AS 1

Configure EIGRP AS 1 for the major networks, 192.168.12.0/24 and 192.168.23.0/24. Do not include the networks falling in the 172.16.0.0/16 range in Figure 3-38. The Class C networks serve as the transit networks for the tunnel network. Make sure that you disable EIGRP automatic summarization:

```
R1(config)# router eigrp 1
R1(config-router)# no auto-summary
R1(config-router)# network 192.168.12.0
R2(config)# router eigrp 1
R2(config-router)# no auto-summary
R2(config-router)# network 192.168.12.0
R2(config-router)# network 192.168.23.0
R3(config)# router eigrp 1
R3(config-router)# no auto-summary
R3(config-router)# network 192.168.23.0
```

Verify that routers R1 and R3 can see the remote transit network with the **show ip route** command. If they cannot see the remote transit network, troubleshoot. Router R2 will not learn any new routes because it is directly connected to both networks.

```
R1# show ip route
Codes: C - connected, S - static, R - RIP, M - mobile, B - BGP
       D - EIGRP, EX - EIGRP external, O - OSPF, IA - OSPF inter area
       N1 - OSPF NSSA external type 1, N2 - OSPF NSSA external type 2
       E1 - OSPF external type 1, E2 - OSPF external type 2
       i - IS-IS, su - IS-IS summary, L1 - IS-IS level-1, L2 - IS-IS level-2
       ia - IS-IS inter area, * - candidate default, U - per-user static route
       o - ODR, P - periodic downloaded static route


Gateway of last resort is not set


C    192.168.12.0/24 is directly connected, Serial0/0/0
     172.16.0.0/24 is subnetted, 1 subnets
C    172.16.1.0 is directly connected, Loopback0
D    192.168.23.0/24 [90/2681856] via 192.168.12.2, 00:00:15, Serial0/0/0
```

```
R2# show ip route
Codes: C - connected, S - static, R - RIP, M - mobile, B - BGP
       D - EIGRP, EX - EIGRP external, O - OSPF, IA - OSPF inter area
       N1 - OSPF NSSA external type 1, N2 - OSPF NSSA external type 2
       E1 - OSPF external type 1, E2 - OSPF external type 2
       i - IS-IS, su - IS-IS summary, L1 - IS-IS level-1, L2 - IS-IS level-2
       ia - IS-IS inter area, * - candidate default, U - per-user static route
       o - ODR, P - periodic downloaded static route

Gateway of last resort is not set

C    192.168.12.0/24 is directly connected, Serial0/0/0
C    192.168.23.0/24 is directly connected, Serial0/0/1
R3# show ip route
Codes: C - connected, S - static, R - RIP, M - mobile, B - BGP
       D - EIGRP, EX - EIGRP external, O - OSPF, IA - OSPF inter area
       N1 - OSPF NSSA external type 1, N2 - OSPF NSSA external type 2
       E1 - OSPF external type 1, E2 - OSPF external type 2
       i - IS-IS, su - IS-IS summary, L1 - IS-IS level-1, L2 - IS-IS level-2
       ia - IS-IS inter area, * - candidate default, U - per-user static route
       o - ODR, P - periodic downloaded static route

Gateway of last resort is not set

D    192.168.12.0/24 [90/2681856] via 192.168.23.2, 00:00:36, Serial0/0/1
     172.16.0.0/24 is subnetted, 1 subnets
C       172.16.3.0 is directly connected, Loopback0
C    192.168.23.0/24 is directly connected, Serial0/0/1
```

Step 3: Configure a GRE Tunnel

Tunnels allow connectivity between remote areas of a network to communicate via a common network protocol and link independent of the native network protocol or routing protocol of their interconnection. For example, consider a company with two locations in which each site connects directly to the Internet with a static IP address. To allow private connections between the two sites, you could easily configure a tunnel between the two remote IP addresses so that private and/or encrypted communications could be sent between the two sites.

In this scenario, router R2 represents the agency providing connectivity between the two sites. Routers R1 and R3 represent the remote sites. A tunnel allows routers R1 and R3 to have a virtual private network (VPN) with each other and route between them. This type of VPN built on GRE encapsulation is not encrypted by default, but it can be encrypted through simple configuration techniques.

When this configuration is complete, router R2 does not need to be informed of the private networks behind R1 or R3, but simply passes IP data traffic between them based on the IP addresses on the packets it is sent. Because tunneled traffic is encapsulated within another IP header in this situation, R2 makes routing decisions based only on the outermost IP header. By running a routing protocol over the tunnel between the two sites, you can ensure that remote sites dynamically learn which remote IP networks are accessible to them.

In this lab, you use a tunnel to establish a VPN between the routers, and then route traffic between the remote sites using the tunnel interface. You use a base configuration without any encryption, although in later labs, we use encryption. In a production network, you would not want to send private network information through the public Internet unencrypted because traffic sniffers are easily able to read unencrypted data traffic.

A tunnel is a logical interface that acts as a logical connection between two endpoints. It is similar to a loopback interface in that it is a *virtual* interface created in software, but not represented by a hardware device. It is different than a loopback interface, however, in that more than one router is involved. You must configure each router at the endpoints of a tunnel with a tunnel interface. GRE stands for generic routing encapsulation, and it is the simplest type of tunnel you can configure.

From global configuration mode, issue the **interface tunnel** *number* command. For simplicity, use tunnel number 0 on both routers. Next, configure an IP address with **ip address** *address subnet-mask*, just like you would do on any other interface. This IP address is used inside the tunnel; it's part of the private network between routers R1 and R3.

Finally, assign a source and destination address for the tunnel with **tunnel source** *address* and **tunnel destination** *address*, respectively. Source can also be specified by interface. These addresses specify the endpoints of the router. GRE traffic is encapsulated out of the source address and deencapsulated on the destination address. We do not need to configure a tunnel mode because the default tunnel mode is GRE:

```
R1(config)# int tunnel0
R1(config-if)# tunnel source serial0/0/0
R1(config-if)# tunnel destination 192.168.23.3
R1(config-if)# ip address 172.16.13.1 255.255.255.0
R3(config)# int tunnel0
R3(config-if)# tunnel source serial0/0/1
R3(config-if)# tunnel destination 192.168.12.1
R3(config-if)# ip address 172.16.13.3 255.255.255.0
```

Verify that you can ping across the tunnel to the other side. If you can do this, you have successfully set up the tunnel.

```
R1# ping 172.16.13.3

Type escape sequence to abort.
Sending 5, 100-byte ICMP Echos to 172.16.13.3, timeout is 2 seconds:
!!!!!
Success rate is 100 percent (5/5), round-trip min/avg/max = 68/69/72 ms
R3# ping 172.16.13.1

Type escape sequence to abort.
Sending 5, 100-byte ICMP Echos to 172.16.13.1, timeout is 2 seconds:
!!!!!
Success rate is 100 percent (5/5), round-trip min/avg/max = 68/68/72 ms
```

When R1 pings 172.16.13.3, and R1 sends the packet toward R2, what is the source address of the packet?

_____

What is the destination address of the packet?

_____

Is this packet encrypted using the commands you entered?

_____

Step 4: Routing EIGRP AS 2 over the Tunnel

Now that you have the tunnel set up, you can set up dynamic routing protocols over it. When the next hop address of a destination network is through the tunnel, the packet is encapsulated in an IP packet, as described in the previous step.

Configure EIGRP AS 2 to route the entire 172.16.0.0 major network over the tunnel, but disable automatic summarization. Remember that router R2 is not participating in this routing process, so it does not need to be configured:

```
R1(config)# router eigrp 2
R1(config-router)# no auto-summary
R1(config-router)# network 172.16.0.0
```

```
R3(config)# router eigrp 2
R3(config-router)# no auto-summary
R3(config-router)# network 172.16.0.0
```

You should see EIGRP neighbors come up with their messages logged to the console. Now, issue the **show ip eigrp neighbors 2** command on routers R1 and R3. The 2 at the end of the command string specifies the AS number. If you omit this, you get neighbor tables for both EIGRP processes.

```
R1# show ip eigrp neighbors 2
IP-EIGRP neighbors for process 2
H    Address                  Interface      Hold Uptime    SRTT    RTO   Q  Seq
                                             (sec)          (ms)          Cnt Num
0    172.16.13.3              Tu0            10 00:01:14    100     5000  0  3
```

```
R3# show ip eigrp neighbors 2
IP-EIGRP neighbors for process 2
H    Address                  Interface      Hold Uptime    SRTT    RTO   Q  Seq
                                             (sec)          (ms)          Cnt Num
0    172.16.13.1              Tu0            13 00:02:47    1608    5000  0  2
```

Notice that the neighbor adjacencies are formed over the tunnel interface, even though no physical connection between the two routers exists. If you issue the **show ip route** command on the three routers, you see that routers R1 and R3 see each other's loopbacks. Although R2 is in the physical path, it has no knowledge of the loopback networks:

```
R1# show ip route
Codes: C - connected, S - static, R - RIP, M - mobile, B - BGP
       D - EIGRP, EX - EIGRP external, O - OSPF, IA - OSPF inter area
       N1 - OSPF NSSA external type 1, N2 - OSPF NSSA external type 2
```

```
            E1 - OSPF external type 1, E2 - OSPF external type 2
            i - IS-IS, su - IS-IS summary, L1 - IS-IS level-1, L2 - IS-IS level-2
            ia - IS-IS inter area, * - candidate default, U - per-user static route
            o - ODR, P - periodic downloaded static route


Gateway of last resort is not set

C    192.168.12.0/24 is directly connected, Serial0/0/0
     172.16.0.0/24 is subnetted, 3 subnets
C       172.16.13.0 is directly connected, Tunnel0
C       172.16.1.0 is directly connected, Loopback0
D       172.16.3.0 [90/297372416] via 172.16.13.3, 00:04:23, Tunnel0
D    192.168.23.0/24 [90/2681856] via 192.168.12.2, 03:06:16, Serial0/0/0
```

R2# **show ip route**
```
Codes: C - connected, S - static, R - RIP, M - mobile, B - BGP
       D - EIGRP, EX - EIGRP external, O - OSPF, IA - OSPF inter area
       N1 - OSPF NSSA external type 1, N2 - OSPF NSSA external type 2
       E1 - OSPF external type 1, E2 - OSPF external type 2
       i - IS-IS, su - IS-IS summary, L1 - IS-IS level-1, L2 - IS-IS level-2
       ia - IS-IS inter area, * - candidate default, U - per-user static route
       o - ODR, P - periodic downloaded static route


Gateway of last resort is not set

C    192.168.12.0/24 is directly connected, Serial0/0/0
C    192.168.23.0/24 is directly connected, Serial0/0/1
```

R3# **show ip route**
```
Codes: C - connected, S - static, R - RIP, M - mobile, B - BGP
       D - EIGRP, EX - EIGRP external, O - OSPF, IA - OSPF inter area
       N1 - OSPF NSSA external type 1, N2 - OSPF NSSA external type 2
       E1 - OSPF external type 1, E2 - OSPF external type 2
       i - IS-IS, su - IS-IS summary, L1 - IS-IS level-1, L2 - IS-IS level-2
       ia - IS-IS inter area, * - candidate default, U - per-user static route
       o - ODR, P - periodic downloaded static route


Gateway of last resort is not set

D    192.168.12.0/24 [90/2681856] via 192.168.23.2, 03:06:54, Serial0/0/1
     172.16.0.0/24 is subnetted, 3 subnets
C       172.16.13.0 is directly connected, Tunnel0
D       172.16.1.0 [90/297372416] via 172.16.13.1, 00:05:12, Tunnel0
C       172.16.3.0 is directly connected, Loopback0
C    192.168.23.0/24 is directly connected, Serial0/0/1
```

You are able to ping the remote loopback addresses from routers R1 and R3. R2 will not be able to ping either address, because no route to the 172.16.0.0 network exists in its routing table:

```
R1# ping 172.16.3.1

Type escape sequence to abort.
Sending 5, 100-byte ICMP Echos to 172.16.3.1, timeout is 2 seconds:
!!!!!
Success rate is 100 percent (5/5), round-trip min/avg/max = 68/68/68 ms
R2# ping 172.16.1.1

Type escape sequence to abort.
Sending 5, 100-byte ICMP Echos to 172.16.1.1, timeout is 2 seconds:
.....
Success rate is 0 percent (0/5)
R2# ping 172.16.3.1

Type escape sequence to abort.
Sending 5, 100-byte ICMP Echos to 172.16.3.1, timeout is 2 seconds:
.....
Success rate is 0 percent (0/5)
R3# ping 172.16.1.1

Type escape sequence to abort.
Sending 5, 100-byte ICMP Echos to 172.16.1.1, timeout is 2 seconds:
!!!!!
Success rate is 100 percent (5/5), round-trip min/avg/max = 68/68/68 ms
```

Why can't R2 ping 172.16.1.1 or 172.16.3.1?

_____

_____

_____

Lab 3-3: Configuring Wireshark and SPAN (3.10.3)

The objectives of this lab are as follows:

- Install Wireshark on a host PC.

- Configure a switch to use the SPAN monitoring tool.

Figure 3-39 illustrates the topology that is used for this lab.

Figure 3-39   Topology Diagram

Scenario

In this lab, you configure a switch to mirror traffic from a certain port out to a destination port for analyzing. In addition, you configure Wireshark on a host PC to monitor the mirrored traffic flow.

Wireshark is a packet-sniffing application that can read and analyze incoming packets. Because it is useful for troubleshooting and verification, Wireshark is used in many of the labs in this course.

Step 1: Configure the Router

Configure the R1 FastEthernet0/0 interface with the IP address shown in Figure 3-39. On the switch ALS1, place all the ports in VLAN 1. Configure EIGRP AS 1 with the 192.168.10.0 network to generate traffic on the wire:

```
R1(config)# interface fastethernet0/0
R1(config-if)# ip address 192.168.10.1 255.255.255.0
R1(config-if)# no shutdown
R1(config-if)# exit
R1(config)# router eigrp 1
R1(config-router)# network 192.168.10.0
```

What kind of packets would you expect R1 to send toward ALS1's Fast Ethernet interface?

Step 2: Install Wireshark and WinPcap

Run the Wireshark installer executable file. If you do not have the installer, download it from http://www.wireshark.org. After the Installation Wizard opens, as shown in Figure 3-40, click **Next**.

Figure 3-40 Wireshark Installation Wizard

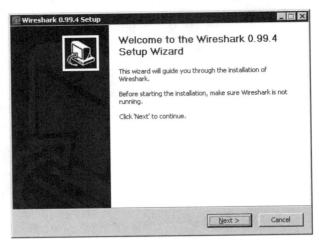

Click **I Agree** to agree to the Wireshark license agreement, as shown in Figure 3-41.

Figure 3-41 Wireshark License Agreement

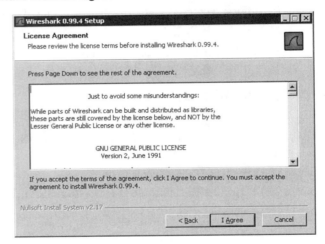

Use the default settings shown in Figure 3-42 and click **Next**.

Figure 3-42 Selecting Wireshark Components

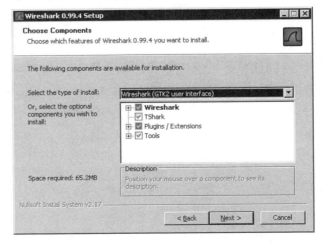

Use your own personal preference to determine where you want the shortcuts to be placed, and check those boxes accordingly. Then click **Next**, as shown in Figure 3-43.

Figure 3-43   Additional Tasks Selection

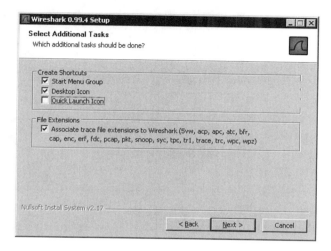

Use the default installation directory and click **Next**, as shown in Figure 3-44.

Figure 3-44   Installation Location Dialog

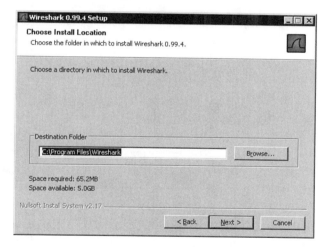

From the dialog shown in Figure 3-45, check the option to install WinPcap, because you need it for Wireshark to work. If you plan to have nonadministrators use Wireshark, choose the Services option, also.

Figure 3-45   WinPcap Installation Options

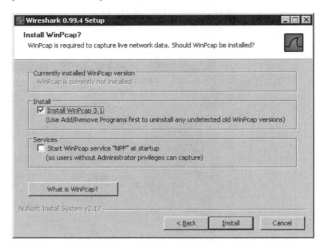

The WinPcap Installation Wizard now runs, as shown in Figure 3-46.

Figure 3-46   Wireshark Installation Progress Indicator

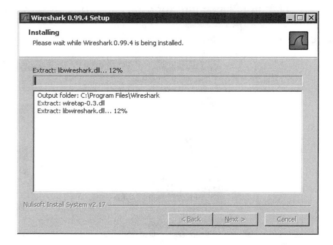

During the install, the WinPcap installer starts up if you selected the launch option earlier. Agree to the license agreement by clicking the **I Agree** button, as shown in Figure 3-47.

Figure 3-47   WinPcap License Agreement

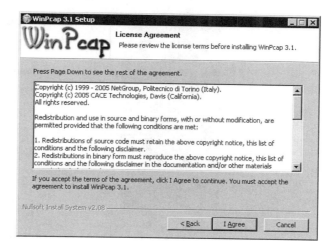

After clicking **I Agree**, WinPcap installs, as shown in Figure 3-48.

Figure 3-48   WinPcap Installation Progress Indicator

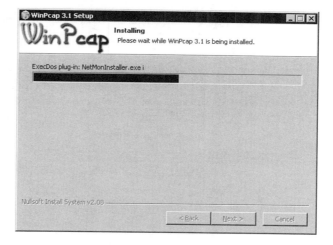

From the screen shown in Figure 3-49, click **Finish** to complete the WinPcap installation, and the Wireshark installer continues.

Figure 3-49   Final WinPcap Installation Window

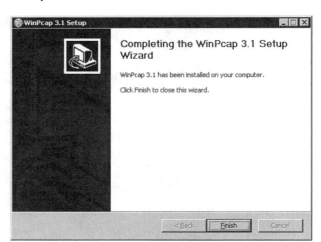

After the Wireshark installer finishes, click **Next** to go to the final screen, as shown in Figure 3-50.

Figure 3-50   Wireshark Installation Progress Indicator

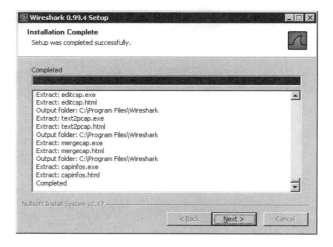

Check **Run Wireshark** if you want to run the program now, and then click **Finish**, as shown in Figure 3-51.

Figure 3-51   Final Wireshark Installation Window

Step 3: Configure SPAN on a Switch

On the Catalyst switch, you need to configure Switched Port Analyzer (SPAN) to mirror traffic going in and out of the router port to the host port. To do this, use the **monitor session** *number* **source interface** *interface-type interface-number* command. This specifies the source interface that is the interface to be monitored. The destination interface is specified in a similar way, using the **monitor session** *number* **destination interface** *interface-type interface-number* command. You must use the same session number in both lines, which indicates that they are the same monitoring session:

```
ALS1(config)# monitor session 1 source interface fastethernet0/1

ALS1(config)# monitor session 1 destination interface fastethernet0/6
```

Note that when an interface is a SPAN destination interface, the switch does not forward any frames at OSI Layer 2 or Layer 3, aside from those captured from the SPAN session. Thus, the destination port does not participate in Dynamic Trunking Protocol (DTP), VLAN Trunking Protocol (VTP), Cisco Discovery Protocol (CDP), Spanning Tree Protocol (STP), or EtherChannel negotiation protocols, such as Port Aggregation Protocol (PAgP) or Link Aggregation Control Protocol (LACP). The only traffic sent out of the destination interface is the traffic from the SPAN session.

Verify the configuration using the **show monitor** command. (In some versions of IOS, the command is **show monitor session**.)

```
ALS1# show monitor
Session 1
---------
Type              : Local Session
Source Ports      :
    Both          : Fa0/1
Destination Ports : Fa0/6
    Encapsulation : Native
          Ingress : Disabled
```

If you had not implemented the following command, would the host still receive the EIGRP hello packets? Explain.

`ALS1(config)# monitor session 1 destination interface fastethernet0/6`

_____

_____

_____

_____

Step 4: Sniff Packets Using Wireshark

Now that the switch is sending SPAN packets to the host, you can show packets generated from R1 in Wireshark. To do this, open Wireshark. It opens with an empty Wireshark window, as shown in Figure 3-52.

Figure 3-52   Wireshark Application Window

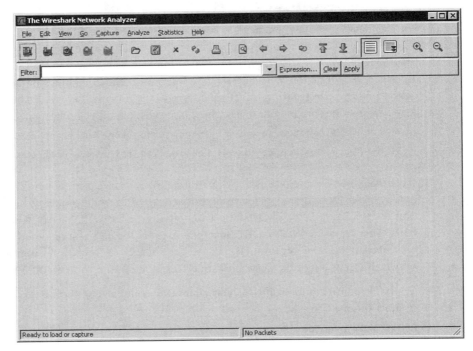

Click **Capture** on the toolbar and click **Interfaces**, as shown in Figure 3-53.

Figure 3-53   Capture Menu

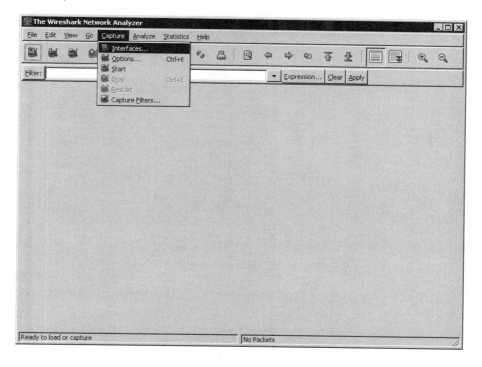

From the screen shown in Figure 3-54, choose the interface on the PC that is connected to the SPAN destination port, and click **Start** for that interface. The IP on the host does not necessarily need to be in the same subnet as the traffic you are sniffing.

Figure 3-54   Interface List

After you sniff a decent amount of traffic (about 30 seconds), click **Stop**, as shown in Figure 3-55. In this list, EIGRP packets are classified as Other.

Figure 3-55   Capture Summary Window

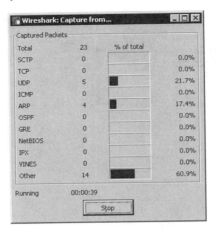

Why are EIGRP packets not classified in any of these protocols?

_____

_____

Wireshark lists all captured packets. In addition, deeper packet information and a raw readout of the packet are available for the selected packet (see Figure 3-56.) Explore the detailed information available for each packet. Note the EIGRP hello multicasts are sent to the host via the SPAN session.

Figure 3-56   Wireshark Packet Detail Window

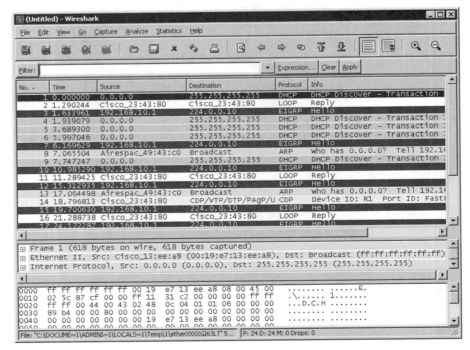

Lab 3-4: Configuring Site-to-Site IPsec VPNs with SDM (3.10.4)

The objectives of this lab are as follows:

- Configure EIGRP on the routers.

- Create a site-to-site IPsec VPN using SDM.

- Verify IPsec operation.

Figure 3-57 illustrates the topology that is used for this lab.

Figure 3-57   Topology Diagram

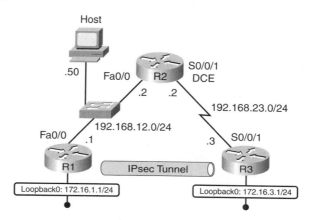

Scenario

In this lab, you configure a site-to-site IPsec VPN. After you configure the VPN, the traffic between the loopback interfaces on routers R1 and R3 becomes encrypted.

For this lab, you use the Cisco SDM. Lab 3-5 involves the same function as this lab, but it's implemented via the command-line interface (CLI).

Step 1: Configure Addressing

Configure the loopback interfaces with the addresses shown in Figure 3-57 and configure the serial interfaces shown in the figure. Set the clock rates on the appropriate interfaces and issue the **no shutdown** command on all physical connections. Verify that you have connectivity across local subnets by using the **ping** command:

```
R1(config)# interface loopback0
R1(config-if)# ip address 172.16.1.1 255.255.255.0
R1(config-if)# interface fastethernet0/0
R1(config-if)# ip address 192.168.12.1 255.255.255.0
R1(config-if)# no shutdown
```

```
R2(config)# interface fastethernet0/0
R2(config-if)# ip address 192.168.12.2 255.255.255.0
R2(config-if)# no shutdown
R2(config-if)# interface serial0/0/1
```

```
R2(config-if)# ip address 192.168.23.2 255.255.255.0
R2(config-if)# clockrate 64000
R2(config-if)# no shutdown
R3(config)# interface loopback0
R3(config-if)# ip address 172.16.3.1 255.255.255.0
R3(config-if)# interface serial0/0/1
R3(config-if)# ip address 192.168.23.3 255.255.255.0
R3(config-if)# no shutdown
```

Step 2: Configure EIGRP

To maintain connectivity between remote networks, configure EIGRP to route between all networks in the figure. Add all connected subnets into the EIGRP autonomous system on every router. Disable automatic summarization:

```
R1(config)# router eigrp 1
R1(config-router)# no auto-summary
R1(config-router)# network 172.16.0.0
R1(config-router)# network 192.168.12.0
R2(config)# router eigrp 1
R2(config-router)# no auto-summary
R2(config-router)# network 192.168.12.0
R2(config-router)# network 192.168.23.0
R3(config)# router eigrp 1
R3(config-router)# no auto-summary
R3(config-router)# network 172.16.0.0
R3(config-router)# network 192.168.23.0
```

At this point, verify that you have full IP connectivity by using the following Toolkit Command Language (TCL) script:

```
tclsh

foreach address {
172.16.1.1
192.168.12.1
192.168.12.2
192.168.23.2
172.16.3.1
192.168.23.3
} { ping $address }

tclquit
```

Compare your output with the output shown in the section, "TCL Script Output." Troubleshoot as necessary.

Step 3: Connect to the Routers via SDM

Configure the IP address shown in Figure 3-57 on the host PC and install SDM to either the router or the PC, as shown in Lab 3-1. Ensure that the PC uses the interface indicated in the figure to forward traffic to remote networks using a default gateway.

From the host, connect to the router using SDM. If you installed the SDM application on the host, connect by launching the SDM application and connecting to 192.168.12.1. When you complete this step for router R3, you will use 192.168.23.3 as the IP address.

Figure 3-58 shows the SDM home page. This page might be shown in an application window if it is installed on the host or in an Internet Explorer window if it is being run from the router.

Figure 3-58   SDM Home Page

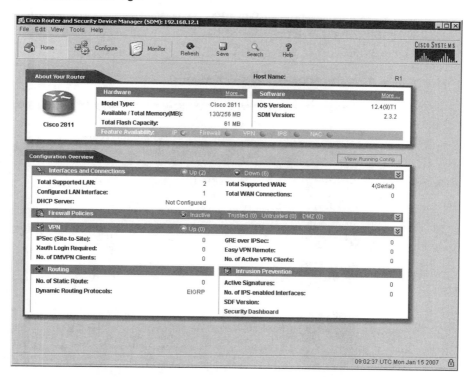

For information on how to configure SDM, refer to Lab 3-1: Configuring SDM on a Router.

Step 4: Configure Site-to-Site IPsec VPN via SDM

IPsec is a framework of open standards developed by the Internet Engineering Task Force (IETF). It provides security for the transmission of sensitive information over unprotected networks, such as the Internet. IPsec acts at the network layer, protecting and authenticating IP packets between participating IPsec devices (peers), such as Cisco routers.

Because IPsec is a framework, it allows us to exchange security protocols as new technologies—including encryption algorithms—are developed.

There are two central configuration elements to the implementation of an IPsec VPN:

- Implement Internet Key Exchange (IKE) parameters

- Implement IPsec parameters

The exchange method employed by IKE is first used to pass and validate IKE policies between peers. Then, the peers exchange and match IPsec policies for the authentication and encryption of data traffic. The IKE policy controls the authentication, encryption algorithm, and key-exchange method used for IKE proposals that are sent and received by the IPsec endpoints. The IPsec policy encrypts data traffic sent through the VPN tunnel.

SDM contains a wizard that makes setting up site-to-site VPNs easier than using the command-line interface (CLI). To access these settings, click the **Configure** heading at the top of the SDM window, below the menu bar. On the taskbar on the far left side of the window, choose **VPN**. In the VPN type list next to it, choose **Site-to-Site VPN**. After choosing the **Create a Site to Site VPN** tab in the main window, click **Launch the selected task** to begin the SDM Site-to-Site VPN wizard, as shown in Figure 3-59.

Figure 3-59   VPN Configuration Screen

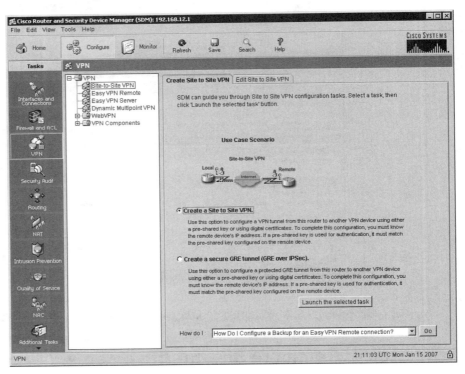

At the next window, shown in Figure 3-60, select **Step by step wizard,** and then click **Next**, so that you have more control over the VPN settings used. If you are in a hurry or don't care about specific VPN settings, you would use the **Quick setup** option.

Figure 3-60   Site-to-Site VPN Wizard

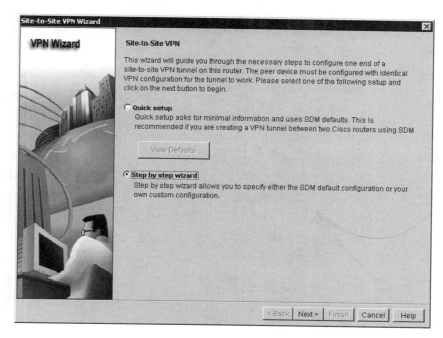

At the next window, shown in Figure 3-61, you can configure some of the basic site-to-site VPN settings. The interface option at the top indicates the outbound interface out of which R1 will send encrypted packets. In this lab topology, R1's outbound VPN interface is FastEthernet0/0. In the Peer Identity section, you select the peer type. Because you are using a static IP peer, you select that option and enter the IP address of the VPN destination. For authentication, click **Preshared keys**, and enter a VPN key. This key is what protects the VPN and keeps it secure, so in the real world, you would want a secure key. Because this is just a lab, use cisco as your VPN key. You could also set up digital certificates as a more scalable solution. Digital certificates would require a more advanced setup, which is beyond the scope of this lab and the CCNP2 curriculum. After you correctly enter these settings, click **Next**.

Figure 3-61   VPN Connection and Authentication Information

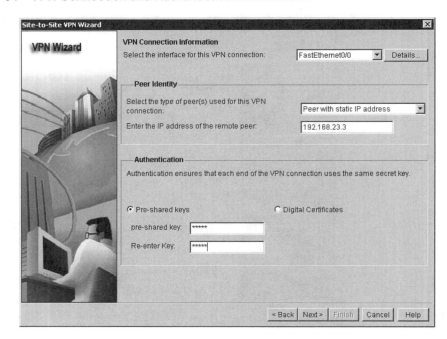

From the next window, shown in Figure 3-62, you can edit the IKE proposals. One is already defined for you as an SDM default. Click **Add** to create your own.

Figure 3-62   IKE Proposals List

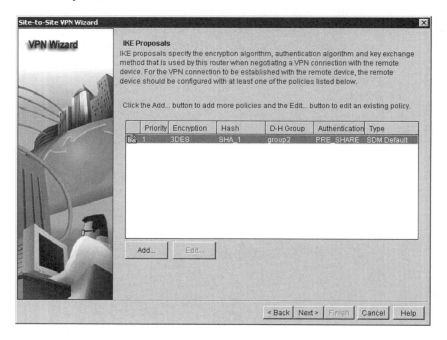

What function does this IKE proposal serve?

_____

IKE policies are used while setting up the control channel between the two VPN endpoints for key exchange. This is also referred to as the IKE security association (SA). In contrast, the IPsec policy is used during IKE Phase 2 to negotiate an IPsec security association to pass target data traffic.

Set up the security settings for this IKE policy, as shown in Figure 3-63. If your IOS image doesn't support all the settings, configure what you can as long as your VPN settings match on both ends of the connection.

Figure 3-63   Add IKE Policy Dialog

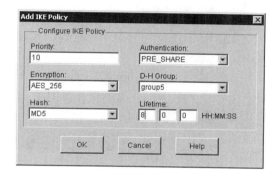

The authentication type can either be preshared keys or digital certificates. The method of preshared keys involves manually typing a secret string on both VPN endpoints during the configuration process. The endpoints will later use that string as part of the authentication process. Make sure you set the authentication type to **PRE_SHARE** so that the preshared keys created earlier will work.

Each of the drop-down boxes shown has multiple protocols or algorithms that can secure the control data.

What is the function of the encryption algorithm in the IKE policy?

_____

_____

What is the purpose of the hash function?

_____

_____

What function does the authentication method serve?

_____

How is the Diffie-Hellman group in the IKE policy used?

_____

_____

What event happens at the end of the IKE policy's lifetime?

_____

Your new IKE proposal has been added to the list, as shown in Figure 3-64. Click **Next**.

Figure 3-64   IKE Proposals with Changes Applied

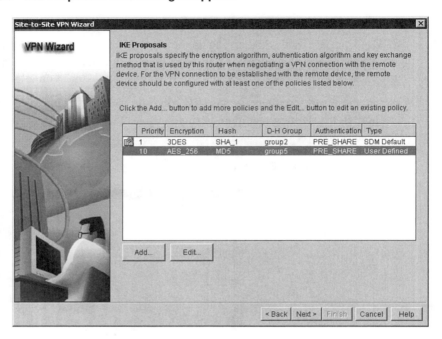

The next window, shown in Figure 3-65, allows you to add an IPsec transform set. Click **Add** to bring up the **Add Transform Set** dialog.

Figure 3-65   IPsec Transform Set List

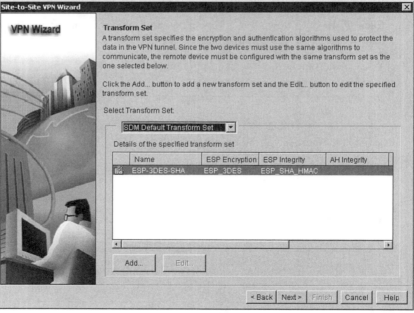

Although the wizard does not explicitly state it, the transform set is the IPsec policy used to encrypt, hash, and authenticate packets that pass through the tunnel.

What is the function of the IPsec transform set?

_____

_____

Use the transform set settings shown in Figure 3-66. If your IOS image doesn't support those settings, configure the VPN settings as closely as possible. Ensure that you match the IPsec policies between the two VPN endpoints.

Figure 3-66   Add IPsec Transform Set Dialog

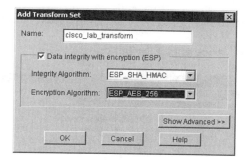

In the drop-down box, choose the transport set you just created, as shown in Figure 3-67. Click **Next** to continue.

Figure 3-67   IPsec Transform Set List with Changes Applied

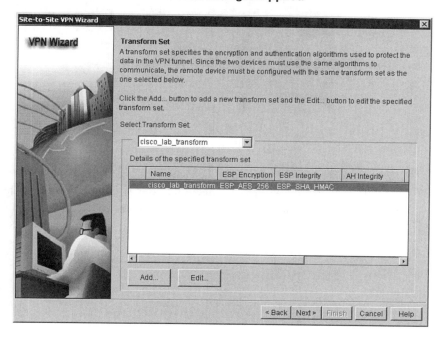

Finally, you must define interesting traffic to be protected through the VPN tunnel. Interesting traffic is defined through an access list when applied to the router. However, SDM allows a common practice to be defined simply using the window shown in Figure 3-68. This window allows users unfamiliar with access lists to define simple access lists based only on source and destination subnets.

If you enter source and destination subnets, such as this configuration has, SDM generates the access lists for you. If not, you can use an existing access list to mark which traffic to encrypt. The source and destination subnets are the loopback networks on routers R1 and R3, respectively.

Ensure that on R1, you define 172.16.1.0/24 as the source subnet and 172.16.3.0/24 as the destination subnet. Use the reverse for R3.

From the screen shown in Figure 3-68, click **Next** after you configure networks and masks.

Figure 3-68   Access List Definition

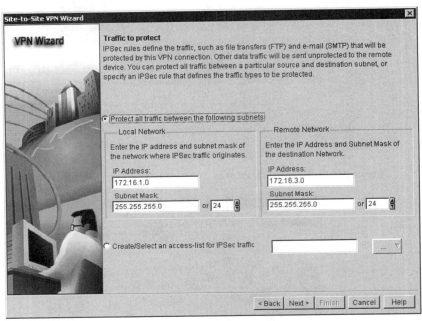

SDM presents a final summary of the changes it is going to make to the router, as shown in Figure 3-69. Do not check **Test VPN connectivity after configuring** because the VPN test will fail because you have not configured R3. Click **Finish**. SDM now modifies R1's configuration based on the parameters you provided in this wizard.

Figure 3-69   Site-to-Site VPN Configuration Summary

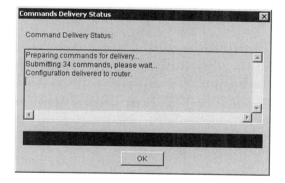

After SDM delivers the configuration to the router, as shown in Figure 3-70, click **OK**. The Site-to-Site VPN wizard closes, and you reenter the VPN configuration window.

Figure 3-70   Command Delivery Progress Indicator

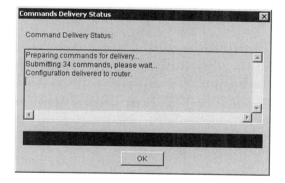

Step 5: Generate a Mirror Configuration for R3

Navigate to the **Edit Site-to-Site VPN** tab, as shown in Figure 3-71.

Figure 3-71   VPN Configuration Screen

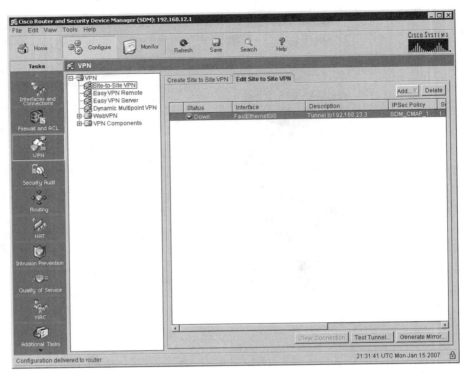

Why is the status of the VPN that you just created "Down"?

_____

_____

_____

Select the VPN policy you just configured and click the **Generate Mirror** button in the lower-right corner of the window to generate the screen shown in Figure 3-72.

Figure 3-72   Mirror VPN Configuration

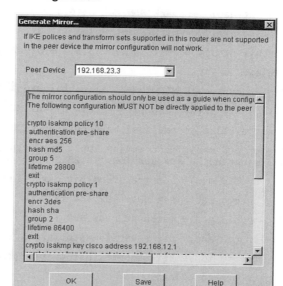

Enter global configuration mode on R3 by issuing the **configure terminal** command. Copy the commands in the SDM window and paste them into your configuration session with R3. You can also copy them by hand, but this method might be prone to error:

```
R3# configure terminal
R3(config)# crypto isakmp policy 10
R3(config-isakmp)# authentication pre-share
R3(config-isakmp)# encr aes 256
R3(config-isakmp)# hash md5
R3(config-isakmp)# group 5
R3(config-isakmp)# lifetime 28800
R3(config-isakmp)# exit
R3(config)# crypto isakmp policy 1
R3(config-isakmp)# authentication pre-share
R3(config-isakmp)# encr 3des
R3(config-isakmp)# hash sha
R3(config-isakmp)# group 2
R3(config-isakmp)# lifetime 86400
R3(config-isakmp)# exit
R3(config)# crypto isakmp key cisco address 192.168.12.1
R3(config)# crypto ipsec transform-set cisco_lab_transform esp-sha-hmac esp-aes 256
R3(cfg-crypto-trans)# mode tunnel
R3(cfg-crypto-trans)# exit
```

```
R3(config)# ip access list extended SDM_1
R3(config-ext-nacl)# remark SDM_ACL Category=4
R3(config-ext-nacl)# remark ipsec Rule
R3(config-ext-nacl)# permit ip 172.16.3.0 0.0.0.255 172.16.1.0 0.0.0.255
R3(config-ext-nacl)# exit
R3(config)# crypto map SDM_CMAP_1 1 ipsec-isakmp
% NOTE: This new crypto map will remain disabled until a peer
        and a valid access list have been configured.
R3(config-crypto-map)# description Apply the crypto map on the peer router's
  interface having IP address 192.168.23.3 that connects to this router.
R3(config-crypto-map)# set transform-set cisco_lab_transform
R3(config-crypto-map)# set peer 192.168.12.1
R3(config-crypto-map)# match address SDM_1
R3(config-crypto-map)# set security-association lifetime seconds 3600
R3(config-crypto-map)# set security-association lifetime kilobytes 4608000
R3(config-crypto-map)# exit
```

You might have noticed the warning in the **Generate Mirror** window, which stated that the configuration generated should only be used as a guide for setting up a site-to-site VPN. Although these configuration commands apply most of the necessary commands to the remote router, they will not apply that configuration to any router interface. Without an associated interface, none of the cryptography settings that you just pasted into R3 are activated. Additionally, if this overwrote some existing IPsec settings, you could potentially destroy one or more existing VPN tunnels.

In this situation, both of your endpoints should not have any VPNs configured before you run the site-to-site VPN wizard or the generated commands for the remote endpoint.

As previously noted, you now need to apply IPsec configuration to an interface. In the generated configuration, SDM_CMAP_1 is the name of the crypto map that was created. Apply this crypto map to the serial interface facing R2 by using the **crypto map** *name* command in interface configuration mode:

```
R3(config)# interface serial 0/0/1
R3(config-if)# crypto map SDM_CMAP_1
*Jan 15 22:00:38.184: %CRYPTO-6-ISAKMP_ON_OFF: ISAKMP is ON
```

This generates a warning that the Internet Security Association and Key Management Protocol (ISAKMP) is now activated.

Step 6: Verify the VPN Configuration Using SDM

Now that you configured R3 for a VPN, use SDM to test the configuration. On the **Edit Site-to-Site VPN** tab, shown in Figure 3-71, choose the VPN you just created and click **Test Tunnel**.

From the screen shown in Figure 3-73, click **Start** to have SDM start troubleshooting the tunnel.

Figure 3-73   VPN Testing Window

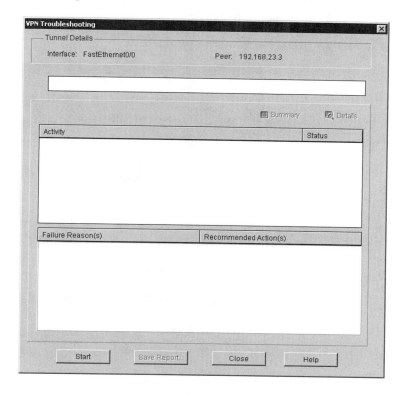

This process might take a few moments, as shown in Figure 3-74.

Figure 3-74   VPN Test In Progress

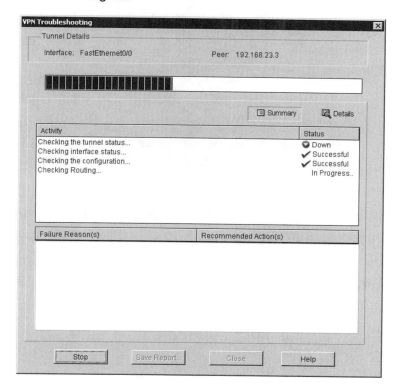

If SDM does not think the tunnel is up, it offers to troubleshoot the problem for you. Click **Yes** to continue, as shown in Figure 3-75.

Figure 3-75   SDM Performance Warning

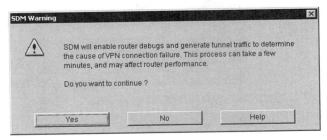

From the screen shown in Figure 3-76, choose the **Have SDM generate VPN traffic** option. Enter R3's loopback address as the destination address. Click **Continue**.

Figure 3-76   Test Traffic Generation Window

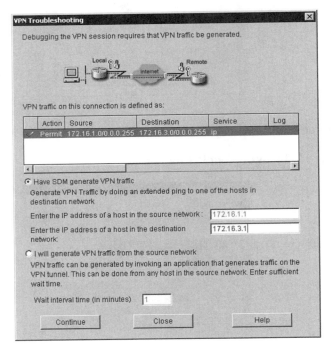

Allow SDM to analyze the situation and continue running the test.

When the test finishes, you should get a message acknowledging that the VPN tunnel is up. Click **OK**.

Figure 3-77 shows a successful test. If you do not receive a successful reply from the test, use SDM's suggestions to troubleshoot.

Figure 3-77   Successful VPN Test Status Window

The status displayed in the window shown in Figure 3-78 should be "Up," which indicates that the VPN connection is now active.

Click **Close** in the VPN Test window to go back to the main SDM console.

Figure 3-78   Detailed VPN Test Results

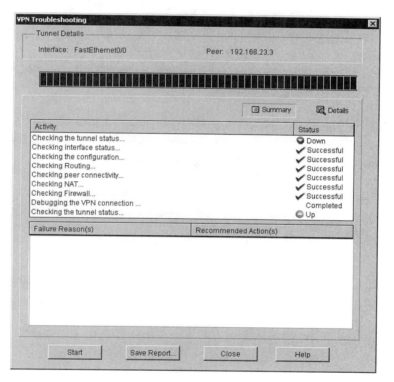

Step 7: Verify the VPN Configuration Using the IOS CLI

Although it is beneficial to have SDM to help troubleshoot a VPN, this is not always possible. There will be times when you have only console or Telnet access to a router. Fortunately, the Cisco IOS has an extensive array of **show** and **debug** commands for analyzing cryptographic configurations.

A useful command for monitoring IPsec VPNs is the **show crypto ipsec sa** command. This command lists all current IPsec security associations and their parameters. Issue this command on R1 and R3:

```
R1# show crypto ipsec sa

interface: FastEthernet0/0
    Crypto map tag: SDM_CMAP_1, local addr 192.168.12.1

  protected vrf: (none)
  local  ident (addr/mask/prot/port): (172.16.1.0/255.255.255.0/0/0)
  remote ident (addr/mask/prot/port): (172.16.3.0/255.255.255.0/0/0)
  current_peer 192.168.23.3 port 500
   PERMIT, flags={origin_is_acl,}
   #pkts encaps: 29, #pkts encrypt: 29, #pkts digest: 29
   #pkts decaps: 29, #pkts decrypt: 29, #pkts verify: 29
   #pkts compressed: 0, #pkts decompressed: 0
   #pkts not compressed: 0, #pkts compr. failed: 0
   #pkts not decompressed: 0, #pkts decompress failed: 0
   #send errors 1, #recv errors 0

    local crypto endpt.: 192.168.12.1, remote crypto endpt.: 192.168.23.3
    path mtu 1500, ip mtu 1500, ip mtu idb FastEthernet0/0
    current outbound spi: 0x487708CA(1215760586)

    inbound esp sas:
     spi: 0xD182B74A(3515004746)
       transform: esp-256-aes esp-sha-hmac ,
       in use settings ={Tunnel, }
       conn id: 2001, flow_id: NETGX:1, crypto map: SDM_CMAP_1
       sa timing: remaining key lifetime (k/sec): (4420862/2990)
       IV size: 16 bytes
       replay detection support: Y
       Status: ACTIVE

    inbound ah sas:

    inbound pcp sas:

    outbound esp sas:
     spi: 0x487708CA(1215760586)
       transform: esp-256-aes esp-sha-hmac ,
       in use settings ={Tunnel, }
       conn id: 2002, flow_id: NETGX:2, crypto map: SDM_CMAP_1
       sa timing: remaining key lifetime (k/sec): (4420862/2989)
```

```
            IV size: 16 bytes
            replay detection support: Y
            Status: ACTIVE


      outbound ah sas:


      outbound pcp sas:

R3# show crypto ipsec sa


interface: Serial0/0/1
    Crypto map tag: SDM_CMAP_1, local addr 192.168.23.3

   protected vrf: (none)
   local  ident (addr/mask/prot/port): (172.16.3.0/255.255.255.0/0/0)
   remote ident (addr/mask/prot/port): (172.16.1.0/255.255.255.0/0/0)
   current_peer 192.168.12.1 port 500
     PERMIT, flags={origin_is_acl,}
    #pkts encaps: 29, #pkts encrypt: 29, #pkts digest: 29
    #pkts decaps: 29, #pkts decrypt: 29, #pkts verify: 29
    #pkts compressed: 0, #pkts decompressed: 0
    #pkts not compressed: 0, #pkts compr. failed: 0
    #pkts not decompressed: 0, #pkts decompress failed: 0
    #send errors 0, #recv errors 0

     local crypto endpt.: 192.168.23.3, remote crypto endpt.: 192.168.12.1
     path mtu 1500, ip mtu 1500, ip mtu idb Serial0/0/1
     current outbound spi: 0xD182B74A(3515004746)

     inbound esp sas:
      spi: 0x487708CA(1215760586)
        transform: esp-256-aes esp-sha-hmac ,
        in use settings ={Tunnel, }
        conn id: 3001, flow_id: NETGX:1, crypto map: SDM_CMAP_1
        sa timing: remaining key lifetime (k/sec): (4467883/2964)
        IV size: 16 bytes
        replay detection support: Y
        Status: ACTIVE

     inbound ah sas:

     inbound pcp sas:
```

```
        outbound esp sas:
         spi: 0xD182B74A(3515004746)
            transform: esp-256-aes esp-sha-hmac ,
            in use settings ={Tunnel, }
            conn id: 3002, flow_id: NETGX:2, crypto map: SDM_CMAP_1
            sa timing: remaining key lifetime (k/sec): (4467883/2962)
            IV size: 16 bytes
            replay detection support: Y
            Status: ACTIVE


        outbound ah sas:


        outbound pcp sas:
```

View the numbers of packets being encrypted and decrypted on each end. You can verify that the correct packets are being encrypted and decrypted by checking that these packet counts increment when traffic is sent. From R1, ping R3's loopback. Then, look at the number of encrypted and decrypted packets on each side:

```
R1# ping 172.16.3.1


Type escape sequence to abort.
Sending 5, 100-byte ICMP Echos to 172.16.3.1, timeout is 2 seconds:
!!!!!
Success rate is 100 percent (5/5), round-trip min/avg/max = 28/28/32 ms


R1# show crypto ipsec sa


interface: FastEthernet0/0
    Crypto map tag: SDM_CMAP_1, local addr 192.168.12.1


  protected vrf: (none)
  local  ident (addr/mask/prot/port): (172.16.1.0/255.255.255.0/0/0)
  remote ident (addr/mask/prot/port): (172.16.3.0/255.255.255.0/0/0)
  current_peer 192.168.23.3 port 500
    PERMIT, flags={origin_is_acl,}
    #pkts encaps: 29, #pkts encrypt: 29, #pkts digest: 29
    #pkts decaps: 29, #pkts decrypt: 29, #pkts verify: 29
<OUTPUT OMITTED>
```

```
R3# show crypto ipsec sa


interface: Serial0/0/1
    Crypto map tag: SDM_CMAP_1, local addr 192.168.23.3
```

```
      protected vrf: (none)
      local  ident (addr/mask/prot/port): (172.16.3.0/255.255.255.0/0/0)
      remote ident (addr/mask/prot/port): (172.16.1.0/255.255.255.0/0/0)
      current_peer 192.168.12.1 port 500
        PERMIT, flags={origin_is_acl,}
       #pkts encaps: 29, #pkts encrypt: 29, #pkts digest: 29
       #pkts decaps: 29, #pkts decrypt: 29, #pkts verify: 29
<OUTPUT OMITTED>
```

Why is the packet count unchanged?

_____

_____

_____

Based on the configuration you enabled on the VPN tunnel, how could you create interesting traffic that would pass through the encrypted tunnel?

The **telnet**, **traceroute**, and extended **ping** commands can all have their packets manipulated so as to be sourced from an explicitly identified interface.

Use an extended **ping** to source packets from R1's loopback interface toward 172.16.3.0/24.

Will these packets be encrypted by the VPN?

_____

Test your answer:

```
R1# ping
Protocol [ip]:
Target IP address: 172.16.3.1
Repeat count [5]:
Datagram size [100]:
Timeout in seconds [2]:
Extended commands [n]: y
Source address or interface: Loopback0
Type of service [0]:
Set DF bit in IP header? [no]:
Validate reply data? [no]:
Data pattern [0xABCD]:
Loose, Strict, Record, Timestamp, Verbose[none]:
Sweep range of sizes [n]:
Type escape sequence to abort.
Sending 5, 100-byte ICMP Echos to 172.16.3.1, timeout is 2 seconds:
```

```
Packet sent with a source address of 172.16.1.1
!!!!!
Success rate is 100 percent (5/5), round-trip min/avg/max = 48/48/48 ms


R1# show crypto ipsec sa


interface: FastEthernet0/0
    Crypto map tag: SDM_CMAP_1, local addr 192.168.12.1


   protected vrf: (none)
   local  ident (addr/mask/prot/port): (172.16.1.0/255.255.255.0/0/0)
   remote ident (addr/mask/prot/port): (172.16.3.0/255.255.255.0/0/0)
   current_peer 192.168.23.3 port 500
     PERMIT, flags={origin_is_acl,}
    #pkts encaps: 34, #pkts encrypt: 34, #pkts digest: 34
    #pkts decaps: 34, #pkts decrypt: 34, #pkts verify: 34
<OUTPUT OMITTED>
```

```
R3# show crypto ipsec sa


interface: Serial0/0/1
    Crypto map tag: SDM_CMAP_1, local addr 192.168.23.3


   protected vrf: (none)
   local  ident (addr/mask/prot/port): (172.16.3.0/255.255.255.0/0/0)
   remote ident (addr/mask/prot/port): (172.16.1.0/255.255.255.0/0/0)
   current_peer 192.168.12.1 port 500
     PERMIT, flags={origin_is_acl,}
    #pkts encaps: 34, #pkts encrypt: 34, #pkts digest: 34
    #pkts decaps: 34, #pkts decrypt: 34, #pkts verify: 34
<OUTPUT OMITTED>
```

Another useful command is **show crypto isakmp sa**, which shows ISAKMP security associations:

```
R1# show crypto isakmp sa
dst             src             state           conn-id slot status
192.168.23.3    192.168.12.1    QM_IDLE               1     0 ACTIVE


R3# show crypto isakmp sa
dst             src             state           conn-id slot status
192.168.23.3    192.168.12.1    QM_IDLE               1     0 ACTIVE
```

Remember that there are two types of security associations necessary to bring this VPN tunnel up. The ISAKMP security association is initiated by IKE Phase 1, and allows the routers to securely exchange IPsec policies. The second type of security association is initiated during IKE Phase 2, and allows the routers to securely send the data traffic.

These are just a few **show** commands. Many other useful **show** and **debug** crypto commands exist.

Challenge: Use Wireshark to Monitor Encryption of Traffic

You can observe packets on the wire using Wireshark and see how their content looks unencrypted and then encrypted. To do this, first configure a SPAN session on the switch and open up Wireshark on a host attached to the SPAN destination port. You can use the host that you used for SDM because you don't need it anymore to configure the VPNs. If you do not know how to do this, refer to Lab 3-3: Configuring Wireshark and SPAN.

Next, you remove the **crypto map** statements on R1 and R3. View the current configuration on the FastEthernet0/0 interface on R1 and Serial0/0/1 as shown in the following code.

Then, issue the **no crypto map** *name* command in interface configuration mode to remove the ISAKMP security association. The router might issue a warning that ISAKMP is now off.

R1:

```
R1# show run interface fastethernet0/0
Building configuration...

Current configuration : 120 bytes
!
interface FastEthernet0/0
 ip address 192.168.12.1 255.255.255.0
 duplex auto
 speed auto
 crypto map SDM_CMAP_1
end


R1# configure terminal
R1(config)# interface fastethernet0/0
R1(config-if)# no crypto map SDM_CMAP_1
*Jan 16 06:02:58.999: %CRYPTO-6-ISAKMP_ON_OFF: ISAKMP is OFF
```

```
R3:
R3# show run interface serial0/0/1
Building configuration...

Current configuration : 91 bytes
!
interface Serial0/0/1
 ip address 192.168.23.3 255.255.255.0
 crypto map SDM_CMAP_1
end


R3# configure terminal
R3(config)# interface serial0/0/1
R3(config-if)# no crypto map SDM_CMAP_1
*Jan 16 06:05:36.038: %CRYPTO-6-ISAKMP_ON_OFF: ISAKMP is OFF
```

Attempt to sniff Telnet traffic from R1 to R3. Enable Telnet access on R3 and configure a secure password to get to configuration mode on R3:

```
R3(config)# enable secret cisco
R3(config)# line vty 0 4
R3(config-line)# password cisco
R3(config-line)# login
```

The routers have now been configured to allow Telnet access.

Have Wireshark start sniffing the packets that it receives via the SPAN session.

Choose **Capture > Interfaces**. Then, click the **Start** button associated with the interface connected to the SPAN destination port. SPAN should start capturing packets on the line, so you can now telnet from R1's loopback to R3's loopback. To source Telnet traffic, use the **telnet** *destination* **/source** *interface* command.

As shown in the previous step, you must source the Telnet session from R1's loopback interface to simulate the interesting traffic that will match the VPN's access list.

First, begin capturing using Wireshark. Then, begin the Telnet session. After you connect to R3, try issuing a command or two and then logging out:

```
R1# telnet 172.16.3.1 /source Loopback0
Trying 172.16.3.1 ... Open


User Access Verification


Password: [cisco]
```

```
R3> en
Password: [cisco]


R3# show ip interface brief
Interface        IP-Address       OK? Method Status                 Protocol
FastEthernet0/0  unassigned       YES unset  administratively down  down
FastEthernet0/1  unassigned       YES unset  administratively down  down
Serial0/0/0      unassigned       YES unset  administratively down  down
Serial0/0/1      192.168.23.3     YES manual up                     up
Serial0/1/0      unassigned       YES unset  administratively down  down
Serial0/1/1      unassigned       YES unset  administratively down  down
Loopback0        172.16.3.1       YES manual up                     up


R3# exit


[Connection to 172.16.3.1 closed by foreign host]
R1#
```

Now, end the capture and look at the output, shown in Figure 3-79 and Figure 3-80. You see a set of Telnet data packets. Some of these, especially the return packets, show entire unencrypted text streams. The reason some return packets having longer text strings is because return packets can be streamed consecutively from the router managing the connection, whereas the text you type into Telnet gets sent in chunks of characters or even character by character, depending on your typing speed.

Figure 3-79   Detailed Packet Data on Telnet String Sent from R1

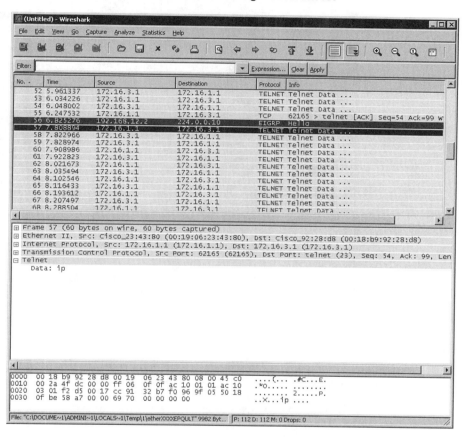

Figure 3-80   Detailed Packet Data on Return Telnet Traffic from R3

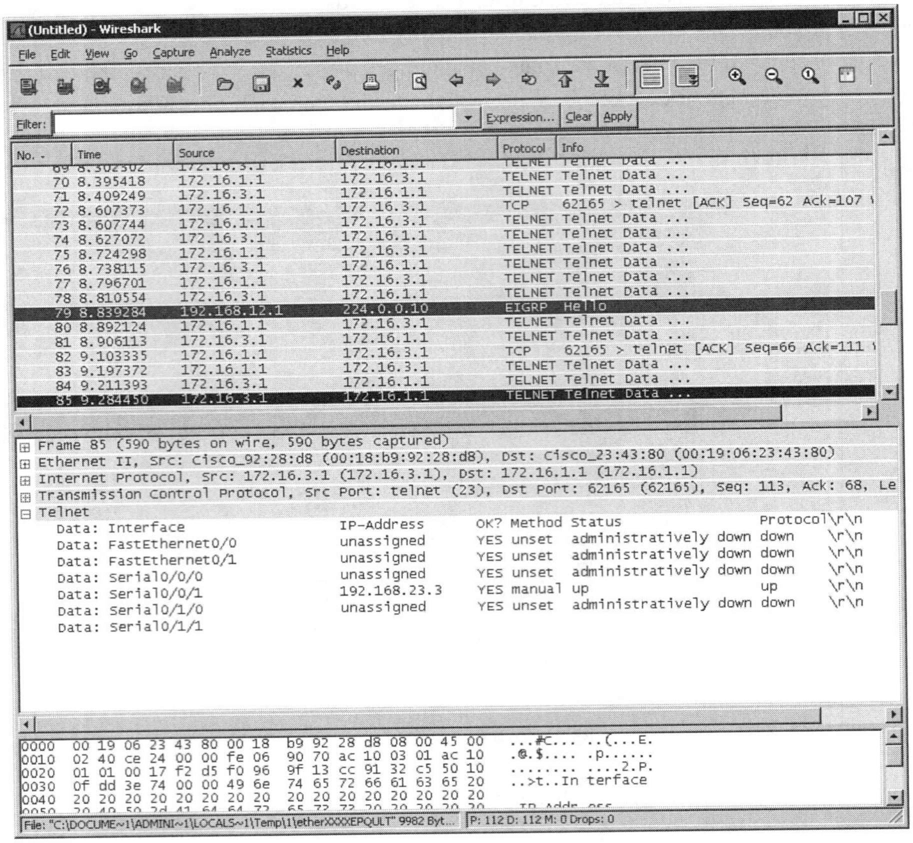

Based on this output, you can see how easy it is for someone who is in the path of sensitive data to view unencrypted or clear-text traffic.

Now, reapply the cryptography settings on R1 and R3 and begin a Telnet session from R1 to R3, as before.

Begin by reapplying the crypto maps you removed earlier on R1 and R3:

```
R1(config)# interface fastethernet0/0
R1(config-if)# crypto map SDM_CMAP_1
*Jan 16 06:36:10.295: %CRYPTO-6-ISAKMP_ON_OFF: ISAKMP is ON
```

```
R3(config)# interface serial0/0/1
R3(config-if)# crypto map SDM_CMAP_1
*Jan 16 06:37:59.798: %CRYPTO-6-ISAKMP_ON_OFF: ISAKMP is ON
```

Start the packet capturing again in Wireshark, and then issue the same Telnet sequence as you did previously:

```
R1# telnet 172.16.3.1 /source Loopback0
Trying 172.16.3.1 ... Open


User Access Verification


Password: [cisco]
```

```
R3> en
Password: [cisco]


R3# show ip interface brief
Interface          IP-Address       OK? Method Status                     Protocol
FastEthernet0/0    unassigned       YES unset  administratively down down
FastEthernet0/1    unassigned       YES unset  administratively down down
Serial0/0/0        unassigned       YES unset  administratively down down
Serial0/0/1        192.168.23.3     YES manual up                         up
Serial0/1/0        unassigned       YES unset  administratively down down
Serial0/1/1        unassigned       YES unset  administratively down down
Loopback0          172.16.3.1       YES manual up                         up


R3# exit


[Connection to 172.16.3.1 closed by foreign host]
R1#
```

End your Wireshark capture when you are finished with the Telnet session.

As far as the user is concerned, the Telnet session seems the same with and without encryption. However, the packet capture from Wireshark shows that the VPN is actively encapsulating and encrypting packets, as shown in Figure 3-81.

Figure 3-81   Detailed Packet Data on Encrypted Telnet String Sent from R1

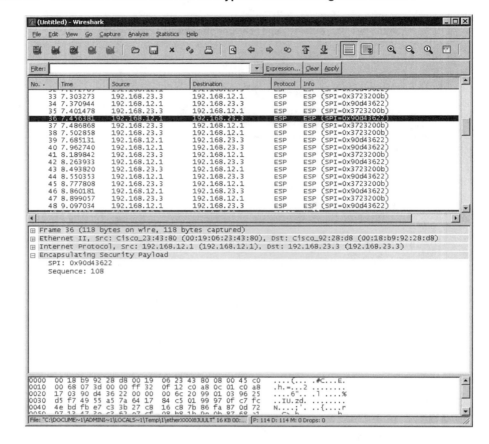

Notice that the protocol is not Telnet (TCP port 23), but the Encapsulating Security Payload (ESP, IP protocol number 50). Remember, all traffic here matches the IPsec access list.

Also, notice that the source and destination are not the actual source and destination of the addresses participating in this Telnet conversation. Rather, they are the VPN endpoints.

Why do you use the VPN endpoints as the source and destination of packets?

_____

_____

Finally, and most important, if you look at the contents of these packets in Wireshark, no matter how you try to format or filter them, you will not be able to see what data was originally inside.

The encryption suite provided by IPsec successfully secures data through authentication, encryption, and data-integrity services.

TCL Script Output

```
R1# tclsh
R1(tcl)# foreach address {
+>(tcl)# 172.16.1.1
+>(tcl)# 192.168.12.1
+>(tcl)# 192.168.12.2
```

```
+>(tcl)# 192.168.23.2
+>(tcl)# 172.16.3.1
+>(tcl)# 192.168.23.3
+>(tcl)# } { ping $address }

Type escape sequence to abort.
Sending 5, 100-byte ICMP Echos to 172.16.1.1, timeout is 2 seconds:
!!!!!
Success rate is 100 percent (5/5), round-trip min/avg/max = 1/1/4 ms
Type escape sequence to abort.
Sending 5, 100-byte ICMP Echos to 192.168.12.1, timeout is 2 seconds:
!!!!!
Success rate is 100 percent (5/5), round-trip min/avg/max = 1/2/4 ms
Type escape sequence to abort.
Sending 5, 100-byte ICMP Echos to 192.168.12.2, timeout is 2 seconds:
!!!!!
Success rate is 100 percent (5/5), round-trip min/avg/max = 1/1/4 ms
Type escape sequence to abort.
Sending 5, 100-byte ICMP Echos to 192.168.23.2, timeout is 2 seconds:
!!!!!
Success rate is 100 percent (5/5), round-trip min/avg/max = 1/2/4 ms
Type escape sequence to abort.
Sending 5, 100-byte ICMP Echos to 172.16.3.1, timeout is 2 seconds:
!!!!!
Success rate is 100 percent (5/5), round-trip min/avg/max = 28/28/32 ms
Type escape sequence to abort.
Sending 5, 100-byte ICMP Echos to 192.168.23.3, timeout is 2 seconds:
!!!!!
Success rate is 100 percent (5/5), round-trip min/avg/max = 28/28/32 ms
R1(tcl)# tclquit
```
```
R2# tclsh
R2(tcl)# foreach address {
+>(tcl)# 172.16.1.1
+>(tcl)# 192.168.12.1
+>(tcl)# 192.168.12.2
+>(tcl)# 192.168.23.2
+>(tcl)# 172.16.3.1
+>(tcl)# 192.168.23.3
+>(tcl)# } { ping $address }

Type escape sequence to abort.
Sending 5, 100-byte ICMP Echos to 172.16.1.1, timeout is 2 seconds:
!!!!!
Success rate is 100 percent (5/5), round-trip min/avg/max = 1/2/4 ms
```

```
Type escape sequence to abort.
Sending 5, 100-byte ICMP Echos to 192.168.12.1, timeout is 2 seconds:
!!!!!
Success rate is 100 percent (5/5), round-trip min/avg/max = 1/2/4 ms
Type escape sequence to abort.
Sending 5, 100-byte ICMP Echos to 192.168.12.2, timeout is 2 seconds:
!!!!!
Success rate is 100 percent (5/5), round-trip min/avg/max = 1/1/4 ms
Type escape sequence to abort.
Sending 5, 100-byte ICMP Echos to 192.168.23.2, timeout is 2 seconds:
!!!!!
Success rate is 100 percent (5/5), round-trip min/avg/max = 56/58/68 ms
Type escape sequence to abort.
Sending 5, 100-byte ICMP Echos to 172.16.3.1, timeout is 2 seconds:
!!!!!
Success rate is 100 percent (5/5), round-trip min/avg/max = 28/28/32 ms
Type escape sequence to abort.
Sending 5, 100-byte ICMP Echos to 192.168.23.3, timeout is 2 seconds:
!!!!!
Success rate is 100 percent (5/5), round-trip min/avg/max = 28/28/28 ms
R2(tcl)# tclquit
```

```
R3# tclsh
R3(tcl)# foreach address {
+>(tcl)# 172.16.1.1
+>(tcl)# 192.168.12.1
+>(tcl)# 192.168.12.2
+>(tcl)# 192.168.23.2
+>(tcl)# 172.16.3.1
+>(tcl)# 192.168.23.3
+>(tcl)# } { ping $address }

Type escape sequence to abort.
Sending 5, 100-byte ICMP Echos to 172.16.1.1, timeout is 2 seconds:
!!!!!
Success rate is 100 percent (5/5), round-trip min/avg/max = 28/28/32 ms
Type escape sequence to abort.
Sending 5, 100-byte ICMP Echos to 192.168.12.1, timeout is 2 seconds:
!!!!!
Success rate is 100 percent (5/5), round-trip min/avg/max = 28/28/32 ms
Type escape sequence to abort.
Sending 5, 100-byte ICMP Echos to 192.168.12.2, timeout is 2 seconds:
!!!!!
Success rate is 100 percent (5/5), round-trip min/avg/max = 28/28/32 ms
Type escape sequence to abort.
```

```
Sending 5, 100-byte ICMP Echos to 192.168.23.2, timeout is 2 seconds:
!!!!!
Success rate is 100 percent (5/5), round-trip min/avg/max = 28/28/32 ms
Type escape sequence to abort.
Sending 5, 100-byte ICMP Echos to 172.16.3.1, timeout is 2 seconds:
!!!!!
Success rate is 100 percent (5/5), round-trip min/avg/max = 1/1/1 ms
Type escape sequence to abort.
Sending 5, 100-byte ICMP Echos to 192.168.23.3, timeout is 2 seconds:
!!!!!
Success rate is 100 percent (5/5), round-trip min/avg/max = 56/58/64 ms
R3(tcl)# tclquit
```

Lab 3-5: Configuring Site-to-Site IPsec VPNs with the IOS CLI (3.10.5)

The objectives of this lab are as follows:

- Configure EIGRP on the routers.

- Create a site-to-site IPsec VPN using IOS.

- Verify IPsec operation.

Figure 3-82 illustrates the topology that is used for this lab.

Figure 3-82   Topology Diagram

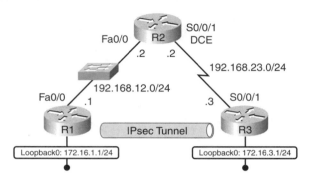

Scenario

In this lab, you configure a site-to-site IPsec VPN. After you configure the VPN, the traffic between the loopback interfaces on routers R1 and R3 is encrypted.

You use the Cisco IOS command-line interface (CLI) for this lab. Lab 3-4 involves the same function as this lab, but it's implemented via the Cisco SDM.

Step 1: Configure Addressing

Configure the loopback interfaces and the serial interfaces with the addresses shown in Figure 3-82. Set the clock rates on the appropriate interfaces and issue the **no shutdown** command on all physical connections. Verify that you have connectivity across local subnets by using the **ping** command:

```
R1(config)# interface loopback0
R1(config-if)# ip address 172.16.1.1 255.255.255.0
R1(config-if)# interface fastethernet0/0
R1(config-if)# ip address 192.168.12.1 255.255.255.0
R1(config-if)# no shutdown
```

```
R2(config)# interface fastethernet0/0
R2(config-if)# ip address 192.168.12.2 255.255.255.0
R2(config-if)# no shutdown
R2(config-if)# interface serial0/0/1
R2(config-if)# ip address 192.168.23.2 255.255.255.0
```

```
R2(config-if)# clockrate 64000
R2(config-if)# no shutdown
R3(config)# interface loopback0
R3(config-if)# ip address 172.16.3.1 255.255.255.0
R3(config-if)# interface serial0/0/1
R3(config-if)# ip address 192.168.23.3 255.255.255.0
R3(config-if)# no shutdown
```

Step 2: Configure EIGRP

To maintain connectivity between remote networks, configure EIGRP to route between all networks in Figure 3-82. Add all connected subnets into the EIGRP autonomous system on every router. Disable automatic summarization:

```
R1(config)# router eigrp 1
R1(config-router)# no auto-summary
R1(config-router)# network 172.16.0.0
R1(config-router)# network 192.168.12.0
R2(config)# router eigrp 1
R2(config-router)# no auto-summary
R2(config-router)# network 192.168.12.0
R2(config-router)# network 192.168.23.0
R3(config)# router eigrp 1
R3(config-router)# no auto-summary
R3(config-router)# network 172.16.0.0
R3(config-router)# network 192.168.23.0
```

At this point, verify that you have full IP connectivity using the following Toolkit Command Language (TCL) script:

```
tclsh

foreach address {
172.16.1.1
192.168.12.1
192.168.12.2
192.168.23.2
172.16.3.1
192.168.23.3
} { ping $address }

tclquit
```

Compare your output with the output shown in the section, "TCL Script Output," for this lab. Troubleshoot as necessary.

Step 3: Create IKE Policies

IPsec is a framework of open standards developed by the Internet Engineering Task Force (IETF). It provides security for the transmission of sensitive information over unprotected networks, such as the Internet. IPsec acts at the network layer, protecting and authenticating IP packets between participating IPsec devices (peers), such as Cisco routers.

Because IPsec is a framework, it allows us to exchange security protocols as new technologies—including encryption algorithms—are developed.

There are two central configuration elements to the implementation of an IPsec VPN:

- Implement Internet Key Exchange (IKE) parameters
- Implement IPsec parameters

The exchange method employed by IKE is first used to pass and validate IKE policies between peers. Then, the peers exchange and match IPsec policies for the authentication and encryption of data traffic. The IKE policy controls the authentication, encryption algorithm, and key exchange method used for IKE proposals that are sent and received by the IPsec endpoints. The IPsec policy encrypts data traffic sent through the VPN tunnel.

IKE needs to be enabled for IPsec to work. IKE is enabled by default on IOS images with cryptographic feature sets. If it is disabled for some reason, enable it with the **crypto isakmp enable** command:

```
R1(config)# crypto isakmp enable
```

If you cannot execute this command on the router, you need to upgrade the IOS image to an image with a feature set that includes the Cisco cryptographic services.

The exchange method employed by IKE is first used to pass and validate IKE policies between peers. Then, the peers exchange and match IPsec policies for the authentication and encryption of data traffic. The IKE policy controls the authentication, encryption algorithm, and key-exchange method that is used by IKE proposals that are sent and received by the IPsec endpoints. The IPsec policy encrypts data traffic that is sent through the VPN tunnel.

To allow IKE Phase 1 negotiation, you must create an Internet Security Association and Key Management Protocol (ISAKMP) policy and configure a peer association involving that ISAKMP policy. An ISAKMP policy defines the authentication and encryption algorithms and hash function used to send control traffic between the two VPN endpoints. When an ISAKMP security association is accepted by the IKE peers, IKE Phase 1 is completed. IKE Phase 2 parameters are configured later in this lab.

Issue the **crypto isakmp policy** *number* command in global configuration mode. This initiates the ISAKMP policy configuration mode. Once in this mode, you can view the various IKE parameters available by typing **?**. Enter into this configuration mode on R1 for policy 10, and view some of the possible settings:

```
R1(config)# crypto isakmp policy 10
R1(config-isakmp)# ?
ISAKMP commands:
  authentication  Set authentication method for protection suite
  default         Set a command to its defaults
  encryption      Set encryption algorithm for protection suite
  exit            Exit from ISAKMP protection suite configuration mode
```

```
group          Set the Diffie-Hellman group
hash           Set hash algorithm for protection suite
lifetime       Set lifetime for ISAKMP security association
no             Negate a command or set its defaults
```

Your choice of an encryption algorithm controls how confidential the control channel between the endpoints will be. The hash algorithm controls data integrity—that is, surety that the data received from a peer has not been tampered with in transit. The authentication type ensures that the packet was indeed sent and signed by the remote peer. The Diffie-Hellman group creates a secret key shared by the peers that has never been sent across the network.

Configure an authentication type of preshared keys. Use AES 256 encryption, SHA as your hash algorithm, and Diffie-Hellman group 5 for this IKE policy.

Give the policy a lifetime of 3600 seconds (1 hour). Configure the same policy on R3. Older versions of the IOS do not support AES 256 encryption and/or SHA as your hash algorithm. Substitute whatever encryption and hashing algorithm your router supports. Be sure the same changes are made on the other VPN endpoint so that they are the same:

```
R1(config-isakmp)# authentication pre-share
R1(config-isakmp)# encryption aes 256
R1(config-isakmp)# hash sha
R1(config-isakmp)# group 5
R1(config-isakmp)# lifetime 3600
R3(config)# crypto isakmp policy 10
R3(config-isakmp)# authentication pre-share
R3(config-isakmp)# encryption aes 256
R3(config-isakmp)# hash sha
R3(config-isakmp)# group 5
R3(config-isakmp)# lifetime 3600
```

Although you only need to configure one policy here, you can configure multiple IKE policies. The different priority numbers refer to how secure a policy is. The lower the policy number, the more secure a policy is. Routers check to verify which security policies are compatible with their peer, starting with the lowest numbered (most secure) policies. You can verify your IKE policy with the **show crypto isakmp policy** command. Note that a default, less secure policy already exists on the router:

```
R1# show crypto isakmp policy

Global IKE policy
Protection suite of priority 10
        encryption algorithm:   AES - Advanced Encryption Standard (256 bit keys).
        hash algorithm:         Secure Hash Standard
        authentication method:  Pre-Shared Key
        Diffie-Hellman group:   #5 (1536 bit)
        lifetime:               3600 seconds, no volume limit
Default protection suite
        encryption algorithm:   DES - Data Encryption Standard (56 bit keys).
        hash algorithm:         Secure Hash Standard
```

```
        authentication method:   Rivest-Shamir-Adleman Signature
        Diffie-Hellman group:    #1 (768 bit)
        lifetime:                86400 seconds, no volume limit
```

```
R3# show crypto isakmp policy

Global IKE policy
Protection suite of priority 10
        encryption algorithm:   AES - Advanced Encryption Standard (256 bit keys).
        hash algorithm:         Secure Hash Standard
        authentication method:  Pre-Shared Key
        Diffie-Hellman group:   #5 (1536 bit)
        lifetime:               3600 seconds, no volume limit
Default protection suite
        encryption algorithm:   DES - Data Encryption Standard (56 bit keys).
        hash algorithm:         Secure Hash Standard
        authentication method:  Rivest-Shamir-Adleman Signature
        Diffie-Hellman group:   #1 (768 bit)
        lifetime:               86400 seconds, no volume limit
```

Step 4: Configure Preshared Keys

Because we chose preshared keys as our authentication method in the IKE policy, we must configure a key on each router corresponding to the other VPN endpoint. These keys must match for authentication to be successful and for the IKE peering to be completed. For simplicity, use the key cisco. A production network should use a more complex key.

Use the global configuration command **crypto isakmp key** *key-string* **address** *address* to enter a pre-shared key. Use the IP address of the remote peer. Ensure that the IP address is the remote interface that the peer would use to route traffic to the local router.

Which IP addresses should you use to configure the IKE peers, given the topology diagram in Figure 3-82?

_____

_____

Each IP address that configures the IKE peers are also referred to as the IP address of the remote VPN endpoint. You can also specify the peer by hostname (substitute the keyword **address** with **hostname**) if the IP address might change dramatically. You either have to statically bind the IP address to the hostname on the router or use a name-lookup service:

```
R1(config)# crypto isakmp key cisco address 192.168.23.3
```

```
R3(config)# crypto isakmp key cisco address 192.168.12.1
```

Step 5: Configure the IPsec Transform Set and Lifetimes

The IPsec transform set is another crypto configuration parameter that routers negotiate to form a security association. In the same way that ISAKMP policies can, multiple transform sets can exist on a router. Routers compare their transform sets to the remote peer until they find a transform set that matches exactly.

Create an IPsec transform set by using the syntax **crypto ipsec transform-set** *tag parameters*. Use **?** to see what parameters are available. For routers R1 and R3, create a transform set with tag 50 and use an ESP transform with an AES 256 cipher first, with Encapsulating Security Payload (ESP) and the SHA hash function, and finally an authentication header using SHA:

```
R1(config)# crypto ipsec transform-set ?
  WORD  Transform set tag


R1(config)# crypto ipsec transform-set 50 ?
  ah-md5-hmac    AH-HMAC-MD5 transform
  ah-sha-hmac    AH-HMAC-SHA transform
  comp-lzs       IP Compression using the LZS compression algorithm
  esp-3des       ESP transform using 3DES(EDE) cipher (168 bits)
  esp-aes        ESP transform using AES cipher
  esp-des        ESP transform using DES cipher (56 bits)
  esp-md5-hmac   ESP transform using HMAC-MD5 auth
  esp-null       ESP transform w/o cipher
  esp-seal       ESP transform using SEAL cipher (160 bits)
  esp-sha-hmac   ESP transform using HMAC-SHA auth


R1(config)# crypto ipsec transform-set 50  esp-aes ?
  128            128 bit keys.
  192            192 bit keys.
  256            256 bit keys.
  ah-md5-hmac    AH-HMAC-MD5 transform
  ah-sha-hmac    AH-HMAC-SHA transform
  comp-lzs       IP Compression using the LZS compression algorithm
  esp-md5-hmac   ESP transform using HMAC-MD5 auth
  esp-sha-hmac   ESP transform using HMAC-SHA auth
  <cr>


R1(config)# crypto ipsec transform-set 50  esp-aes 256 ?
  ah-md5-hmac    AH-HMAC-MD5 transform
  ah-sha-hmac    AH-HMAC-SHA transform
  comp-lzs       IP Compression using the LZS compression algorithm
  esp-md5-hmac   ESP transform using HMAC-MD5 auth
  esp-sha-hmac   ESP transform using HMAC-SHA auth
  <cr>


R1(config)# crypto ipsec transform-set 50  esp-aes 256 esp-sha-hmac ?
  ah-md5-hmac    AH-HMAC-MD5 transform
  ah-sha-hmac    AH-HMAC-SHA transform
  comp-lzs       IP Compression using the LZS compression algorithm
  <cr>
```

Executing these commands sends you into the transform set configuration mode, although you can just type **exit** to leave it because you do not need to configure any additional transform parameters:

```
R1(config)# crypto ipsec transform-set 50 esp-aes 256 esp-sha-hmac ah-sha-hmac
R1(cfg-crypto-trans)# exit
R1(config)#
R3(config)# crypto ipsec transform-set 50 esp-aes 256 esp-sha-hmac ah-sha-hmac
R3(cfg-crypto-trans)# exit
R3(config)#
```

What is the function of the IPsec transform set?

_____

_____

_____

You can also change the IPsec security association lifetimes from its default, which is 3600 seconds or 4,608,000 kilobytes, whichever comes first. Change this with the global configuration command **crypto ipsec security-association lifetime seconds** *seconds* or **crypto ipsec security-association lifetime kilobytes** *kilobytes*. On R1 and R3, set the IPsec security association lifetime to 30 minutes (or 1800 seconds).

```
R1(config)# crypto ipsec security-association lifetime seconds 1800
R3(config)# crypto ipsec security-association lifetime seconds 1800
```

Step 6: Define Interesting Traffic

Now that most of the encryption settings are in place, define extended access lists to tell the router which traffic to encrypt. Like other access lists used to define "interesting traffic" rather than packet filtering, **permit** and **deny** do not have the usual meaning of a filtering access list. A packet that is permitted by an access list used for defining IPsec traffic will get encrypted if the IPsec session is configured correctly. A packet that is denied by one of these access lists is not dropped; it is sent unencrypted. Also, like any other access list, there is an implicit **deny** at the end, which, in this case, means the default action is to not encrypt traffic. If no IPsec security association is correctly configured, no traffic is encrypted, but traffic is forwarded as unencrypted traffic.

In this scenario, the traffic you want to encrypt is traffic going from R1's loopback network to R3's loopback network or vice versa. These access lists are used outbound on the VPN endpoint interfaces, so configure them accordingly. The configuration of R1's access list needs to be mirrored exactly on R3 for this to work properly:

```
R1(config)# access-list 101 permit ip 172.16.1.0 0.0.0.255 172.16.3.0 0.0.0.255
R3(config)# access-list 101 permit ip 172.16.3.0 0.0.0.255 172.16.1.0 0.0.0.255
```

Does IPsec evaluate whether the access lists are mirrored as a requirement to negotiate its security association?

_____

_____

Step 7: Create and Apply Crypto Maps

Now that you have created all of these small configuration modules, you can bring them together in a crypto map. A crypto map is a mapping that associates traffic matching an access list (like the one we created earlier) to a peer and various IKE and IPsec settings. Crypto maps can have multiple map statements, so you can have traffic that matches a certain access list being encrypted and sent to one IPsec peer, and have other traffic that matches a different access list being encrypted toward a different peer. After a crypto map is created, it can be applied to one or more interfaces. The interface(s) that it is applied to should be the one(s) facing the IPsec peer.

To create a crypto map, use the global configuration command **crypto map** *name sequence-num type* to enter the crypto map configuration mode for that sequence number. Multiple crypto map statements can belong to the same crypto map, and they are evaluated in ascending numerical order.

Use a type of **ipsec-isakmp**, which means that IKE establishes IPsec security associations (SA). Under normal circumstances, you would want to use this mode instead of the **ipsec-manual** type. If **ipsec-manual** is used, IKE is not used to configure the IPsec SA. (This mode is beyond the scope of this lab.) Name the crypto map MYMAP, and use 10 as the sequence number. Enter the crypto map configuration mode on R1. When you do this, the crypto map is created, and this command generates a warning that a peer must be fully configured before the crypto map is considered valid and can be actively applied:

```
R1(config)# crypto map MYMAP 10 ipsec-isakmp
% NOTE: This new crypto map will remain disabled until a peer
        and a valid access list have been configured.
```

Use the **match address** *access-list* command to specify which access list defines which traffic to encrypt. If you have ever configured route maps or similar maps on a router before, some of these map-related commands might seem familiar:

```
R1(config-crypto-map)# match address 101
```

You can do many possible **set** commands in a crypto map. To view the list of possibilities, use the **?** help character:

```
R1(config-crypto-map)# set ?
  identity             Identity restriction.
  ip                   Interface Internet Protocol config commands
  isakmp-profile       Specify isakmp Profile
  nat                  Set NAT translation
  peer                 Allowed Encryption/Decryption peer.
  pfs                  Specify pfs settings
  security-association Security association parameters
  transform-set        Specify list of transform sets in priority order
```

Setting a peer IP or hostname is required, so set it to R3's remote VPN endpoint interface using the **set peer** *address* command. Hardcode the transform set to be used with this peer by using the **set transform-set** *tag* command.

Set the perfect forwarding secrecy type by using the **set pfs** *type* command, and modify the default IPsec security association lifetime with the **set security-association lifetime seconds** *seconds* command. As you can see, in the previous output of **?**, you can change more settings in this crypto map. Create a congruent crypto map on R3 by using the mirrored access list to define interesting traffic:

```
R1(config-crypto-map)# set peer 192.168.23.3
R1(config-crypto-map)# set pfs group5
R1(config-crypto-map)# set transform-set 50
R1(config-crypto-map)# set security-association lifetime seconds 900
```

```
R3(config)# crypto map MYMAP 10 ipsec-isakmp
% NOTE: This new crypto map will remain disabled until a peer
        and a valid access list have been configured.
R3(config-crypto-map)# match address 101
R3(config-crypto-map)# set peer 192.168.12.1
R3(config-crypto-map)# set pfs group5
R3(config-crypto-map)# set transform-set 50
R3(config-crypto-map)# set security-association lifetime seconds 900
```

Now that the crypto maps are created, the final step in the process of creating site-to-site VPNs is applying the maps to interfaces. This is done with the interface level **crypto map** *name* command. Note that the SAs will not be established until the crypto map is activated by interesting traffic. Do not create interesting traffic yet, because you want to enable some debugging during the next step. The router generates a notification that crypto is now on:

```
R1(config)# interface fastethernet0/0
R1(config-if)# crypto map MYMAP
*Jan 17 04:09:09.150: %CRYPTO-6-ISAKMP_ON_OFF: ISAKMP is ON
```

```
R3(config)# interface serial0/0/1
R3(config-if)# crypto map MYMAP
*Jan 17 04:10:54.138: %CRYPTO-6-ISAKMP_ON_OFF: ISAKMP is ON
```

Step 8: Verify IPsec Configuration

In Step 3, you used the **show crypto isakmp policy** command to show the configured ISAKMP policies on the router. Similarly, the **show crypto ipsec transform-set** command displays the configured IPsec policies in the form of the transport sets:

```
R1# show crypto ipsec transform-set
Transform set 50: { ah-sha-hmac  }
   will negotiate = { Tunnel,  },
   { esp-256-aes esp-sha-hmac  }
   will negotiate = { Tunnel,  },
```

```
R3# show crypto ipsec transform-set
Transform set 50: { ah-sha-hmac  }
   will negotiate = { Tunnel,  },
   { esp-256-aes esp-sha-hmac  }
   will negotiate = { Tunnel,  },
```

Use the **show crypto map** command to display the crypto maps that will be applied to the router:

```
R1# show crypto map
Crypto Map "MYMAP" 10 ipsec-isakmp
        Peer = 192.168.23.3
        Extended IP access list 101
```

```
        access-list 101 permit ip 172.16.1.0 0.0.0.255 172.16.3.0 0.0.0.255
        Current peer: 192.168.23.3
        Security association lifetime: 4608000 kilobytes/900 seconds
        PFS (Y/N): Y
        DH group:  group5
        Transform sets={
                50,
        }
        Interfaces using crypto map MYMAP:
                FastEthernet0/0
R3# show crypto map
Crypto Map "MYMAP" 10 ipsec-isakmp
        Peer = 192.168.12.1
        Extended IP access list 101
            access-list 101 permit ip 172.16.3.0 0.0.0.255 172.16.1.0 0.0.0.255
        Current peer: 192.168.12.1
        Security association lifetime: 4608000 kilobytes/900 seconds
        PFS (Y/N): Y
        DH group:  group5
        Transform sets={
                50,
        }
        Interfaces using crypto map MYMAP:
                Serial0/0/1
```

The output of these **show** commands does not change if interesting traffic goes across the connection.

Step 9: Verify IPsec Operation

If you use the **show crypto isakmp sa** command, it reveals that no IKE SAs exist yet. After we send some interesting traffic later in this lab, this command output changes:

```
R1# show crypto isakmp sa
dst             src             state           conn-id slot status
R3# show crypto isakmp sa
dst             src             state           conn-id slot status
```

If you use the **show crypto ipsec sa** command, it shows the unused SA between routers R1 and R3. Note the number of packets sent across and the lack of any security associations listed toward the bottom of the output:

```
R1# show crypto ipsec sa

interface: FastEthernet0/0
    Crypto map tag: MYMAP, local addr 192.168.12.1

    protected vrf: (none)
    local  ident (addr/mask/prot/port): (172.16.1.0/255.255.255.0/0/0)
```

```
      remote ident (addr/mask/prot/port): (172.16.3.0/255.255.255.0/0/0)
    current_peer 192.168.23.3 port 500
      PERMIT, flags={origin_is_acl,}
      #pkts encaps: 0, #pkts encrypt: 0, #pkts digest: 0
      #pkts decaps: 0, #pkts decrypt: 0, #pkts verify: 0
      #pkts compressed: 0, #pkts decompressed: 0
      #pkts not compressed: 0, #pkts compr. failed: 0
      #pkts not decompressed: 0, #pkts decompress failed: 0
      #send errors 0, #recv errors 0

      local crypto endpt.: 192.168.12.1, remote crypto endpt.: 192.168.23.3
      path mtu 1500, ip mtu 1500, ip mtu idb FastEthernet0/0
      current outbound spi: 0x0(0)

      inbound esp sas:

      inbound ah sas:

      inbound pcp sas:

      outbound esp sas:

      outbound ah sas:

      outbound pcp sas:
```

```
R3# show crypto ipsec sa

interface: Serial0/0/1
    Crypto map tag: MYMAP, local addr 192.168.23.3

    protected vrf: (none)
    local  ident (addr/mask/prot/port): (172.16.3.0/255.255.255.0/0/0)
    remote ident (addr/mask/prot/port): (172.16.1.0/255.255.255.0/0/0)
    current_peer 192.168.12.1 port 500
      PERMIT, flags={origin_is_acl,}
      #pkts encaps: 0, #pkts encrypt: 0, #pkts digest: 0
      #pkts decaps: 0, #pkts decrypt: 0, #pkts verify: 0
      #pkts compressed: 0, #pkts decompressed: 0
      #pkts not compressed: 0, #pkts compr. failed: 0
      #pkts not decompressed: 0, #pkts decompress failed: 0
      #send errors 0, #recv errors 0
```

```
    local crypto endpt.: 192.168.23.3, remote crypto endpt.: 192.168.12.1
    path mtu 1500, ip mtu 1500, ip mtu idb Serial0/0/1
    current outbound spi: 0x0(0)

    inbound esp sas:

    inbound ah sas:

    inbound pcp sas:

    outbound esp sas:

    outbound ah sas:

    outbound pcp sas:
```

Why have no SAs been negotiated?

_____

_____

How could you force the IPsec peers to negotiate their security association?

_____

_____

Step 10: Interpret IPsec Event Debugging

In terms of the actual communication between the VPN endpoints, ISAKMP prescribes stringent rules as to how an SA can be established. IKE Phase 1 (ISAKMP) negotiates the secure channel between the endpoints, authenticates the neighbor as having the correct secret key, and authenticates the remote endpoint through the secure channel. IKE Phase 1 uses main mode, which consists of six messages in three event-driven exchanges. The result is one bidirectional ISAKMP security association. The exchanges are input/output-driven, so every event is recorded in the debug as an input event from either the local router or the remote router.

IKE Phase 2 (IPsec) negotiates the IPsec tunnel between the two endpoints, authenticates the peers, and encrypts data traffic between them through the encrypted tunnel. IKE Phase 2 uses a process called quick mode to perform its exchange to establish two unidirectional security associations.

On R1, enable two debug commands: **debug crypto isakmp** and **debug crypto ipsec**:

```
R1# debug crypto isakmp
Crypto ISAKMP debugging is on
R1# debug crypto ipsec
Crypto IPSEC debugging is on
```

Now, send an extended ping from R1's loopback to R3's loopback, and watch the debug outputs on both routers. You see both ISAKMP negotiation and IPsec SAs being established. This output is *very* verbose:

```
R1# ping
Protocol [ip]:
Target IP address: 172.16.3.1
Repeat count [5]:
Datagram size [100]:
Timeout in seconds [2]:
Extended commands [n]: y
Source address or interface: 172.16.1.1
Type of service [0]:
Set DF bit in IP header? [no]:
Validate reply data? [no]:
Data pattern [0xABCD]:
Loose, Strict, Record, Timestamp, Verbose[none]:
Sweep range of sizes [n]:
```

At this point, the packets are sent. What happens next?

```
Type escape sequence to abort.
Sending 5, 100-byte ICMP Echos to 172.16.3.1, timeout is 2 seconds:
Packet sent with a source address of 172.16.1.1

*Jan 17 05:11:39.142: IPSEC(sa_request): ,
  (key eng. msg.) OUTBOUND local= 192.168.12.1, remote= 192.168.23.3,
    local_proxy= 172.16.1.0/255.255.255.0/0/0 (type=4),
    remote_proxy= 172.16.3.0/255.255.255.0/0/0 (type=4),
    protocol= ESP, transform= NONE   (Tunnel),
    lifedur= 900s and 4608000kb,
    spi= 0x0(0), conn_id= 0, keysize= 256, flags= 0x0
...
```

When R1 detects interesting traffic going toward R3, the **crypto map** statement defined on R1's Fast Ethernet interface invokes an IPsec state change from inactive to active. The IPsec suite attempts to raise a SA between R1 and R3 to pass secure traffic with the IPsec parameters that were previously configured. The ISAKMP processes on each of the VPN endpoints are now aware that a SA will be attempted and prepare to send ISAKMP policies:

```
...
*Jan 17 05:11:39.146: ISAKMP:(0): SA request profile is (NULL)
*Jan 17 05:11:39.146: ISAKMP: Created a peer struct for 192.168.23.3, peer port 500
*Jan 17 05:11:39.146: ISAKMP: New peer created peer = 0x46F56220 peer_handle =
  0x80000002
*Jan 17 05:11:39.146: ISAKMP: Locking peer struct 0x46F56220, refcount 1 for
  isakmp_initiator
*Jan 17 05:11:39.146: ISAKMP: local port 500, remote port 500
*Jan 17 05:11:39.146: ISAKMP: set new node 0 to QM_IDLE
*Jan 17 05:11:39.146: insert sa successfully sa = 477B9850
...
```

The Cisco IOS Software builds an ISAKMP peer structure in memory, which provides a means to store parameters and policies related to IKE Phase 1 key exchanges. The peers communicate on port 500 on both ends between the IP addresses of the encrypting interfaces on each router. ISAKMP creates and inserts a memory structure representing the ISAKMP SA into the peer structure it just created:

```
...
*Jan 17 05:11:39.146: ISAKMP:(0):Can not start Aggressive mode, trying Main mode
*Jan 17 05:11:39.146: ISAKMP:(0):found peer pre-shared key matching 192.168.23.3
*Jan 17 05:11:39.146: ISAKMP:(0): constructed NAT-T vendor-07 ID
*Jan 17 05:11:39.150: ISAKMP:(0): constructed NAT-T vendor-03 ID
*Jan 17 05:11:39.150: ISAKMP:(0): constructed NAT-T vendor-02 ID
*Jan 17 05:11:39.150: ISAKMP:(0):Input = IKE_MESG_FROM_IPSEC, IKE_SA_REQ_MM
*Jan 17 05:11:39.150: ISAKMP:(0):Old State = IKE_READY  New State = IKE_I_MM1
...
```

Aggressive mode is an exchange process in which all IKE Phase 1 is negotiated with one exchange. This aggressive mode is clearly less secure than main mode, which relies on three exchanges: the ISAKMP policy exchange, the Diffie-Hellman key exchange, and an encrypted authentication test that initiates the ISAKMP security association used for Phase II. In main mode, less information is given to the remote node before the remote node must communicate and can be authenticated:

```
...
*Jan 17 05:11:39.150: ISAKMP:(0): beginning Main Mode exchange
*Jan 17 05:11:39.150: ISAKMP:(0): sending packet to 192.168.23.3 my_port 500
  peer_port 500 (I) MM_NO_STATE
*Jan 17 05:11:39.282: ISAKMP (0:0): received packet from 192.168.23.3 dport 500
  sport 500 Global (I) MM_NO_STATE
*Jan 17 05:11:39.286: ISAKMP:(0):Input = IKE_MESG_FROM_PEER, IKE_MM_EXCH
*Jan 17 05:11:39.286: ISAKMP:(0):Old State = IKE_I_MM1  New State = IKE_I_MM2
*Jan 17 05:11:39.286: ISAKMP:(0): processing SA payload. message ID = 0


.!!!!

Success rate is 80 percent (4/5), round-trip min/avg/max = 52/54/56 ms


R1#


*Jan 17 05:11:39.286: ISAKMP:(0): processing vendor id payload
*Jan 17 05:11:39.286: ISAKMP:(0): vendor ID seems Unity/DPD but major 245 mismatch
*Jan 17 05:11:39.286: ISAKMP (0:0): vendor ID is NAT-T v7
*Jan 17 05:11:39.286: ISAKMP:(0):found peer pre-shared key matching 192.168.23.3
*Jan 17 05:11:39.286: ISAKMP:(0): local preshared key found
*Jan 17 05:11:39.286: ISAKMP : Scanning profiles for xauth ...
*Jan 17 05:11:39.286: ISAKMP:(0):Checking ISAKMP transform 1 against priority 10
  policy
*Jan 17 05:11:39.286: ISAKMP:       encryption AES-CBC
*Jan 17 05:11:39.286: ISAKMP:       keylength of 256
*Jan 17 05:11:39.286: ISAKMP:       hash SHA
```

```
*Jan 17 05:11:39.286: ISAKMP:       default group 5
*Jan 17 05:11:39.286: ISAKMP:       auth pre-share
*Jan 17 05:11:39.286: ISAKMP:       life type in seconds
*Jan 17 05:11:39.286: ISAKMP:       life duration (basic) of 3600
*Jan 17 05:11:39.286: ISAKMP:(0):atts are acceptable. Next payload is 0
*Jan 17 05:11:39.286: ISAKMP:(0): processing vendor id payload
*Jan 17 05:11:39.286: ISAKMP:(0): vendor ID seems Unity/DPD but major 245 mismatch
*Jan 17 05:11:39.286: ISAKMP (0:0): vendor ID is NAT-T v7
*Jan 17 05:11:39.290: ISAKMP:(0):Input = IKE_MESG_INTERNAL, IKE_PROCESS_MAIN_MODE
*Jan 17 05:11:39.290: ISAKMP:(0):Old State = IKE_I_MM2  New State = IKE_I_MM2
...
```

During the first exchange, the initiator sends its policy to the endpoint of the ISAKMP SA in the first message, and the endpoint responds with its ISAKMP security policy in the second message.

Notice that each of the IKE peers sends the ISAKMP security policy to the other. R1 then processes the payload of the packet it received from R3 and determines that it has a preshared key associated with R3's address. R1 matches the ISAKMP transform set (policy) from R3 against its own priority 10 policy. After this check is performed, R1 determines that the attributes of the ISAKMP policy are acceptable and signals the ISAKMP process to continue to the next main mode exchange. Finally, R1 informs R3 that it has accepted the policy and entered the second exchange by beginning the second exchange with R3.

If R1 rejected R3's ISAKMP policy, you would see the following error in the debug output:

```
ISAKMP (0): atts are not acceptable. Next payload is 0
ISAKMP (0): no offers accepted!
ISAKMP (0): SA not acceptable!
```

Also, note that the Internet Control Message Protocol (ICMP) packets passed through the tunnel, although the debug output has not finished displaying to the screen. The entire exchange took about 1 second to perform, according to the timestamps on the debug messages:

```
...
*Jan 17 05:11:39.290: ISAKMP:(0): sending packet to 192.168.23.3 my_port 500
  peer_port 500 (I) MM_SA_SETUP
*Jan 17 05:11:39.290: ISAKMP:(0):Input = IKE_MESG_INTERNAL, IKE_PROCESS_COMPLETE
*Jan 17 05:11:39.290: ISAKMP:(0):Old State = IKE_I_MM2  New State = IKE_I_MM3
*Jan 17 05:11:39.502: ISAKMP (0:0): received packet from 192.168.23.3 dport 500
  sport 500 Global (I) MM_SA_SETUP
*Jan 17 05:11:39.502: ISAKMP:(0):Input = IKE_MESG_FROM_PEER, IKE_MM_EXCH
*Jan 17 05:11:39.502: ISAKMP:(0):Old State = IKE_I_MM3  New State = IKE_I_MM4
*Jan 17 05:11:39.506: ISAKMP:(0): processing KE payload. message ID = 0
*Jan 17 05:11:39.638: ISAKMP:(0): processing NONCE payload. message ID = 0
*Jan 17 05:11:39.638: ISAKMP:(0):found peer pre-shared key matching 192.168.23.3
*Jan 17 05:11:39.642: ISAKMP:(1001): processing vendor id payload
*Jan 17 05:11:39.642: ISAKMP:(1001): vendor ID is Unity
*Jan 17 05:11:39.642: ISAKMP:(1001): processing vendor id payload
*Jan 17 05:11:39.642: ISAKMP:(1001): vendor ID is DPD
*Jan 17 05:11:39.642: ISAKMP:(1001): processing vendor id payload
```

```
*Jan 17 05:11:39.642: ISAKMP:(1001): speaking to another IOS box!
*Jan 17 05:11:39.642: ISAKMP:(1001):Input = IKE_MESG_INTERNAL, IKE_PROCESS_MAIN_MODE
*Jan 17 05:11:39.642: ISAKMP:(1001):Old State = IKE_I_MM4  New State = IKE_I_MM4
...
```

During main mode's second exchange, the ISAKMP initiator sends the remote endpoint an RSA nonce (random number) to be used in the Diffie-Hellman algorithm and the key it receives as the output of the Diffie-Hellman function. This is the third message in the main mode process. The remote endpoint R3 then replies in the fourth message of main mode with its respective nonce and key. R1 and R3 authenticate each other as both sharing the same preshared key used to generate the key it received from the peer.

If the peers did not have matching preshared keys, you would see the following error in the debug output:

```
%CRYPTO-4-IKMP_BAD_MESSAGE: IKE message from 192.168.23.3 failed its
       sanity check or is malformed
%CRYPTO-6-IKMP_MODE_FAILURE: Processing of Main Mode failed with peer
       at 192.168.23.3
```

At this point, R1 prepares to send a packet to R3 that will be passed through the secure channel. This packet will be used by R3 to authenticate R1 as the remote end of the ISAKMP SA:

```
...
*Jan 17 05:11:39.642: ISAKMP:(1001):Send initial contact
*Jan 17 05:11:39.646: ISAKMP:(1001):SA is doing pre-shared key authentication using
  id type ID_IPV4_ADDR
*Jan 17 05:11:39.646: ISAKMP (0:1001): ID payload
        next-payload : 8
        type         : 1
        address      : 192.168.12.1
        protocol     : 17
        port         : 500
        length       : 12
*Jan 17 05:11:39.646: ISAKMP:(1001):Total payload length: 12
*Jan 17 05:11:39.646: ISAKMP:(1001): sending packet to 192.168.23.3 my_port 500
  peer_port 500 (I) MM_KEY_EXCH
*Jan 17 05:11:39.646: ISAKMP:(1001):Input = IKE_MESG_INTERNAL, IKE_PROCESS_COMPLETE
*Jan 17 05:11:39.646: ISAKMP:(1001):Old State = IKE_I_MM4  New State = IKE_I_MM5
*Jan 17 05:11:39.690: ISAKMP (0:1001): received packet from 192.168.23.3 dport 500
  sport 500 Global (I) MM_KEY_EXCH
*Jan 17 05:11:39.690: ISAKMP:(1001): processing ID payload. message ID = 0
*Jan 17 05:11:39.690: ISAKMP (0:1001): ID payload
        next-payload : 8
        type         : 1
        address      : 192.168.23.3
        protocol     : 17
        port         : 500
        length       : 12
```

```
*Jan 17 05:11:39.690: ISAKMP:(0):: peer matches *none* of the profiles
*Jan 17 05:11:39.690: ISAKMP:(1001): processing HASH payload. message ID = 0
*Jan 17 05:11:39.690: ISAKMP:(1001):SA authentication status:
      authenticated
*Jan 17 05:11:39.690: ISAKMP:(1001):SA has been authenticated with 192.168.23.3
...
```

When R1 receives the authentication packet from R3, it checks the ID payload and hash value of the packet. If ISAKMP authenticates the SA through the encrypted channel, IKE Phase 1 is complete and the security association is established:

```
...
*Jan 17 05:11:39.690: ISAKMP: Trying to insert a peer 192.168.12.1/192.168.23.3/500/,
   and inserted successfully 46F56220.
*Jan 17 05:11:39.690: ISAKMP:(1001):Input = IKE_MESG_FROM_PEER, IKE_MM_EXCH
*Jan 17 05:11:39.690: ISAKMP:(1001):Old State = IKE_I_MM5  New State = IKE_I_MM6
*Jan 17 05:11:39.694: ISAKMP:(1001):Input = IKE_MESG_INTERNAL, IKE_PROCESS_MAIN_MODE
*Jan 17 05:11:39.694: ISAKMP:(1001):Old State = IKE_I_MM6  New State = IKE_I_MM6
*Jan 17 05:11:39.694: ISAKMP:(1001):Input = IKE_MESG_INTERNAL, IKE_PROCESS_COMPLETE
*Jan 17 05:11:39.694: ISAKMP:(1001):Old State = IKE_I_MM6  New State = IKE_P1_
   COMPLETE
...
```

Finally, R1 inserts the peer into the memory structure reserved at the beginning of the ISAKMP negotiation. R1 begins IKE Phase 2 over the ISAKMP SA created in IKE Phase 1:

```
...
*Jan 17 05:11:39.694: ISAKMP:(1001):beginning Quick Mode exchange, M-ID of 787769575
*Jan 17 05:11:39.694: ISAKMP:(1001):QM Initiator gets spi
*Jan 17 05:11:39.698: ISAKMP:(1001): sending packet to 192.168.23.3 my_port 500
   peer_port 500 (I) QM_IDLE
*Jan 17 05:11:39.698: ISAKMP:(1001):Node 787769575, Input = IKE_MESG_INTERNAL,
   IKE_INIT_QM
*Jan 17 05:11:39.698: ISAKMP:(1001):Old State = IKE_QM_READY  New State =
   IKE_QM_I_QM1
*Jan 17 05:11:39.698: ISAKMP:(1001):Input = IKE_MESG_INTERNAL, IKE_PHASE1_COMPLETE
*Jan 17 05:11:39.698: ISAKMP:(1001):Old State = IKE_P1_COMPLETE  New State =
   IKE_P1_COMPLETE
...
```

Quick mode uses three messages to create an IPsec SA. The initiator, R1, sends the first message including the hash, IPsec SA policies, a nonce, and a key created using the preshared keys and two ID payloads. R3 processes R1's IPsec proposal and replies with a message with its values for the parameters:

```
...
*Jan 17 05:11:40.014: ISAKMP (0:1001): received packet from 192.168.23.3 dport 500
   sport 500 Global (I) QM_IDLE
*Jan 17 05:11:40.018: ISAKMP:(1001): processing HASH payload. message ID = 787769575
*Jan 17 05:11:40.018: ISAKMP:(1001): processing SA payload. message ID = 787769575
*Jan 17 05:11:40.018: ISAKMP:(1001):Checking IPSec proposal 1
```

```
*Jan 17 05:11:40.018: ISAKMP: transform 1, AH_SHA
*Jan 17 05:11:40.018: ISAKMP:    attributes in transform:
*Jan 17 05:11:40.018: ISAKMP:      encaps is 1 (Tunnel)
*Jan 17 05:11:40.018: ISAKMP:      SA life type in seconds
*Jan 17 05:11:40.018: ISAKMP:      SA life duration (basic) of 900
*Jan 17 05:11:40.018: ISAKMP:      SA life type in kilobytes
*Jan 17 05:11:40.018: ISAKMP:      SA life duration (VPI) of  0x0 0x46 0x50 0x0
*Jan 17 05:11:40.018: ISAKMP:      group is 5
*Jan 17 05:11:40.018: ISAKMP:      authenticator is HMAC-SHA
*Jan 17 05:11:40.018: ISAKMP:(1001):atts are acceptable.
*Jan 17 05:11:40.018: ISAKMP:(1001):Checking IPSec proposal 1
*Jan 17 05:11:40.018: ISAKMP: transform 1, ESP_AES
*Jan 17 05:11:40.018: ISAKMP:    attributes in transform:
*Jan 17 05:11:40.018: ISAKMP:      encaps is 1 (Tunnel)
*Jan 17 05:11:40.018: ISAKMP:      SA life type in seconds
*Jan 17 05:11:40.018: ISAKMP:      SA life duration (basic) of 900
*Jan 17 05:11:40.018: ISAKMP:      SA life type in kilobytes
*Jan 17 05:11:40.018: ISAKMP:      SA life duration (VPI) of  0x0 0x46 0x50 0x0
*Jan 17 05:11:40.018: ISAKMP:      authenticator is HMAC-SHA
*Jan 17 05:11:40.018: ISAKMP:      key length is 256
*Jan 17 05:11:40.018: ISAKMP:      group is 5
*Jan 17 05:11:40.018: ISAKMP:(1001):atts are acceptable.
...
```

R3 responds with a second similar message containing the same properties. R1 processes the hash and IPsec policy, as just shown. R1 determines that the IPsec proposal from R3 is acceptable with the attributes in its own IPsec policies.

Notice that two transforms will be used, with an authentication header (AH) applied to the ESP-encapsulated and encrypted data. A packet routed on R1 from 172.16.1.1 to 172.16.3.1 will first be encrypted and encapsulated as the payload of an ESP packet, and then the AH will be applied. The packet will be sent with a source IP address of 192.168.12.1 and a destination IP address of 192.168.23.3:

```
...
*Jan 17 05:11:40.018: IPSEC(validate_proposal_request): proposal part #1
*Jan 17 05:11:40.018: IPSEC(validate_proposal_request): proposal part #1,
  (key eng. msg.) INBOUND local= 192.168.12.1, remote= 192.168.23.3,
    local_proxy= 172.16.1.0/255.255.255.0/0/0 (type=4),
    remote_proxy= 172.16.3.0/255.255.255.0/0/0 (type=4),
    protocol= AH, transform= ah-sha-hmac  (Tunnel),
    lifedur= 0s and 0kb,
    spi= 0x0(0), conn_id= 0, keysize= 0, flags= 0x0
*Jan 17 05:11:40.018: IPSEC(validate_proposal_request): proposal part #2
*Jan 17 05:11:40.018: IPSEC(validate_proposal_request): proposal part #2,
  (key eng. msg.) INBOUND local= 192.168.12.1, remote= 192.168.23.3,
    local_proxy= 172.16.1.0/255.255.255.0/0/0 (type=4),
```

```
    remote_proxy= 172.16.3.0/255.255.255.0/0/0 (type=4),
    protocol= ESP, transform= esp-aes 256 esp-sha-hmac  (Tunnel),
    lifedur= 0s and 0kb,
    spi= 0x0(0), conn_id= 0, keysize= 256, flags= 0x0
*Jan 17 05:11:40.022: Crypto mapdb : proxy_match
       src addr     : 172.16.1.0
       dst addr     : 172.16.3.0
       protocol     : 0
       src port     : 0
       dst port     : 0
*Jan 17 05:11:40.022: ISAKMP:(1001): processing NONCE payload. message ID = 787769575
*Jan 17 05:11:40.022: ISAKMP:(1001): processing KE payload. message ID = 787769575
*Jan 17 05:11:40.158: ISAKMP:(1001): processing ID payload. message ID = 787769575
*Jan 17 05:11:40.158: ISAKMP:(1001): processing ID payload. message ID = 787769575
...
```

R1 checks the proposal against its own IPsec policies, including the access lists on each end. If the access lists were not mirrors of each other, you would receive the following error:

```
    IPSEC(validate_transform_proposal): proxy identities not supported
    ISAKMP: IPSec policy invalidated proposal
```

The crypto map database could also evaluate the transport protocol or the source and destination ports using other properties in the extended access list, but these were unused in the access list you supplied.

The nonce and keyed payload validate that two peers have the same keys. When the processing of this second message is complete, R1 must create the IPsec SAs so that interesting data can be encrypted using the policies negotiated.

Because two transforms exist in the transform set, two security associations and two proposals need to be created for each unidirectional path between the endpoints:

```
...
*Jan 17 05:11:40.158: ISAKMP:(1001): Creating IPSec SAs
*Jan 17 05:11:40.158:          inbound SA from 192.168.23.3 to 192.168.12.1 (f/i)
  0/ 0
       (proxy 172.16.3.0 to 172.16.1.0)
*Jan 17 05:11:40.158:          has spi 0x588AA60C and conn_id 0
*Jan 17 05:11:40.158:          lifetime of 900 seconds
*Jan 17 05:11:40.158:          lifetime of 4608000 kilobytes
*Jan 17 05:11:40.158:          outbound SA from 192.168.12.1 to 192.168.23.3 (f/i)
  0/0
       (proxy 172.16.1.0 to 172.16.3.0)
*Jan 17 05:11:40.162:          has spi  0x897F9209 and conn_id 0
*Jan 17 05:11:40.162:          lifetime of 900 seconds
*Jan 17 05:11:40.162:          lifetime of 4608000 kilobytes
*Jan 17 05:11:40.162: ISAKMP:(1001): Creating IPSec SAs
*Jan 17 05:11:40.162:          inbound SA from 192.168.23.3 to 192.168.12.1 (f/i)
  0/ 0
```

```
                    (proxy 172.16.3.0 to 172.16.1.0)
*Jan 17 05:11:40.162:          has spi 0x2E2954C0 and conn_id 0
*Jan 17 05:11:40.162:          lifetime of 900 seconds
*Jan 17 05:11:40.162:          lifetime of 4608000 kilobytes
*Jan 17 05:11:40.162:          outbound SA from 192.168.12.1 to 192.168.23.3 (f/i) 0/0
                    (proxy 172.16.1.0 to 172.16.3.0)
*Jan 17 05:11:40.162:          has spi  0xAE4C8E5A and conn_id 0
*Jan 17 05:11:40.162:          lifetime of 900 seconds
*Jan 17 05:11:40.162:          lifetime of 4608000 kilobytes
*Jan 17 05:11:40.162: ISAKMP:(1001): sending packet to 192.168.23.3 my_port 500
  peer_port 500 (I) QM_IDLE
*Jan 17 05:11:40.162: ISAKMP:(1001):deleting node 787769575 error FALSE reason "No
  Error"
*Jan 17 05:11:40.162: ISAKMP:(1001):Node 787769575, Input = IKE_MESG_FROM_PEER,
  IKE_QM_EXCH
*Jan 17 05:11:40.162: ISAKMP:(1001):Old State = IKE_QM_I_QM1  New State =
  IKE_QM_PHASE2_COMPLETE
*Jan 17 05:11:40.166: IPSEC(key_engine): got a queue event with 1 KMI message(s)
*Jan 17 05:11:40.166: Crypto mapdb : proxy_match
        src addr    : 172.16.1.0
        dst addr    : 172.16.3.0
        protocol    : 0
        src port    : 0
        dst port    : 0
*Jan 17 05:11:40.166: IPSEC(crypto_IPSec_sa_find_ident_head): reconnecting with the
  same proxies and peer 192.168.23.3
*Jan 17 05:11:40.166: IPSEC(policy_db_add_ident): src 172.16.1.0, dest 172.16.3.0,
  dest_port 0


*Jan 17 05:11:40.166: IPSEC(create_sa): sa created,
   (sa) sa_dest= 192.168.12.1, sa_proto= 51,
     sa_spi= 0x588AA60C(1485481484),
     sa_trans= ah-sha-hmac , sa_conn_id= 2001
*Jan 17 05:11:40.166: IPSEC(create_sa): sa created,
   (sa) sa_dest= 192.168.23.3, sa_proto= 51,
     sa_spi= 0x897F9209(2306839049),
     sa_trans= ah-sha-hmac , sa_conn_id= 2002
*Jan 17 05:11:40.166: IPSEC(create_sa): sa created,
   (sa) sa_dest= 192.168.12.1, sa_proto= 50,
     sa_spi= 0x2E2954C0(774460608),
     sa_trans= esp-aes 256 esp-sha-hmac , sa_conn_id= 2001
*Jan 17 05:11:40.166: IPSEC(create_sa): sa created,
   (sa) sa_dest= 192.168.23.3, sa_proto= 50,
     sa_spi= 0xAE4C8E5A(2924252762),
     sa_trans= esp-aes 256 esp-sha-hmac , sa_conn_id= 2002
```

```
*Jan 17 05:11:40.166: IPSEC(update_current_outbound_sa): updated peer 192.168.23.3
  current outbound sa to SPI AE4C8E5A
*Jan 17 05:12:30.162: ISAKMP:(1001):purging node 787769575
```

R1 has now established four security associations with R3: two in the outbound direction and two in the inbound direction. One in each direction is used for the AH transform, and the other is used for the ESP transform. At this point, the ICMP replies are passing naturally through the IPsec tunnel.

Disable debugging after you finish:

R1# **undebug all**

```
All possible debugging has been turned off
```

As you can see, the output from the debugs is extensive and verbose. However, it can really help you if you are troubleshooting an IPsec problem. As mentioned earlier, we can view **crypto** commands and see that they now are populated with data:

R1# **show crypto isakmp sa**

```
dst             src             state         conn-id slot status
192.168.23.3    192.168.12.1    QM_IDLE         1001     0 ACTIVE


R1# show crypto ipsec sa

interface: FastEthernet0/0
    Crypto map tag: MYMAP, local addr 192.168.12.1

   protected vrf: (none)
   local  ident (addr/mask/prot/port): (172.16.1.0/255.255.255.0/0/0)
   remote ident (addr/mask/prot/port): (172.16.3.0/255.255.255.0/0/0)
   current_peer 192.168.23.3 port 500
     PERMIT, flags={origin_is_acl,}
    #pkts encaps: 4, #pkts encrypt: 4, #pkts digest: 4
    #pkts decaps: 4, #pkts decrypt: 4, #pkts verify: 4
    #pkts compressed: 0, #pkts decompressed: 0
    #pkts not compressed: 0, #pkts compr. failed: 0
    #pkts not decompressed: 0, #pkts decompress failed: 0
    #send errors 1, #recv errors 0

     local crypto endpt.: 192.168.12.1, remote crypto endpt.: 192.168.23.3
     path mtu 1500, ip mtu 1500, ip mtu idb FastEthernet0/0
     current outbound spi: 0xAE4C8E5A(2924252762)

     inbound esp sas:
      spi: 0x2E2954C0(774460608)
        transform: esp-256-aes esp-sha-hmac ,
        in use settings ={Tunnel, }
        conn id: 2001, flow_id: NETGX:1, crypto map: MYMAP
        sa timing: remaining key lifetime (k/sec): (4506913/334)
```

```
                  IV size: 16 bytes
                  replay detection support: Y
                  Status: ACTIVE

            inbound ah sas:
             spi: 0x588AA60C(1485481484)
                  transform: ah-sha-hmac ,
                  in use settings ={Tunnel, }
                  conn id: 2001, flow_id: NETGX:1, crypto map: MYMAP
                  sa timing: remaining key lifetime (k/sec): (4506913/332)
                  replay detection support: Y
                  Status: ACTIVE

            inbound pcp sas:

            outbound esp sas:
             spi: 0xAE4C8E5A(2924252762)
                  transform: esp-256-aes esp-sha-hmac ,
                  in use settings ={Tunnel, }
                  conn id: 2002, flow_id: NETGX:2, crypto map: MYMAP
                  sa timing: remaining key lifetime (k/sec): (4506913/332)
                  IV size: 16 bytes
                  replay detection support: Y
                  Status: ACTIVE

            outbound ah sas:
             spi: 0x897F9209(2306839049)
                  transform: ah-sha-hmac ,
                  in use settings ={Tunnel, }
                  conn id: 2002, flow_id: NETGX:2, crypto map: MYMAP
                  sa timing: remaining key lifetime (k/sec): (4506913/332)
                  replay detection support: Y
                  Status: ACTIVE

            outbound pcp sas:
R3# show crypto isakmp sa
dst              src            state         conn-id slot status
192.168.23.3     192.168.12.1   QM_IDLE            1    0 ACTIVE


R3# show crypto ipsec sa

interface: Serial0/0/1
      Crypto map tag: MYMAP, local addr 192.168.23.3
```

```
protected vrf: (none)
local  ident (addr/mask/prot/port): (172.16.3.0/255.255.255.0/0/0)
remote ident (addr/mask/prot/port): (172.16.1.0/255.255.255.0/0/0)
current_peer 192.168.12.1 port 500
  PERMIT, flags={origin_is_acl,}
 #pkts encaps: 4, #pkts encrypt: 4, #pkts digest: 4
 #pkts decaps: 4, #pkts decrypt: 4, #pkts verify: 4
 #pkts compressed: 0, #pkts decompressed: 0
 #pkts not compressed: 0, #pkts compr. failed: 0
 #pkts not decompressed: 0, #pkts decompress failed: 0
 #send errors 0, #recv errors 0

  local crypto endpt.: 192.168.23.3, remote crypto endpt.: 192.168.12.1
  path mtu 1500, ip mtu 1500, ip mtu idb Serial0/0/1
  current outbound spi: 0x2E2954C0(774460608)

  inbound esp sas:
   spi: 0xAE4C8E5A(2924252762)
     transform: esp-256-aes esp-sha-hmac ,
     in use settings ={Tunnel, }
     conn id: 3001, flow_id: NETGX:1, crypto map: MYMAP
     sa timing: remaining key lifetime (k/sec): (4385199/319)
     IV size: 16 bytes
     replay detection support: Y
     Status: ACTIVE

  inbound ah sas:
   spi: 0x897F9209(2306839049)
     transform: ah-sha-hmac ,
     in use settings ={Tunnel, }
     conn id: 3001, flow_id: NETGX:1, crypto map: MYMAP
     sa timing: remaining key lifetime (k/sec): (4385199/318)
     replay detection support: Y
     Status: ACTIVE

  inbound pcp sas:

  outbound esp sas:
   spi: 0x2E2954C0(774460608)
     transform: esp-256-aes esp-sha-hmac ,
     in use settings ={Tunnel, }
     conn id: 3002, flow_id: NETGX:2, crypto map: MYMAP
     sa timing: remaining key lifetime (k/sec): (4385199/318)
     IV size: 16 bytes
```

```
        replay detection support: Y
        Status: ACTIVE


    outbound ah sas:
     spi: 0x588AA60C(1485481484)
        transform: ah-sha-hmac ,
        in use settings ={Tunnel, }
        conn id: 3002, flow_id: NETGX:2, crypto map: MYMAP
        sa timing: remaining key lifetime (k/sec): (4385199/318)
        replay detection support: Y
        Status: ACTIVE


    outbound pcp sas:
```

Why are there four security associations on each router?

_____

_____

Challenge: Use Wireshark to Monitor Encryption of Traffic

You can observe packets on the wire using Wireshark and see how their content looks unencrypted and then encrypted. To do this, first configure a SPAN session on the switch and open up Wireshark on a host attached to the SPAN destination port. You can use the host that you used for SDM because you don't need it anymore to configure the VPNs. If you do not know how to do this, refer to Lab 3-3: Configuring Wireshark and SPAN.

Next, you remove the **crypto map** statements on R1 and R3. View the current configuration on the FastEthernet0/0 interface on R1 and Serial0/0/1 as shown in the following code.

Then, issue the **no crypto map** *name* command in interface configuration mode to remove the ISAKMP SA. The router might issue a warning that ISAKMP is now off.
R1:

```
R1# show run interface fastethernet0/0
Building configuration...

Current configuration : 120 bytes
!
interface FastEthernet0/0
 ip address 192.168.12.1 255.255.255.0
 duplex auto
 speed auto
 crypto map SDM_CMAP_1
end


R1# configure terminal
R1(config)# interface fastethernet0/0
```

```
R1(config-if)# no crypto map SDM_CMAP_1
*Jan 16 06:02:58.999: %CRYPTO-6-ISAKMP_ON_OFF: ISAKMP is OFF
```

R3:

```
R3# show run interface serial0/0/1
Building configuration...

Current configuration : 91 bytes
!
interface Serial0/0/1
 ip address 192.168.23.3 255.255.255.0
 crypto map SDM_CMAP_1
end


R3# configure terminal
R3(config)# interface serial0/0/1
R3(config-if)# no crypto map SDM_CMAP_1
*Jan 16 06:05:36.038: %CRYPTO-6-ISAKMP_ON_OFF: ISAKMP is OFF
```

Attempt to sniff Telnet traffic from R1 to R3. Enable Telnet access on R3 and configure a secure password to get to configuration mode on R3:

```
R3(config)# enable secret cisco
R3(config)# line vty 0 4
R3(config-line)# password cisco
R3(config-line)# login
```

The routers have now been configured to allow Telnet access.

Have Wireshark start sniffing the packets that it receives via the SPAN session.

Choose **Capture > Interfaces**. Then, click the **Start** button associated with the interface connected to the SPAN destination port. SPAN should start capturing packets on the line, so you can now telnet from R1's loopback to R3's loopback. To source Telnet traffic, use the **telnet** *destination* **/source** *interface* command.

As shown in the previous step, you must source the Telnet session from R1's loopback interface to simulate the interesting traffic that will match the VPN's access list.

First, begin capturing using Wireshark. Then, begin the Telnet session. After you connect to R3, try issuing a command or two and then logging out:

```
R1# telnet 172.16.3.1 /source Loopback0
Trying 172.16.3.1 ... Open


User Access Verification


Password: [cisco]
R3> en
Password: [cisco]
```

```
R3# show ip interface brief
Interface           IP-Address       OK? Method Status                   Protocol
FastEthernet0/0     unassigned       YES unset  administratively down    down
FastEthernet0/1     unassigned       YES unset  administratively down    down
Serial0/0/0         unassigned       YES unset  administratively down    down
Serial0/0/1         192.168.23.3     YES manual up                       up
Serial0/1/0         unassigned       YES unset  administratively down    down
Serial0/1/1         unassigned       YES unset  administratively down    down
Loopback0           172.16.3.1       YES manual up                       up

R3# exit


[Connection to 172.16.3.1 closed by foreign host]
R1#
```

Now, end the capture and look at the output, shown in Figure 3-83 and Figure 3-84. You see a set of Telnet data packets. Some of these, especially the return packets, show entire unencrypted text streams. The reason some return packets have longer text strings is because return packets can be streamed consecutively from the router managing the connection, whereas the text you type into Telnet gets sent in chunks of characters or even character by character, depending on your typing speed.

Figure 3-83   Detailed Packet Data on Telnet String Sent from R1

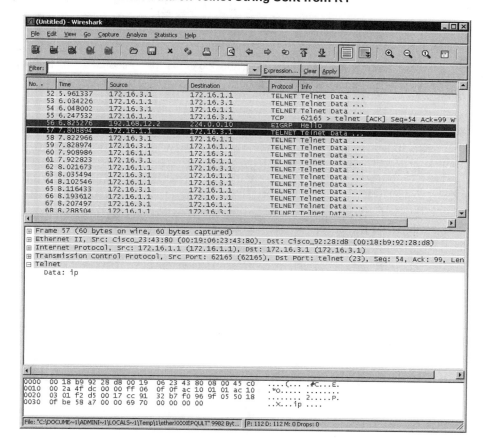

Figure 3-84   Detailed Packet Data on Return Telnet Traffic from R3

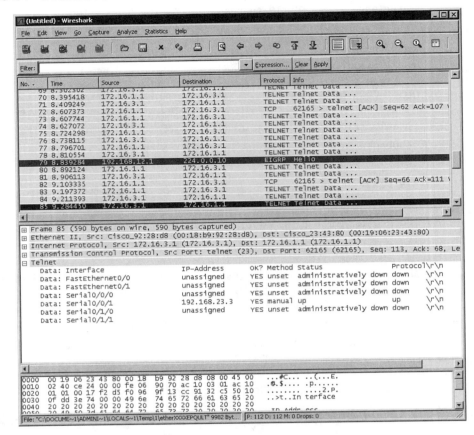

Based on this output, you can see how easy it is for someone who is in the path of sensitive data to view unencrypted or clear-text traffic.

Now, reapply the cryptography settings on R1 and R3 and begin a Telnet session from R1 to R3, as before.

Begin by reapplying the crypto maps you removed earlier on R1 and R3:

```
R1(config)# interface fastethernet0/0
R1(config-if)# crypto map SDM_CMAP_1
*Jan 16 06:36:10.295: %CRYPTO-6-ISAKMP_ON_OFF: ISAKMP is ON
```

```
R3(config)# interface serial0/0/1
R3(config-if)# crypto map SDM_CMAP_1
*Jan 16 06:37:59.798: %CRYPTO-6-ISAKMP_ON_OFF: ISAKMP is ON
```

Start the packet capturing again in Wireshark, and then issue the same Telnet sequence that you did previously:

```
R1# telnet 172.16.3.1 /source Loopback0
Trying 172.16.3.1 ... Open


User Access Verification


Password: [cisco]
R3> en
Password: [cisco]


R3# show ip interface brief
Interface            IP-Address      OK? Method Status                    Protocol
FastEthernet0/0      unassigned      YES unset  administratively down     down
FastEthernet0/1      unassigned      YES unset  administratively down     down
Serial0/0/0          unassigned      YES unset  administratively down     down
Serial0/0/1          192.168.23.3    YES manual up                        up
Serial0/1/0          unassigned      YES unset  administratively down     down
Serial0/1/1          unassigned      YES unset  administratively down     down
Loopback0            172.16.3.1      YES manual up                        up


R3# exit


[Connection to 172.16.3.1 closed by foreign host]
R1#
```

End your Wireshark capture when you are finished with the Telnet session.

As far as the user is concerned, the Telnet session seems the same with and without encryption. However, the packet capture from Wireshark in Figure 3-85 shows that the VPN is actively encapsulating and encrypting packets.

Figure 3-85   Detailed Packet Data on Encrypted Telnet String Sent from R1

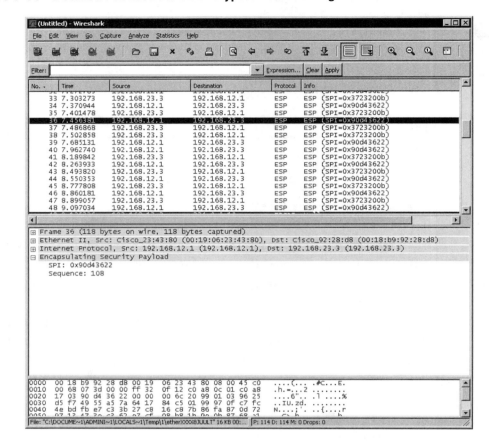

Notice that the protocol is not Telnet (TCP port 23), but the Encapsulating Security Protocol (ESP, IP protocol number 50). Remember, all traffic here matches the IPsec access list.

Also, notice that the source and destination are not the actual source and destination of the addresses participating in this Telnet conversation. Rather, they are the VPN endpoints.

Why do you use the VPN endpoints as the source and destination of packets?

Finally, and most important, if you look at the contents of these packets in Wireshark, no matter how you try to format or filter them, you will not be able to see what data was originally inside.

The encryption suite provided by IPsec successfully secures data through authentication, encryption, and data-integrity services.

TCL Script Output

```
R1# tclsh
R1(tcl)#foreach address {
+>(tcl)#172.16.1.1
+>(tcl)#192.168.12.1
+>(tcl)#192.168.12.2
+>(tcl)#192.168.23.2
+>(tcl)#172.16.3.1
+>(tcl)#192.168.23.3
+>(tcl)#} { ping $address }


Type escape sequence to abort.
Sending 5, 100-byte ICMP Echos to 172.16.1.1, timeout is 2 seconds:
!!!!!
Success rate is 100 percent (5/5), round-trip min/avg/max = 1/1/4 ms
Type escape sequence to abort.
Sending 5, 100-byte ICMP Echos to 192.168.12.1, timeout is 2 seconds:
!!!!!
Success rate is 100 percent (5/5), round-trip min/avg/max = 1/2/4 ms
Type escape sequence to abort.
Sending 5, 100-byte ICMP Echos to 192.168.12.2, timeout is 2 seconds:
!!!!!
Success rate is 100 percent (5/5), round-trip min/avg/max = 1/1/4 ms
Type escape sequence to abort.
Sending 5, 100-byte ICMP Echos to 192.168.23.2, timeout is 2 seconds:
!!!!!
Success rate is 100 percent (5/5), round-trip min/avg/max = 1/2/4 ms
Type escape sequence to abort.
Sending 5, 100-byte ICMP Echos to 172.16.3.1, timeout is 2 seconds:
!!!!!
Success rate is 100 percent (5/5), round-trip min/avg/max = 28/28/32 ms
Type escape sequence to abort.
Sending 5, 100-byte ICMP Echos to 192.168.23.3, timeout is 2 seconds:
!!!!!
Success rate is 100 percent (5/5), round-trip min/avg/max = 28/28/32 ms
R1(tcl)# tclquit
```

```
R2# tclsh
R2(tcl)#foreach address {
+>(tcl)#172.16.1.1
+>(tcl)#192.168.12.1
+>(tcl)#192.168.12.2
+>(tcl)#192.168.23.2
+>(tcl)#172.16.3.1
```

```
+>(tcl)#192.168.23.3
+>(tcl)#} { ping $address }

Type escape sequence to abort.
Sending 5, 100-byte ICMP Echos to 172.16.1.1, timeout is 2 seconds:
!!!!!
Success rate is 100 percent (5/5), round-trip min/avg/max = 1/2/4 ms
Type escape sequence to abort.
Sending 5, 100-byte ICMP Echos to 192.168.12.1, timeout is 2 seconds:
!!!!!
Success rate is 100 percent (5/5), round-trip min/avg/max = 1/2/4 ms
Type escape sequence to abort.
Sending 5, 100-byte ICMP Echos to 192.168.12.2, timeout is 2 seconds:
!!!!!
Success rate is 100 percent (5/5), round-trip min/avg/max = 1/1/4 ms
Type escape sequence to abort.
Sending 5, 100-byte ICMP Echos to 192.168.23.2, timeout is 2 seconds:
!!!!!
Success rate is 100 percent (5/5), round-trip min/avg/max = 56/58/68 ms
Type escape sequence to abort.
Sending 5, 100-byte ICMP Echos to 172.16.3.1, timeout is 2 seconds:
!!!!!
Success rate is 100 percent (5/5), round-trip min/avg/max = 28/28/32 ms
Type escape sequence to abort.
Sending 5, 100-byte ICMP Echos to 192.168.23.3, timeout is 2 seconds:
!!!!!
Success rate is 100 percent (5/5), round-trip min/avg/max = 28/28/28 ms
R2(tcl)# tclquit
```

```
R3# tclsh
R3(tcl)#foreach address {
+>(tcl)#172.16.1.1
+>(tcl)#192.168.12.1
+>(tcl)#192.168.12.2
+>(tcl)#192.168.23.2
+>(tcl)#172.16.3.1
+>(tcl)#192.168.23.3
+>(tcl)#} { ping $address }

Type escape sequence to abort.
Sending 5, 100-byte ICMP Echos to 172.16.1.1, timeout is 2 seconds:
!!!!!
Success rate is 100 percent (5/5), round-trip min/avg/max = 28/28/32 ms
Type escape sequence to abort.
```

```
Sending 5, 100-byte ICMP Echos to 192.168.12.1, timeout is 2 seconds:
!!!!!
Success rate is 100 percent (5/5), round-trip min/avg/max = 28/28/32 ms
Type escape sequence to abort.
Sending 5, 100-byte ICMP Echos to 192.168.12.2, timeout is 2 seconds:
!!!!!
Success rate is 100 percent (5/5), round-trip min/avg/max = 28/28/32 ms
Type escape sequence to abort.
Sending 5, 100-byte ICMP Echos to 192.168.23.2, timeout is 2 seconds:
!!!!!
Success rate is 100 percent (5/5), round-trip min/avg/max = 28/28/32 ms
Type escape sequence to abort.
Sending 5, 100-byte ICMP Echos to 172.16.3.1, timeout is 2 seconds:
!!!!!
Success rate is 100 percent (5/5), round-trip min/avg/max = 1/1/1 ms
Type escape sequence to abort.
Sending 5, 100-byte ICMP Echos to 192.168.23.3, timeout is 2 seconds:
!!!!!
Success rate is 100 percent (5/5), round-trip min/avg/max = 56/58/64 ms
R3(tcl)# tclquit
```

Lab 3-6: Configuring a Secure GRE Tunnel with SDM (3.10.6)

The objectives of this lab are as follows:

- Configure EIGRP on the routers.

- Use SDM to configure a secure GRE tunnel.

Figure 3-86 illustrates the topology that is used for this lab.

Figure 3-86   Topology Diagram

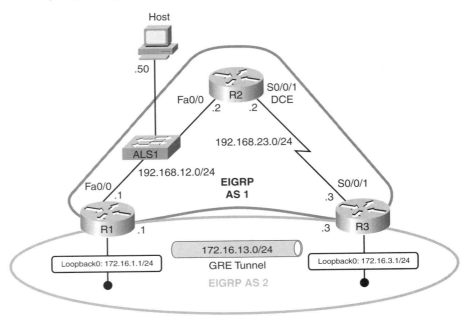

Scenario

In this lab, you use the Cisco SDM to configure a secure GRE tunnel using IPsec. It helps if you have previously completed Lab 3-2, Lab 3-4, and Lab 3-5, because this lab builds on concepts covered in those labs.

Step 1: Configure Addressing

Configure the loopback interfaces with the addresses shown in Figure 3-86. Also, configure the serial interfaces shown in Figure 3-86. Do not forget to set the clock rates on the appropriate interfaces and issue the **no shutdown** command on all serial connections. Verify that you have connectivity across the local subnet by using the **ping** command. Do not set up the tunnel interface until the next step:

```
R1# configure terminal
R1(config)# interface loopback 0
R1(config-if)# ip address 172.16.1.1 255.255.255.0
R1(config-if)# interface fastethernet 0/0
```

```
R1(config-if)# ip address 192.168.12.1 255.255.255.0
R1(config-if)# no shutdown
```

```
R2# configure terminal
R2(config)# interface fastethernet 0/0
R2(config-if)# ip address 192.168.12.2 255.255.255.0
R2(config-if)# no shutdown
R2(config-if)# interface serial0/0/1
R2(config-if)# ip address 192.168.23.2 255.255.255.0
R2(config-if)# clockrate 64000
R2(config-if)# no shutdown
```

```
R3# configure terminal
R3(config)# interface loopback 0
R3(config-if)# ip address 172.16.3.1 255.255.255.0
R3(config-if)# interface serial0/0/1
R3(config-if)# ip address 192.168.23.3 255.255.255.0
R3(config-if)# no shutdown
```

Step 2: Configure EIGRP AS 1

Configure EIGRP AS 1 for the major networks 192.168.12.0/24 and 192.168.23.0/24. Do not include
the networks falling in the 172.16.0.0/16 range in Figure 3-86. The Class C networks serve as the
transit networks for the tunnel network. Make sure you disable EIGRP automatic summarization:

```
R1(config)# router eigrp 1
R1(config-router)# no auto-summary
R1(config-router)# network 192.168.12.0
```

```
R2(config)# router eigrp 1
R2(config-router)# no auto-summary
R2(config-router)# network 192.168.12.0
R2(config-router)# network 192.168.23.0
```

```
R3(config)# router eigrp 1
R3(config-router)# no auto-summary
R3(config-router)# network 192.168.23.0
```

Given this configuration, will the 172.16.1.0/24 network be reachable from R3? Explain.

Will the 172.16.3.0/24 network be reachable from R1?

Step 3: Connect to the Router Using SDM

Prepare R1 for access using SDM as described in Lab 3-1: Configuring SDM on a Router.

Configure the IP address shown in Figure 3-87 on the host PC, and install SDM to either the router or the PC. Connect to the router using SDM so that you are at the SDM home screen. For information on how to configure SDM, refer to Lab 3-1: Configuring SDM on a Router.

Figure 3-87   SDM Home Screen

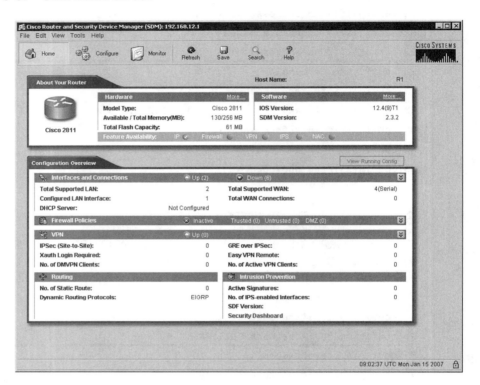

Step 4: Configure an IPsec VTI Using SDM

SDM contains a wizard that makes configuring an IPsec virtual tunnel interface (VTI) simple. Click the **Configure** tab at the top, and then choose **VPN** on the left-side bar. In the second column from the left, click **Site-to-Site VPN**, and then, in the **Create Site-to-Site VPN** tab, choose **Create a secure GRE tunnel (GRE over IPsec)**, as shown in Figure 3-88. Click the **Launch the selected task** button.

Figure 3-88   Site-to-Site VPN Tab

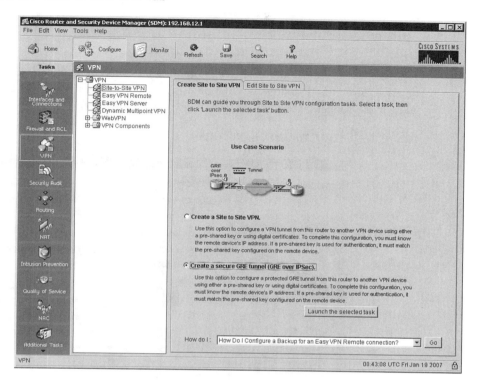

After reading the brief introduction to IPsec VTIs, as shown in Figure 3-89, click **Next** to start the wizard.

Figure 3-89   Secure GRE Wizard

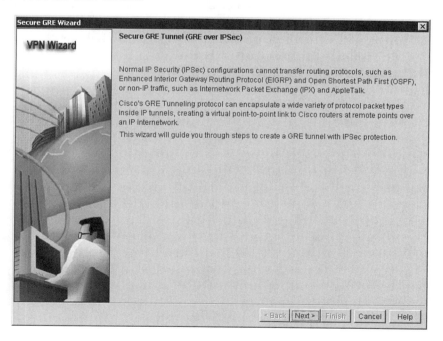

What IP addresses should you use as the endpoints for your GRE tunnel? Why?

_____

_____

From the screen shown in Figure 3-90, configure the tunnel source using the FastEthernet0/0 interface on R1. Choose the IP address destination using the closest interface on R3 to R1. The internal IP address and subnet mask of the tunnel are given in Figure 3-86.

Figure 3-90   GRE Tunnel Configuration

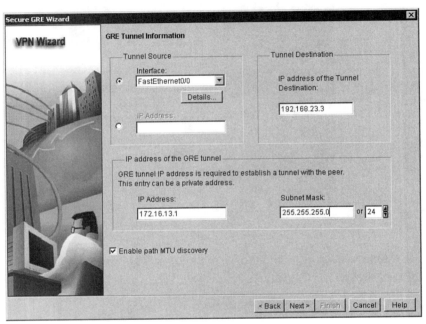

At the next prompt in the wizard, shown in Figure 3-91, do not check **Create a backup GRE tunnel for resilience**. Just click the **Next** button.

Figure 3-91   Backup GRE Tunnel Options

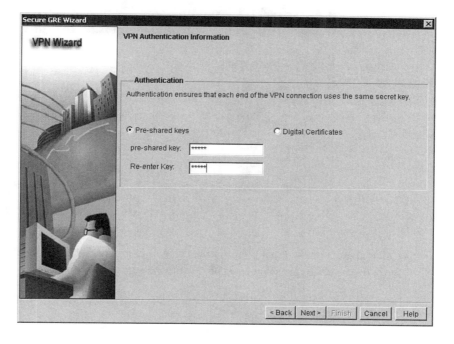

From the screen shown in Figure 3-92, click **Preshared keys** for the authentication method and use **cisco** as your preshared key.

Figure 3-92   VPN Authentication Information

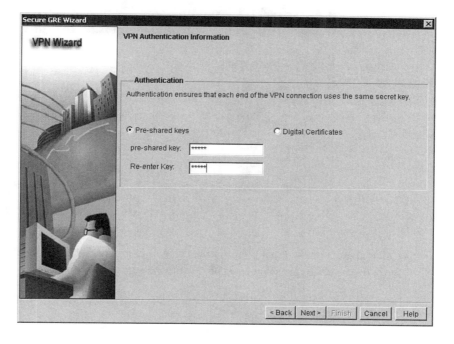

What is a preshared key? What purpose does it serve?

_____

_____

_____

Based on your work on the IPsec VPN labs, what is the function of the Internet Key Exchange (IKE) protocol?

_____

_____

What attributes might be configured in an IKE policy? Enumerate at least three attributes.

_____

_____

Create a new IKE policy by clicking the **Add** button, as shown in Figure 3-93.

Figure 3-93   IKE Proposals List

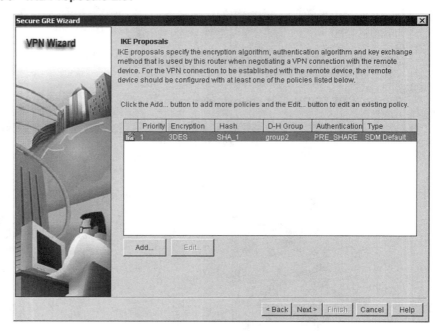

Create the new policy using the settings shown in Figure 3-94. If your IOS image doesn't support all the settings, configure what you can. Just make sure your VPN settings match on both ends of the connection.

Then, click **OK**.

Figure 3-94   Add IKE Policy Dialog

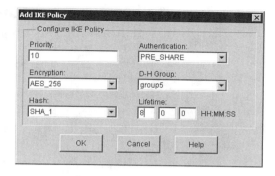

You should now see your new IKE proposal in the list, as shown in Figure 3-95. Click **Next** to continue.

Figure 3-95   IKE Proposals with Changes Applied

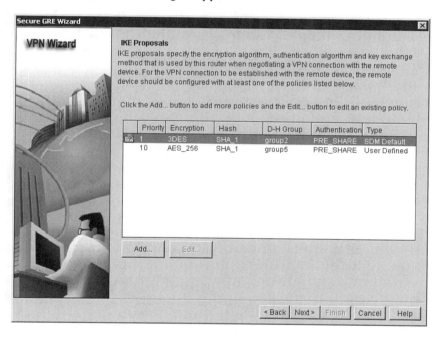

On the Transform Set page shown in Figure 3-96, create a new transform set by clicking **Add**.

Figure 3-96   IPsec Transform Set List

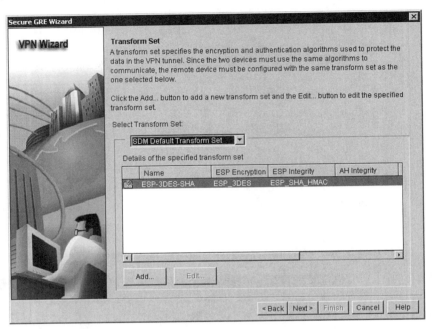

What is the function of an IPsec transform set?

_____

_____

_____

What are the main differences between the authentication header (AH) and the Encapsulating Security Payload (ESP) as methods to ensure data integrity?

_____

_____

Create a new transform set using the name mytrans. Use the settings shown in Figure 3-97. If these settings are not supported on your router, use whichever settings you can. However, remember to keep the settings consistent on both sides of the tunnel.

Figure 3-97   Add IPsec Transform Set Dialog

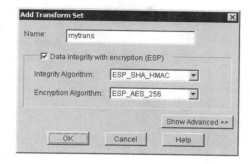

You should see your new transform set appear in the window, as shown in Figure 3-98. Click **Next**.

Figure 3-98   IPsec Transform Set List with Changes Applies

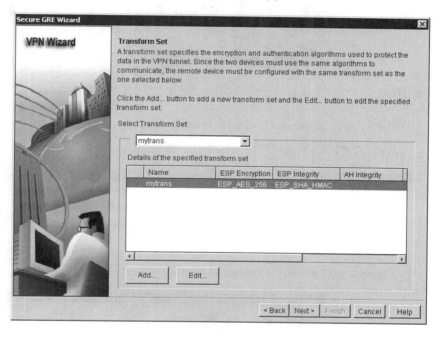

From the screen shown in Figure 3-99, choose **EIGRP** as the routing protocol and click **Next**.

Figure 3-99   Routing Protocol Selection

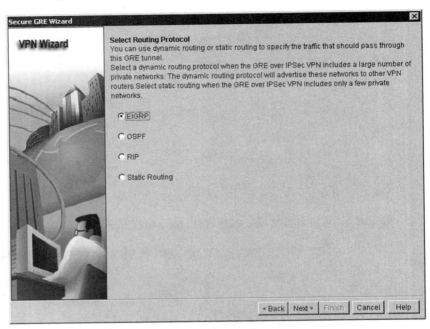

Use EIGRP AS number 2 to route over the tunnel.

Will EIGRP AS 1 and EIGRP AS 2 automatically redistribute routes between autonomous systems?

Add the entire 172.16.0.0 major network into this EIGRP autonomous system on R1, as shown in Figure 3-100.

Figure 3-100 Advanced Routing Protocol Configuration

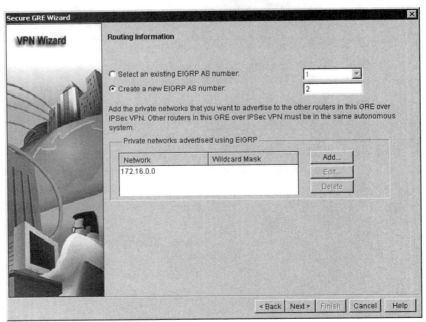

From the screen shown in Figure 3-101, click **Finish** to deliver the configuration to the router. Do not test VPN connectivity yet, because the other endpoint of the tunnel is not configured.

Figure 3-101 Site-to-Site IPsec GRE Configuration Summary

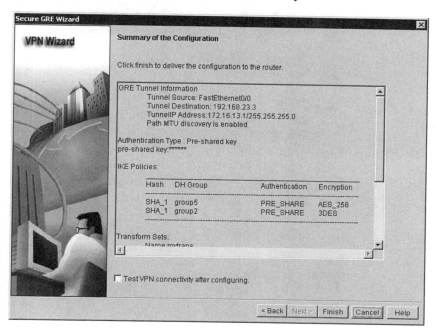

SDM delivers the configuration changes to the router. When the configuration changes are complete, click **OK**, as shown in Figure 3-102.

Figure 3-102 Command Delivery Progress Indicator

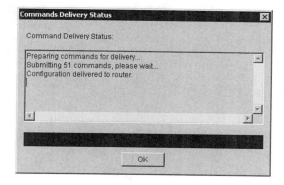

Step 5: Generate a Mirror Configuration for R3

In the **Edit Site-to-Site VPN** tab of SDM, as shown in Figure 3-103, click the **Generate Mirror** button. An incomplete mirror configuration for R3 is generated.

Figure 3-103 Edit Site-to-Site VPN Tab

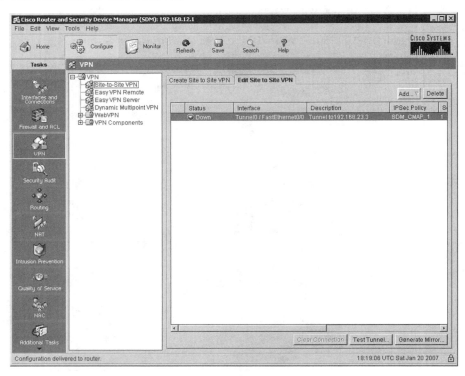

Copy the commands shown in the dimmed text box, shown in Figure 3-104, to the Windows clipboard.

Figure 3-104 Mirror Router Configuration Script

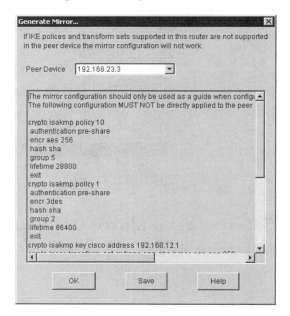

In global configuration mode on R3, paste in this configuration:

```
R3(config)# crypto isakmp policy 10
R3(config-isakmp)# authentication pre-share
R3(config-isakmp)# encr aes 256
R3(config-isakmp)# hash sha
R3(config-isakmp)# group 5
R3(config-isakmp)# lifetime 28800
R3(config-isakmp)# exit
R3(config)# crypto isakmp policy 1
R3(config-isakmp)# authentication pre-share
R3(config-isakmp)# encr 3des
R3(config-isakmp)# hash sha
R3(config-isakmp)# group 2
R3(config-isakmp)# lifetime 86400
R3(config-isakmp)# exit
R3(config)# crypto isakmp key cisco address 192.168.12.1
R3(config)# crypto ipsec transform-set mytrans esp-sha-hmac esp-aes 256
R3(cfg-crypto-trans)# mode tunnel
R3(cfg-crypto-trans)# exit
R3(config)# ip access-list extended SDM_1
R3(config-ext-nacl)# remark SDM_ACL Category=4
R3(config-ext-nacl)# permit gre host 192.168.23.3 host 192.168.12.1
R3(config-ext-nacl)# exit
R3(config)# crypto map SDM_CMAP_1 1 ipsec-isakmp
% NOTE: This new crypto map will remain disabled until a peer
        and a valid access list have been configured.
R3(config-crypto-map)# description Apply the crypto map on the peer router's
   interface having IP address 192.168.23.3 that connects to this router.
R3(config-crypto-map)# set transform-set mytrans
R3(config-crypto-map)# set peer 192.168.12.1
R3(config-crypto-map)# match address SDM_1
R3(config-crypto-map)# set security-association lifetime seconds 3600
R3(config-crypto-map)# set security-association lifetime kilobytes 4608000
R3(config-crypto-map)# exit
```

Unfortunately, the configuration generated from SDM is incomplete. There is no GRE tunnel interface, and the crypto map must also be applied to the physical interface on R3. The EIGRP AS 2 routing process is also missing from the configuration. To get a general idea of how the tunnel configuration should look, look at R1's tunnel interface:

```
R1# show run interface tunnel 0
Building configuration...

Current configuration : 190 bytes
!
```

```
interface Tunnel0
 ip address 172.16.13.1 255.255.255.0
 ip mtu 1420
 tunnel source FastEthernet0/0
 tunnel destination 192.168.23.3
 tunnel path-mtu-discovery
 crypto map SDM_CMAP_1
end
```

Reuse this configuration, but swap the IP addresses and interfaces as necessary. You might see a warning about IKE failing because there is no key for the remote peer with that IP address. This is normal:

```
R3(config)# interface Tunnel 0
R3(config-if)# ip address 172.16.13.3 255.255.255.0
R3(config-if)# ip mtu 1420
R3(config-if)# tunnel source Serial0/0/1
R3(config-if)# tunnel destination 192.168.12.1
R3(config-if)# tunnel path-mtu-discovery
R3(config-if)# crypto map SDM_CMAP_1
```

Apply the crypto map that was created to the serial interface to encrypt GRE traffic:

```
R3(config)# interface serial 0/0/1
R3(config-if)# crypto map SDM_CMAP_1
```

Finally, create the EIGRP AS 2 process on R3. Disable automatic summarization and add the entire 172.16.0.0/16 major network to it. You should see the EIGRP adjacency come up over the tunnel interface:

```
R3(config)# router eigrp 2
R3(config-router)# no auto-summary
R3(config-router)# network 172.16.0.0
```

Will the 172.16.13.0/24 network be reachable from R2?

_____

_____

Step 6: Verify Tunnel Configuration Through SDM

You can use SDM to verify the tunnel configuration. To do this, click the **Test Tunnel** button on the **Edit Site-to-Site VPN** tab, as shown in Figure 3-105.

Figure 3-105 Edit Site-to-Site VPN Tab

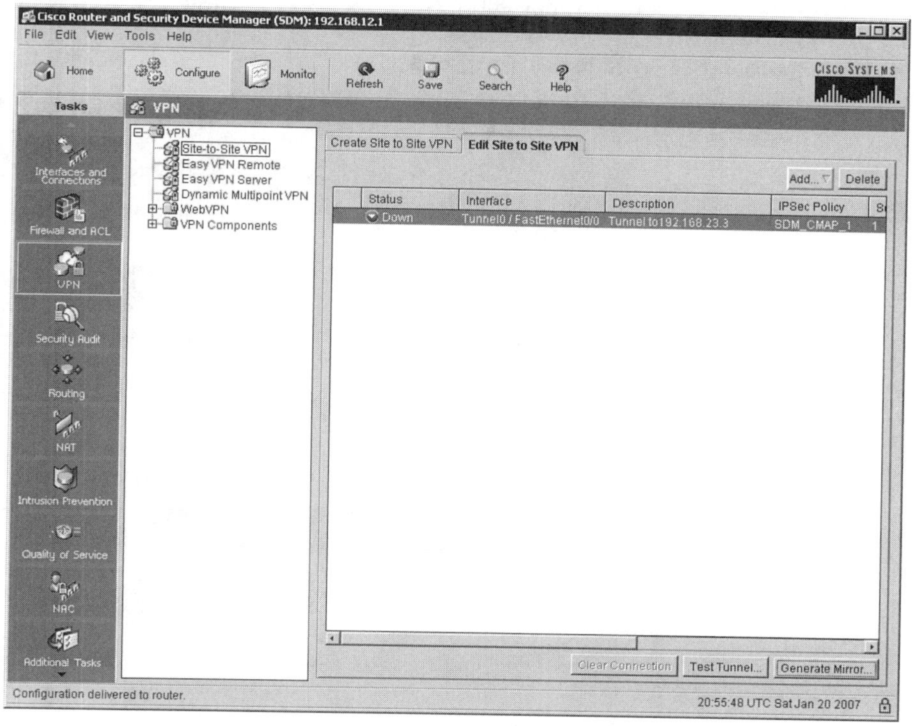

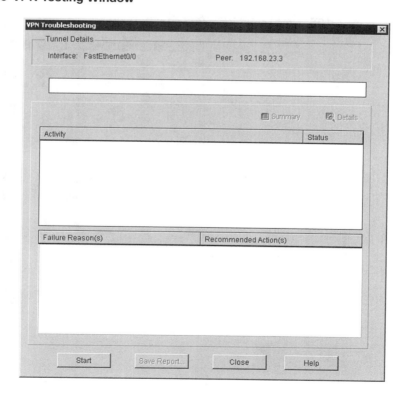

From the screen shown in Figure 3-106, click **Start**, and SDM verifies the tunnel status.

Figure 3-106 VPN Testing Window

When verification (shown in progress in Figure 3-107) is complete, a success message should appear, as shown in Figure 3-108. Click **OK**.

Figure 3-107 VPN Test In Progress

Figure 3-108 Successful VPN Test Status Window

The status of "up" should be displayed in the screen shown in Figure 3-109. Click **Close** when you are done reading this window. You are returned to the main SDM window.

Figure 3-109 Detailed VPN Test Results

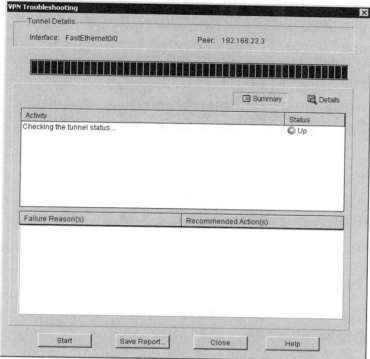

At this point, verify that you have partial IP connectivity with the following Toolkit Command Language (TCL) script:

```
tclsh

foreach address {
172.16.1.1
172.16.3.1
172.16.13.1
172.16.13.3
192.168.12.1
192.168.12.2
192.168.23.2
192.168.23.3
} { ping $address }

tclquit
```

Compare your output with the output shown in the section, "TCL Script Output," for this lab. Troubleshoot as necessary. Remember that R2 should not be able to reach any subnets of the 172.16.0.0/16 network.

Challenge: Use Wireshark to Monitor Encryption of Traffic

You can observe packets on the wire using Wireshark and see how their content looks unencrypted and then encrypted. To do this, first configure a SPAN session on the switch and open up Wireshark on a host attached to the SPAN destination port. You can use the host that you used for SDM because you don't need it anymore to configure the VPNs. If you do not know how to do this, refer to Lab 3-3: Configuring Wireshark and SPAN.

Next, you remove the **crypto map** statements on R1 and R3. View the current configuration on the FastEthernet0/0 interface on R1 and Serial0/0/1, as shown in the following code.

Then, issue the **no crypto map** *name* command in interface configuration mode to remove the Internet Security Association and Key Management Protocol (ISAKMP) security association (SA). The router might issue a warning that ISAKMP is now off:

```
R1# show run interface fastethernet 0/0
Building configuration...

Current configuration : 120 bytes
!
interface FastEthernet0/0
 ip address 192.168.12.1 255.255.255.0
 duplex auto
 speed auto
 crypto map SDM_CMAP_1
end


R1# configure terminal
R1(config)# interface fastethernet0/0
R1(config-if)# no crypto map SDM_CMAP_1
*Jan 16 06:02:58.999: %CRYPTO-6-ISAKMP_ON_OFF: ISAKMP is OFF
```

```
R3# show run interface serial 0/0/1
Building configuration...

Current configuration : 91 bytes
!
interface Serial0/0/1
 ip address 192.168.23.3 255.255.255.0
 crypto map SDM_CMAP_1
end
```

```
R3# configure terminal
R3(config)# interface serial0/0/1
R3(config-if)# no crypto map SDM_CMAP_1
*Jan 16 06:05:36.038: %CRYPTO-6-ISAKMP_ON_OFF: ISAKMP is OFF
```

The traffic we want to sniff is Telnet traffic, so enable Telnet access and an enable password on R3, if you haven't already:

```
R3(config)# enable secret cisco
R3(config)# line vty 0 4
R3(config-line)# password cisco
R3(config-line)# login
```

Have Wireshark start sniffing packets that it receives via the SPAN session.

Choose **Capture > Interfaces**. Then, click the **Start** button associated with the interface connected to the SPAN destination port. SPAN should start capturing packets on the line, so you can now telnet from R1's loopback to R3's loopback. To send Telnet traffic, use the **telnet** *destination* command.

Do you need to use the **/source** attribute in the **telnet** command? Explain.

_____

_____

_____

_____

_____

First, begin capturing using Wireshark. Then, begin the Telnet session. After you connect to R3, try issuing a command or two and then logging out.

The packets are routed through the tunnel interface toward the loopback on R3, so Wireshark displays the GRE packets. Remember to have Wireshark capturing when you start the Telnet session. After you connect to the remote router, try issuing a command or two and then logging out:

```
R1# telnet 172.16.3.1
Trying 172.16.3.1 ... Open


User Access Verification


Password:
R3> enable
Password:
R3# show ip interface brief
Interface            IP-Address      OK? Method Status                  Protocol
FastEthernet0/0      unassigned      YES unset  administratively down   down
FastEthernet0/1      unassigned      YES unset  administratively down   down
Serial0/0/0          unassigned      YES unset  administratively down   down
Serial0/0/1          192.168.23.3    YES manual up                      up
Serial0/1/0          unassigned      YES unset  administratively down   down
Serial0/1/1          unassigned      YES unset  administratively down   down
Loopback0            172.16.3.1      YES manual up                      up
Tunnel0              172.16.13.3     YES manual up                      up
R3# exit
```

```
[Connection to 172.16.3.1 closed by foreign host]
R1#
```

Now, look at the output. Notice that Wireshark is smart enough to classify these packets as Telnet traffic, even though the actual packets are GRE. Looking in the middle pane in Wireshark, as shown in Figure 3-110, it shows the multiple layers of encapsulation, including the GRE information. Notice that because you disabled encryption, you can easily read the plain-text strings of the Telnet session in Wireshark.

Figure 3-110 Detailed Packet Data on Telnet String Sent from R1

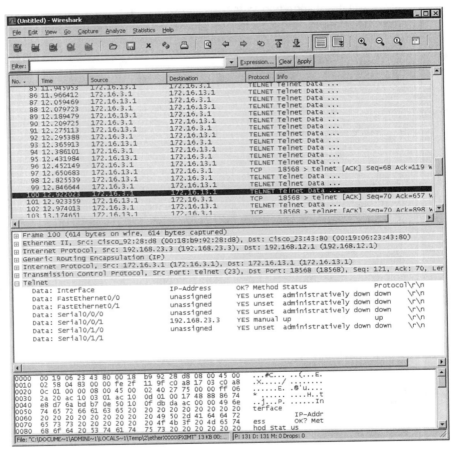

Based on this output, you can see how easy it is for someone who is in the path of sensitive data to view unencrypted or clear-text traffic.

Now, reapply the cryptography settings on R1 and R3 and begin a Telnet session from R1 to R3, as before.

Begin by reapplying the crypto maps you removed earlier on R1 and R3:

```
R1(config)# interface fastethernet 0/0
R1(config-if)# crypto map SDM_CMAP_1
```

```
R3(config)# interface serial0/0/1
R3(config-if)# crypto map SDM_CMAP_1
```

Start the packet capturing again in Wireshark, and then issue the same Telnet sequence that you did previously:

```
R1# telnet 172.16.3.1
Trying 172.16.3.1 ... Open


User Access Verification


Password:
```

```
R3> enable
Password:
R3# show ip interface brief
Interface                IP-Address      OK? Method Status                Protocol
FastEthernet0/0          unassigned      YES unset  administratively down down
FastEthernet0/1          unassigned      YES unset  administratively down down
Serial0/0/0              unassigned      YES unset  administratively down down
Serial0/0/1              192.168.23.3    YES manual up                    up
Serial0/1/0              unassigned      YES unset  administratively down down
Serial0/1/1              unassigned      YES unset  administratively down down
Loopback0                172.16.3.1      YES manual up                    up
Tunnel0                  172.16.13.3     YES manual up                    up
R3#exit


[Connection to 172.16.3.1 closed by foreign host]
R1#
```

End your Wireshark capture when you are finished with the Telnet session.

As far as the user is concerned, the Telnet session seems the same with and without encryption. However, the packet capture from Wireshark in Figure 3-111 shows that the VPN is actively encapsulating and encrypting packets.

Figure 3-111 Detailed Packet Data on Encrypted Telnet String Sent from R1

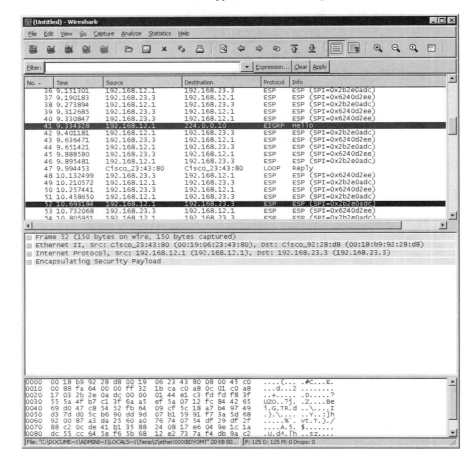

Notice that the protocol is not Telnet (TCP port 23), but the Encapsulating Security Payload (ESP, IP protocol number 50). Remember, all traffic here matches the IPsec access list.

Also, notice that the source and destination are not the actual source and destination of the addresses participating in this Telnet conversation. Rather, they are the VPN endpoints.

Finally, and most important, if you look at the contents of these packets in Wireshark, no matter how you try to format or filter them, you will not be able to see what data was originally inside.

The encryption suite provided by IPsec successfully secures data through authentication, encryption, and data-integrity services.

TCL Script Output

```
tclsh

foreach address {
172.16.1.1
172.16.3.1
172.16.13.1
172.16.13.3
192.168.12.1
```

```
    192.168.12.2
    192.168.23.2
    192.168.23.3
    } { ping $address }

R1# tclsh
R1(tcl)#
R1(tcl)#foreach address {
+>(tcl)#172.16.1.1
+>(tcl)#172.16.3.1
+>(tcl)#172.16.13.1
+>(tcl)#172.16.13.3
+>(tcl)#192.168.12.1
+>(tcl)#192.168.12.2
+>(tcl)#192.168.23.2
+>(tcl)#192.168.23.3
+>(tcl)#} { ping $address }

Type escape sequence to abort.
Sending 5, 100-byte ICMP Echos to 172.16.1.1, timeout is 2 seconds:
!!!!!
Success rate is 100 percent (5/5), round-trip min/avg/max = 1/1/4 ms
Type escape sequence to abort.
Sending 5, 100-byte ICMP Echos to 172.16.3.1, timeout is 2 seconds:
!!!!!
Success rate is 100 percent (5/5), round-trip min/avg/max = 68/68/72 ms
Type escape sequence to abort.
Sending 5, 100-byte ICMP Echos to 172.16.13.1, timeout is 2 seconds:
!!!!!
Success rate is 100 percent (5/5), round-trip min/avg/max = 1/1/1 ms
Type escape sequence to abort.
Sending 5, 100-byte ICMP Echos to 172.16.13.3, timeout is 2 seconds:
!!!!!
Success rate is 100 percent (5/5), round-trip min/avg/max = 68/69/72 ms
Type escape sequence to abort.
Sending 5, 100-byte ICMP Echos to 192.168.12.1, timeout is 2 seconds:
!!!!!
Success rate is 100 percent (5/5), round-trip min/avg/max = 56/56/60 ms
Type escape sequence to abort.
Sending 5, 100-byte ICMP Echos to 192.168.12.2, timeout is 2 seconds:
!!!!!
Success rate is 100 percent (5/5), round-trip min/avg/max = 28/28/32 ms
Type escape sequence to abort.
```

```
Sending 5, 100-byte ICMP Echos to 192.168.23.2, timeout is 2 seconds:
!!!!!
Success rate is 100 percent (5/5), round-trip min/avg/max = 28/28/28 ms
Type escape sequence to abort.
Sending 5, 100-byte ICMP Echos to 192.168.23.3, timeout is 2 seconds:
!!!!!
Success rate is 100 percent (5/5), round-trip min/avg/max = 56/56/56 ms
R1(tcl)# tclquit
```

```
R2# tclsh
R2(tcl)#
R2(tcl)#foreach address {
+>(tcl)#172.16.1.1
+>(tcl)#172.16.3.1
+>(tcl)#172.16.13.1
+>(tcl)#172.16.13.3
+>(tcl)#192.168.12.1
+>(tcl)#192.168.12.2
+>(tcl)#192.168.23.2
+>(tcl)#192.168.23.3
+>(tcl)#} { ping $address }

Type escape sequence to abort.
Sending 5, 100-byte ICMP Echos to 172.16.1.1, timeout is 2 seconds:
.....
Success rate is 0 percent (0/5)
Type escape sequence to abort.
Sending 5, 100-byte ICMP Echos to 172.16.3.1, timeout is 2 seconds:
.....
Success rate is 0 percent (0/5)
Type escape sequence to abort.
Sending 5, 100-byte ICMP Echos to 172.16.13.1, timeout is 2 seconds:
.....
Success rate is 0 percent (0/5)
Type escape sequence to abort.
Sending 5, 100-byte ICMP Echos to 172.16.13.3, timeout is 2 seconds:
.....
Success rate is 0 percent (0/5)
Type escape sequence to abort.
Sending 5, 100-byte ICMP Echos to 192.168.12.1, timeout is 2 seconds:
!!!!!
Success rate is 100 percent (5/5), round-trip min/avg/max = 28/28/32 ms
Type escape sequence to abort.
Sending 5, 100-byte ICMP Echos to 192.168.12.2, timeout is 2 seconds:
!!!!!
```

```
Success rate is 100 percent (5/5), round-trip min/avg/max = 52/56/64 ms
Type escape sequence to abort.
Sending 5, 100-byte ICMP Echos to 192.168.23.2, timeout is 2 seconds:
!!!!!
Success rate is 100 percent (5/5), round-trip min/avg/max = 56/59/64 ms
Type escape sequence to abort.
Sending 5, 100-byte ICMP Echos to 192.168.23.3, timeout is 2 seconds:
!!!!!
Success rate is 100 percent (5/5), round-trip min/avg/max = 28/29/36 ms
R2(tcl)# tclquit
```

```
R3# tclsh
R3(tcl)#
R3(tcl)#foreach address {
+>(tcl)#172.16.1.1
+>(tcl)#172.16.3.1
+>(tcl)#172.16.13.1
+>(tcl)#172.16.13.3
+>(tcl)#192.168.12.1
+>(tcl)#192.168.12.2
+>(tcl)#192.168.23.2
+>(tcl)#192.168.23.3
+>(tcl)#} { ping $address }

Type escape sequence to abort.
Sending 5, 100-byte ICMP Echos to 172.16.1.1, timeout is 2 seconds:
!!!!!
Success rate is 100 percent (5/5), round-trip min/avg/max = 68/69/72 ms
Type escape sequence to abort.
Sending 5, 100-byte ICMP Echos to 172.16.3.1, timeout is 2 seconds:
!!!!!
Success rate is 100 percent (5/5), round-trip min/avg/max = 1/1/1 ms
Type escape sequence to abort.
Sending 5, 100-byte ICMP Echos to 172.16.13.1, timeout is 2 seconds:
!!!!!
Success rate is 100 percent (5/5), round-trip min/avg/max = 68/68/72 ms
Type escape sequence to abort.
Sending 5, 100-byte ICMP Echos to 172.16.13.3, timeout is 2 seconds:
!!!!!
Success rate is 100 percent (5/5), round-trip min/avg/max = 1/1/4 ms
Type escape sequence to abort.
Sending 5, 100-byte ICMP Echos to 192.168.12.1, timeout is 2 seconds:
!!!!!
Success rate is 100 percent (5/5), round-trip min/avg/max = 56/56/56 ms
Type escape sequence to abort.
```

```
Sending 5, 100-byte ICMP Echos to 192.168.12.2, timeout is 2 seconds:
!!!!!
Success rate is 100 percent (5/5), round-trip min/avg/max = 28/28/28 ms
Type escape sequence to abort.
Sending 5, 100-byte ICMP Echos to 192.168.23.2, timeout is 2 seconds:
!!!!!
Success rate is 100 percent (5/5), round-trip min/avg/max = 28/28/32 ms
Type escape sequence to abort.
Sending 5, 100-byte ICMP Echos to 192.168.23.3, timeout is 2 seconds:
!!!!!
Success rate is 100 percent (5/5), round-trip min/avg/max = 56/59/64 ms
R3(tcl)# tclquit
```

Lab 3-7: Configuring a Secure GRE Tunnel with the IOS CLI (3.10.7)

The objectives of this lab are as follows:

- Configure EIGRP on the routers.

- Create a GRE tunnel between two routers.

- Use IPsec to secure the GRE tunnel.

Figure 3-112 illustrates the topology that is used for this lab.

Figure 3-112 Topology Diagram

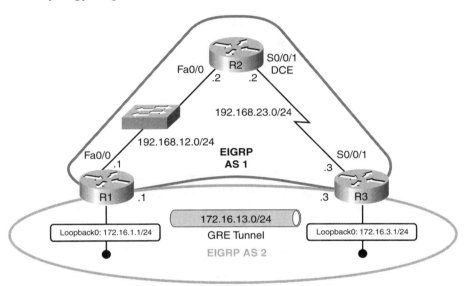

Scenario

In this lab, you configure a secure GRE tunnel using IPsec. You also use IPsec to secure traffic going through the tunnel. It helps you to have previously completed Lab 3.2 and Lab 3.5, because this lab combines the two. Lab 3-8: Configuring IPsec VTIs, also addresses a newer way to configure this type of tunnel. This newer method combines encryption into the tunnel configuration.

Step 1: Configure Addressing

Configure the loopback interfaces with the addresses shown in Figure 3-112. Also, configure the serial interfaces shown in the figure. Set the clock rates on the appropriate interfaces and issue the **no shutdown** command on all serial connections. Verify that you have connectivity across the local subnet by using the **ping** command. Do not set up the tunnel interface until the next step:

```
R1# configure terminal
R1(config)# interface loopback0
R1(config-if)# ip address 172.16.1.1 255.255.255.0
R1(config-if)# interface fastethernet0/0
```

```
R1(config-if)# ip address 192.168.12.1 255.255.255.0
R1(config-if)# no shutdown
R2# configure terminal
R2(config)# interface fastethernet0/0
R2(config-if)# ip address 192.168.12.2 255.255.255.0
R2(config-if)# no shutdown
R2(config-if)# interface serial0/0/1
R2(config-if)# ip address 192.168.23.2 255.255.255.0
R2(config-if)# clockrate 64000
R2(config-if)# no shutdown
R3# configure terminal
R3(config)# interface loopback0
R3(config-if)# ip address 172.16.3.1 255.255.255.0
R3(config-if)# interface serial0/0/1
R3(config-if)# ip address 192.168.23.3 255.255.255.0
R3(config-if)# no shutdown
```

Step 2: Configure EIGRP AS 1

Configure EIGRP AS 1 for the major networks 192.168.12.0/24 and 192.168.23.0/24. Do not include the networks falling in the 172.16.0.0/16 range in Figure 3-112. The Class C networks serve as the transit networks for the tunnel network. Make sure you disable EIGRP automatic summarization:

```
R1(config)# router eigrp 1
R1(config-router)# no auto-summary
R1(config-router)# network 192.168.12.0
R2(config)# router eigrp 1
R2(config-router)# no auto-summary
R2(config-router)# network 192.168.12.0
R2(config-router)# network 192.168.23.0
R3(config)# router eigrp 1
R3(config-router)# no auto-summary
R3(config-router)# network 192.168.23.0
```

Verify that routers R1 and R3 can see the remote transit network with the **show ip route** command.

Step 3: Configure the GRE Tunnel

To configure a GRE tunnel, enter interface configuration mode with the **interface tunnel** *number* command from global configuration mode. For simplicity, use tunnel number 0 on both routers. Next, configure an IP address with **ip address** *address mask* the way you would on any other interface. Finally, assign a source and destination address for the tunnel with **tunnel source** *address* and **tunnel destination** *address*, respectively. The source can also be specified by the interface. These addresses specify the endpoints of the router, so our GRE traffic will be encapsulated with the source address and decapsulated at the destination address. You do not need to configure a tunnel mode because the default tunnel mode is GRE:

```
R1(config)# interface tunnel 0
R1(config-if)# ip address 172.16.13.1 255.255.255.0
R1(config-if)# tunnel source fastethernet0/0
R1(config-if)# tunnel destination 192.168.23.3
```
```
R3(config)# interface tunnel0
R3(config-if)# ip address 172.16.13.3 255.255.255.0
R3(config-if)# tunnel source serial0/0/1
R3(config-if)# tunnel destination 192.168.12.1
```

Verify that you can **ping** across the tunnel to the other side. If you can do this, you have successfully set up the tunnel:

```
R1# ping 172.16.13.3

Type escape sequence to abort.
Sending 5, 100-byte ICMP Echos to 172.16.13.3, timeout is 2 seconds:
!!!!!
Success rate is 100 percent (5/5), round-trip min/avg/max = 68/69/72 ms
```
```
R3# ping 172.16.13.1

Type escape sequence to abort.
Sending 5, 100-byte ICMP Echos to 172.16.13.1, timeout is 2 seconds:
!!!!!
Success rate is 100 percent (5/5), round-trip min/avg/max = 68/68/72 ms
```

With what source and destination IP address are these packets sent out of the FastEthernet0/0 interface on R1? Why?

_____

_____

_____

What IP protocol number do these packets have?

_____

Step 4: Configure EIGRP AS 2 over the Tunnel

Now that you set up the GRE tunnel, implement routing through it the way you would any other interface. Configure EIGRP AS 2 to route the entire 172.16.0.0/16 major network. Disable automatic summarization. Remember that R2 is not participating in this routing process, and it will not need to be configured with EIGRP AS 2:

```
R1(config)# router eigrp 2
R1(config-router)# no auto-summary
R1(config-router)# network 172.16.0.0
```
```
R3(config)# router eigrp 2
R3(config-router)# no auto-summary
R3(config-router)# network 172.16.0.0
```

You should observe EIGRP neighbor adjacencies become active with messages logged to the console. If not, troubleshoot by ensuring that you can ping from 192.168.12.1 to 192.168.23.3 and vice versa. Also, check that you have correctly configured these tunnel interfaces.

If you configured this step correctly, you should be able to successfully ping from R1's loopback interface to R3's loopback.

Step 5: Create IKE Policies and Peers

Configure an Internet Key Exchange (IKE) policy and peer key. Create an IKE policy using the information that follows. If your IOS image doesn't support all the settings, configure what you can. Just make sure that your VPN settings match on both ends of the connection:

```
R1(config)# crypto isakmp policy 10
R1(config-isakmp)# authentication pre-share
R1(config-isakmp)# encryption aes 256
R1(config-isakmp)# hash sha
R1(config-isakmp)# group 5
R1(config-isakmp)# lifetime 3600
```
```
R3(config)# crypto isakmp policy 10
R3(config-isakmp)# authentication pre-share
R3(config-isakmp)# encryption aes 256
R3(config-isakmp)# hash sha
R3(config-isakmp)# group 5
R3(config-isakmp)# lifetime 3600
```

Of the three authentication methods available, which method is considered the weakest?

_____

What is currently the most secure encryption algorithm?

_____

What is currently the most secure hash algorithm?

_____

Which of the Diffie-Hellman groups is considered the weakest?

_____

_____

Next, configure each peer using the key cisco for Internet Security Association and Key Management Protocol (ISAKMP):

```
RR1(config)# crypto isakmp key cisco address 192.168.23.3
```
```
R3(config)# crypto isakmp key cisco address 192.168.12.1
```

Step 6: Create IPsec Transform Sets

On both endpoint routers, create an IPsec transform set with the following settings. If your routers do not support these settings, use whichever settings you can. Just keep it consistent on both routers.

```
R1(config)# crypto ipsec transform-set mytrans esp-aes 256 esp-sha-hmac ah-sha-hmac
R1(cfg-crypto-trans)# exit
R1(config)#
```
```
R3(config)# crypto ipsec transform-set mytrans esp-aes 256 esp-sha-hmac ah-sha-hmac
R3(cfg-crypto-trans)# exit
R3(config)#
```

Step 7: Define the Traffic to Be Encrypted

On both endpoint routers, define traffic to be encrypted by IPsec to be GRE traffic with the source and destination as the tunnel endpoint addresses. Remember to keep the correct order of these networks on each router:

```
R1(config)# access-list 101 permit gre host 192.168.12.1 host 192.168.23.3
```
```
R3(config)# access-list 101 permit gre host 192.168.23.3 host 192.168.12.1
```

Step 8: Create and Apply Crypto Maps

On both endpoint routers, you need to create and apply an IPsec crypto map to the outgoing interfaces to encrypt the GRE tunnel traffic. The EIGRP neighbor adjacency might flap (go down and come back up) while the crypto map is configured on one router and not the other:

```
R1(config)# crypto map mymap 10 ipsec-isakmp
% NOTE: This new crypto map will remain disabled until a peer
        and a valid access list have been configured.
R1(config-crypto-map)# match address 101
R1(config-crypto-map)# set peer 192.168.23.3
R1(config-crypto-map)# set transform-set mytrans
R1(config-crypto-map)# exit
R1(config)# interface fastethernet 0/0
R1(config-if)# crypto map mymap
*Jan 22 07:01:30.147: %CRYPTO-6-ISAKMP_ON_OFF: ISAKMP is ON
```
```
R3(config)# crypto map mymap 10 ipsec-isakmp
% NOTE: This new crypto map will remain disabled until a peer
        and a valid access list have been configured.
R3(config-crypto-map)# match address 101
R3(config-crypto-map)# set peer 192.168.12.1
R3(config-crypto-map)# set transform-set mytrans
R3(config-crypto-map)# interface serial 0/0/1
R3(config-if)# crypto map mymap
*Jan 22 07:02:47.726: %CRYPTO-6-ISAKMP_ON_OFF: ISAKMP is ON
```

Note: On certain older IOS releases, you might also need to apply the crypto map to the tunnel interface.

Step 9: Verify Crypto Operation

Verify that the number of packets is increasing by issuing the **show crypto ipsec sa** command and monitoring the number of packet differences after issuing the command on a router:

```
R1# show crypto ipsec sa

interface: FastEthernet0/0
    Crypto map tag: mymap, local addr 192.168.12.1

    protected vrf: (none)
    local  ident (addr/mask/prot/port): (192.168.12.1/255.255.255.255/47/0)
    remote ident (addr/mask/prot/port): (192.168.23.3/255.255.255.255/47/0)
    current_peer 192.168.23.3 port 500
      PERMIT, flags={origin_is_acl,}
     #pkts encaps: 8, #pkts encrypt: 8, #pkts digest: 8
     #pkts decaps: 8, #pkts decrypt: 8, #pkts verify: 8
...
```

Wait a few seconds, and then reissue the **show crypto ipsec sa** command:

```
R1# show crypto ipsec sa

interface: FastEthernet0/0
    Crypto map tag: mymap, local addr 192.168.12.1

    protected vrf: (none)
    local  ident (addr/mask/prot/port): (192.168.12.1/255.255.255.255/47/0)
    remote ident (addr/mask/prot/port): (192.168.23.3/255.255.255.255/47/0)
    current_peer 192.168.23.3 port 500
      PERMIT, flags={origin_is_acl,}
     #pkts encaps: 10, #pkts encrypt: 10, #pkts digest: 10
     #pkts decaps: 10, #pkts decrypt: 10, #pkts verify: 10
...
```

Although you have not issued another ping, packets are still being encrypted in the GRE tunnel and the IPsec VPN.

Based on your knowledge of the configuration on R1 and R3, what packets are causing the packet count to increment as time passes?

_____

_____

_____

For more crypto verification commands, refer to Lab 3-5: Configuring Site-to-Site IPsec VPNs with the IOS CLI.

Challenge: Use Wireshark to Monitor Encryption of Traffic

You can observe packets on the wire using Wireshark and see how their content looks unencrypted and then encrypted. To do this, first configure a SPAN session on the switch and open up Wireshark on a host attached to the SPAN destination port. You can use the host that you used for SDM because you don't need it anymore to configure the VPNs. If you do not know how to do this, refer to Lab 3-3: Configuring Wireshark and SPAN.

Next, you remove the **crypto map** statements on R1 and R3. View the current configuration on the FastEthernet0/0 interface on R1 and Serial0/0/1, as shown in the following code.

Then, issue the **no crypto map** *name* command in interface configuration mode to remove the ISAKMP SA. The router might issue a warning that ISAKMP is now off:

```
R1# show run interface fastethernet 0/0
Building configuration...

Current configuration : 120 bytes
!
interface FastEthernet0/0
 ip address 192.168.12.1 255.255.255.0
 duplex auto
 speed auto
 crypto map mymap
end


R1# configure terminal
R1(config)# interface fastethernet0/0
R1(config-if)# no crypto map mymap
*Jan 16 06:02:58.999: %CRYPTO-6-ISAKMP_ON_OFF: ISAKMP is OFF
R3# show run interface serial 0/0/1
Building configuration...

Current configuration : 91 bytes
!
interface Serial0/0/1
 ip address 192.168.23.3 255.255.255.0
 crypto map mymap
end


R3# configure terminal
R3(config)# interface serial0/0/1
R3(config-if)# no crypto map mymap
*Jan 16 06:05:36.038: %CRYPTO-6-ISAKMP_ON_OFF: ISAKMP is OFF
```

The traffic we want to sniff is Telnet traffic, so if you haven't already, enable Telnet access and an enable password on R3:

```
R3(config)# enable secret cisco
R3(config)# line vty 0 4
R3(config-line)# password cisco
R3(config-line)# login
```

Have Wireshark start sniffing packets that it receives via the SPAN session.

Choose **Capture > Interfaces**. Then, click the **Start** button associated with the interface connected to the SPAN destination port. SPAN should start capturing packets on the line, so you can now telnet from R1's loopback to R3's loopback. To send Telnet traffic, use the **telnet** *destination* command.

Do you need to use the **/source** attribute in the **telnet** command? Explain.

_____

_____

_____

_____

First, begin capturing packets using Wireshark. Then, begin the Telnet session. After you connect to R3, issue a command or two, and then log out. The packets are routed through the tunnel interface toward the loopback on R3, so Wireshark displays the GRE packets:

```
R1# telnet 172.16.3.1
Trying 172.16.3.1 ... Open


User Access Verification


Password:
R3> enable
Password:
R3# show ip interface brief
Interface              IP-Address      OK? Method Status                 Protocol
FastEthernet0/0        unassigned      YES unset  administratively down down
FastEthernet0/1        unassigned      YES unset  administratively down down
Serial0/0/0            unassigned      YES unset  administratively down down
Serial0/0/1            192.168.23.3    YES manual up                     up
Serial0/1/0            unassigned      YES unset  administratively down down
Serial0/1/1            unassigned      YES unset  administratively down down
Loopback0              172.16.3.1      YES manual up                     up
Tunnel0                172.16.13.3     YES manual up                     up
R3# exit


[Connection to 172.16.3.1 closed by foreign host]
R1#
```

Now, look at the output shown in Figure 3-113. Notice that Wireshark is smart enough to classify these packets as Telnet traffic, even though the actual packets are GRE. Looking in the middle pane in Wireshark, it shows the multiple layers of encapsulation, including the GRE information. Notice that because you disabled encryption, you can easily read the plain-text strings of the Telnet session in Wireshark.

Figure 3-113 Detailed Packet Data on Telnet String Sent from R1

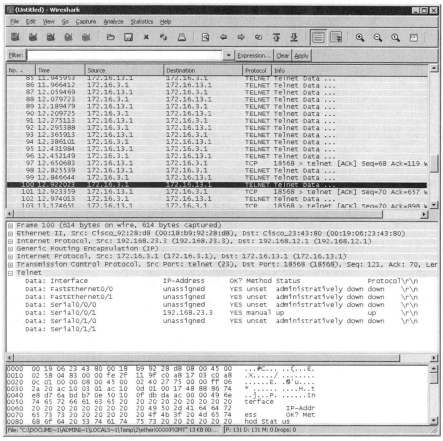

Based on this output, you can see how easy it is for someone who is in the path of sensitive data to view unencrypted or clear-text traffic.

Now, you reapply the cryptography settings on R1 and R3 and begin a Telnet session from R1 to R3, as before.

Begin by reapplying the crypto maps you removed earlier on R1 and R3:

```
R1(config)# interface fastethernet 0/0
R1(config-if)# crypto map mymap
```

```
R3(config)# interface serial0/0/1
R3(config-if)# crypto map mymap
```

Start the packet capturing again in Wireshark, and then issue the same Telnet sequence that you did previously:

```
R1# telnet 172.16.3.1
Trying 172.16.3.1 ... Open


User Access Verification


Password:
```

```
R3> enable
Password:
R3# show ip interface brief
Interface               IP-Address      OK? Method Status                Protocol
FastEthernet0/0         unassigned      YES unset  administratively down down
FastEthernet0/1         unassigned      YES unset  administratively down down
Serial0/0/0             unassigned      YES unset  administratively down down
Serial0/0/1             192.168.23.3    YES manual up                    up
Serial0/1/0             unassigned      YES unset  administratively down down
Serial0/1/1             unassigned      YES unset  administratively down down
Loopback0               172.16.3.1      YES manual up                    up
Tunnel0                 172.16.13.3     YES manual up                    up
R3# exit


[Connection to 172.16.3.1 closed by foreign host]
R1#
```

End your Wireshark capture when you are finished with the Telnet session.

As far as the user is concerned, the Telnet session seems the same with and without encryption. However, the packet capture from Wireshark in Figure 3-114 shows that the VPN is actively encapsulating and encrypting packets.

Figure 3-114 Detailed Packet Data on Encrypted Telnet String Sent from R1

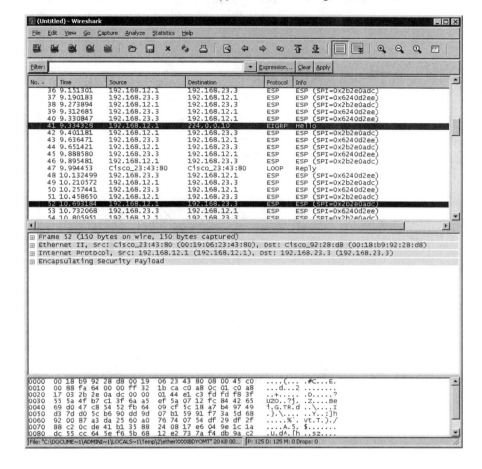

Notice that the protocol is not Telnet (TCP port 23), but the Encapsulating Security Payload (ESP, IP protocol number 50). Remember, all traffic here matches the IPsec access list.

Also, notice that the source and destination are not the actual source and destination of the addresses participating in this Telnet conversation. Rather, they are the VPN endpoints.

Finally, and most important, if you look at the contents of these packets in Wireshark, no matter how you try to format or filter them, you will not be able to see what data was originally inside.

The encryption suite provided by IPsec successfully secures data through authentication, encryption, and data-integrity services.

Lab 3-8: Configuring IPsec VTIs (3.10.8)

The objectives of this lab are as follows:

- Configure EIGRP on a router.

- Configure an IPsec VTI.

- Configure the VTI to be used for backup purposes only.

Figure 3-115 illustrates the topology that is used for this lab.

Figure 3-115 Topology Diagram

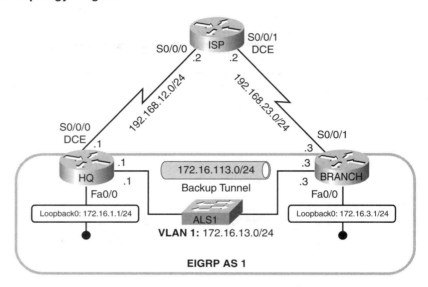

Scenario

The headquarters and branch-office routers of International Travel Agency are connected over a leased line, which they receive as an Ethernet connection. They also both have slower, serial links connecting them to the Internet. This lab covers configuring an IPsec virtual tunnel interface (VTI) to be used as a backup connection, running over the public Internet.

If you have previously completed Lab 3-7, in which you created secure GRE tunnels, the results are similar; however, this newer method is the preferred method. If you run an older IOS release, this feature might not be supported. It is highly recommended that you have previously configured GRE tunnels and IPsec VPNs to understand the commands used in this lab.

Step 1: Configure Addressing

Configure the loopback interfaces with the addresses shown in Figure 3-115. Also, configure the serial interfaces shown in the figure. Set the clock rates on the appropriate interfaces and issue the **no shutdown** command on all serial connections. Verify that you have connectivity across the local subnet by using the **ping** command. Do not set up the tunnel interface until Step 7:

```
HQ# configure terminal
HQ(config)# interface loopback 0
HQ(config-if)# ip address 172.16.1.1 255.255.255.0
HQ(config-if)# interface fastethernet 0/0
```

```
HQ(config-if)# ip address 172.16.13.1 255.255.255.0
HQ(config-if)# no shutdown
HQ(config-if)# interface serial 0/0/0
HQ(config-if)# ip address 192.168.12.1 255.255.255.0
HQ(config-if)# clockrate 64000
HQ(config-if)# no shutdown
```
```
ISP# configure terminal
ISP(config-if)# interface serial 0/0/0
ISP(config-if)# ip address 192.168.12.2 255.255.255.0
ISP(config-if)# no shutdown
ISP(config-if)# interface serial 0/0/1
ISP(config-if)# ip address 192.168.23.2 255.255.255.0
ISP(config-if)# clockrate 64000
ISP(config-if)# no shutdown
```
```
BRANCH# configure terminal
BRANCH(config)# interface loopback 0
BRANCH(config-if)# ip address 172.16.3.1 255.255.255.0
BRANCH(config-if)# interface fastethernet 0/0
BRANCH(config-if)# ip address 172.16.13.3 255.255.255.0
BRANCH(config-if)# no shutdown
BRANCH(config-if)# interface serial 0/0/1
BRANCH(config-if)# ip address 192.168.23.3 255.255.255.0
BRANCH(config-if)# no shutdown
```

Step 2: Configure EIGRP AS 1

Configure EIGRP for AS1 on HQ and BRANCH. Add the whole major network 172.16.0.0 and disable automatic summarization. ISP will not participate in this routing process:

```
HQ(config)# router eigrp 1
HQ(config-router)# no auto-summary
HQ(config-router)# network 172.16.0.0
```
```
BRANCH(config)# router eigrp 1
BRANCH(config-router)# no auto-summary
BRANCH(config-router)# network 172.16.0.0
```

EIGRP neighbor adjacencies should form. If not, troubleshoot by checking your interface configuration, EIGRP configuration, and physical connectivity.

Step 3: Configure Static Routing

On the HQ and BRANCH routers, add a static default route pointing toward ISP through the serial interfaces. This simulates a connection to the Internet. Remember that this route will not be preferred over routes learned via EIGRP, because the EIGRP routes will be more specific and are therefore preferred. We also do not need to configure any static routes on ISP because it has connected routes to route between the 192.168.X.0/24 networks, HQ and BRANCH:

```
HQ(config)# ip route 0.0.0.0 0.0.0.0 192.168.12.2
```

```
BRANCH(config)# ip route 0.0.0.0 0.0.0.0 192.168.23.2
```

Now, everything is in place for configuring the backup tunnel to run over the Internet. Before starting, be sure that both HQ and BRANCH can successfully ping each other's Internet-facing interface (which should be routed via ISP) and the other's loopback interface. Compare the output of the **show ip route** command on your devices to the following output:

```
HQ# ping 192.168.23.3


Type escape sequence to abort.
Sending 5, 100-byte ICMP Echos to 192.168.23.3, timeout is 2 seconds:
!!!!!
Success rate is 100 percent (5/5), round-trip min/avg/max = 56/56/56 ms


HQ# ping 172.16.3.1


Type escape sequence to abort.
Sending 5, 100-byte ICMP Echos to 172.16.3.1, timeout is 2 seconds:
!!!!!
Success rate is 100 percent (5/5), round-trip min/avg/max = 1/2/4 ms


HQ# show ip route
Codes: C - connected, S - static, R - RIP, M - mobile, B - BGP
       D - EIGRP, EX - EIGRP external, O - OSPF, IA - OSPF inter area
       N1 - OSPF NSSA external type 1, N2 - OSPF NSSA external type 2
       E1 - OSPF external type 1, E2 - OSPF external type 2
       i - IS-IS, su - IS-IS summary, L1 - IS-IS level-1, L2 - IS-IS level-2
       ia - IS-IS inter area, * - candidate default, U - per-user static route
       o - ODR, P - periodic downloaded static route


Gateway of last resort is 192.168.12.2 to network 0.0.0.0


C    192.168.12.0/24 is directly connected, Serial0/0/0
     172.16.0.0/24 is subnetted, 3 subnets
C       172.16.13.0 is directly connected, FastEthernet0/0
C       172.16.1.0 is directly connected, Loopback0
D       172.16.3.0 [90/156160] via 172.16.13.3, 00:01:56, FastEthernet0/0
S*   0.0.0.0/0 [1/0] via 192.168.12.2
```

```
BRANCH# ping 192.168.12.1


Type escape sequence to abort.
Sending 5, 100-byte ICMP Echos to 192.168.12.1, timeout is 2 seconds:
!!!!!
Success rate is 100 percent (5/5), round-trip min/avg/max = 56/56/56 ms
```

```
BRANCH# ping 172.16.1.1

Type escape sequence to abort.
Sending 5, 100-byte ICMP Echos to 172.16.1.1, timeout is 2 seconds:
!!!!!
Success rate is 100 percent (5/5), round-trip min/avg/max = 1/1/4 ms

BRANCH# show ip route
Codes: C - connected, S - static, R - RIP, M - mobile, B - BGP
       D - EIGRP, EX - EIGRP external, O - OSPF, IA - OSPF inter area
       N1 - OSPF NSSA external type 1, N2 - OSPF NSSA external type 2
       E1 - OSPF external type 1, E2 - OSPF external type 2
       i - IS-IS, su - IS-IS summary, L1 - IS-IS level-1, L2 - IS-IS level-2
       ia - IS-IS inter area, * - candidate default, U - per-user static route
       o - ODR, P - periodic downloaded static route

Gateway of last resort is 192.168.23.2 to network 0.0.0.0

      172.16.0.0/24 is subnetted, 3 subnets
C        172.16.13.0 is directly connected, FastEthernet0/0
D        172.16.1.0 [90/156160] via 172.16.13.1, 00:02:32, FastEthernet0/0
C        172.16.3.0 is directly connected, Loopback0
C     192.168.23.0/24 is directly connected, Serial0/0/1
S*    0.0.0.0/0 [1/0] via 192.168.23.2
```

Step 4: Create IKE Policies and Peers

Because you will be using Internet Security Association and Key Management Protocol (ISAKMP) with IPsec, configure Internet Key Exchange (IKE) policies and IKE peers on both tunnel endpoints. Create an IKE policy, as shown in the following output. If your IOS image doesn't support all the settings, configure what you can. Just make sure that your VPN settings match on both ends of the connection:

```
HQ(config)# crypto isakmp policy 10
HQ(config-isakmp)# authentication pre-share
HQ(config-isakmp)# encryption aes 256
HQ(config-isakmp)# hash sha
HQ(config-isakmp)# group 5
HQ(config-isakmp)# lifetime 3600
```

```
BRANCH(config)# crypto isakmp policy 10
BRANCH(config-isakmp)# authentication pre-share
BRANCH(config-isakmp)# encryption aes 256
BRANCH(config-isakmp)# hash sha
BRANCH(config-isakmp)# group 5
BRANCH(config-isakmp)# lifetime 3600
```

Which of the options ensures data confidentiality in the tunnel?

_____

_____

Which of the options ensures data integrity in the tunnel?

_____

_____

Which of the options controls the strength of keying information during the ISAKMP exchange?

_____

_____

Now, configure each peer using the key cisco for ISAKMP:

```
HQ(config)# crypto isakmp key cisco address 192.168.23.3
```

```
BRANCH(config)# crypto isakmp key cisco address 192.168.12.1
```

Step 5: Create IPsec Transform Sets

On both endpoint routers, create an IPsec transform set using the following settings. An IPsec profile is a set of parameters used to negotiate an IPsec VPN tunnel between two endpoints, including data encapsulation, authentication, and integrity:

```
HQ(config)# crypto ipsec transform-set mytrans esp-aes 256 esp-sha-hmac ah-sha-hmac
HQ(cfg-crypto-trans)# exit
HQ(config)#
```

```
BRANCH(config)# crypto ipsec transform-set mytrans esp-aes 256 esp-sha-
   hmac
BRANCH(cfg-crypto-trans)# exit
BRANCH(config)#
```

If your routers do not support these settings, use whichever settings you can. Just keep it consistent on both routers.

Step 6: Create an IPsec Profile

Now that you created the transform set, create an IPsec profile. An IPsec profile is similar to a crypto map in that it binds the set of independent parameters and associations negotiated in IKE Phase 1 with the transform sets for Phase 2. It also creates a structure that can, like a crypto map, be applied to an interface. However, an IPsec profile differs from a crypto map in that no **match** clause exists, only **set** statements, because it is applied to an interface. All traffic sent into or out of the tunnel interface is encrypted.

To begin configuring an IPsec profile, use the global configuration command **crypto ipsec profile** *name*. In this configuration, use myprof as the profile name:

```
HQ(config)# crypto ipsec profile myprof
```

In the IPsec profile configuration submode, type **set ?** to find various attributes you can set with an IPsec profile:

```
HQ(ipsec-profile)# set ?
  identity              Identity restriction.
  isakmp-profile        Specify isakmp Profile
  pfs                   Specify pfs settings
  security-association  Security association parameters
  transform-set         Specify list of transform sets in priority order
```

As you can see, the **set** parameters are similar to the parameters you can set in a crypto map. In this case, we only set the transform set to the transform set we configured earlier. Apply the same configuration to BRANCH:

```
HQ(ipsec-profile)# set transform-set mytrans
```
```
BRANCH(config)# crypto ipsec profile myprof
BRANCH(ipsec-profile)# set transform-set mytrans
```

Step 7: Create the IPsec VTI

HQ and BRANCH need to have a tunnel interface on them, which has the standard tunnel IP address, source, and destination. The source and destination should be the serial connections to router ISP. In addition to this, you should change the mode of the tunnel by using the interface level command **tunnel mode** *mode*, and in this case, the mode is ipsec with IPv4. To apply the IPsec profile created earlier, use the interface level command **tunnel protection ipsec profile** *name*:

```
HQ(config)# interface tunnel 0
HQ(config-if)# ip address 172.16.113.1 255.255.255.0
HQ(config-if)# tunnel source serial 0/0/0
HQ(config-if)# tunnel destination 192.168.23.3
HQ(config-if)# tunnel mode ipsec ipv4
HQ(config-if)# tunnel protection ipsec profile myprof
```
```
BRANCH(config)# interface tunnel 0
BRANCH(config-if)# ip address 172.16.113.3 255.255.255.0
BRANCH(config-if)# tunnel source serial 0/0/1
BRANCH(config-if)# tunnel destination 192.168.12.1
BRANCH(config-if)# tunnel mode ipsec ipv4
BRANCH(config-if)# tunnel protection ipsec profile myprof
```

If the endpoints of the tunnel are the serial interfaces facing ISP, when will routed traffic to the private 172.16.0.0/24 network be sent through the tunnel?

_____

_____

Use the **show crypto ipsec sa** command to verify that the packet counters are incrementing with EIGRP hello packets across the tunnel. Also, verify that the EIGRP neighbor adjacency is up with the **show ip eigrp neighbors** command:

```
HQ# show crypto ipsec sa

interface: Tunnel0
    Crypto map tag: Tunnel0-head-0, local addr 192.168.12.1

    protected vrf: (none)
    local  ident (addr/mask/prot/port): (0.0.0.0/0.0.0.0/0/0)
    remote ident (addr/mask/prot/port): (0.0.0.0/0.0.0.0/0/0)
    current_peer 192.168.23.3 port 500
      PERMIT, flags={origin_is_acl,}
     #pkts encaps: 14, #pkts encrypt: 14, #pkts digest: 14
     #pkts decaps: 16, #pkts decrypt: 16, #pkts verify: 16
<OUTPUT OMITTED>


HQ# show crypto ipsec sa

interface: Tunnel0
    Crypto map tag: Tunnel0-head-0, local addr 192.168.12.1

    protected vrf: (none)
    local  ident (addr/mask/prot/port): (0.0.0.0/0.0.0.0/0/0)
    remote ident (addr/mask/prot/port): (0.0.0.0/0.0.0.0/0/0)
    current_peer 192.168.23.3 port 500
      PERMIT, flags={origin_is_acl,}
     #pkts encaps: 15, #pkts encrypt: 15, #pkts digest: 15
     #pkts decaps: 17, #pkts decrypt: 17, #pkts verify: 17
<OUTPUT OMITTED>


HQ# show ip eigrp neighbors
IP-EIGRP neighbors for process 1
```

H	Address	Interface	Hold Uptime (sec)	SRTT (ms)	RTO	Q Cnt	Seq Num
1	172.16.113.3	Tu0	11 00:03:40	118	5000	0	15
0	172.16.13.3	Fa0/0	10 01:04:20	1	200	0	13

```
BRANCH# show crypto ipsec sa

interface: Tunnel0
    Crypto map tag: Tunnel0-head-0, local addr 192.168.23.3

    protected vrf: (none)
    local  ident (addr/mask/prot/port): (0.0.0.0/0.0.0.0/0/0)
```

```
      remote ident (addr/mask/prot/port): (0.0.0.0/0.0.0.0/0/0)
      current_peer 192.168.12.1 port 500
        PERMIT, flags={origin_is_acl,}
       #pkts encaps: 40, #pkts encrypt: 40, #pkts digest: 40
       #pkts decaps: 39, #pkts decrypt: 39, #pkts verify: 39
<OUTPUT OMITTED>


BRANCH# show crypto ipsec sa


interface: Tunnel0
    Crypto map tag: Tunnel0-head-0, local addr 192.168.23.3


    protected vrf: (none)
    local  ident (addr/mask/prot/port): (0.0.0.0/0.0.0.0/0/0)
    remote ident (addr/mask/prot/port): (0.0.0.0/0.0.0.0/0/0)
    current_peer 192.168.12.1 port 500
      PERMIT, flags={origin_is_acl,}
     #pkts encaps: 41, #pkts encrypt: 41, #pkts digest: 41
     #pkts decaps: 41, #pkts decrypt: 41, #pkts verify: 41
<OUTPUT OMITTED>


BRANCH# show ip eigrp neighbors
IP-EIGRP neighbors for process 1
H   Address                Interface      Hold Uptime   SRTT   RTO   Q  Seq
                                          (sec)         (ms)        Cnt Num
1   172.16.113.1           Tu0             11 00:03:48  118    5000  0  12
0   172.16.13.1            Fa0/0           12 01:04:28  333    1998  0  11
```

Step 8: Verify Proper EIGRP Behavior

On HQ, issue a **show ip route** command and make sure that the preferred route to the BRANCH loopback is through the leased line (FastEthernet0/0):

```
HQ# show ip route
Codes: C - connected, S - static, R - RIP, M - mobile, B - BGP
       D - EIGRP, EX - EIGRP external, O - OSPF, IA - OSPF inter area
       N1 - OSPF NSSA external type 1, N2 - OSPF NSSA external type 2
       E1 - OSPF external type 1, E2 - OSPF external type 2
       i - IS-IS, su - IS-IS summary, L1 - IS-IS level-1, L2 - IS-IS level-2
       ia - IS-IS inter area, * - candidate default, U - per-user static route
       o - ODR, P - periodic downloaded static route


Gateway of last resort is 192.168.12.2 to network 0.0.0.0
```

```
C    192.168.12.0/24 is directly connected, Serial0/0/0
     172.16.0.0/24 is subnetted, 4 subnets
C       172.16.13.0 is directly connected, FastEthernet0/0
C       172.16.1.0 is directly connected, Loopback0
D       172.16.3.0 [90/156160] via 172.16.13.3, 00:13:29, FastEthernet0/0
C       172.16.113.0 is directly connected, Tunnel0
S*   0.0.0.0/0 [1/0] via 192.168.12.2
```

Now, shut down the leased-line connection on BRANCH:

```
BRANCH(config)# interface fastethernet 0/0
BRANCH(config-if)# shutdown
```

On HQ, try issuing a **show ip route** command again, after the neighbor adjacency expires:

```
*Jan 23 02:14:17.931: %DUAL-5-NBRCHANGE: IP-EIGRP(0) 1: Neighbor 172.16.13.3
(FastEthernet0/0) is down: holding time expired
```

```
HQ# show ip route
Codes: C - connected, S - static, R - RIP, M - mobile, B - BGP
       D - EIGRP, EX - EIGRP external, O - OSPF, IA - OSPF inter area
       N1 - OSPF NSSA external type 1, N2 - OSPF NSSA external type 2
       E1 - OSPF external type 1, E2 - OSPF external type 2
       i - IS-IS, su - IS-IS summary, L1 - IS-IS level-1, L2 - IS-IS level-2
       ia - IS-IS inter area, * - candidate default, U - per-user static route
       o - ODR, P - periodic downloaded static route


Gateway of last resort is 192.168.12.2 to network 0.0.0.0


C    192.168.12.0/24 is directly connected, Serial0/0/0
     172.16.0.0/24 is subnetted, 4 subnets
C       172.16.13.0 is directly connected, FastEthernet0/0
C       172.16.1.0 is directly connected, Loopback0
D       172.16.3.0 [90/297372416] via 172.16.113.3, 00:00:44, Tunnel0
C       172.16.113.0 is directly connected, Tunnel0
S*   0.0.0.0/0 [1/0] via 192.168.12.2
```

Shutting down the Fast Ethernet interface on BRANCH simulates the leased line being disconnected. As you can see, the network reconverges to use the protected tunnel through the ISP router.

What happens to IP traffic passing through the tunnel?

_____

_____

Of course, this transport path is slower than the leased line, and it is only preferred as a temporary backup, not a permanent solution. Open the FastEthernet0/0 interface that you shut down earlier, and verify on HQ that the transit path is back to the way it was:

```
BRANCH(config)# interface fastethernet 0/0
BRANCH(config-if)# no shutdown


*Jan 23 02:18:56.959: %DUAL-5-NBRCHANGE: IP-EIGRP(0) 1: Neighbor 172.16.13.3
(FastEthernet0/0) is up: new adjacency


HQ# show ip route
Codes: C - connected, S - static, R - RIP, M - mobile, B - BGP
       D - EIGRP, EX - EIGRP external, O - OSPF, IA - OSPF inter area
       N1 - OSPF NSSA external type 1, N2 - OSPF NSSA external type 2
       E1 - OSPF external type 1, E2 - OSPF external type 2
       i - IS-IS, su - IS-IS summary, L1 - IS-IS level-1, L2 - IS-IS level-2
       ia - IS-IS inter area, * - candidate default, U - per-user static route
       o - ODR, P - periodic downloaded static route


Gateway of last resort is 192.168.12.2 to network 0.0.0.0


C    192.168.12.0/24 is directly connected, Serial0/0/0
     172.16.0.0/24 is subnetted, 4 subnets
C        172.16.13.0 is directly connected, FastEthernet0/0
C        172.16.1.0 is directly connected, Loopback0
D        172.16.3.0 [90/156160] via 172.16.13.3, 00:00:29, FastEthernet0/0
C        172.16.113.0 is directly connected, Tunnel0
S*   0.0.0.0/0 [1/0] via 192.168.12.2
```

You can understand why EIGRP prefers the path through the Fast Ethernet network, if you look at the default bandwidth and delay on the Fast Ethernet and tunnel interfaces with the **show interfaces** *interface-type interface-number* command. Remember that EIGRP prefers the path with the minimum composite metric of minimum path bandwidth and lowest total delay. As the output shows, there are radical differences in these attributes between Fast Ethernet and tunnel interfaces. If you needed to change these to make the routes preferred in a certain way, you could modify the attributes with the interface level commands **bandwidth** *bandwidth* and **delay** *delay*, although these commands are outside the scope of this lab:

```
HQ# show interfaces fastethernet 0/0
FastEthernet0/0 is up, line protocol is up
  Hardware is MV96340 Ethernet, address is 0019.0623.4380 (bia 0019.0623.4380)
  Internet address is 172.16.13.1/24
  MTU 1500 bytes, BW 100000 Kbit, DLY 100 usec,


HQ# show interfaces tunnel 0
Tunnel0 is up, line protocol is up
  Hardware is Tunnel
  Internet address is 172.16.113.1/24
  MTU 1514 bytes, BW 9 Kbit, DLY 500000 usec,
```

Lab 3-9: Configuring Easy VPN with SDM (3.10.9)

The objectives of this lab are as follows:

- Configure EIGRP on a router.

- Configure Easy VPN using SDM.

- Install the Cisco VPN Client to a host.

- Connect to the VPN using Cisco VPN Client.

- Verify VPN operation using SDM.

Figure 3-116 illustrates the topology that is used for this lab.

Figure 3-116 Topology Diagram

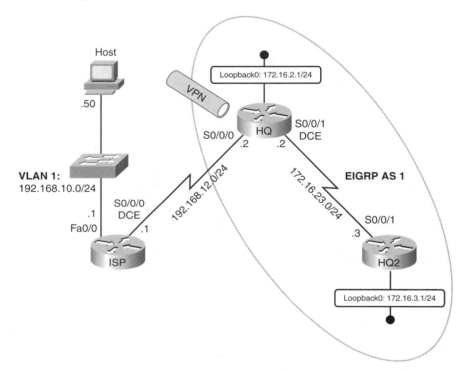

Scenario

In this lab, you set up Easy VPN using SDM for the International Travel Agency. The host simulates an employee connecting from home over the Internet. The router ISP simulates an Internet router representing the Internet connection for both the home user and the company headquarters.

Step 1: Configure Addressing

Configure the loopback interfaces with the addresses shown in Figure 3-116. Also, configure the serial interfaces shown in the figure. Set the clock rate on the appropriate interfaces and issue the **no shutdown** command on all serial connections. Verify that you have connectivity across the local subnet by using the **ping** command. Do not set up the tunnel interface:

```
ISP# configure terminal
ISP(config)# interface fastethernet0/0
ISP(config-if)# ip address 192.168.10.1 255.255.255.0
ISP(config-if)# no shutdown
ISP(config-if)# interface serial 0/0/0
ISP(config-if)# ip address 192.168.12.1 255.255.255.0
ISP(config-if)# clockrate 64000
ISP(config-if)# no shutdown
```
```
HQ# configure terminal
HQ(config)# interface loopback 0
HQ(config-if)# ip address 172.16.2.1 255.255.255.0
HQ(config-if)# interface serial0/0/0
HQ(config-if)# ip address 192.168.12.2 255.255.255.0
HQ(config-if)# no shutdown
HQ(config-if)# interface serial 0/0/1
HQ(config-if)# ip address 172.16.23.2 255.255.255.0
HQ(config-if)# clockrate 64000
HQ(config-if)# no shutdown
```
```
HQ2# configure terminal
HQ2(config)# interface loopback 0
HQ2(config-if)# ip address 172.16.3.1 255.255.255.0
HQ2(config-if)# interface serial 0/0/1
HQ2(config-if)# ip address 172.16.23.3 255.255.255.0
HQ2(config-if)# no shutdown
```

Step 2: Configure EIGRP AS 1

Configure EIGRP for AS1 on HQ and HQ2. Add the entire 172.16.0.0/16 major network and disable automatic summarization. The router ISP will not participate in this routing process:

```
HQ(config)# router eigrp 1
HQ(config-router)# no auto-summary
HQ(config-router)# network 172.16.0.0
```
```
HQ2(config)# router eigrp 1
HQ2(config-router)# no auto-summary
HQ2(config-router)# network 172.16.0.0
```

An EIGRP neighbor adjacency should form between HQ and HQ2. If not, troubleshoot by checking your interface configuration, EIGRP configuration, and physical connectivity.

Step 3: Configure a Static Default Route

Because the router ISP represents an Internet connection, send all traffic whose destination network does not exist in the routing tables at company headquarters out this connection via a default route. This route can be statically created on HQ, but it will need to be redistributed into EIGRP so HQ2 will learn the route as well:

```
HQ(config)# ip route 0.0.0.0 0.0.0.0 192.168.12.1
HQ(config)# router eigrp 1
HQ(config-router)# redistribute static
```

For which types of routes is it unnecessary to assign a default/seed metric when redistributing into EIGRP?

_____

_____

How else could you configure HQ to advertise the default route?

_____

Step 4: Connect to HQ Through SDM

Prepare the HQ router to allow connection and configuration via SDM, as you did in Lab 3-1: Configuring SDM on a Router.

Configure the host to connect to HQ using SDM. Configure the host with the IP address shown in Figure 3-116, and ensure that its default gateway is set to ISP so that traffic from the host to HQ gets routed properly. Remember that you should only be able to connect to HQ's outside interface (192.168.12.2) using SDM because the interfaces inside the EIGRP domain are not reachable from ISP and the PC. If you do not know how to configure the host IP address and connect using SDM, refer to Lab 3-1.

Step 5: Configure Easy VPN Server Through SDM

After you are at the SDM home screen for HQ (see Figure 3-117), click the **Configure** icon at the top and choose **VPN** on the left side bar. Choose **Easy VPN Server** in the VPN types list. Notice from the screen in Figure 3-118 that there is a prerequisite task to configure authentication, authorization, and accounting (AAA). Click **Enable AAA** to allow SDM to fulfill this task for you.

Figure 3-117 SDM Home Screen

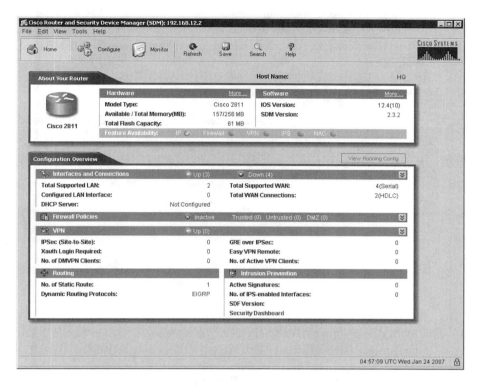

Figure 3-118 Create Easy VPN Server Tab

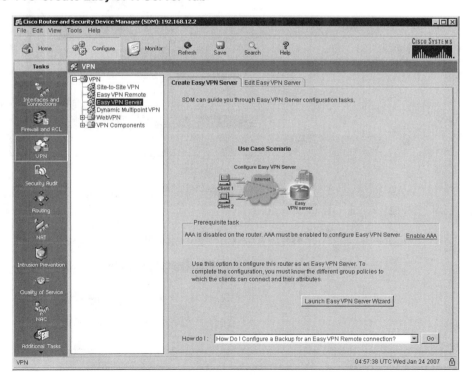

As Figure 3-119 shows, SDM warns you about the changes it will make in addition to enabling AAA. (This prevents you from getting locked out of the router.) When you understand the implications of acknowledgment, click **Yes** to continue. Note that now, when accessing HQ, you need to use a user-name/password pair configured on the router. You already have configured one to use with SDM, so you can reuse it.

Figure 3-119 AAA Configuration Prompt

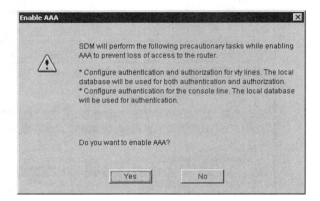

SDM delivers the AAA commands to the router, as shown in Figure 3-120. Click **OK** when the delivery process is complete.

Figure 3-120 Command Delivery Progress Indicator

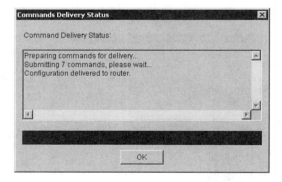

After delivery is complete, SDM notifies you that enabling AAA was successful, as shown in Figure 3-121. Click **OK** to continue.

Figure 3-121 Successful AAA Configuration Report

Now that AAA is enabled, start the Easy VPN Server Wizard by clicking the **Launch Easy VPN Server Wizard** button from the screen shown in Figure 3-122.

Figure 3-122 Create Easy VPN Server Tab

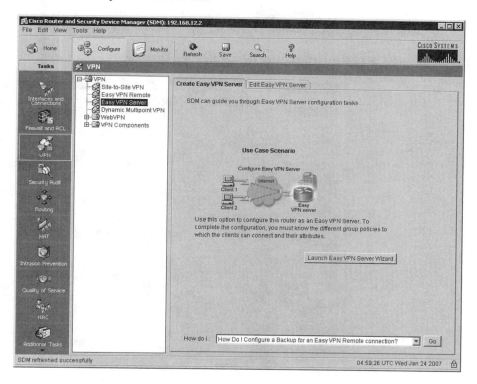

After reading the brief introduction to the wizard, as shown in Figure 3-123, click **Next**.

Figure 3-123 Easy VPN Server Wizard

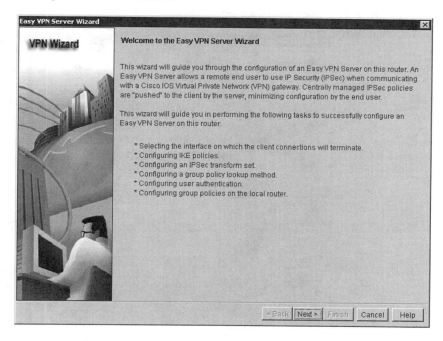

Choose to run the Easy VPN Server on the ISP-facing interface of HQ. Use preshared keys as the authentication type because we will not be using a certificate server. Click **Next** when you are finished with the screen, as shown in Figure 3-124.

Figure 3-124 Interface and Authentication Options

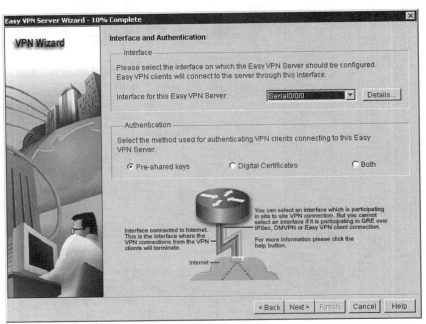

From the screen shown in Figure 3-125, use the default SDM IKE proposal and click **Next**.

Figure 3-125 IKE Proposals List

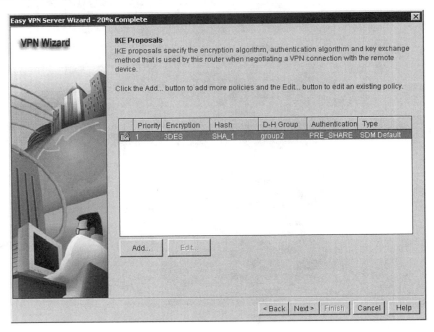

From the screen shown in Figure 3-126, use the default SDM IPsec transform set and click **Next**.

Figure 3-126 IPsec Transform Set List

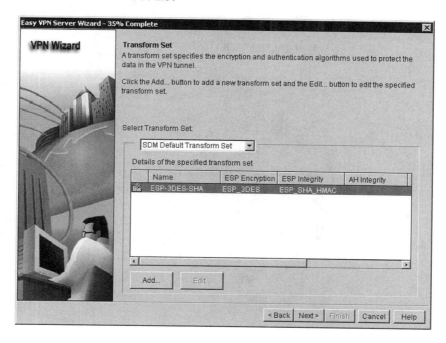

From the screen shown in Figure 3-127, choose **Local** in **Method List for Group Policy Lookup**, and then click **Next**.

Figure 3-127 Authorization and Policy Options

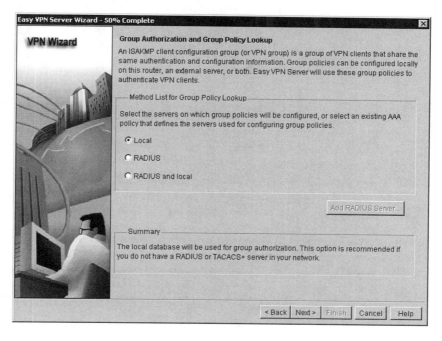

Enable user authentication from a local database. From the screen shown in Figure 3-128, click **Add User Credentials** to add a username for VPN access.

Figure 3-128 User Authentication Options

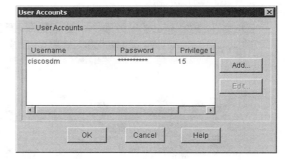

From the screen shown in Figure 3-129, click **Add** to create a new user.

Figure 3-129 Local User Accounts

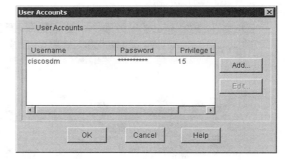

Create a username of **ciscouser** with a password of **ciscouser**. You can leave this user at privilege level 1 because it is only going to be used for VPN access. Encrypting this password is optional and not required.

If you clicked **Encrypt password using MD5 hash algorithm**, how would the password be stored?

_____

_____

_____

From the screen shown in Figure 3-130, click **OK** when you are done, and then click **Next** in the user authentication window.

Figure 3-130 Add User Account Dialog

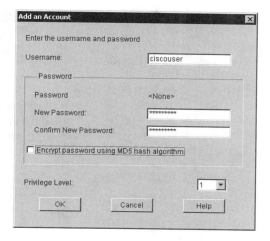

You need to create a group for our Easy VPN Clients. To do this, from the screen shown in Figure 3-131, click **Add**. Also, add a preshared key for the group.

Figure 3-131 VPN Client Authorization Configuration

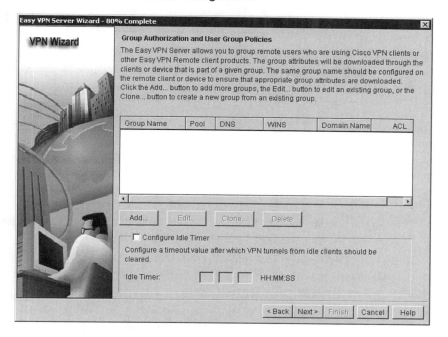

From the screen shown in Figure 3-132, make the group name and preshared key **ciscogroup**. Create an IP pool for clients and use the range 172.16.2.100–172.16.2.200, with a subnet mask of 24 bits. (Later versions of SDM do not have subnet mask length as an option.) Notice that this range falls under HQ's loopback network. Click the **Split Tunneling** tab after completing these fields.

Figure 3-132 VPN Group Policy Configuration

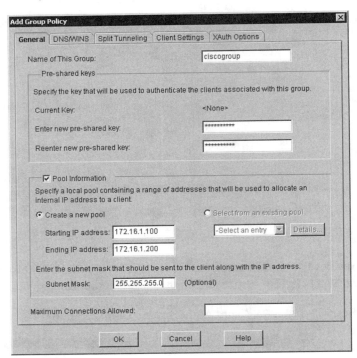

Why would you want to use an IP network associated with a loopback interface for your VPN pool?

_____

_____

How will HQ2 route traffic to the VPN clients?

_____

_____

From the screen shown in Figure 3-133, enable split tunneling to advertise the entire 172.16.0.0 network into the route table of VPN clients. Click the **Add** button and add the network with the appropriate wildcard mask. When complete, click **OK**. Later versions of SDM provide a warning about the IP range being the same as the user IP pool.

Figure 3-133 Split Tunneling Tab

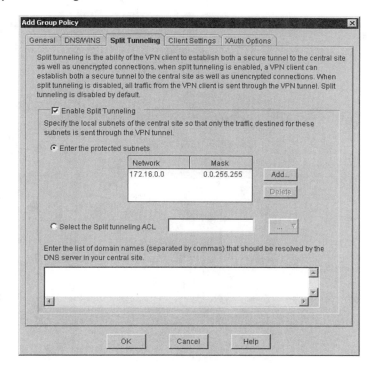

From the screen shown in Figure 3-134, you should see the new group information added. Configure an idle timer of 8 hours and click **Next**.

Figure 3-134 VPN Client Authorization Configuration with Changes Applied

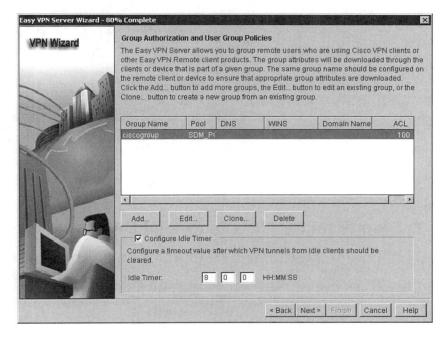

From the screen shown in Figure 3-135, review what SDM will send to the router and click **Finish**.

Figure 3-135 Summary of Easy VPN Configuration

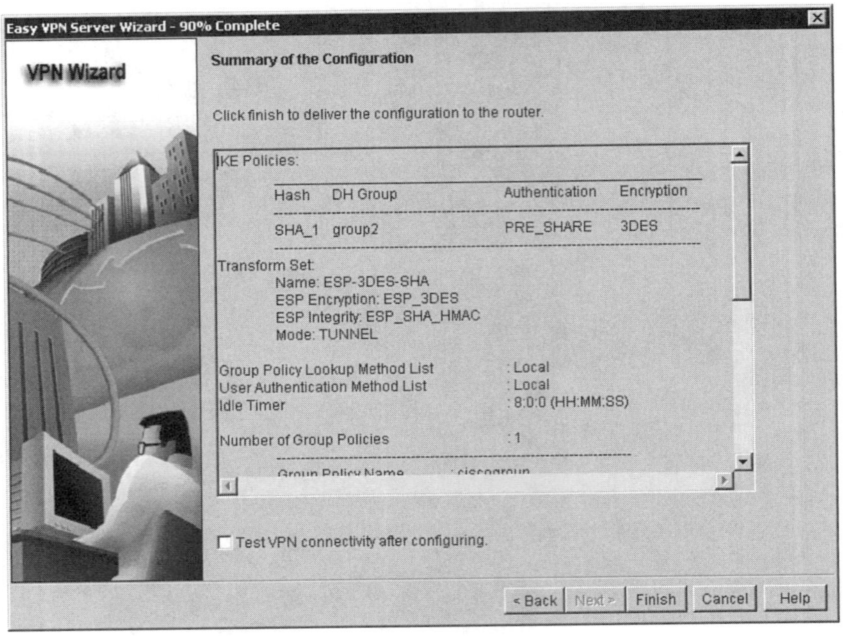

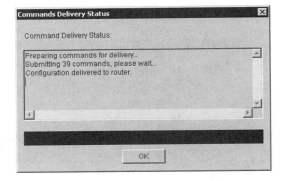

As shown in Figure 3-136, SDM delivers the configuration to the router. Click **OK** when delivery is complete.

Figure 3-136 Command Delivery Progress Indicator

You have now successfully configured Easy VPN Server.

Step 6: Install the Cisco VPN Client

Now that HQ has been set up as an Easy VPN Server, the host changes its role from management host to a VPN client connecting across the Internet to HQ. Before you can connect, you must install the Cisco VPN Client if you haven't already. If you have already installed the VPN Client, go to Step 7.

To begin installation, download the VPN Client from Cisco, and extract it to a temporary directory. Run the setup.exe file in the temporary directory to start installation. Click **Next** when the installer welcomes you, as shown in Figure 3-137.

Figure 3-137 VPN Client Installation Wizard

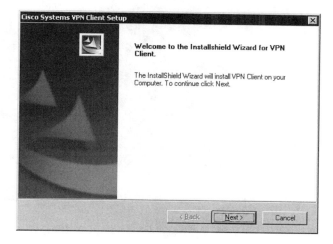

From the screen shown in Figure 3-138, click **Yes** after reading the software license agreement.

Figure 3-138 Cisco VPN Client License Agreement

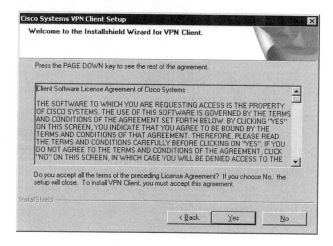

From the screen shown in Figure 3-139, click **Next** to use the default installation.

Figure 3-139 VPN Client Installation Location

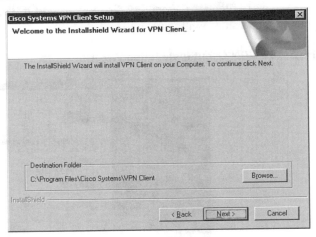

From the screen shown in Figure 3-140, choose the default program group and click **Next**.

Figure 3-140 Start Menu Program Folder Selection

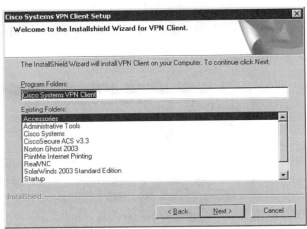

Allow the wizard to install all necessary files. At the end of the process, the wizard adds the virtual network interfaces required for VPN use, as shown in Figure 3-141. This might take some time.

Figure 3-141 VPN Client Installation Progress Indicator

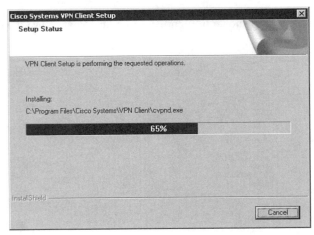

At the end of the installer, you are required to restart. From the screen shown in Figure 3-142, click **Finish** to restart your computer.

Figure 3-142 Final Installation Wizard Window

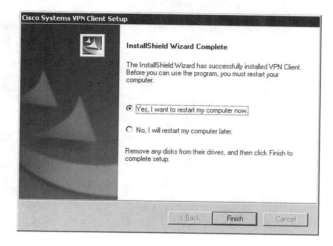

Step 7: Test Access from Client Without VPN Connection

After restarting the host with VPN Client installed, open up a command prompt. Click the **Start** button, choose **Run**, enter **cmd**, and then click **OK**. Try pinging HQ2's loopback address, as shown in Figure 3-143. The pings should fail.

Figure 3-143 Unsuccessful Pings Without VPN

Step 8: Connect to the VPN

Start the Cisco VPN Client by clicking the **Start** button and choosing **Programs > Cisco Systems VPN Client > VPN Client**, as shown in Figure 3-144.

Figure 3-144 Launching the VPN Client

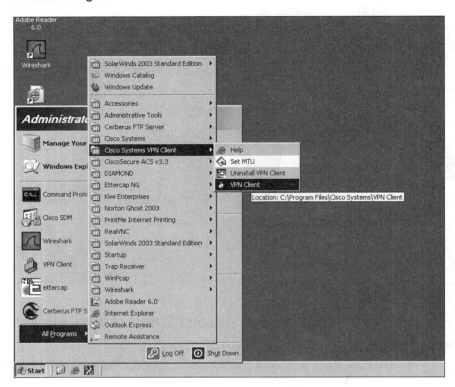

Figure 3-145 shows the resulting VPN Client application window.

Figure 3-145 VPN Client Application

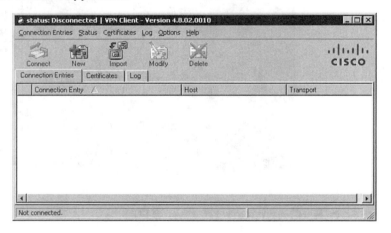

After the VPN Client opens, you need to create a new connection profile with which to connect to HQ. Click the **New** button. Create the new connection with any name and description you want. For host, enter the IP of HQ's Serial0/0/0 interface, 192.168.12.2. The host IP address represents the IP address of the VPN server or concentrator to which you want to connect. In this case, HQ is running the Easy VPN Server and functions as such. Use the group name and password previously configured in the Easy VPN wizard, as shown in Figure 3-146. Click **Save** when you finish configuring.

Figure 3-146 Create New VPN Connection Dialog

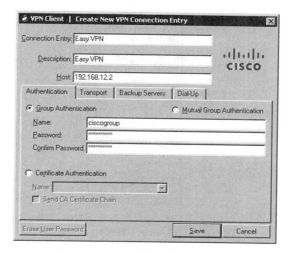

You should see your new profile appear in the profiles list. Before connecting, click the **Log** tab so you can enable logging before attempting to connect, as shown in Figure 3-147. Logging is not normally required, but it is helpful in this lab to watch the VPN client connect.

Figure 3-147 VPN Client Log Tab

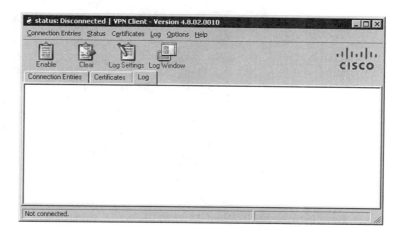

Click **Log Window** to open up logging in a separate window, as shown in Figure 3-148.

Figure 3-148 Log Window

While you have the log window open, go back to the main VPN Client window and click **Log Settings**. From the window shown in Figure 3-149, change the logging settings for IKE and IPsec to **3 – High**. Click **OK** to apply these settings.

Figure 3-149 Logging Settings

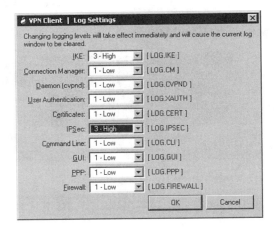

Click **Enable** to enable logging. The **Enable** button should change to a **Disable** button, as shown in Figure 3-150.

Figure 3-150 Log Tab with Logging Enabled

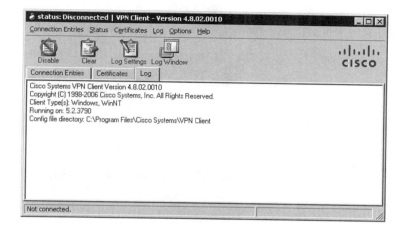

Click the **Connection Entries** tab, as shown in Figure 3-151, and double-click the entry or click **Connect** to connect to this profile.

Figure 3-151 VPN Client Connections Tab

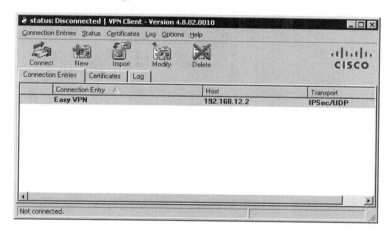

While the VPN client tries to connect to the VPN, it prompts you for a username and password. Enter the user credentials you specified earlier during the VPN Client wizard, as shown in Figure 3-152.

Figure 3-152 User Authentication Prompt

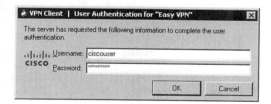

When the VPN successfully connects, you see a locked padlock icon in the system tray, as shown in Figure 3-153.

Figure 3-153 VPN Client System Tray Icon, Status: Connected

You can also see that your connection has populated the log window with information. After reviewing the information in the window shown in Figure 3-154, click **Close** to close this window. This logging functionality can be useful when troubleshooting VPN client problems.

Figure 3-154 Log Window, Populated with Connection Messages

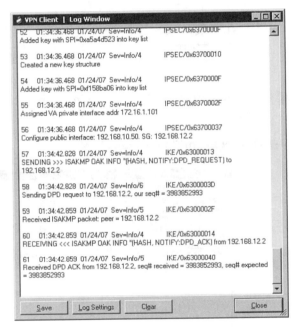

To view VPN connection statistics, right-click the padlock icon in the system tray and click **Statistics** to display the screen shown in Figure 3-155.

Figure 3-155 VPN Client Statistics

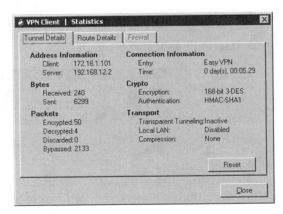

Click the **Route Details** tab to view routes sent out through split tunneling, as shown in Figure 3-156.

Figure 3-156 Route Details Tab

VPN Client | Statistics
Tunnel Details
Route Details
Firewall
Local LAN Routes
Network
Subnet Mask
Secured Routes
Network
Subnet Mask
172.16.0.0
255.255.0.0
Close

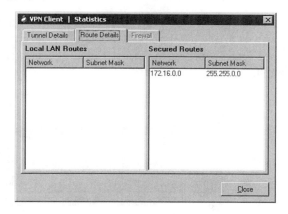

When done, close the **Statistics** window.

Step 9: Test Network Access with VPN Connectivity

Now that the host has connected to the VPN, open up the command prompt again (see earlier steps if you don't remember) and ping HQ2's loopback, as shown in Figure 3-157. This time, it should be successful.

Figure 3-157 Successful Pings with VPN

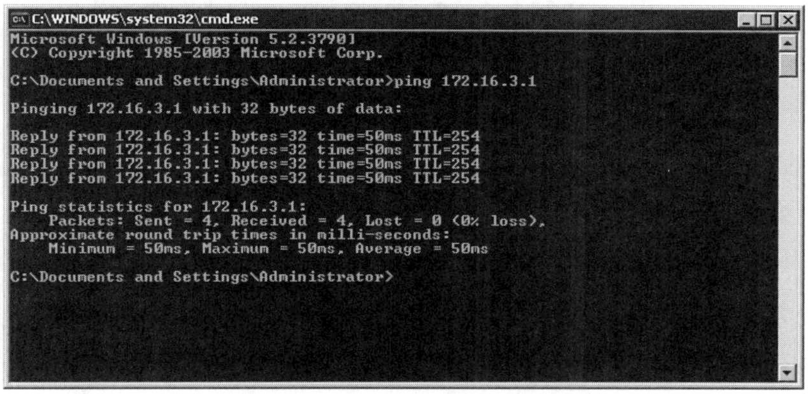

C:\WINDOWS\system32\cmd.exe
Microsoft Windows [Version 5.2.3790]
(C) Copyright 1985-2003 Microsoft Corp.
C:\Documents and Settings\Administrator>ping 172.16.3.1
Pinging 172.16.3.1 with 32 bytes of data:
Reply from 172.16.3.1: bytes=32 time=50ms TTL=254
Reply from 172.16.3.1: bytes=32 time=50ms TTL=254
Reply from 172.16.3.1: bytes=32 time=50ms TTL=254
Reply from 172.16.3.1: bytes=32 time=50ms TTL=254
Ping statistics for 172.16.3.1:
Packets: Sent = 4, Received = 4, Lost = 0 (0% loss),
Approximate round trip times in milli-seconds:
Minimum = 50ms, Maximum = 50ms, Average = 50ms
C:\Documents and Settings\Administrator>

Step 10: Verify Easy VPN Functionality with SDM

While connected through the VPN, open up SDM again on the host and connect to HQ. This time, you can connect to any interface on HQ, not just the external one, because you are inside the VPN. On the home screen, note the number of active VPN clients under the VPN section, as shown in Figure 3-158.

Figure 3-158 SDM Home Screen

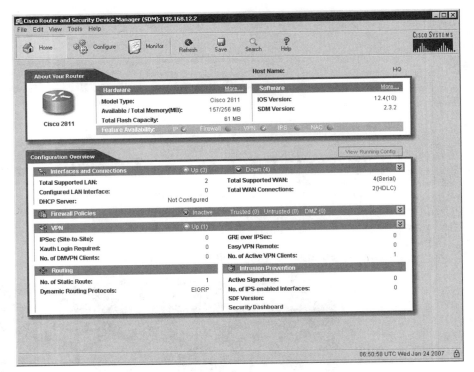

Click the **Configure** icon, and then click **VPN** on the left-side bar. Choose **Easy VPN Server** from the VPN types. Click the **Edit Easy VPN Server** tab, and then click the **Test VPN Server** button, as shown in Figure 3-159.

Figure 3-159 Edit Easy VPN Server Tab

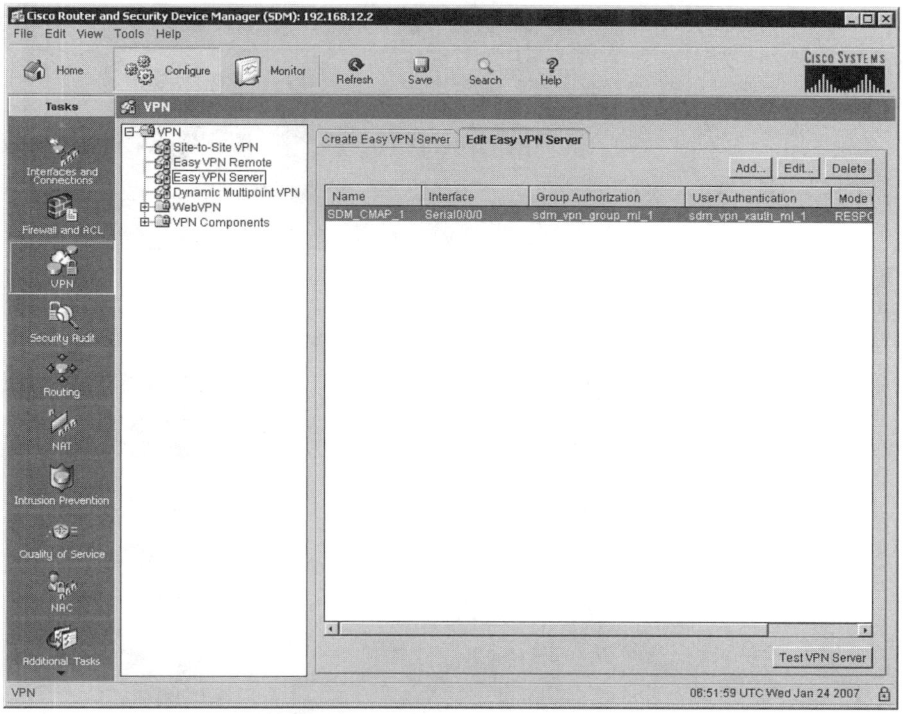

From the screen in Figure 3-160, click **Start**.

Figure 3-160 VPN Testing Window

The tests should be successful, as shown in Figure 3-161.

Figure 3-161 VPN Test In Progress

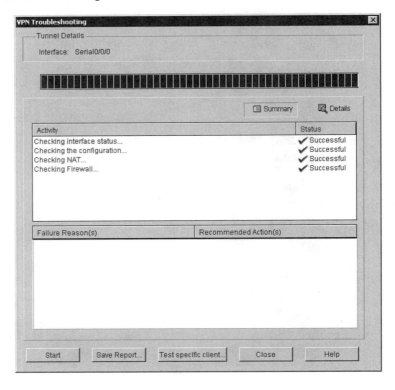

Click **OK** after the success message appears, as shown in Figure 3-162.

Figure 3-162 Successful VPN Test Status Window

Click **Close** when you are finished, and then close SDM.

Step 11: Disconnect the VPN Client

Right-click the padlock icon in the system tray and click **Disconnect**, as shown in Figure 3-163. The VPN client disconnnects.

Figure 3-163 Disconnecting from the VPN via the System Tray Icon

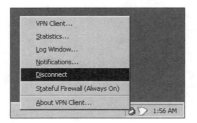

The padlock should first change to a padlock with an X through it, which indicates that it is disconnecting. It changes to an unlocked icon, which indicates no VPN connection. Finally, right-click the padlock and click **Exit** to quit the VPN client, as shown in Figure 3-164.

Figure 3-164 Exiting the VPN Client via the System Tray Icon

Lab 3-10: Configuring Easy VPN with the IOS CLI

The objectives of this lab are as follows:

- Configure EIGRP on a router.

- Configure Easy VPN Server.

- Install the Cisco VPN Client to a host.

- Connect to the VPN using Cisco VPN Client.

- Verify VPN operation.

Figure 3-165 illustrates the topology that is used for this lab.

Figure 3-165 Topology Diagram

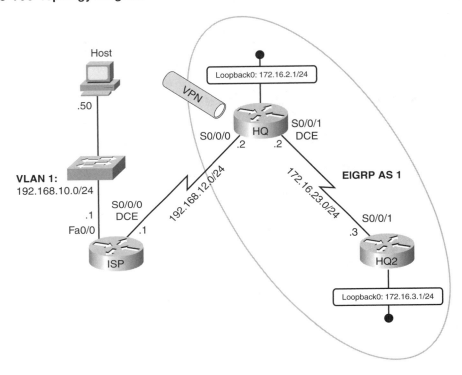

Scenario

In this lab, you set up Easy VPN for the International Travel Agency and connect to Headquarters (HQ) using the IOS command-line interface (CLI). The host simulates an employee connecting from home over the Internet. ISP simulates an Internet router representing the Internet connection for both the home user and the company HQ.

Step 1: Configure Addressing

Configure the loopback interfaces with the addresses shown in Figure 3-165. Also, configure the serial interfaces shown in the figure. Set the clock rate on the appropriate interfaces and issue the **no shutdown** command on all serial connections. Verify that you have connectivity across the local subnet by using the **ping** command. Do not set up the tunnel interface:

```
ISP# configure terminal
ISP(config)# interface fastethernet 0/0
ISP(config-if)# ip address 192.168.10.1 255.255.255.0
ISP(config-if)# no shutdown
ISP(config-if)# interface serial 0/0/0
ISP(config-if)# ip address 192.168.12.1 255.255.255.0
ISP(config-if)# clockrate 64000
ISP(config-if)# no shutdown
```
```
HQ# configure terminal
HQ(config)# interface loopback 0
HQ(config-if)# ip address 172.16.2.1 255.255.255.0
HQ(config-if)# interface serial0/0/0
HQ(config-if)# ip address 192.168.12.2 255.255.255.0
HQ(config-if)# no shutdown
HQ(config-if)# interface serial 0/0/1
HQ(config-if)# ip address 172.16.23.2 255.255.255.0
HQ(config-if)# clockrate 64000
HQ(config-if)# no shutdown
```
```
HQ2# configure terminal
HQ2(config)# interface loopback 0
HQ2(config-if)# ip address 172.16.3.1 255.255.255.0
HQ2(config-if)# interface serial 0/0/1
HQ2(config-if)# ip address 172.16.23.3 255.255.255.0
HQ2(config-if)# no shutdown
```

Step 2: Configure EIGRP AS 1

Configure EIGRP for AS1 on HQ and HQ2. Add the entire 172.16.0.0/16 major network and disable automatic summarization. ISP will not participate in this routing process:

```
HQ(config)# router eigrp 1
HQ(config-router)# no auto-summary
HQ(config-router)# network 172.16.0.0
```
```
HQ2(config)# router eigrp 1
HQ2(config-router)# no auto-summary
HQ2(config-router)# network 172.16.0.0
```

An EIGRP neighbor adjacency should form between HQ and HQ2. If not, troubleshoot by checking your interface configuration, EIGRP configuration, and physical connectivity.

Step 3: Configure a Static Default Route

Because ISP represents a connection to the Internet, send all traffic whose destination network does not exist in the routing tables at company HQ out this connection via a default route. This route can be statically created on HQ, but it will need to be redistributed into EIGRP so HQ2 will learn the route as well:

```
HQ(config)# ip route 0.0.0.0 0.0.0.0 192.168.12.1
HQ(config)# router eigrp 1
HQ(config-router)# redistribute static
```

For which types of routes is it unnecessary to assign a default/seed metric when redistributing into EIGRP?

_____

_____

How else could you configure HQ to advertise the default route?

_____

Step 4: Enable AAA on HQ

To run Easy VPN Server, authentication, authorization, and accounting (AAA) must be enabled on the router. To prevent getting locked out of the router, create a local username and make sure that authentication is performed through the local database. HQ will be the Easy VPN Server, so this is where it must be configured:

```
HQ(config)# username cisco password cisco
HQ(config)# aaa new-model
HQ(config)# aaa authentication login default local none
```

Step 5: Create the IP Pool

Create a pool that VPN clients will draw their IP addresses from using the command **ip local pool** *name low-address high-address*. Use addresses from 172.16.2.100 to 172.16.2.200:

```
HQ(config)# ip local pool VPNCLIENTS 172.16.2.100 172.16.2.200
```

Step 6: Configure the Group Authorization

Use the AAA authorization command **aaa authorization network** *name types* to configure the VPN group authentication list. This list authenticates remote users connecting to the VPN using the group set up in their client. Use the local group list, which is configured in the next step:

```
HQ(config)# aaa authorization network VPNAUTH local
```

Step 7: Create an IKE Policy and Group

Just like previous crypto configurations, you must set up ISAKMP policies to be used during IKE Phase 1 negotiation. Use the following settings. If your version of IOS does not support the same settings that appear here, try to make them as similar as possible:

```
HQ(config)# crypto isakmp policy 10
HQ(config-isakmp)# authentication pre-share
HQ(config-isakmp)# encryption aes 256
HQ(config-isakmp)# group 2
```

Because you don't know specific peers, you cannot statically associate ISAKMP keys with IP address-es or hosts. Rather, VPN clients could connect from anywhere on the Internet. So instead, we config-ure an ISAKMP client group. The group exists locally on the router, as specified by the AAA network authorization command in the previous step.

To enter the ISAKMP group configuration mode, use the global configuration command **crypto isakmp client configuration group** *name*. Use the name **ciscogroup**. Once in this mode, use **?** to find what options you have available:

```
HQ(config)# crypto isakmp client configuration group ciscogroup
HQ(config-isakmp-group)# ?
ISAKMP group policy config commands:
  access-restrict   Restrict clients in this group to an interface
  acl               Specify split tunneling inclusion access-list number
  backup-gateway    Specify backup gateway
  dns               Specify DNS Addresses
  domain            Set default domain name to send to client
  exit              Exit from ISAKMP client group policy configuration mode
  firewall          Enforce group firewall feature
  group-lock        Enforce group lock feature
  include-local-lan Enable Local LAN Access with no split tunnel
  key               pre-shared key/IKE password
  max-logins        Set maximum simultaneous logins for users in this group
  max-users         Set maximum number of users for this group
  netmask           netmask used by the client for local connectivity
  no                Negate a command or set its defaults
  pfs               The client should propose PFS
  pool              Set name of address pool
  save-password     Allows remote client to save XAUTH password
  split-dns         DNS name to append for resolution
  wins              Specify WINS Addresses
```

Configure a preshared key to be the same as the group name. Also, associate the address pool created earlier with this group. In addition, specify an access list to be used as the split tunneling list; this enables split tunneling in this configuration. This access list doesn't exist yet, but you create it momentarily. Finally, set the network mask, because the IP pool does not specify one:

```
HQ(config-isakmp-group)# key ciscogroup
HQ(config-isakmp-group)# pool VPNCLIENTS
HQ(config-isakmp-group)# acl 100
HQ(config-isakmp-group)# netmask 255.255.255.0
```

Now that you have referenced the split tunneling access list, create it. Source networks permitted by the access list are sent to the VPN clients and injected into their IP tables. Create an access list allow-ing traffic sourced from the entire 172.16.0.0/16 network:

```
HQ(config)# access-list 100 permit ip 172.16.0.0 0.0.255.255 any
```

Step 8: Configure the IPsec Transform Set

Configure an IPsec transform set for use with the VPN. Use the 3DES algorithm for encryption and the SHA-HMAC hash function for data integrity:

```
R1(config)# crypto ipsec transform-set mytrans esp-3des esp-sha-hmac
R1(cfg-crypto-trans)# exit
```

Step 9: Create a Dynamic Crypto Map

As in previous IPsec configurations, you must set up a crypto map. However, this type of crypto map is different than earlier configurations. Previously, you configured static crypto maps, which configure certain traffic to establish VPNs with certain peers. However, because you don't know what the peers will be and what the triggering traffic will be, create and apply a dynamic crypto map.

Use the global configuration command **crypto dynamic-map** *name sequence*, similar to a regular crypto map. Use the name mymap and the sequence number 10. After you enter crypto map configuration mode, set the transform set you configured in the previous step. Use the command **reverse-route,** which ensures that a route is installed on the local router for the remote VPN peer:

```
HQ(config)# crypto dynamic-map mymap 10
HQ(config-crypto-map)# set transform-set mytrans
HQ(config-crypto-map)# reverse-route
```

After creating the map, more commands modify it. The first of these commands, the **crypto map** *name* **client configuration address respond** command, makes the map respond to VPN requests. The next command is **crypto map** *name* **isakmp authorization list** *name*, which associates an AAA group authorization list with the map. The final command creates a regular crypto map using the dynamic one created earlier:

```
HQ(config)# crypto map mymap client configuration address respond
HQ(config)# crypto map mymap isakmp authorization list VPNAUTH
HQ(config)# crypto map mymap 10 ipsec-isakmp dynamic mymap
```

Finally, apply the crypto map to the interface that is facing ISP:

```
HQ(config)# int serial0/0/0
HQ(config-if)# crypto map mymap
```

Step 10: Enable IKE DPD and User Authentication

IKE Dead Peer Detection (DPD) is a keepalive mechanism for checking VPN connections. This is beneficial when a VPN server has to manage many connections that are potentially on unstable connections. To configure IKE DPD, use the global configuration command **crypto isakmp keepalive** *seconds retry-time*, where *seconds* is how often to send a keepalive packet and *retry-time* is how soon to retry if one is missed. Use a keepalive timer of 30 seconds and a retry-time of 5 seconds:

```
HQ(config)# crypto isakmp keepalive 30 5
```

Extended authentication (Xauth) is the method used to authenticate VPN clients on a per-user basis, in addition to the group authentication. To configure this, use the AAA login authentication command **aaa authentication login** *group types*. We reuse the name VPNAUTH (the last time we used it, it was for network authentication, not login authentication), and keep the authentication type as local. Also, add a user for VPN access with the username/password of ciscouser/ciscouser:

```
HQ(config)# aaa authentication login VPNAUTH local
HQ(config)# username ciscouser password ciscouser
```

Globally configure the Xauth timeout to be 60 seconds using the **crypto isakmp xauth timeout** *seconds* command. This controls the amount of time that the VPN server waits before terminating the IKE session with a client if user authentication is not performed:

```
HQ(config)# crypto isakmp xauth timeout 60
```

Finally, associate the AAA login list with the crypto map configured earlier:

```
HQ(config)# crypto map mymap client authentication list VPNAUTH
```

Step 11: Install the Cisco VPN Client

Now that HQ has been set up as an Easy VPN Server, the host changes its role from management host to a VPN client connecting across the Internet to HQ. Before you can connect, you must install the Cisco VPN Client, if you haven't already. If you have already installed the VPN client, go to Step 12.

To begin the installation, download the VPN Client from Cisco, and extract it to a temporary directory. Run the setup.exe file in the temporary directory to start installation. Click **Next** when the installer welcomes you, as shown in Figure 3-166.

Figure 3-166 VPN Client Installation Wizard

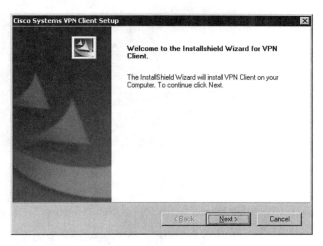

Click **Yes** after reading the software license agreement shown in Figure 3-167.

Figure 3-167 Cisco VPN Client License Agreement

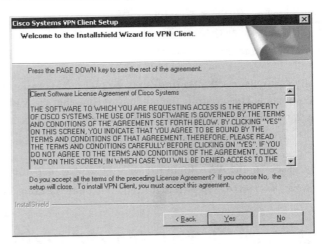

From the screen shown in Figure 3-168, click **Next** to use the default installation.

Figure 3-168 VPN Client Installation Location

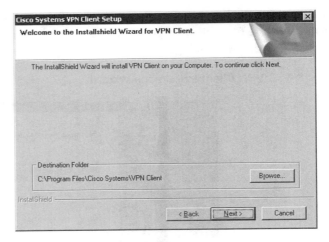

From the screen shown in Figure 3-169, choose the default program group and click **Next**.

Figure 3-169 Start Menu Program Folder Selection

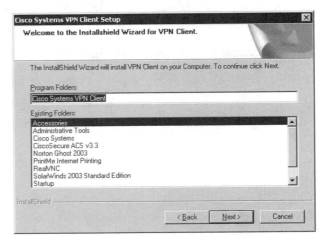

Allow the wizard to install all the necessary files. Toward the end of the process, the wizard tries to add the virtual network interfaces required for VPN use, as shown in Figure 3-170. This might take some time.

Figure 3-170 VPN Client Installation Progress Indicator

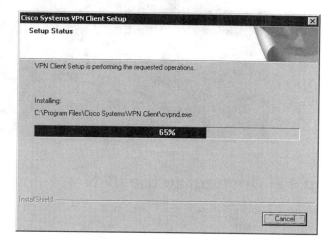

At the end of the installer, you are required to restart. Click **Finish** to restart your computer, as shown in Figure 3-171.

Figure 3-171 Final Installation Wizard Window

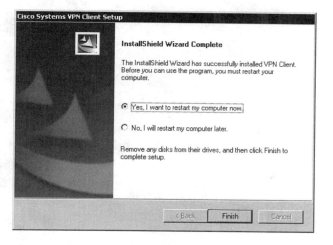

Step 12: Test Access from Client Without VPN Connection

After restarting the host with the VPN Client installed, open up a command prompt. Click the **Start** button, choose **Run**, enter **cmd**, and click **OK**. Try pinging HQ2's loopback address. The pings should fail, as shown in Figure 3-172.

Figure 3-172 Unsuccessful Pings Without VPN

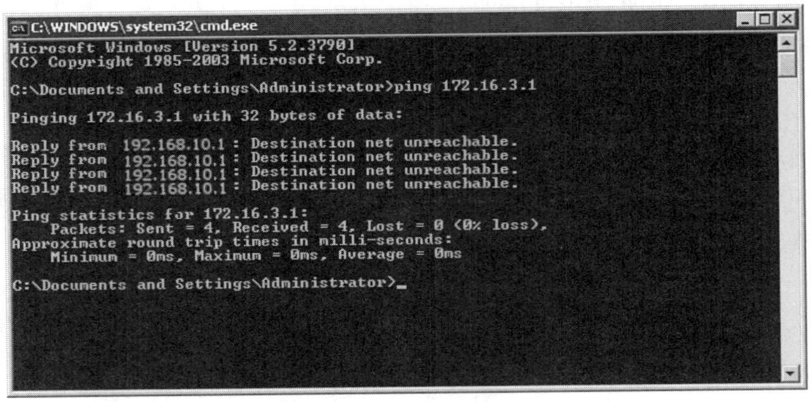

C:\WINDOWS\system32\cmd.exe
Microsoft Windows [Version 5.2.3790]
(C) Copyright 1985-2003 Microsoft Corp.
C:\Documents and Settings\Administrator>ping 172.16.3.1
Pinging 172.16.3.1 with 32 bytes of data:
Reply from 192.168.10.1 : Destination net unreachable.
Reply from 192.168.10.1 : Destination net unreachable.
Reply from 192.168.10.1 : Destination net unreachable.
Reply from 192.168.10.1 : Destination net unreachable.
Ping statistics for 172.16.3.1:
Packets: Sent = 4, Received = 4, Lost = 0 (0% loss),
Approximate round trip times in milli-seconds:
Minimum = 0ms, Maximum = 0ms, Average = 0ms
C:\Documents and Settings\Administrator>_

Step 13: Connect to the VPN

To start the Cisco VPN Client, click the **Start** button and choose **Programs > Cisco Systems VPN Client > VPN Client**, as shown in Figure 3-173.

Figure 3-173 Launching the VPN Client

SolarWinds 2003 Standard Edition
Windows Catalog
Windows Update
Accessories
Administrative Tools
Cerberus FTP Server
Cisco Systems
Cisco Systems VPN Client
CiscoSecure ACS v3.3
DIAMOND
Ettercap NG
Kiwi Enterprises
Norton Ghost 2003
PrintMe Internet Printing
RealVNC
SolarWinds 2003 Standard Edition
Startup
Trap Receiver
WinPcap
Wireshark
Adobe Reader 6.0
Internet Explorer
Outlook Express
Remote Assistance
Help
Set MTU
Uninstall VPN Client
VPN Client
Location: C:\Program Files\Cisco Systems\VPN Client
Manage Your
Windows Expl
Command Prom
Cisco SDM
Wireshark
VPN Client
ettercap
Cerberus FTP S
All Programs
Log Off
Shut Down
Start

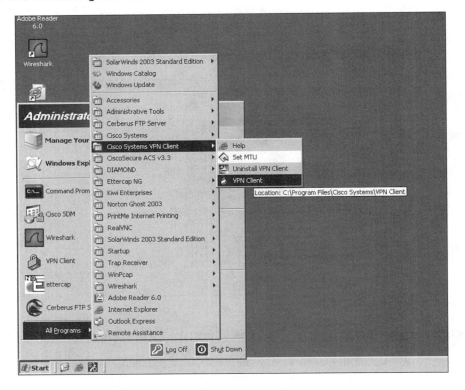

After the VPN Client opens, as shown in Figure 3-174, you need to create a new connection profile to connect to HQ.

Figure 3-174 VPN Client Application

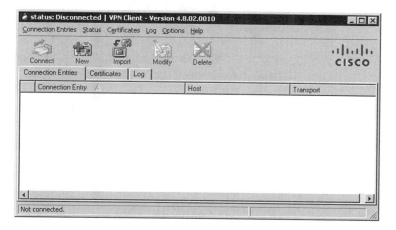

Click the **New** button. Create the new connection with any name and description you want. For host, enter the IP of HQ's Serial0/0/0 interface, 192.168.12.2. The host IP address represents the IP address of the VPN server or concentrator to which you want to connect. In this case, HQ is running the Easy VPN Server and functions as such. Use the group name and password previously configured in the Easy VPN wizard, as shown in Figure 3-175. Click **Save** when you finish configuring.

Figure 3-175 Create New VPN Connection Dialog

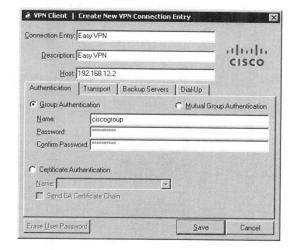

You should see your new profile appear in the profiles list. Before connecting, click the **Log** tab from the screen shown in Figure 3-176 so you can enable logging before attempting to connect. Logging is not normally required, but it is helpful in this lab to watch the VPN client connect.

Figure 3-176 VPN Client Log Tab

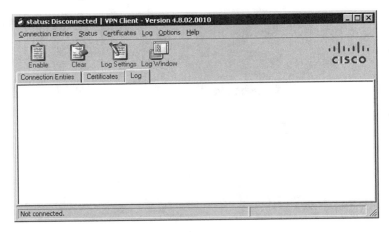

Click **Log Window** to open up logging in a separate window, as shown in Figure 3-177.

Figure 3-177 Log Window

While you have the log window open, go back to the main VPN client window and click **Log Settings**. Change the logging settings for IKE and IPsec to **3 – High**, as shown in Figure 3-178. Click **OK** to apply these settings.

Figure 3-178 Logging Settings

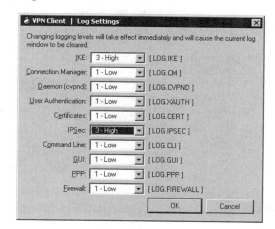

Click **Enable** to enable logging. The **Enable** button should change to a **Disable** button, as shown in Figure 3-179.

Figure 3-179 Log Tab with Logging Enabled

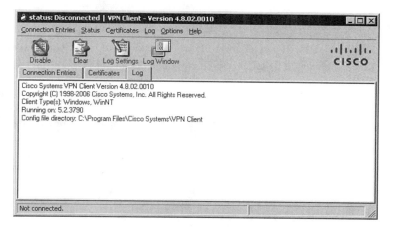

From the screen shown in Figure 3-180, click the **Connection Entries** tab, and double-click the entry or click **Connect** to connect to this profile.

Figure 3-180 VPN Client Connections Tab

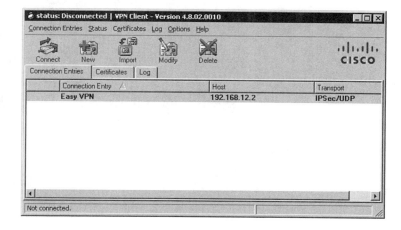

While the VPN client tries to connect to the VPN, it prompts you for a username and password. From the screen shown in Figure 3-181, enter the user credentials you specified earlier during the VPN Client wizard.

Figure 3-181 User Authentication Prompt

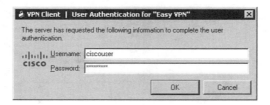

When the VPN has successfully connected, you should see a locked padlock icon in the system tray, as shown in Figure 3-182.

Figure 3-182 VPN Client System Tray Icon, Status: Connected

You can also see that your connection has populated the log window with information, as shown in Figure 3-183. After reviewing the information here, click **Close** to close this window. This logging functionality can be useful when troubleshooting VPN client problems.

Figure 13-183   Log Window, Populated with Connection Messages

To view VPN connection statistics, right-click the padlock icon in the system tray and click **Statistics** to generate the window shown in Figure 3-184.

Figure 3-184 VPN Client Statistics

VPN Client | Statistics
Tunnel Details
Route Details
Firewall
Address Information
Client: 172.16.1.101
Server: 192.168.12.2
Bytes
Received: 240
Sent: 6299
Packets
Encrypted: 50
Decrypted: 4
Discarded: 0
Bypassed: 2133
Connection Information
Entry: Easy VPN
Time: 0 day(s), 00:05.29
Crypto
Encryption: 168-bit 3-DES
Authentication: HMAC-SHA1
Transport
Transparent Tunneling: Inactive
Local LAN: Disabled
Compression: None
Reset
Close

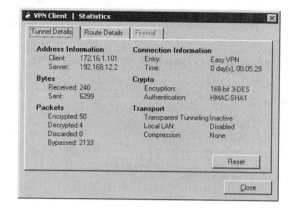

Click the **Route Details** tab to view routes sent out through split tunneling, as shown in Figure 3-185.

Figure 3-185 Route Details Tab

VPN Client | Statistics
Tunnel Details
Route Details
Firewall
Local LAN Routes
Network
Subnet Mask
Secured Routes
Network
Subnet Mask
172.16.0.0
255.255.0.0
Close

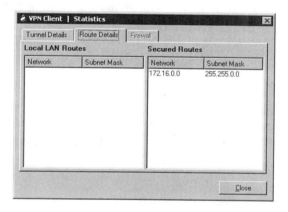

Close the Statistics window when done.

Step 14: Test Inside VPN Connectivity

Now that the host has connected to the VPN, open up the command prompt again (see earlier steps if you don't remember how) and ping HQ2's loopback. This time, it should be successful, as shown in Figure 3-186.

Figure 3-186 Successful Pings with VPN

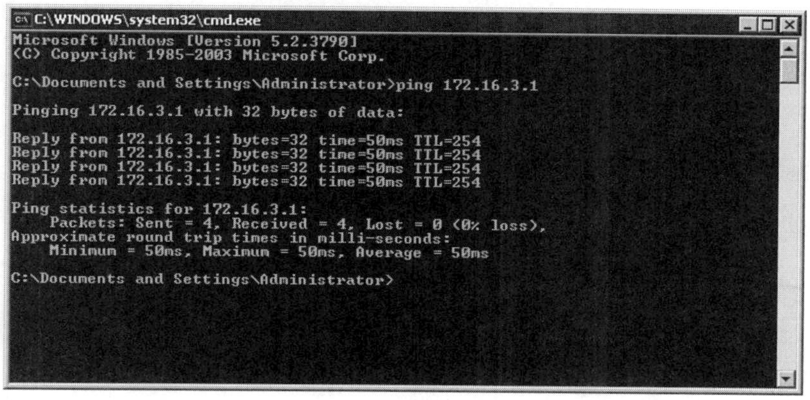

C:\WINDOWS\system32\cmd.exe
Microsoft Windows [Version 5.2.3790]
(C) Copyright 1985-2003 Microsoft Corp.
C:\Documents and Settings\Administrator>ping 172.16.3.1
Pinging 172.16.3.1 with 32 bytes of data:
Reply from 172.16.3.1: bytes=32 time=50ms TTL=254
Reply from 172.16.3.1: bytes=32 time=50ms TTL=254
Reply from 172.16.3.1: bytes=32 time=50ms TTL=254
Reply from 172.16.3.1: bytes=32 time=50ms TTL=254
Ping statistics for 172.16.3.1:
Packets: Sent = 4, Received = 4, Lost = 0 (0% loss),
Approximate round trip times in milli-seconds:
Minimum = 50ms, Maximum = 50ms, Average = 50ms
C:\Documents and Settings\Administrator>

Step 15: Verify VPN Operation Using the CLI

You can use many command-line **show** commands to verify VPN configuration. You can use the **show crypto isakmp sa** and **show crypto ipsec sa** commands to verify crypto security associations:

```
HQ# show crypto isakmp sa
dst             src             state          conn-id slot status
192.168.12.2    192.168.10.50   QM_IDLE             1    0 ACTIVE


HQ# show crypto ipsec sa

interface: Serial0/0/0
    Crypto map tag: mymap, local addr 192.168.12.2

  protected vrf: (none)
  local  ident (addr/mask/prot/port): (0.0.0.0/0.0.0.0/0/0)
  remote ident (addr/mask/prot/port): (172.16.2.100/255.255.255.255/0/0)
  current_peer 192.168.10.50 port 1471
   PERMIT, flags={}
  #pkts encaps: 4, #pkts encrypt: 4, #pkts digest: 4
  #pkts decaps: 44, #pkts decrypt: 44, #pkts verify: 44
  #pkts compressed: 0, #pkts decompressed: 0
  #pkts not compressed: 0, #pkts compr. failed: 0
  #pkts not decompressed: 0, #pkts decompress failed: 0
  #send errors 0, #recv errors 0

    local crypto endpt.: 192.168.12.2, remote crypto endpt.: 192.168.10.50
    path mtu 1500, ip mtu 1500, ip mtu idb Serial0/0/0
    current outbound spi: 0xECC953E1(3972617185)

    inbound esp sas:
     spi: 0xB18FB7F1(2978985969)
       transform: esp-3des esp-sha-hmac ,
       in use settings ={Tunnel, }
       conn id: 3001, flow_id: NETGX:1, crypto map: mymap
       sa timing: remaining key lifetime (k/sec): (4600939/3552)
       IV size: 8 bytes
       replay detection support: Y
       Status: ACTIVE

    inbound ah sas:

    inbound pcp sas:

    outbound esp sas:
     spi: 0xECC953E1(3972617185)
```

```
transform: esp-3des esp-sha-hmac ,
in use settings ={Tunnel, }
conn id: 3002, flow_id: NETGX:2, crypto map: mymap
sa timing: remaining key lifetime (k/sec): (4600946/3551)
IV size: 8 bytes
replay detection support: Y
Status: ACTIVE


outbound ah sas:


outbound pcp sas:
```

Use the command **show ip local pool** to view IP pool information:

HQ# **show ip local pool**

Pool	Begin	End	Free	In use
VPNCLIENTS	172.16.2.100	172.16.2.200	100	1

Step 16: Disconnect the VPN Client

Right-click the padlock icon in the system tray and click **Disconnect**, as shown in Figure 3-187. The VPN client disconnects.

Figure 3-187 Disconnecting from the VPN via the System Tray Icon

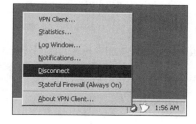

The padlock should first change to a padlock with an X through it, which indicates that it is disconnecting. It changes to an unlocked icon, which indicates no VPN connection. Finally, right-click the padlock and click **Exit** to quit the VPN client, as shown in Figure 3-188.

Figure 3-188 Exiting the VPN Client via the System Tray Icon

Lab 3-11: IPsec Challenge Lab

Your network topology employs dual links to each of your data centers. One link is a dedicated, serial 128-kbps link, while the other is a rate-limited Internet link presented to the offices in the form of Fast Ethernet. For this scenario, imagine that the Ethernet VLAN that connects the four routers represents a nonbroadcast Layer 3 Internet cloud.

The routers at those data centers, R2 and R3, control all traffic between each branch office. In this scenario, model two separate branch offices with R1 and R4.

Internal subnets are represented in the 172.17.0.0/16 network. Public subnets are represented in the 172.16.0.0/16 network.

Your goal is to configure this network to secure routed traffic flowing between the sites. Consider the following restriction: R3 does not support AES encryption or Diffie-Hellman group 5 authentication. However, secure tunnels to R2 with the best possible authentication and encryption schemes that are supported on these routers.

Implement the topology shown in Figure 3-189 and Figure 3-190, according to the following requirements:

- Configure all interfaces shown in the topology diagram with the IP addresses shown.

- Set the clock speed on all serial DCE interfaces to 2000 Kbps.

- Configure EIGRP AS 1 to route over the internal network between the two data centers and their branch offices.

- Employ IPsec tunnels to R2 using ISAKMP negotiation with the following conditions:

    - Use IPsec VTIs to connect the branch offices to the data centers.

    - Use AES encryption to protect traffic sent over the Internet subnet to R2.

    - Use 3DES encryption to protect traffic sent over the Internet subnet to R3.

- Tunnels to R2 must use the preshared key cisco for authentication.

- Tunnels to R3 must use the preshared key systems for authentication.

- All IPsec tunnels must use the most secure methods of source authentication and data integrity to verify traffic.

- For routing purposes, prefer the IPsec VTI tunnels for data center connectivity over the 128-kbps serial connections.

- Secure the serial links using the authentication scheme, which uses a three-way handshake. Use the password incorporated. Do not use AAA methods for authentication.

Figure 3-189 Topology Diagram

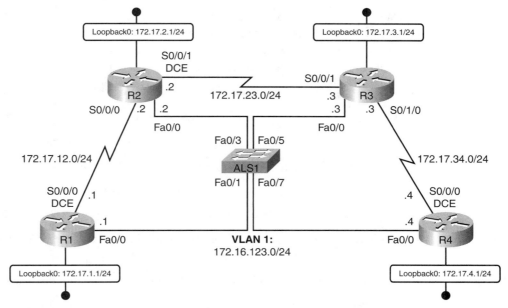

Figure 3-190 Tunnel Diagram

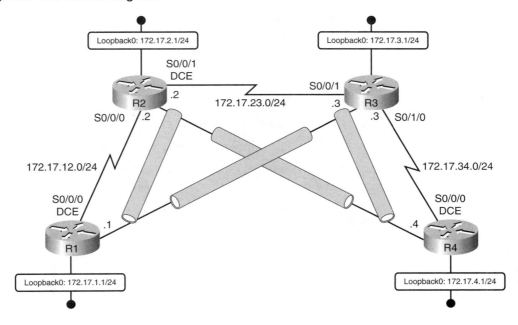

Use the following commands to verify your configurations:

- **show ip route**
- **show ip interfaces brief**
- **show crypto isakmp sa**
- **show crypto ipsec sa**

Lab 3-12: IPsec Troubleshooting Lab

In this lab, you troubleshoot existing configurations to get a working topology. Copy and paste the initial configurations into your routers. (You can download the configurations at ciscopress.com/title/158713215x, under the More Information section.) Your goal is to use troubleshooting techniques to fix anything in the scenario that prevents fulfillment of the following requirements:

- All links and tunnels configured for security must completely authenticate.

- Employ IPsec tunnels to R2 using ISAKMP negotiation with the following conditions:

  - Use IPsec VTIs to connect the branch offices to the data centers.

  - Use AES encryption to protect traffic sent over the Internet subnet to R2.

  - Use 3DES encryption to protect traffic sent over the Internet subnet to R3.

- EIGRP must prefer tunneled routes to remote subnets over the physical links themselves.

If you don't know where to start, try pinging remote addresses and see which ones are reachable (either manually performing pings or using a TCL script).

Use the default switch configuration on ALS1 by erasing your configuration and reloading.

Turn up the debugging output for the various processes as you attempt to find and solve the problems.

Figure 3-191 and Figure 3-192 show the network topology and tunnel diagram for this lab.

Figure 3-191 Topology Diagram

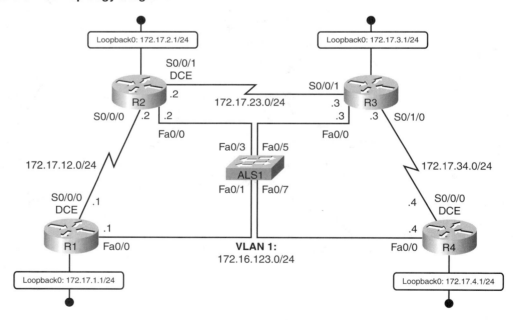

Figure 3-192 Tunnel Diagram

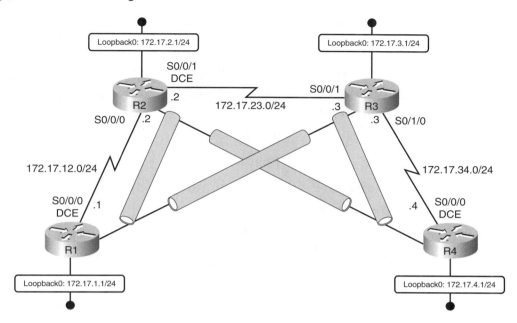

Initial Configurations

```
R1# show run
!
hostname R1
!
username R3 password 0 incorporated
!
crypto isakmp policy 10
 encr aes 256
 authentication pre-share
 group 5
 lifetime 3600
!
crypto isakmp policy 20
 encr 3des
 authentication pre-share
 group 2
 lifetime 3600
crypto isakmp key cisco address 172.16.123.2
crypto isakmp key systems address 172.16.123.3
!
crypto ipsec transform-set R2 ah-sha-hmac esp-aes 256 esp-sha-hmac
crypto ipsec transform-set R3 ah-sha-hmac esp-3des esp-sha-hmac
!
```

```
crypto ipsec profile R2
 set transform-set R2
!
crypto ipsec profile R3
 set transform-set R3
!
interface Loopback0
 ip address 172.17.1.1 255.255.255.0
 shutdown
!
interface Tunnel12
 ip unnumbered Loopback0
 tunnel source FastEthernet0/0
 tunnel destination 172.16.123.2
 tunnel protection ipsec profile R2
!
interface Tunnel13
 ip unnumbered Loopback0
 tunnel source FastEthernet0/0
 tunnel destination 172.16.123.3
 tunnel mode ipsec ipv4
 tunnel protection ipsec profile R2
!
interface FastEthernet0/0
 ip address 172.16.123.1 255.255.255.0
 duplex auto
 speed auto
!
interface Serial0/0/0
 ip address 172.17.12.1 255.255.255.0
 encapsulation ppp
 clock rate 2000000
 ppp authentication chap
!
router eigrp 1
 network 172.16.0.0
 no auto-summary
!
end
```

R2# **show run**
```
!
hostname R2
!
```

```
username R3 password 0 incorporated
username R1 password 0 incorporated
!
crypto isakmp policy 10
 encr aes 256
 authentication pre-share
 group 5
crypto isakmp key cisco address 172.16.123.4
crypto isakmp key cisco address 172.16.123.1
!
crypto ipsec transform-set R2 ah-sha-hmac esp-aes 256 esp-sha-hmac
!
crypto ipsec profile R2
 set transform-set R2
!
interface Loopback0
 ip address 172.17.2.1 255.255.255.0
!
interface Tunnel12
 ip unnumbered Loopback0
 tunnel source FastEthernet0/0
 tunnel destination 172.16.123.1
 tunnel mode ipsec ipv4
 tunnel protection ipsec profile R2
!
interface Tunnel24
 ip unnumbered Loopback0
 tunnel source FastEthernet0/0
 tunnel destination 172.16.123.4
 tunnel mode ipsec ipv4
 tunnel protection ipsec profile R2
!
interface FastEthernet0/0
 ip address 172.16.123.2 255.255.255.0
 duplex auto
 speed auto
!
interface Serial0/0/0
 ip address 172.17.12.2 255.255.255.0
 no fair-queue
!
interface Serial0/0/1
 ip address 172.17.23.2 255.255.255.0
 encapsulation ppp
```

```
  clock rate 2000000
  ppp authentication chap
 !
 router eigrp 1
  network 172.17.0.0
  no auto-summary
 !
 end
```

```
R3# show run
 !
 hostname R3
 !
 username R4 password 0 incorporated
 username R2 password 0 incorporated
 !
 crypto isakmp policy 10
  encr 3des
  authentication pre-share
  group 2
  lifetime 3600
 crypto isakmp key systems address 172.16.123.1
 !
 crypto ipsec transform-set R3 ah-sha-hmac esp-3des esp-sha-hmac
 !
 crypto ipsec profile R3
  set transform-set R3
 !
 interface Loopback0
  ip address 172.17.3.1 255.255.255.0
 !
 interface Tunnel13
  ip unnumbered Loopback0
  tunnel source FastEthernet0/0
  tunnel destination 172.16.123.1
  tunnel mode ipsec ipv4
  tunnel protection ipsec profile R3
 !
 interface Tunnel34
  ip unnumbered Loopback0
  tunnel source FastEthernet0/0
  tunnel destination 172.16.123.4
  tunnel protection ipsec profile R3
 !
```

```
interface FastEthernet0/0
 ip address 172.16.123.3 255.255.255.0
 duplex auto
 speed auto
!
interface Serial0/0/0
 no ip address
 shutdown
 no fair-queue
 clock rate 2000000
!
interface Serial0/0/1
 ip address 172.17.23.3 255.255.255.0
 encapsulation ppp
 ppp authentication chap
!
interface Serial0/1/0
 ip address 172.17.34.3 255.255.255.0
 encapsulation ppp
 clock rate 2000000
 ppp authentication chap
!
end
```

```
R4# show run
!
hostname R4
!
username R3 password 0 corporate
!
crypto isakmp policy 10
 encr aes 256
 authentication pre-share
 group 5
 lifetime 3600
!
crypto isakmp policy 20
 encr 3des
 authentication pre-share
 group 2
 lifetime 3600
crypto isakmp key cisco address 172.16.123.2
crypto isakmp key systems address 172.16.123.3
!
```

```
crypto ipsec transform-set R2 ah-sha-hmac esp-aes 256
crypto ipsec transform-set R3 ah-sha-hmac esp-3des esp-sha-hmac
!
crypto ipsec profile R2
 set transform-set R2
!
crypto ipsec profile R3
 set transform-set R3
!
interface Loopback0
 ip address 172.17.4.1 255.255.255.0
!
interface Tunnel24
 ip unnumbered Loopback0
 tunnel source FastEthernet0/0
 tunnel destination 172.16.123.2
 tunnel mode ipsec ipv4
 tunnel protection ipsec profile R2
!
interface Tunnel34
 ip unnumbered FastEthernet0/0
tunnel source FastEthernet0/0
 tunnel destination 172.16.123.3
 tunnel mode ipsec ipv4
 tunnel protection ipsec profile R3
!
interface FastEthernet0/0
 ip address 172.16.123.4 255.255.255.0
 duplex auto
 speed auto
!
interface Serial0/0/0
 ip address 172.17.34.4 255.255.255.0
 encapsulation ppp
 no fair-queue
 ppp authentication chap
!
 router eigrp 1
 network 172.17.0.0
 no auto-summary
 !
 End
```

CHAPTER 4

Frame Mode MPLS Implementation

Lab 4-1: Configuring Frame Mode MPLS (4.5.1)

In this lab, you learn how to do the following:

- Configure EIGRP on a router.
- Configure LDP on a router.
- Change the size of the MTU.
- Verify MPLS behavior.

Figure 4-1 illustrates the topology that is used for this lab.

Figure 4-1   Topology Diagram

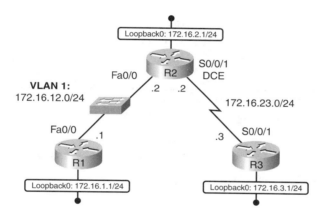

Scenario

In this lab, you configure a simple Enhanced Interior Gateway Routing Protocol (EIGRP) network to route IP packets. You run Multiprotocol Label Switching (MPLS) over the IP internetwork to fast-switch Layer 2 frames.

Step 1: Configure Addressing

Configure the loopback interfaces with the addresses shown in Figure 4-1. Also, configure the serial interfaces shown in the figure. Set the clock rate on the appropriate interface and issue the **no shutdown** command on all serial connections. Verify that you have connectivity across the local subnet by using the **ping** command:

```
R1(config)# interface loopback 0
R1(config-if)# ip address 172.16.1.1 255.255.255.0
R1(config-if)# interface fastethernet 0/0
R1(config-if)# ip address 172.16.12.1 255.255.255.0
R1(config-if)# no shutdown
```

```
R2(config)# interface loopback 0
R2(config-if)# ip address 172.16.2.1 255.255.255.0
R2(config-if)# interface fastethernet 0/0
R2(config-if)# ip address 172.16.12.2 255.255.255.0
R2(config-if)# no shutdown
R2(config-if)# interface serial 0/0/1
R2(config-if)# ip address 172.16.23.2 255.255.255.0
R2(config-if)# clockrate 64000
R2(config-if)# no shutdown
```

```
R3(config)# interface loopback 0
R3(config-if)# ip address 172.16.3.1 255.255.255.0
R3(config-if)# interface serial 0/0/1
R3(config-if)# ip address 172.16.23.3 255.255.255.0
R3(config-if)# no shutdown
```

Step 2: Configure EIGRP AS 1

Configure EIGRP for AS1 on all three routers. Add the whole major network 172.16.0.0 and disable automatic summarization:

```
R1(config)# router eigrp 1
R1(config-router)# no auto-summary
R1(config-router)# network 172.16.0.0
```

```
R2(config)# router eigrp 1
R2(config-router)# no auto-summary
R2(config-router)# network 172.16.0.0
```

```
R3(config)# router eigrp 1
R3(config-router)# no auto-summary
R3(config-router)# network 172.16.0.0
```

EIGRP neighbor adjacencies should form between R1 and R2 and between R2 and R3. If the adjacencies do not form, troubleshoot by checking your interface configuration, EIGRP configuration, and physical connectivity.

What impact does IP connectivity have on MPLS?

_____

_____

_____

Step 3: Observe CEF Operation

Because all the routers have EIGRP adjacencies and are advertising the entire major 172.16.0.0 network, all routers should have full routing tables:

```
R1# show ip route
Codes: C - connected, S - static, R - RIP, M - mobile, B - BGP
       D - EIGRP, EX - EIGRP external, O - OSPF, IA - OSPF inter area
       N1 - OSPF NSSA external type 1, N2 - OSPF NSSA external type 2
       E1 - OSPF external type 1, E2 - OSPF external type 2
       i - IS-IS, su - IS-IS summary, L1 - IS-IS level-1, L2 - IS-IS level-2
       ia - IS-IS inter area, * - candidate default, U - per-user static route
       o - ODR, P - periodic downloaded static route


Gateway of last resort is not set


     172.16.0.0/24 is subnetted, 5 subnets
D        172.16.23.0 [90/2172416] via 172.16.12.2, 00:01:56, FastEthernet0/0
C        172.16.12.0 is directly connected, FastEthernet0/0
C        172.16.1.0 is directly connected, Loopback0
D        172.16.2.0 [90/156160] via 172.16.12.2, 00:01:56, FastEthernet0/0
D        172.16.3.0 [90/2300416] via 172.16.12.2, 00:01:51, FastEthernet0/0
```

On R1, if you perform a **traceroute** to the R3's loopback, you see the path that the packet follows. This output changes slightly after you configure MPLS:

```
R1# traceroute 172.16.3.1


Type escape sequence to abort.
Tracing the route to 172.16.3.1


  1 172.16.12.2 0 msec 0 msec 0 msec
  2 172.16.23.3 16 msec 12 msec *
```

Cisco Express Forwarding (CEF) is the Cisco proprietary Layer 3 switching algorithm for Cisco IOS routers. CEF allows forwarding to be distributed throughout the line cards on Cisco models, such as the Catalyst 6500. CEF also provides quicker switching than switching based on the routing table (process switching) or switching based on a standards-compliant forwarding information base (fast-switching).

What is the function of CEF?

_____

_____

_____

_____

Which information does CEF view as significant in making a forwarding determination for an IP packet?

_____

You can also see that CEF is enabled by default by using the **show ip cef command**:

```
R1# show ip cef
Prefix                Next Hop          Interface
0.0.0.0/0             drop              Null0 (default route handler entry)
0.0.0.0/32            receive
172.16.1.0/24         attached          Loopback0
172.16.1.0/32         receive
172.16.1.1/32         receive
172.16.1.255/32       receive
172.16.2.0/24         172.16.12.2       FastEthernet0/0
172.16.3.0/24         172.16.12.2       FastEthernet0/0
172.16.12.0/24        attached          FastEthernet0/0
172.16.12.0/32        receive
172.16.12.1/32        receive
172.16.12.2/32        172.16.12.2       FastEthernet0/0
172.16.12.255/32      receive
172.16.23.0/24        172.16.12.2       FastEthernet0/0
224.0.0.0/4           drop
224.0.0.0/24          receive
255.255.255.255/32    receive
```

Another important CEF command is the **show ip cef non-recursive** command, which allows the user to display CEF forwarding information for prefixes installed in the routing table:

```
R1# show ip cef non-recursive
Prefix                Next Hop          Interface
172.16.1.0/24         attached          Loopback0
172.16.2.0/24         172.16.12.2       FastEthernet0/0
172.16.3.0/24         172.16.12.2       FastEthernet0/0
172.16.12.0/24        attached          FastEthernet0/0
172.16.12.2/32        172.16.12.2       FastEthernet0/0
172.16.23.0/24        172.16.12.2       FastEthernet0/0
```

CEF records both the Layer 3 next-hop information and the Layer 2 frame next-hop information. CEF currently supports the following Layer 2 protocols: Asynchronous Transfer Mode (ATM), Frame Relay, Ethernet, Fiber Distributed Data Interface (FDDI), Point-to-Point Protocol (PPP), High-Level Data Link Control (HDLC), and tunnels.

CEF is critical to the operation of MPLS on Cisco routers because MPLS packets must be forwarded based on label. Because the CEF architecture can support multiple protocols, such as IPv4 and IPv6, CEF switching could naturally be extended to support MPLS labels.

CEF should be enabled by default. If CEF is not enabled, issue the **ip cef** command in global configuration mode on each router.

Step 4: Enable MPLS on All Physical Interfaces

MPLS is a standardized protocol that allows routers to switch packets based on labels, rather than route switch packets based on standards in the protocol's routing formula. Under normal IP routing, every intermediate system looks up the destination prefix of an IP packet in the Routing Information Base (RIB) of a router or in the Forwarding Information Base (FIB) of a fast switch at every Layer 3 node. Instead of switching that is based on prefix, the first router running MPLS can encapsulate the IP packet in an MPLS frame and then further encapsulate the packet in the Layer 2 frame before sending it across one of many supported Layer 2 media. At the next MPLS-enabled label switch router (LSR), the MPLS frame is read, and the IP packet is switched as an MPLS frame from router to router with little rewrite at each node.

This allows routers to switch multiple protocols (hence, the name) by using the same switching mechanism, as well as perform some other functionality not available in traditional destination-based forwarding, including Layer 2 VPNs (AToM), Layer 3 VPNs, and traffic engineering. MPLS runs between Layers 2 and 3 of the OSI model and, because of this, it is sometimes said to run at Layer 2 1/2. The MPLS header is 4 bytes long and includes a 20-bit label.

Configuring the interface-level command **mpls ip** on an interface tells the router to switch MPLS packets inbound and outbound on that interface and attempt to bring up MPLS adjacencies with the Label Distribution Protocol (LDP) out that egress interface. LDP facilitates communication between MPLS peers by allowing them to inform each other of labels to assign packets to particular destinations based on Layer 2, Layer 3, or other significant information.

Configure MPLS on all physical interfaces in the topology.

Note: If you run Cisco IOS Software Release 12.4 on your routers, use the **mpls ip** command in this lab. However, when Cisco first developed packet-labeling technology, it was called tag switching. Therefore, if you run an older version of IOS, you might see one of two different variations: The first variation is that your router accepts the **mpls ip** command. However, the commands are stored in IOS as **tag-switching** commands. The second variation is that your router won't accept the **mpls ip** command. In this event, the **mpls ip** command can be entered as the **tag-switching ip** command. Try the newer commands first, beginning with the **mpls** keyword.

```
R1(config)# interface fastethernet0/0
R1(config-if)# mpls ip
```

```
R2(config)# interface fastethernet0/0
R2(config-if)# mpls ip
*Jan 31 08:28:54.315: %LDP-5-NBRCHG: LDP Neighbor 172.16.1.1:0 (1) is UP
R2(config-if)# interface serial0/0/1
R2(config-if)# mpls ip
```

```
R3(config)# interface serial0/0/1
R3(config-if)# mpls ip
*Jan 31 08:32:11.571: %LDP-5-NBRCHG: LDP Neighbor 172.16.2.1:0 (1) is UP
```

Notice that as you configure MPLS on both ends of a connection, IOS logs a messages to the console on both routers, which indicates that an LDP neighbor adjacency has formed.

Although you are going to use LDP in this lab, another Cisco proprietary label-exchanging protocol exists: Tag Distribution Protocol (TDP), which was part of the Cisco tag-switching architecture. To change the protocol being used, use the **mpls label protocol** *protocol* command either on a global level at the global configuration prompt or on a per-interface basis, using the interface-level version of this command. Cisco TDP and MPLS LDP are nearly identical in functionality, but they use incompatible message formats and some different procedures. Cisco is changing from TDP to a fully compliant LDP.

Step 5: Verify MPLS Configuration

MPLS has many **show** commands that you can use to verify proper MPLS operation. Issue the **show mpls interfaces** command to see a quick summary of interfaces configured with MPLS. Keep in mind that you see this output because you applied the **mpls ip** command to these interfaces:

```
R1# show mpls interfaces
Interface            IP          Tunnel   Operational
FastEthernet0/0      Yes (ldp)   No       Yes
```

```
R2# show mpls interfaces
Interface            IP          Tunnel   Operational
FastEthernet0/0      Yes (ldp)   No       Yes
Serial0/0/1          Yes (ldp)   No       Yes
```

```
R3# show mpls interfaces
Interface            IP          Tunnel   Operational
Serial0/0/1          Yes (ldp)   No       Yes
```

Issue the **show mpls ldp discovery** command to find out local sources for LDP exchanges and the **show mpls ldp neighbor** command to show LDP adjacencies. Notice that MPLS chooses its IDs based on loopback interfaces, similar to other protocols, such as Open Shortest Path First (OSPF) Protocol and Border Gateway Protocol (BGP):

```
R1# show mpls ldp discovery
 Local LDP Identifier:
    172.16.1.1:0
    Discovery Sources:
    Interfaces:
        FastEthernet0/0 (ldp): xmit/recv
            LDP Id: 172.16.2.1:0; no host route
```

```
R1# show mpls ldp neighbor
    Peer LDP Ident: 172.16.2.1:0; Local LDP Ident 172.16.1.1:0
        TCP connection: 172.16.2.1.49525 - 172.16.1.1.646
        State: Oper; Msgs sent/rcvd: 29/26; Downstream
        Up time: 00:16:40
        LDP discovery sources:
          FastEthernet0/0, Src IP addr: 172.16.12.2
```

```
            Addresses bound to peer LDP Ident:
                172.16.12.2      172.16.23.2      172.16.2.1
R2# show mpls ldp discovery
  Local LDP Identifier:
      172.16.2.1:0
  Discovery Sources:
  Interfaces:
      FastEthernet0/0 (ldp): xmit/recv
          LDP Id: 172.16.1.1:0; no host route
      Serial0/0/1 (ldp): xmit/recv
          LDP Id: 172.16.3.1:0; no host route


R2# show mpls ldp neighbor
    Peer LDP Ident: 172.16.1.1:0; Local LDP Ident 172.16.2.1:0
        TCP connection: 172.16.1.1.646 - 172.16.2.1.49525
        State: Oper; Msgs sent/rcvd: 27/30; Downstream
        Up time: 00:17:06
        LDP discovery sources:
          FastEthernet0/0, Src IP addr: 172.16.12.1
        Addresses bound to peer LDP Ident:
            172.16.12.1      172.16.1.1
    Peer LDP Ident: 172.16.3.1:0; Local LDP Ident 172.16.2.1:0
        TCP connection: 172.16.3.1.34352 - 172.16.2.1.646
        State: Oper; Msgs sent/rcvd: 27/26; Downstream
        Up time: 00:16:23
        LDP discovery sources:
          Serial0/0/1, Src IP addr: 172.16.23.3
        Addresses bound to peer LDP Ident:
172.16.3.1
R3# show mpls ldp discovery
  Local LDP Identifier:
      172.16.3.1:0
  Discovery Sources:
  Interfaces:
      Serial0/0/1 (ldp): xmit/recv
          LDP Id: 172.16.2.1:0; no host route
R3# show mpls ldp neighbor
    Peer LDP Ident: 172.16.2.1:0; Local LDP Ident 172.16.3.1:0
        TCP connection: 172.16.2.1.646 - 172.16.3.1.34352
        State: Oper; Msgs sent/rcvd: 27/28; Downstream
        Up time: 00:17:19
        LDP discovery sources:
```

```
      Serial0/0/1, Src IP addr: 172.16.23.2
   Addresses bound to peer LDP Ident:
      172.16.12.2      172.16.23.2      172.16.2.1
```

What interface does LDP use on R1 to identify itself to other LDP peers?

_____

_____

_____

What transport protocol does LDP use to communicate with other LDP peers?

_____

_____

In the configuration you set up in Step 4, all routers are acting as LSRs and running LDP. On LSRs, each forwarding equivalence class (in this case, each routable IP prefix) is assigned an MPLS label. LDP automatically distributes labels to peers to be used when sending traffic to specific destinations through the LSR. After the labels are distributed, switching for MPLS packets is done through the Label Information Base (LIB).

Display the contents of the LIB by using the **show mpls ldp bindings** command. A binding exists for every routed prefix; however, the bindings can vary from router to router because they can get swapped at each hop. In a larger network, the way labels are swapped is easier to see. The LIB is also referred to on Cisco routers as the TIB, which is a legacy name from tag switching. Do not be alarmed to see the LIB entries listed instead as TIB entries; this does not signal that TDP is the protocol being used for distribution:

```
R1# show mpls ldp bindings
  tib entry: 172.16.1.0/24, rev 6
        local binding:  tag: imp-null
        remote binding: tsr: 172.16.2.1:0, tag: 16
  tib entry: 172.16.2.0/24, rev 8
        local binding:  tag: 17
        remote binding: tsr: 172.16.2.1:0, tag: imp-null
  tib entry: 172.16.3.0/24, rev 10
        local binding:  tag: 18
        remote binding: tsr: 172.16.2.1:0, tag: 17
  tib entry: 172.16.12.0/24, rev 4
        local binding:  tag: imp-null
        remote binding: tsr: 172.16.2.1:0, tag: imp-null
  tib entry: 172.16.23.0/24, rev 2
        local binding:  tag: 16
        remote binding: tsr: 172.16.2.1:0, tag: imp-null
R2# show mpls ldp bindings
  tib entry: 172.16.1.0/24, rev 6
        local binding:  tag: 16
        remote binding: tsr: 172.16.1.1:0, tag: imp-null
        remote binding: tsr: 172.16.3.1:0, tag: 17
```

```
     tib entry: 172.16.2.0/24, rev 8
          local binding:  tag: imp-null
          remote binding: tsr: 172.16.1.1:0, tag: 17
          remote binding: tsr: 172.16.3.1:0, tag: 18
     tib entry: 172.16.3.0/24, rev 10
          local binding:  tag: 17
          remote binding: tsr: 172.16.1.1:0, tag: 18
          remote binding: tsr: 172.16.3.1:0, tag: imp-null
     tib entry: 172.16.12.0/24, rev 4
          local binding:  tag: imp-null
          remote binding: tsr: 172.16.1.1:0, tag: imp-null
          remote binding: tsr: 172.16.3.1:0, tag: 16
     tib entry: 172.16.23.0/24, rev 2
          local binding:  tag: imp-null
          remote binding: tsr: 172.16.1.1:0, tag: 16
          remote binding: tsr: 172.16.3.1:0, tag: imp-null
R3# show mpls ldp bindings
     tib entry: 172.16.1.0/24, rev 6
          local binding:  tag: 17
          remote binding: tsr: 172.16.2.1:0, tag: 16
     tib entry: 172.16.2.0/24, rev 8
          local binding:  tag: 18
          remote binding: tsr: 172.16.2.1:0, tag: imp-null
     tib entry: 172.16.3.0/24, rev 10
          local binding:  tag: imp-null
          remote binding: tsr: 172.16.2.1:0, tag: 17
     tib entry: 172.16.12.0/24, rev 4
          local binding:  tag: 16
          remote binding: tsr: 172.16.2.1:0, tag: imp-null
     tib entry: 172.16.23.0/24, rev 2
          local binding:  tag: imp-null
          remote binding: tsr: 172.16.2.1:0, tag: imp-null
```

The local bindings are generated by LDP on an LSR when LDP is enabled. A label is generated for every prefix in the routing table. These labels are then sent to all the router's LDP peers. A tag of implicit-NULL (imp-null in the output of the command **show mpls ldp bindings**) is advertised when the packet will not be forwarded locally based on label, but based on prefix. This situation regularly occurs with connected networks.

For example, assume R2 and R3 have already peered with each other using LDP. Now R1 begins running MPLS and attempts to peer to R2:

- R1 generates the locally bound label, namely 18, for the prefix 172.16.3.0/24 in its routing table.

- R1 advertises the local binding to its LDP peer, R2.

- R2 enters R1's binding for the 172.16.3.0/24 prefix, now classified as a remote binding, into its LIB, regardless of whether it uses it to reach the destination network. The remote binding for this IP prefix through R1 is label 18.

- Based on the routing table, R2 will use R3 as the next hop for 172.16.3.0/24. R2 will not forward IP packets inside an MPLS encapsulation, but rather simply as IP packets because R3 has advertised the label of implicit-NULL to R2.

What is the significance of the local binding entry?

_____

_____

What is the significance of a remote binding entry?

_____

_____

_____

On R2, why is there more than one remote binding for each of the networks in Figure 4-1?

_____

_____

_____

Note that LDP assigns local labels to *all* Interior Gateway Protocol (IGP) prefixes and advertises the bindings to *all* LDP peers. The concept of split horizon does not exist; an LDP peer assigns its own local label to a prefix and advertises that back to the other LDP peer, even though that other LDP peer owns the prefix (it is a connected prefix) or that other LDP peer is the downstream LSR.

What is the meaning of the implicit-NULL label?

_____

_____

_____

_____

As previously mentioned, **traceroute** would differ slightly after MPLS is set up. The output now includes labels for each hop. Unfortunately, because of the size of this network, you only see one label. In a larger network, you would see more hops and, therefore, more labels:

```
R1# traceroute 172.16.3.1

Type escape sequence to abort.
Tracing the route to 172.16.3.1

  1 172.16.12.2 [MPLS: Label 17 Exp 0] 44 msec 44 msec 48 msec
  2 172.16.23.3 12 msec 12 msec *
```

Step 6: Change MPLS MTU

Because you are adding extra header information to packets, the maximum transmission unit (MTU) of packets can change. Remember that each MPLS header is 4 bytes. The default MTU size of MPLS packets is taken from the interface it is running on, which, in the case of Ethernet, is 1500 bytes. To verify this, use the **show mpls interfaces** *interface-type interface-number* **detail** command to see the Ethernet connections of R1 and R2:

```
R1# show mpls interfaces fastethernet 0/0 detail
Interface FastEthernet0/0:
        IP labeling enabled (ldp):
          Interface config
        LSP Tunnel labeling not enabled
        BGP tagging not enabled
        Tagging operational
        Fast Switching Vectors:
          IP to MPLS Fast Switching Vector
          MPLS Turbo Vector
        MTU = 1500
```

```
R2# show mpls interfaces fastethernet 0/0 detail
Interface FastEthernet0/0:
        IP labeling enabled (ldp):
          Interface config
        LSP Tunnel labeling not enabled
        BGP tagging not enabled
        Tagging operational
        Fast Switching Vectors:
          IP to MPLS Fast Switching Vector
          MPLS Turbo Vector
        MTU = 1500
```

For this lab, we change the Ethernet connection between R1 and R2 to support two MPLS headers, so we will change the MPLS MTU to 1508 on their Fast Ethernet interfaces. To change the MPLS MTU, use the **mpls mtu** *size* command in interface configuration mode. Verify the change by using the **show mpls interfaces** *interface* **detail** command previously used:

```
R1(config)# interface fastethernet 0/0
R1(config-if)# mpls mtu 1508
```

```
R2(config)# interface fastethernet0/0
RR2(config-if)# mpls mtu 1508
```

```
R1# show mpls interface fastethernet 0/0 detail
Interface FastEthernet0/0:
        IP labeling enabled (ldp):
          Interface config
        LSP Tunnel labeling not enabled
        BGP tagging not enabled
        Tagging operational
```

```
        Fast Switching Vectors:
          IP to MPLS Fast Switching Vector
          MPLS Turbo Vector
        MTU = 1508
```

R2# **show mpls interface fastethernet 0/0 detail**

```
Interface FastEthernet0/0:
        IP labeling enabled (ldp):
          Interface config
        LSP Tunnel labeling not enabled
        BGP tagging not enabled
        Tagging operational
        Fast Switching Vectors:
          IP to MPLS Fast Switching Vector
          MPLS Turbo Vector
        MTU = 1508
```

Lab 4-2: Challenge Lab: Implementing MPLS VPNs (4.5.2)

This lab qualifies as a challenge lab rather than a required lab because the implementation of this lab is out of the scope of the CCNP2: Implementing Secure Converged WANs course. The requirement for the CCNP2 course is that individuals be able to *describe* MPLS VPN technology. There is no requirement to be able to *configure* it. The Border Gateway Protocol (BGP) commands used in this lab are beyond the scope of the commands learned in the CCNP1 course. Because MPLS VPN config-uration typically takes place as part of an internal ISP network, this level of configuration knowledge is not required at the CCNP level.

Also, the lab requires five Layer 3 devices to show the distributed configuration and nature of MPLS. This is more equipment than is required in the Networking Academy bundle. There is nothing extraor-dinary about the configurations on the HQ and Branch routers; therefore, it is possible to solve this issue by using either Layer 3 switches or older routers. Only SP1, SP2, and SP3 need to be MPLS-capable routers. However, no required lab can exceed the standard equipment bundle.

This lab is included because, from a pedagogical perspective, it is often easier to understand difficult concepts through hands-on practice. If you choose not to actually configure devices, just reading through the configurations helps you understand and describe MPLS VPN technology.

Also, some CCNPs are called upon to configure MPLS VPNs in the core of large enterprise networks or at ISPs. They will benefit from being exposed to this configuration in a lab environment.

In this lab, you learn how to do the following:

- Configure OSPF and EIGRP on a router.

- Enable MPLS on a router.

- Verify MPLS implementation.

- Configure a VRF instance.

- Use MBGP to exchange VPN routing updates.

- Verify VPN activity.

Figure 4-2 illustrates the topology that is used for this lab.

Figure 4-2   Topology Diagram

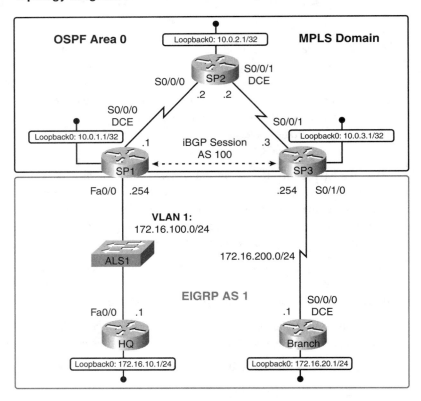

Scenario

As a network engineer at a service-provider corporation, you suggest rolling out MPLS as a new transport technology to facilitate VPNs between customer sites that connect through your network. Your CIO has asked you to implement proof-of-concept in a lab environment, starting with a small implementation of MPLS VPNs before moving up to more moderately sized test cases.

MPLS VPN technology is a powerful technology that leverages the multiprotocol aspect of MPLS to switch MPLS frames between VPN endpoints while hiding the customer networks from the MPLS transport network that connects them. In other words, the intermediate transport network has no knowledge of the customer's IP networks, but it is still able to label-switch frames based on information it receives from MPLS Label Distribution Protocol (LDP) relationships.

You decide to model one of your current customer's connections and then show how MPLS VPNs can carry customer traffic through the provider network. The International Travel Agency currently uses your network to connect from its corporate headquarters to a remote branch office, so you choose this customer network to model in your demonstration.

First, set up the model of both the service provider's network and the agency's network. Then, use appropriate routing and forwarding techniques to set up a MPLS VPN between the provider edge routers to which the customer connects.

SP1, SP2, and SP3 represent a service-provider network, and HQ and BRANCH represent the International Travel Agency routers at their headquarters and at a branch site.

Step 1: Configure Addressing

Configure the loopback interfaces with the addresses shown in Figure 4-2. Also, configure the serial interfaces shown in Figure 4-2. Set the clock rate on the appropriate interfaces and issue the **no shutdown** command on all physical interfaces. Verify that you have connectivity across the local subnet by using the **ping** command inside the service-provider domain. Wait to configure the interface on SP1 facing HQ and the interface on SP3 facing BRANCH. These are configured later:

```
SP1(config)# interface loopback 0
SP1(config-if)# ip address 10.0.1.1 255.255.255.255
SP1(config-if)# interface serial 0/0/0
SP1(config-if)# ip address 10.0.12.1 255.255.255.0
SP1(config-if)# no shutdown
```

```
SP2(config)# interface loopback 0
SP2(config-if)# ip address 10.0.2.1 255.255.255.255
SP2(config-if)# interface serial 0/0/0
SP2(config-if)# ip address 10.0.12.2 255.255.255.0
SP2(config-if)# no shutdown
SP2(config-if)# interface serial 0/0/1
SP2(config-if)# ip address 10.0.23.2 255.255.255.0
SP2(config-if)# clockrate 64000
SP2(config-if)# no shutdown
```

```
SP3(config)# interface loopback 0
SP3(config-if)# ip address 10.0.3.1 255.255.255.255
SP3(config-if)# interface serial 0/0/1
SP3(config-if)# ip address 10.0.23.3 255.255.255.0
SP3(config-if)# no shutdown
```

Configure customer sites HQ and BRANCH:

```
HQ(config)# interface loopback 0
HQ(config-if)# ip address 172.16.10.1 255.255.255.0
HQ(config-if)# interface fastethernet 0/0
HQ(config-if)# ip address 172.16.100.1 255.255.255.0
HQ(config-if)# no shutdown
```

```
BRANCH(config)# interface loopback 0
BRANCH(config-if)# ip address 172.16.20.1 255.255.255.0
BRANCH(config-if)# interface serial 0/0/0
BRANCH(config-if)# ip address 172.16.200.1 255.255.255.0
BRANCH(config-if)# clockrate 64000
BRANCH(config-if)# no shutdown
```

Step 2: Configure Routing in the Service-Provider Domain

Your service-provider network uses OSPF as its routing protocol, advertising internal loopback interfaces and transit networks. Configure OSPF to model the service-provider domain. Add all the interfaces addressed within the 10.0.0.0 major network into Area 0 of the OSPF process. You only need to configure OSPF in this manner on the service-provider routers—namely SP1, SP2, and SP3:

```
SP1(config)# router ospf 1
SP1(config-router)# network 10.0.0.0 0.255.255.255 area 0
```

```
SP2(config)# router ospf 1
SP2(config-router)# network 10.0.0.0 0.255.255.255 area 0
```

```
SP3(config)# router ospf 1
SP3(config-router)# network 10.0.0.0 0.255.255.255 area 0
```

Verify that all of your Open Shortest Path First (OSPF) adjacencies come up. OSPF adjacencies should form between SP1 and SP2 and between SP2 and SP3. If the adjacencies do not form, troubleshoot by checking your interface configuration, OSPF configuration, and physical connectivity.

What purpose does OSPF serve in the preceding configurations?

Consider that you will deploy BGP in the SP domain later in this lab using loopback addresses as the sources for BGP updates. Why do you need to deploy an Interior Gateway Protocol (IGP) in the SP domain?

Step 3: Configure MPLS in the SP Domain

On all the service-provider routers, force MPLS to use the Loopback 0 interface as the router ID for LDP adjacencies. The loopback interface would be chosen by each router automatically, but it is advisable to force the ID so that the value is persistent through topology changes and reloads. To force LDP's selection of the loopback interface as the router ID, use the **mpls ldp router-id** *interface* **force** command in global configuration mode. Also, enable MPLS on all the physical interfaces in the MPLS domain with the **mpls ip** command:

```
SP1(config)# mpls ldp router-id loopback0 force
SP1(config)# interface serial0/0/0
SP1(config-if)# mpls ip
```

```
SP2(config)# mpls ldp router-id loopback0 force
SP2(config)# interface serial0/0/0
SP2(config-if)# mpls ip
SP2(config-if)# interface serial0/0/1
SP2(config-if)# mpls ip
```

```
SP3(config)# mpls ldp router-id loopback0 force
SP3(config)# interface serial0/0/1
SP3(config-if)# mpls ip
```

You should see console messages notifying you that the MPLS-enabled routers have become adjacent with each other via LDP. Verify that these adjacencies have formed using the **show mpls ldp neighbor** command:

```
SP1# show mpls ldp neighbor
    Peer LDP Ident: 10.0.2.1:0; Local LDP Ident 10.0.1.1:0
        TCP connection: 10.0.2.1.62676 - 10.0.1.1.646
        State: Oper; Msgs sent/rcvd: 9/9; Downstream
        Up time: 00:01:43
        LDP discovery sources:
          Serial0/0/0, Src IP addr: 10.0.12.2
        Addresses bound to peer LDP Ident:
          10.0.12.2       10.0.23.2        10.0.2.1
```

```
SP2# show mpls ldp neighbor
    Peer LDP Ident: 10.0.1.1:0; Local LDP Ident 10.0.2.1:0
        TCP connection: 10.0.1.1.646 - 10.0.2.1.62676
        State: Oper; Msgs sent/rcvd: 10/10; Downstream
        Up time: 00:02:03
        LDP discovery sources:
          Serial0/0/0, Src IP addr: 10.0.12.1
        Addresses bound to peer LDP Ident:
          10.0.12.1       10.0.1.1
    Peer LDP Ident: 10.0.3.1:0; Local LDP Ident 10.0.2.1:0
        TCP connection: 10.0.3.1.42919 - 10.0.2.1.646
        State: Oper; Msgs sent/rcvd: 10/10; Downstream
        Up time: 00:01:58
        LDP discovery sources:
          Serial0/0/1, Src IP addr: 10.0.23.3
        Addresses bound to peer LDP Ident:
          10.0.23.3       10.0.3.1
```

```
SP3# show mpls ldp neighbor
    Peer LDP Ident: 10.0.2.1:0; Local LDP Ident 10.0.3.1:0
        TCP connection: 10.0.2.1.646 - 10.0.3.1.42919
        State: Oper; Msgs sent/rcvd: 10/10; Downstream
        Up time: 00:02:08
        LDP discovery sources:
          Serial0/0/1, Src IP addr: 10.0.23.2
        Addresses bound to peer LDP Ident:
          10.0.12.2       10.0.23.2        10.0.2.1
```

Step 4: Configure a VRF

An MPLS VPN is a Layer 3 VPN that allows packet routing through a MPLS core. This type of VPN provides a customer with connections to multiple sites through a service provider's network. The service provider not only provides the physical connection, but the ability to dynamically route between the VPN endpoints. This is especially impressive when one considers that the customers might not be using globally unique Layer 3 addresses. For example, different customers can use private addresses, as defined by RFC 1918, but still use the same transit provider to route their specific endpoints without translation. As shown in Figure 4-3, the routers at the provider's edge run the same routing protocol as the customer's network and allow the customer offices to interface with the provider.

Figure 4-3   MPLS VPNs Conceptual Diagram

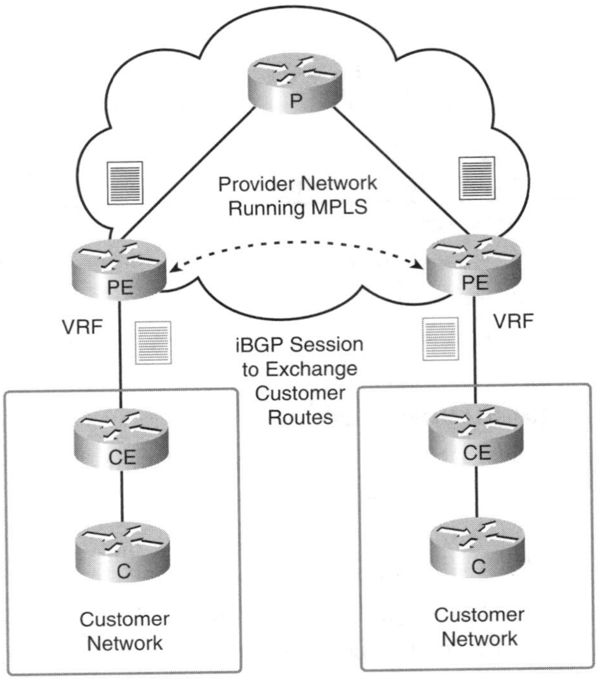

The standard model for MPLS VPNs uses the following designations:

- **Provider (P).** Routers owned by the service provider (SP) that act as label switch routers (LSR) to provide transit across the provider backbone. P routers do not carry customer routes in their routing tables.

- **Customer (C).** Routers owned by the customer that provide transit through the normal customer network.

- **Customer edge (CE).** The CE router is installed at the customer site. Depending on the business model of the Internet service provider (ISP), this router can be managed by the customer, the ISP, or both. The CE router connects to, and communicates with, the service-provider routers, and it allows the service provider to participate in customer routing.

- **Provider edge (PE).** Routers owned by the provider that actively participate in customer routing, guaranteeing optimum routing between customer sites. PE routers use a separate virtual routing table for each customer, which results in perfect isolation between customers.

Note that neither the C nor the CE routers need any special configuration. The P routers require only a simple MPLS LDP configuration.

In this lab, SP2 models the P router, and SP1 and SP3 model the PE routers. HQ and BRANCH are both CE routers with loopback networks to simulate connections to other C routers.

The PE routers control the entire MPLS VPN from end to end. You might be asking numerous relevant questions: How can a single router determine which routes in its table belong to the service provider's internal network, and which routes belong to each customer? How can the PE device allow customers to use existing networks, including private addressing without creating routing problems?

The answer to all of these questions lies in the ability of routers to maintain virtual routing and forwarding (VRF) instances. Each VRF uses and maintains its own routing information base (RIB) and Cisco Express Forwarding (CEF) table. Interfaces are either assigned to specific VRF instances or they use the default RIB and CEF tables. The VRF instance's RIB fulfills the role of control plane while the VRF's CEF table fulfills the role of the data forwarding plane. Routing protocols between the PE and CE routers populate the VRF RIB and CEF makes forwarding decisions based on the routes in the VRF RIB. When an IP packet arrives on an interface that has been associated with a VRF, the packet is routed according to the CEF table for that VRF instance. CEF is the only IP switching protocol supported for VRF, so CEF should be enabled globally with the **ip cef** command and on the interfaces associated with the VRF instance.

However, PE routers must now be connected through the provider network to perform routing and forwarding between customer sites. The most efficient and only scalable method to achieve this is to use the multiprotocol extensions to BGP (MP-BGP) that enable the provider network to carry routes for different routed protocols. PE routers establish iBGP sessions with other PEs in your carrier network to exchange for each VPN routes. This helps populate the VRF routing tables on each PE router with the VRF tables from other customer sites. CEF tables will be updated with the RIB information so that forwarding can occur between customer sites after the label-switched paths have been created through the provider network.

PE routers advertise routes that are part of their VPN by using a new traffic class to distinguish these routes from internal routes in the provider's network. BGP uses a new address family called VPNv4 to carry MPLS VPN routes to IPv4 networks. The VPNv4 address family is a 12-byte address consisting of an 8-byte route distinguisher (RD) and a 4-byte IPv4 address. The RD acts as a unique prefix when appended with the IPv4 address. Each VRF must have an RD for unique advertisement.

VRFs use the route target attribute to control the import and export of VPNv4 routes through iBGP. The route target is an extended BGP community that indicates which routes should be imported from MP-BGP into the VRF. Exporting a route target (RT) means that the exported VPNv4 route receives an additional BGP extended community—this is the route target—when the route is redistributed from the VRF RIB into MP-BGP. Importing an RT means that the received VPNv4 route from MP-BGP is checked for a matching extended community—this is the route target—with the ones in the configuration.

To configure a VRF instance on the PE routers, use the **ip vrf** *name* command in global configuration mode on SP1 and SP3. At the VRF configuration prompt, create a VRF named customer. Each VRF instance needs an RD and an RT. The RD and RT are each 8 bytes in length, with a colon separating 4 bytes on either side. There are various conventions for allocating RDs for MPLS VPNs; the most useful of which is ASN:nn. Another popular notation is IP address:nn. In each of these cases, nn represents an arbitrary value assigned by the network administrator. In this lab, use 100:1 as the RD. The RT is also an arbitrary 8-byte value used later in BGP.

Configure an RD of 100:1 and RT of 1:100 using the commands **rd** *ASN:nn* and **route-target** {**import** | **export** | **both**} *nn:nn*. In this case, you need to use the **both** keyword because you want PEs to import and export from that VRF:

```
SP1(config)# ip vrf customer
SP1(config-vrf)# rd 100:1
SP1(config-vrf)# route-target both 1:100
```

```
SP3(config)# ip vrf customer
SP3(config-vrf)# rd 100:1
SP3(config-vrf)# route-target both 1:100
```

Imagine that SP1 is running MP-BGP, and it receives a VPNv4 route with an RT of 100:100. Given the previous configuration, should BGP import the route into the *customer* VRF routing table?

After creating the VRFs, add interfaces to the VRF by using the interface-level **ip vrf forwarding** *name* command, where name is the VRF instance name. Use this command on the interfaces of SP1 and SP3 (the PE routers) facing the CE routers. Add the IP address, as shown in the figure, to those interfaces:

```
SP1(config)# interface fastethernet 0/0
SP1(config-if)# ip vrf forwarding customer
SP1(config-if)# ip address 172.16.100.254 255.255.255.0
SP1(config-if)# no shut
SP3(config)# interface serial 0/1/0
SP3(config-if)# ip vrf forwarding customer
SP3(config-if)# ip address 172.16.200.254 255.255.255.0
SP3(config-if)# no shutdown
```

You should now be able to ping across those the PE-CE links because you configured the other end of these links in Step 1. However, because these are not in the default routing table, you must use the **ping vrf** *name address* command. Because the VRF is transparent to the customer routers, you can use a traditional **ping** command when you ping from the C and CE routers:

```
SP1# ping vrf customer 172.16.100.1

Type escape sequence to abort.
Sending 5, 100-byte ICMP Echos to 172.16.100.1, timeout is 2 seconds:
!!!!!
Success rate is 100 percent (5/5), round-trip min/avg/max = 1/1/4 ms
HQ# ping 172.16.100.254

Type escape sequence to abort.
Sending 5, 100-byte ICMP Echos to 172.16.100.254, timeout is 2 seconds:
!!!!!
Success rate is 100 percent (5/5), round-trip min/avg/max = 1/2/8 ms
SP3# ping vrf customer 172.16.200.1

Type escape sequence to abort.
Sending 5, 100-byte ICMP Echos to 172.16.200.1, timeout is 2 seconds:
!!!!!
Success rate is 100 percent (5/5), round-trip min/avg/max = 28/28/32 ms
BRANCH# ping 172.16.200.254
```

```
Type escape sequence to abort.
Sending 5, 100-byte ICMP Echos to 172.16.200.254, timeout is 2 seconds:
!!!!!
Success rate is 100 percent (5/5), round-trip min/avg/max = 28/28/28 ms
```

Step 5: Configure EIGRP AS 1

The service provider by whom you are employed uses the BGP AS 100. Your customer, the International Travel Agency, uses the BGP AS 1. To keep the configuration logically consistent, use the AS number 100 for EIGRP and BGP in the provider's network, and use the AS number 1 for EIGRP and BGP in the customer's network. You configure EIGRP AS 1 on the PE routers from within the configuration of the global EIGRP AS 100.

On the customer routers, configure EIGRP AS 1 for the major network 172.16.0.0. Disable automatic summarization:

```
HQ(config)# router eigrp 1
HQ(config-router)# no auto-summary
HQ(config-router)# network 172.16.0.0
```

```
BRANCH(config)# router eigrp 1
BRANCH(config-router)# no auto-summary
BRANCH(config-router)# network 172.16.0.0
```

Given only this information, will EIGRP immediately form any adjacencies?

_____

_____

On the PE routers, the configuration is more complex. Every IGP has a different method of configuring a VRF for it. To implement EIGRP for VRFs, start the EIGRP process by configuring EIGRP AS 100. Remember, this AS belongs to the provider and is not significant to the customer. If you were using EIGRP as the service provider's IGP instead of OSPF, you would configure your network statements at this point:

```
SP1(config)# router eigrp 100
```

```
SP3(config)# router eigrp 100
```

Now, to configure EIGRP for an individual VRF instance, use the command **address-family ipv4 vrf** *name*, where *name* is the name of the VRF instance. Although each VPN must be logically separate from other IPv4 address spaces using VRF, this separation must extend not only to the routing table but also to the routing protocols. The **address-family** command creates a logical segment of a routing protocol and its routes and adjacencies to separate it from other sets of routes and adjacencies. In this case, you separate an EIGRP autonomous system from the EIGRP instance initiated with the **router eigrp 100** command. Networks learned via this new autonomous system are injected into the VRF routing table associated with the isolated EIGRP AS. It is important to note that these networks will not be advertised to any neighbors in EIGRP AS 100; it is completely separate from the rest of the EIGRP domain:

```
SP1(config-router)# address-family ipv4 vrf customer
SP1(config-router-af)# autonomous-system 1
SP1(config-router-af)# no auto-summary
SP1(config-router-af)# network 172.16.0.0
```

```
SP3(config-router)# address-family ipv4 vrf customer
SP3(config-router-af)# autonomous-system 1
SP3(config-router-af)# no auto-summary
SP3(config-router-af)# network 172.16.0.0
```

On the PE routers, display the default routing table with the **show ip route** command. Notice that the PE routers do not possess any routes from the 172.16.0.0/16 major network in the default routing table. Display the VRF routing table with the **show ip route vrf** *name* command, where *name* is the VRF instance name:

```
SP1# show ip route
Codes: C - connected, S - static, R - RIP, M - mobile, B - BGP
       D - EIGRP, EX - EIGRP external, O - OSPF, IA - OSPF inter area
       N1 - OSPF NSSA external type 1, N2 - OSPF NSSA external type 2
       E1 - OSPF external type 1, E2 - OSPF external type 2
       i - IS-IS, su - IS-IS summary, L1 - IS-IS level-1, L2 - IS-IS level-2
       ia - IS-IS inter area, * - candidate default, U - per-user static route
       o - ODR, P - periodic downloaded static route


Gateway of last resort is not set


     10.0.0.0/8 is variably subnetted, 5 subnets, 2 masks
C       10.0.12.0/24 is directly connected, Serial0/0/0
O       10.0.3.1/32 [110/129] via 10.0.12.2, 05:29:59, Serial0/0/0
O       10.0.2.1/32 [110/65] via 10.0.12.2, 05:29:59, Serial0/0/0
C       10.0.1.1/32 is directly connected, Loopback0
O       10.0.23.0/24 [110/128] via 10.0.12.2, 05:29:59, Serial0/0/0


SP1# show ip route vrf customer


Routing Table: customer
Codes: C - connected, S - static, R - RIP, M - mobile, B - BGP
       D - EIGRP, EX - EIGRP external, O - OSPF, IA - OSPF inter area
       N1 - OSPF NSSA external type 1, N2 - OSPF NSSA external type 2
       E1 - OSPF external type 1, E2 - OSPF external type 2
       i - IS-IS, su - IS-IS summary, L1 - IS-IS level-1, L2 - IS-IS level-2
       ia - IS-IS inter area, * - candidate default, U - per-user static route
       o - ODR, P - periodic downloaded static route


Gateway of last resort is not set


     172.16.0.0/24 is subnetted, 2 subnets
D       172.16.10.0 [90/156160] via 172.16.100.1, 00:03:29, FastEthernet0/0
C       172.16.100.0 is directly connected, FastEthernet0/0
SP3# show ip route
Codes: C - connected, S - static, R - RIP, M - mobile, B - BGP
```

```
        D - EIGRP, EX - EIGRP external, O - OSPF, IA - OSPF inter area
        N1 - OSPF NSSA external type 1, N2 - OSPF NSSA external type 2
        E1 - OSPF external type 1, E2 - OSPF external type 2
        i - IS-IS, su - IS-IS summary, L1 - IS-IS level-1, L2 - IS-IS level-2
        ia - IS-IS inter area, * - candidate default, U - per-user static route
        o - ODR, P - periodic downloaded static route


Gateway of last resort is not set


     10.0.0.0/8 is variably subnetted, 5 subnets, 2 masks
O        10.0.12.0/24 [110/128] via 10.0.23.2, 05:30:42, Serial0/0/1
C        10.0.3.1/32 is directly connected, Loopback0
O        10.0.2.1/32 [110/65] via 10.0.23.2, 05:30:42, Serial0/0/1
O        10.0.1.1/32 [110/129] via 10.0.23.2, 05:30:42, Serial0/0/1
C        10.0.23.0/24 is directly connected, Serial0/0/1
SP3# show ip route vrf customer


Routing Table: customer
Codes: C - connected, S - static, R - RIP, M - mobile, B - BGP
        D - EIGRP, EX - EIGRP external, O - OSPF, IA - OSPF inter area
        N1 - OSPF NSSA external type 1, N2 - OSPF NSSA external type 2
        E1 - OSPF external type 1, E2 - OSPF external type 2
        i - IS-IS, su - IS-IS summary, L1 - IS-IS level-1, L2 - IS-IS level-2
        ia - IS-IS inter area, * - candidate default, U - per-user static route
        o - ODR, P - periodic downloaded static route


Gateway of last resort is not set


     172.16.0.0/24 is subnetted, 2 subnets
C        172.16.200.0 is directly connected, Serial0/1/0
D        172.16.20.0 [90/2297856] via 172.16.200.1, 00:02:06, Serial0/1/0
```

The SP1 and HQ routers do not possess routes to the customer networks on SP3 and BRANCH and vice versa. Explain why this occurs, even though EIGRP adjacencies have formed.

_____

_____

_____

Step 6: Configure BGP

Now that the PE routers are routing to the CE routers over VRF tables, you can set up the PE routers to exchange routes through BGP. First, configure BGP between SP1 and SP3 and have them peer between their loopback addresses. Synchronization should be disabled by default on newer IOS releases. If synchronization is not already disabled, explicitly disable it by using the **no synchronization** command. For more information on configuring BGP, refer to CCNP1:

```
SP1(config)# router bgp 100
SP1(config-router)# neighbor 10.0.3.1 remote-as 100
SP1(config-router)# neighbor 10.0.3.1 update-source loopback0
```
```
SP3(config)# router bgp 100
SP3(config-router)# neighbor 10.0.1.1 remote-as 100
SP3(config-router)# neighbor 10.0.1.1 update-source loopback0
```

To configure the exchange of VPNv4 routes over BGP, use the **address-family vpnv4** command. At the address family prompt, activate the BGP neighbor for this address family with **neighbor** *address* **activate** command. Activating a neighbor for an address family allows BGP to send routes to and receive routes from the designated neighbor using the specified address family. By default, neighbors are only activated for IPv4.

The RTs are translated as extended BGP communities, so you must allow SP1 and SP3 to send both standard and extended communities over MP-BGP using the **neighbor** *address* **send-community both** command. The adjacencies might flap (temporarily go down and then come back up) when you activate the address family.

```
SP1(config-router)# address-family vpnv4
SP1(config-router-af)# neighbor 10.0.3.1 activate
SP1(config-router-af)# neighbor 10.0.3.1 send-community both
SP1(config-router-af)# exit
```
```
SP3(config-router)# address-family vpnv4
SP3(config-router-af)# neighbor 10.0.1.1 activate
SP3(config-router-af)# neighbor 10.0.1.1 send-community both
SP3(config-router-af)# exit
```

Finally, you need to configure BGP to redistribute the EIGRP routes in the VRF RIB into the BGP protocol so that these routes are advertised to the remote PE. Under the main BGP configuration prompt, enter another address family associated only with the routing table for the VRF *customer*. Redistribute the EIGRP routes that are associated with this VRF into BGP:

```
SP1(config-router)# address-family ipv4 vrf customer
SP1(config-router-af)# redistribute eigrp 1
SP1(config-router-af)# exit
SP1(config-router)# exit
```
```
SP3(config-router)# address-family ipv4 vrf customer
SP3(config-router-af)# redistribute eigrp 1
SP3(config-router-af)# exit
SP3(config-router)# exit
```

Based on the previous configuration, will SP1's VRF RIB contain the 172.16.20.0/24 route that was originated by EIGRP on BRANCH? Explain.

_____

_____

Will HQ learn the same routes via EIGRP? Explain.

_____

_____

Do you expect to see the redistributed routes as internal or external EIGRP routes on the CE routers? Explain.

_____

_____

_____

_____

Enter the EIGRP instance that contains the VRF configuration on SP1 and SP3, and configure it to redistribute BGP routes. Because you are redistributing into EIGRP from BGP, the metrics are not comparable. Add a seed metric with a bandwidth of 64 kbps, 100 microseconds, reliability of 255/255, load of 1/255, and MTU of 1500 bytes:

```
SP1(config)# router eigrp 100
SP1(config-router)# address-family ipv4 vrf customer
SP1(config-router-af)# redistribute bgp 100 metric 64 1000 255 1 1500
SP3(config)# router eigrp 100
SP3(config-router)# address-family ipv4 vrf customer
SP3(config-router-af)# redistribute bgp 100 metric 64 1000 255 1 1500
```

Step 7: Investigate Control Plane Operation

Remember that MPLS differentiates the control plane from the forwarding plane. The control plane, represented by the routing table (the RIB) and the routing protocols, must operate so that the VRF routes reach remote PEs and are installed as necessary in the VRF routing tables. Not only the prefixes, but also the accompanying metrics and tags are important to the reconstruction of the route at the remote PE. Fortunately, MP-BGP allows you to send these metrics in the Network Layer Reachability Information (NLRI).

Through this step and Step 8, you investigate the routing and forwarding information associated with the route to 172.16.20.0/24.

Verify that the routes have propagated to the remote PE routers. Issue the **show ip route vrf** *name* command to see the VRF RIB. Notice the source of the routes on the PE routers:

```
SP1# show ip route vrf customer

Routing Table: customer
Codes: C - connected, S - static, R - RIP, M - mobile, B - BGP
       D - EIGRP, EX - EIGRP external, O - OSPF, IA - OSPF inter area
       N1 - OSPF NSSA external type 1, N2 - OSPF NSSA external type 2
       E1 - OSPF external type 1, E2 - OSPF external type 2
       i - IS-IS, su - IS-IS summary, L1 - IS-IS level-1, L2 - IS-IS level-2
       ia - IS-IS inter area, * - candidate default, U - per-user static route
       o - ODR, P - periodic downloaded static route

Gateway of last resort is not set
```

```
      172.16.0.0/24 is subnetted, 4 subnets
B        172.16.200.0 [200/0] via 10.0.3.1, 00:06:44
B        172.16.20.0 [200/2297856] via 10.0.3.1, 00:06:44
D        172.16.10.0 [90/156160] via 172.16.100.1, 00:17:34, FastEthernet0/0
C        172.16.100.0 is directly connected, FastEthernet0/0
SP3# show ip route vrf customer


Routing Table: customer
Codes: C - connected, S - static, R - RIP, M - mobile, B - BGP
       D - EIGRP, EX - EIGRP external, O - OSPF, IA - OSPF inter area
       N1 - OSPF NSSA external type 1, N2 - OSPF NSSA external type 2
       E1 - OSPF external type 1, E2 - OSPF external type 2
       i - IS-IS, su - IS-IS summary, L1 - IS-IS level-1, L2 - IS-IS level-2
       ia - IS-IS inter area, * - candidate default, U - per-user static route
       o - ODR, P - periodic downloaded static route


Gateway of last resort is not set

      172.16.0.0/24 is subnetted, 4 subnets
C        172.16.200.0 is directly connected, Serial0/1/0
D        172.16.20.0 [90/2297856] via 172.16.200.1, 16:47:37, Serial0/1/0
B        172.16.10.0 [200/156160] via 10.0.1.1, 00:17:28
B        172.16.100.0 [200/0] via 10.0.1.1, 00:17:28
```

You might ask, "Why does the source of the route to 172.16.20.0/24 on SP1 point to 10.0.3.1, because that address would be routed based on the default routing table?" Consider that, when an internally generated route is sent to an iBGP peer, BGP sets the next-hop attribute to be the advertising router. In this case, SP3 generates the route in BGP by redistribution. The BGP peers are communicating between loopback interfaces, so the next-hop is set to the IP address of the BGP peer's source interface. Thus, the VRF RIB points to an interface that must be reached through the default global RIB. We will investigate the forwarding for packets destined for these networks in the next step.

On the CE routers, issue the **show ip route** command to see a full routing table:

```
HQ# show ip route
Codes: C - connected, S - static, R - RIP, M - mobile, B - BGP
       D - EIGRP, EX - EIGRP external, O - OSPF, IA - OSPF inter area
       N1 - OSPF NSSA external type 1, N2 - OSPF NSSA external type 2
       E1 - OSPF external type 1, E2 - OSPF external type 2, E - EGP
       i - IS-IS, su - IS-IS summary, L1 - IS-IS level-1, L2 - IS-IS level-2
       ia - IS-IS inter area, * - candidate default, U - per-user static route
       o - ODR, P - periodic downloaded static route


Gateway of last resort is not set
```

```
      172.16.0.0/24 is subnetted, 4 subnets
D        172.16.200.0
            [90/2172416] via 172.16.100.254, 00:05:17, FastEthernet0/0
D        172.16.20.0 [90/2300416] via 172.16.100.254, 00:05:17, FastEthernet0/0
C        172.16.10.0 is directly connected, Loopback0
C        172.16.100.0 is directly connected, FastEthernet0/0
```
```
BRANCH# show ip route
Codes: C - connected, S - static, R - RIP, M - mobile, B - BGP
       D - EIGRP, EX - EIGRP external, O - OSPF, IA - OSPF inter area
       N1 - OSPF NSSA external type 1, N2 - OSPF NSSA external type 2
       E1 - OSPF external type 1, E2 - OSPF external type 2
       i - IS-IS, su - IS-IS summary, L1 - IS-IS level-1, L2 - IS-IS level-2
       ia - IS-IS inter area, * - candidate default, U - per-user static route
       o - ODR, P - periodic downloaded static route

Gateway of last resort is not set

      172.16.0.0/24 is subnetted, 4 subnets
C        172.16.200.0 is directly connected, Serial0/0/0
C        172.16.20.0 is directly connected, Loopback0
D        172.16.10.0 [90/2300416] via 172.16.200.254, 00:02:02, Serial0/0/0
D        172.16.100.0 [90/2172416] via 172.16.200.254, 00:02:02, Serial0/0/0
```

On both the CE and PE routers, notice that the routes you redistributed from BGP into EIGRP are *internal* EIGRP routes because BGP preserves features of the EIGRP route while advertising the route to the other PEs. The PE encodes as much EIGRP information as possible into new extended communities—TLV tuples (type, length, value)—to preserve route characteristics through the VPN. This enables the remote PE router to reconstruct the EIGRP route with all of its characteristics, including the metric components, AS, TAG, and, for external routes, the remote AS number, the remote ID, the remote protocol, and the remote metric. These are the EIGRP characteristics of a prefix that you can find in the topology table. If the EIGRP-advertised route is internal, the route is advertised as an internal route into the remote site if the destination AS matches the source AS carried by the BGP extended community attributes.

Display information on the VPNv4 BGP routes on SP1 with the **show bgp vpnv4 unicast all** command:

```
SP1# show bgp vpnv4 unicast all
BGP table version is 9, local router ID is 10.0.1.1
Status codes: s suppressed, d damped, h history, * valid, > best, i - internal,
              r RIB-failure, S Stale
Origin codes: i - IGP, e - EGP, ? - incomplete


   Network          Next Hop          Metric LocPrf Weight Path
Route Distinguisher: 100:1 (default for vrf customer)
*> 172.16.10.0/24   172.16.100.1        156160        32768 ?
*>i172.16.20.0/24   10.0.3.1           2297856    100     0 ?
```

```
*> 172.16.100.0/24  0.0.0.0              0          32768 ?
*>i172.16.200.0/24  10.0.3.1             0    100     0 ?
```

```
SP3# show bgp vpnv4 unicast all
BGP table version is 9, local router ID is 10.0.3.1
Status codes: s suppressed, d damped, h history, * valid, > best, i - internal,
              r RIB-failure, S Stale
Origin codes: i - IGP, e - EGP, ? - incomplete

   Network          Next Hop         Metric LocPrf Weight Path
Route Distinguisher: 100:1 (default for vrf customer)
*>i172.16.10.0/24   10.0.1.1          156160   100     0 ?
*> 172.16.20.0/24   172.16.200.1     2297856         32768 ?
*>i172.16.100.0/24  10.0.1.1               0   100     0 ?
*> 172.16.200.0/24  0.0.0.0                0         32768 ?
```

Notice that the metric (MED value) in BGP is the metric advertised through EIGRP for that route as well.

What does the value of the NEXT-HOP attribute for the 172.16.200.0/24 network on SP3 indicate?

_____

What is the value of the BGP NEXT-HOP attribute for the 172.16.20.0/24 route on SP1?

_____

By which routing protocol, and from which router, was the route to 10.0.3.1/32 installed in the default routing table on SP1?

_____

View more specific detail on a particular prefix by using **show bgp vpnv4 unicast all** *ip-address* command. Notice that the MPLS label information is included. Execute this on both of the PEs. Remember that SP3 is advertising the 172.16.20.0/24 prefix through BGP, while SP1 is receiving the route through BGP NLRI:

```
SP1# show bgp vpnv4 unicast all 172.16.20.0/24
BGP routing table entry for 100:1:172.16.20.0/24, version 15
Paths: (1 available, best #1, table customer)
Flag: 0x820
  Not advertised to any peer
  Local
    10.0.3.1 (metric 129) from 10.0.3.1 (10.0.3.1)
      Origin incomplete, metric 2297856, localpref 100, valid, internal, best
      Extended Community: RT:1:100
        Cost:pre-bestpath:128:2297856 (default-2145185791) 0x8800:32768:0
        0x8801:1:640000 0x8802:65281:1657856 0x8803:65281:1500
      mpls labels in/out nolabel/20
```

```
SP3# show bgp vpnv4 unicast all 172.16.20.1
BGP routing table entry for 100:1:172.16.20.0/24, version 15
Paths: (1 available, best #1, table customer)
```

```
Advertised to update-groups:
   1
Local
  172.16.200.1 from 0.0.0.0 (10.0.3.1)
    Origin incomplete, metric 2297856, localpref 100, weight 32768, valid, sourced,
      best
    Extended Community: RT:1:100
      Cost:pre-bestpath:128:2297856 (default-2145185791) 0x8800:32768:0
      0x8801:1:640000 0x8802:65281:1657856 0x8803:65281:1500
    mpls labels in/out 20/nolabel
```

Notice that multiple values are in the BGP extended communities. Recall that BGP sends the route information in NLRI as extended communities. These values are TLVs, indicating such EIGRP attributes as the TAG, AS number, bandwidth, delay, reliability, load, MTU, and hop count.

Why is the origin code "incomplete?"

_____

_____

What type of attribute carries the route target information in MP-BGP NLRI?

_____

Notice the MPLS labels indicated for this BGP route. The in-label of nolabel on SP1 indicates that SP1 is not advertising a label for the prefix 172.16.20.0/24. The out-label of 21 is advertised by SP3 and received by SP1. This label is significant only on the path between SP1 and SP3. This label has been allocated by BGP on SP3.

View the list of MPLS labels that are being used with BGP using **show bgp vpnv4 unicast all labels**:

```
SP1# show bgp vpnv4 unicast all labels
   Network           Next Hop        In label/Out label
Route Distinguisher: 100:1 (customer)
   172.16.10.0/24    172.16.100.1      19/nolabel
   172.16.20.0/24    10.0.3.1          nolabel/20
   172.16.100.0/24   0.0.0.0           20/aggregate(customer)
   172.16.200.0/24   10.0.3.1          nolabel/19
```

```
SP3# show bgp vpnv4 unicast all labels
   Network           Next Hop        In label/Out label
Route Distinguisher: 100:1 (customer)
   172.16.10.0/24    10.0.1.1          nolabel/19
   172.16.20.0/24    172.16.200.1      20/nolabel
   172.16.100.0/24   10.0.1.1          nolabel/20
   172.16.200.0/24   0.0.0.0           19/aggregate(customer)
```

How has SP1 learned the VPN label, label 20?

_____

Will SP1 or SP2 learn the label via LDP?

_____

Has the P router SP2 learned about label 20 from SP3? Explain.

_____

_____

Finally, display the route attributes for the same prefix, 172.16.20.0/24, in the EIGRP topology table on SP1 with the **show ip eigrp vrf customer topology** *ip-prefix/mask* command. Verify this against the originator of the EIGRP route in BGP, SP3:

```
SP1# show ip eigrp vrf customer topology 172.16.20.0/24
IP-EIGRP (AS 1): Topology entry for 172.16.20.0/24
  State is Passive, Query origin flag is 1, 1 Successor(s), FD is 2297856
  Routing Descriptor Blocks:
  10.0.3.1, from VPNv4 Sourced, Send flag is 0x0
      Composite metric is (2297856/0), Route is Internal (VPNv4 Sourced)
      Vector metric:
        Minimum bandwidth is 1544 Kbit
        Total delay is 25000 microseconds
        Reliability is 255/255
        Load is 1/255
        Minimum MTU is 1500
        Hop count is 1
```

```
SP3# show ip eigrp vrf customer topology 172.16.20.0/24
IP-EIGRP (AS 1): Topology entry for 172.16.20.0/24
  State is Passive, Query origin flag is 1, 1 Successor(s), FD is 2297856
  Routing Descriptor Blocks:
  172.16.200.1 (Serial0/1/0), from 172.16.200.1, Send flag is 0x0
      Composite metric is (2297856/128256), Route is Internal
      Vector metric:
        Minimum bandwidth is 1544 Kbit
        Total delay is 25000 microseconds
        Reliability is 255/255
        Load is 1/255
        Minimum MTU is 1500
        Hop count is 1
```

There is absolutely no difference in the EIGRP route parameters between SP1 and SP3. BGP encodes and decodes the information on the PE routers with no changes.

Remember that SP2—a P router—has no knowledge of individual routes in the VRF tables on the PE routers. You can verify this with the **show** commands previously performed:

```
SP2# show ip route
Codes: C - connected, S - static, R - RIP, M - mobile, B - BGP
       D - EIGRP, EX - EIGRP external, O - OSPF, IA - OSPF inter area
       N1 - OSPF NSSA external type 1, N2 - OSPF NSSA external type 2
       E1 - OSPF external type 1, E2 - OSPF external type 2
       i - IS-IS, su - IS-IS summary, L1 - IS-IS level-1, L2 - IS-IS level-2
```

```
          ia - IS-IS inter area, * - candidate default, U - per-user static route
          o - ODR, P - periodic downloaded static route

Gateway of last resort is not set

      10.0.0.0/8 is variably subnetted, 5 subnets, 2 masks
C        10.0.12.0/24 is directly connected, Serial0/0/0
O        10.0.3.1/32 [110/65] via 10.0.23.3, 1d00h, Serial0/0/1
C        10.0.2.1/32 is directly connected, Loopback0
O        10.0.1.1/32 [110/65] via 10.0.12.1, 1d00h, Serial0/0/0
C        10.0.23.0/24 is directly connected, Serial0/0/1


SP2# show ip route vrf customer
% IP routing table customer does not exist
```

Ping between the CE routers to verify connectivity through the MPLS VPN:

```
HQ# ping 172.16.20.1

Type escape sequence to abort.
Sending 5, 100-byte ICMP Echos to 172.16.20.1, timeout is 2 seconds:
!!!!!
Success rate is 100 percent (5/5), round-trip min/avg/max = 84/89/93 ms
BRANCH# ping 172.16.10.1

Type escape sequence to abort.
Sending 5, 100-byte ICMP Echos to 172.16.10.1, timeout is 2 seconds:
!!!!!
Success rate is 100 percent (5/5), round-trip min/avg/max = 84/86/88 ms
```

Step 8: Investigate Forwarding Plane Operation

Recall that MPLS has two tables: the Label Information Base (LIB) and the Label Forwarding Information Base (LFIB). Normally, LDP-allocated labels are advertised to LDP peers. BGP-allocated labels are advertised to BGP peers. BGP-allocated labels will be used by BGP peers as an MPLS label on packets destined for that network through the VPN. The BGP-allocated labels are only significant to the ingress and egress routers. P routers that are not BGP peers with the PE routers will not see the VPN label for the networks known by BGP.

To traverse the MPLS cloud, the packets need to be label-switched at every hop based on advertised labels. To ensure that VPN packets that reach the egress PE have the MPLS label needed to switch the packets after they arrive, the labels are stacked at the ingress PE. However, the packet still needs to be sent along the label-switched path.

Recall that the VRF RIB's next hop for the networks is known via the VPN to the loopback on the egress PE. CEF uses the inuse label for the BGP next hop as the outermost label for packets traveling through the MPLS VPN. First, however, CEF must push on the VPN label that will be used at the egress PE. Thus, CEF stacks the label in a sequential manner so that the VPN label is available at the egress PE, but the label to traverse the label-switched path through the P routers is pushed as the outermost label.

Take some time to study and understand the details of how this is possible. BGP, LDP, CEF, the LFIB, and the provider's IGP are all involved in the use of MPLS labels as a VPN technology.

Once BGP learns the MPLS label to use as the VPN label, this information is entered into the CEF forwarding table on the ingress PE. Display the CEF forwarding entry for 172.16.20.0/24 on SP1 with the **show ip cef vrf name** *ip-address* command:

```
SP1# show ip cef vrf customer 172.16.20.0
172.16.20.0/24, version 12, epoch 0, cached adjacency to Serial0/0/0
0 packets, 0 bytes
  tag information set
    local tag: VPN-route-head
    fast tag rewrite with Se0/0/0, point2point, tags imposed: {16 20}
  via 10.0.3.1, 0 dependencies, recursive
    next hop 10.0.12.2, Serial0/0/0 via 10.0.3.1/32
    valid cached adjacency
    tag rewrite with Se0/0/0, point2point, tags imposed: {16 20}
```

CEF resolves the recursive lookup to the BGP next hop. Based on the labels learned by LDP, CEF might or might not apply the forwarding label to reach 10.0.3.1/32. In this case, LDP on SP2 has advertised a forwarding label to SP1. View the labels advertised to SP1 via LDP using the **show mpls ip binding** command:

```
SP1# show mpls ip binding
  10.0.1.1/32
        in label:     imp-null
        out label:    17          lsr: 10.0.2.1:0
  10.0.2.1/32
        in label:     16
        out label:    imp-null lsr: 10.0.2.1:0          inuse
  10.0.3.1/32
        in label:     17
        out label:    16          lsr: 10.0.2.1:0       inuse
  10.0.12.0/24
        in label:     imp-null
        out label:    imp-null lsr: 10.0.2.1:0
  10.0.23.0/24
        in label:     18
        out label:    imp-null lsr: 10.0.2.1:0          inuse
```

CEF pushes the label of 20 onto the packet first, and then pushes the outer label of 16. The CEF forwarding table decides which path to use based, of course, on the default RIB. The route has been installed in the RIB by OSPF. Thus, the ingress PE imposes two labels in the sequence {16, 20}, as shown in this CEF forwarding table.

Because the incoming VPN packets from SP1 are encapsulated in MPLS frames, SP2 acts according to the directives in its LFIB. SP2 is also the penultimate hop in the label-switched path from SP1 to SP3's loopback interface, and therefore pops the outermost label from the MPLS frame. Display the LFIB with the **show mpls forwarding-table** command:

```
SP2# show mpls forwarding-table
```

Local tag	Outgoing tag or VC	Prefix or Tunnel Id	Bytes tag switched	Outgoing interface	Next Hop
16	Pop tag	10.0.3.1/32	5175	Se0/0/1	point2point
17	Pop tag	10.0.1.1/32	8079	Se0/0/0	point2point

Notice that the LFIB does not care whether there is an inner label or not; it simply performs the operation specified in the column labeled Outgoing, tag or VC.

If you enable MPLS packet debugging on SP2 using **debug mpls packets**, and then issue a ping from one CE to the other, you can see the MPLS packets being label-switched. The ICMP packets are forwarded inside MPLS frames through SP2. Notice in the debug output that each ICMP echo request receives a reply, which is label-switched on its return path through the MPLS network. When you are done, disable debugging:

```
SP2# debug mpls packets
MPLS packet debugging is on
HQ# ping 172.16.20.1

Type escape sequence to abort.
Sending 5, 100-byte ICMP Echos to 172.16.20.1, timeout is 2 seconds:
!!!!!
Success rate is 100 percent (5/5), round-trip min/avg/max = 84/87/92 ms
SP2#
*Feb  3 20:55:57.422: MPLS: Se0/0/0: recvd: CoS=0, TTL=254, Label(s)=16/20
*Feb  3 20:55:57.422: MPLS: Se0/0/1: xmit: CoS=0, TTL=253, Label(s)=20
!
! These 2 messages indicate the label-switching of the ICMP echo request
!
*Feb  3 20:55:57.478: MPLS: Se0/0/1: recvd: CoS=0, TTL=254, Label(s)=17/20
*Feb  3 20:55:57.478: MPLS: Se0/0/0: xmit: CoS=0, TTL=253, Label(s)=20
!
! These 2 messages indicate the label-switching of the ICMP echo reply
!
*Feb  3 20:55:57.510: MPLS: Se0/0/0: recvd: CoS=0, TTL=254, Label(s)=16/20
*Feb  3 20:55:57.510: MPLS: Se0/0/1: xmit: CoS=0, TTL=253, Label(s)=20
*Feb  3 20:55:57.566: MPLS: Se0/0/1: recvd: CoS=0, TTL=254, Label(s)=17/20
*Feb  3 20:55:57.566: MPLS: Se0/0/0: xmit: CoS=0, TTL=253, Label(s)=20
*Feb  3 20:55:57.598: MPLS: Se0/0/0: recvd: CoS=0, TTL=254, Label(s)=16/20
*Feb  3 20:55:57.598: MPLS: Se0/0/1: xmit: CoS=0, TTL=253, Label(s)=20
*Feb  3 20:55:57.654: MPLS: Se0/0/1: recvd: CoS=0, TTL=254, Label(s)=17/20
*Feb  3 20:55:57.654: MPLS: Se0/0/0: xmit: CoS=0, TTL=253, Label(s)=20
```

```
*Feb  3 20:55:57.686: MPLS: Se0/0/0: recvd: CoS=0, TTL=254, Label(s)=16/20
*Feb  3 20:55:57.686: MPLS: Se0/0/1: xmit: CoS=0, TTL=253, Label(s)=20
*Feb  3 20:55:57.742: MPLS: Se0/0/1: recvd: CoS=0, TTL=254, Label(s)=17/20
*Feb  3 20:55:57.742: MPLS: Se0/0/0: xmit: CoS=0, TTL=253, Label(s)=20
*Feb  3 20:55:57.774: MPLS: Se0/0/0: recvd: CoS=0, TTL=254, Label(s)=16/20
*Feb  3 20:55:57.774: MPLS: Se0/0/1: xmit: CoS=0, TTL=253, Label(s)=20
*Feb  3 20:55:57.830: MPLS: Se0/0/1: recvd: CoS=0, TTL=254, Label(s)=17/20
*Feb  3 20:55:57.830: MPLS: Se0/0/0: xmit: CoS=0, TTL=253, Label(s)=20
```

```
SP2# undebug all
All possible debugging has been turned off
```

Continue tracing the label-switched path through the provider network to the egress PE, SP3.

Based on which forwarding table will the VPN packet be switched at SP3? Explain.

_____

_____

Display the MPLS LFIB on SP3 using the **show mpls forwarding-table** command that you used on SP2 previously:

```
SP3# show mpls forwarding-table
```

Local tag	Outgoing tag or VC	Prefix or Tunnel Id	Bytes tag switched	Outgoing interface	Next Hop
16	Pop tag	10.0.12.0/24	0	Se0/0/1	point2point
17	Pop tag	10.0.2.1/32	0	Se0/0/1	point2point
18	17	10.0.1.1/32	0	Se0/0/1	point2point
19	Aggregate	172.16.200.0/24[V] \			
			2704		
20	Untagged	172.16.20.0/24[V]	2704	Se0/1/0	point2point

Notice that SP3 forwards the decapsulated IP packet untagged to the Serial 0/1/0 egress interface because it was received with a label of 20. This is the label that BGP advertised to SP1. SP1's CEF forwarding table encapsulated the IP packets within two MPLS labels {16 20} and then forwarded the packet to SP2.

Conclusion

Issue the **traceroute** command from one CE to another to find that it is going through multiple Layer 3 hops. This is an important debugging tool because it can also be issued from a PE router with reference to a VRF:

```
HQ# traceroute 172.16.20.1
```

```
Type escape sequence to abort.
Tracing the route to 172.16.20.1
```

```
1 172.16.100.254 0 msec 0 msec 0 msec
2 10.0.12.2 126 msec 117 msec 126 msec
3 172.16.200.254 59 msec 50 msec 50 msec
4 172.16.200.1 50 msec 42 msec *
```

Fill in Table 4-1, tracing the path of packets from 172.16.100.1 to 172.16.20.1 to trace the packet's path.

Table 4-1   Path of Packets Through the Network

Router	Incoming (MPLS/IP)	Outgoing (MPLS/IP)	Switched By (CEF/LFIB)	Incoming Label(s)	Outgoing Label(s)
HQ	—			—	—
SP1				—	
SP2					
SP3					—
BRANCH		—		—	—

Given the following output on each of the routers, trace the return path from 172.16.20.1 to 172.16.100.1 by filling in the chart shown in Table 4-2:

```
BRANCH# show ip cef 172.16.100.1
172.16.100.0/24, version 22, epoch 0, cached adjacency to Serial0/0/0
0 packets, 0 bytes
  via 172.16.200.254, Serial0/0/0, 0 dependencies
    next hop 172.16.200.254, Serial0/0/0
    valid cached adjacency
```

```
SP3# show ip cef vrf customer 172.16.100.1
172.16.100.0/24, version 6, epoch 0, cached adjacency to Serial0/0/1
0 packets, 0 bytes
  tag information set
    local tag: VPN-route-head
    fast tag rewrite with Se0/0/1, point2point, tags imposed: {17 20}
  via 10.0.1.1, 0 dependencies, recursive
    next hop 10.0.23.2, Serial0/0/1 via 10.0.1.1/32
    valid cached adjacency
    tag rewrite with Se0/0/1, point2point, tags imposed: {17 20}
```

```
SP2# show mpls forwarding-table
Local  Outgoing    Prefix         Bytes tag  Outgoing   Next Hop
tag    tag or VC   or Tunnel Id   switched   interface
16     Pop tag     10.0.3.1/32    15601      Se0/0/1    point2point
17     Pop tag     10.0.1.1/32    25413      Se0/0/0    point2point
```

```
SP1# show mpls forwarding-table
Local  Outgoing    Prefix         Bytes tag  Outgoing   Next Hop
tag    tag or VC   or Tunnel Id   switched   interface
16     Pop tag     10.0.2.1/32    0          Se0/0/0    point2point
```

```
17    16          10.0.3.1/32        0          Se0/0/0    point2point
18    Pop tag     10.0.23.0/24       0          Se0/0/0    point2point
19    Untagged    172.16.10.0/24[V]  0          Fa0/0      172.16.100.1
20    Aggregate   172.16.100.0/24[V]   \0
```

Table 4-2   Return Path of Packets Through the Network

Router	Incoming (MPLS/IP)	Outgoing (MPLS/IP)	Switched By (CEF/LFIB)	Incoming Label(s)	Outgoing Label(s)
BRANCH	—			—	—
SP3				—	
SP2					
SP1					—
HQ		—		—	—

CHAPTER 5

Cisco Device Hardening

Lab 5-1: Using SDM One-Step Lockdown (5.12.1)

The objectives of this lab are as follows:

- Install the Nmap application on a host.

- Use Cisco SDM One-Step Lockdown.

- Use Nmap before and after to verify results.

Figure 5-1 illustrates the topology that is used for this lab.

Figure 5-1   Topology Diagram

Scenario

Your CIO rolls out a new security policy in the corporate network. Your manager notes that several of the requirements in the security policy can be accomplished automatically using a feature of Cisco Security Device Manager (SDM) called One-Step Lockdown. One-Step Lockdown allows automatic configuration of best-practice security commands.

To rapidly implement the security policy, implement One-Step Lockdown using SDM and verify the results using Nmap, which is a tool that allows you to identify remote system types with a port scan.

Step 1: Configure Addressing

Configure the router interface shown in Figure 5-1:

```
R1(config)# interface fastethernet0/0
R1(config-if)# ip address 192.168.10.1 255.255.255.0
R1(config-if)# no shutdown
```

On the host, download Nmap for Windows from this URL: http://insecure.org/Nmap/download.html.

After you download the file, configure the host with the IP address 192.168.10.50, as shown in the figure. If you do not know how to change an IP address in Windows, see Lab 3-1: Configuring SDM on a Router.

If you use a switch to connect routers to hosts, erase the switch's configuration and leave the switch in its default configuration for the entirety of this lab. By default, the switch assigns all switchports to VLAN 1. Thus, R1 and the PC host shown in the figure communicate across VLAN 1. If you are remotely accessing your equipment, follow your instructor's instructions concerning the switch configuration.

Step 2: Install Nmap on the Host

Run the installer program. Click **I Agree** to accept the licensing agreement for Nmap, as shown in Figure 5-2. The Nmap software is constantly updated. If you install a newer version of Nmap, the screen shots might look different. Also, functionality changes over time, and some features might have been added and others deleted. What follows is suggestive. Your actual results can vary.

Note: At the time this lab was written, Nmap only partially works on computers running Microsoft Windows XP Service Pack 2. This might change in the future, so check the Nmap download page for updates.

Figure 5-2   Nmap License Agreement

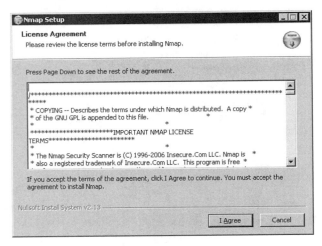

On the **Choose Components** page (see Figure 5-3), do not change the default components that are checked. Click **Next** to install the defaults.

Figure 5-3   Nmap Setup, Components Selection

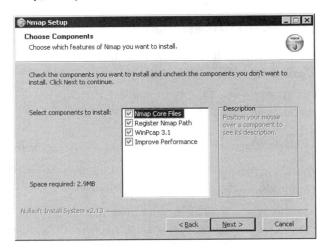

Use the default installation directory, as shown in Figure 5-4. Click **Install**.

Figure 5-4   Nmap Installation Location

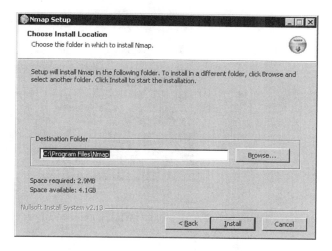

If you have previously installed other security tools that use WinPcap, a popup window might appear notifying you that WinPcap is already installed and will be skipped as part of the Nmap installation. If this notification appears, as shown in Figure 5-5, click **OK,** and skip to Figure 5-7. If this notification does not appear, proceed normally through this step.

Figure 5-5   WinPcap Installed Notification

Click **I Agree** to accept the license agreement for WinPcap, as shown in Figure 5-6.

Figure 5-6   WinPcap License Agreement

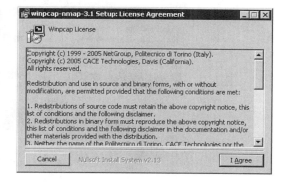

Accept the default installation directory, or choose your own installation directory, and then click **Install**, as shown in Figure 5-7.

Figure 5-7 **WinPcap Installation Location Dialog**

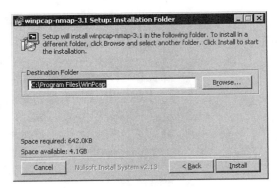

Click **Close** to complete the WinPcap installation (see Figure 5-8). You return to the Nmap installation.

Figure 5-8 **WinPcap Installation Progress Indicator**

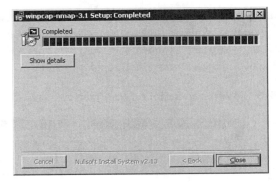

When the Nmap installation is complete (see Figure 5-9), click **Close** to end the installation wizard.

Figure 5-9 **Nmap Installation Progress Indicator**

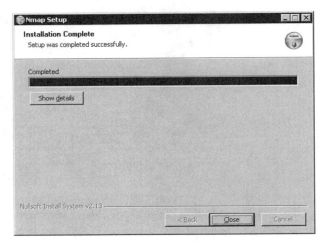

Step 3: Run a Port Scan with Nmap

Nmap for Windows runs as a text-based command-line program. To run Nmap, open the Microsoft Windows command-line terminal. Click the **Start** button, and then choose **Run**. Type **cmd** in the Open field, and then click **OK**. Once in the command prompt, navigate to the Nmap installation directory and run Nmap for R1 using **nmap** *address*. Some versions of Windows do not support running scans against itself. Depending on which version you run, the following might *not* work:

```
Microsoft Windows [Version 5.2.3790]
(C) Copyright 1985-2003 Microsoft Corp.


C:\Documents and Settings\Administrator> cd ..


C:\Documents and Settings> cd ..


C:\> cd Program Files


C:\Program Files> cd Nmap


C:\Program Files\Nmap> nmap 192.168.10.1


Starting Nmap 4.20 ( http://insecure.org ) at 2007-02-05 03:48 Eastern Standard
Time
Interesting ports on 192.168.10.1:
Not shown: 1695 closed ports
PORT    STATE SERVICE
23/tcp open  telnet
80/tcp open  http
MAC Address: 00:19:06:23:43:80 (Cisco Systems)


Nmap finished: 1 IP address (1 host up) scanned in 3.843 seconds
```

Step 4: Prepare a Router for SDM

Recall that a router must be prepared for SDM connectivity before the SDM management interface can configure a router.

Which protocols does SDM use to connect to a router? Provide the name and number layer of the OSI model at which each protocol operates:

- Internet Protocol (IP). Layer 3 = network layer.

- Transmission Control Protocol (TCP). Layer 4 = transport layer.

- TCP establishes the HTTPS and SSH connections over IP.

- Secure Hypertext Transfer Protocol (HTTPS). Layer 7 = application layer.

- Secure Shell Protocol (SSH). Layer 7 = application layer.

Prepare the router for SDM connectivity with the following configuration:

```
username ciscosdm privilege 15 password 7 030752180500324843
ip http authentication local
ip http secure-server
line vty 0 4
 transport input ssh
```

For more information on the commands used here, see "Step 2, Prepare the Router for SDM" in Lab 3-1: Configuring SDM on a Router.

Step 5: Use SDM One-Step Lockdown

One-Step Lockdown is an automatic procedure used to secure a router. It is only available through the SDM interface and not on the router itself in the command-line interface (CLI). Thus, SDM must deliver the One-Step Lockdown functionality over SSH as an expanded set of configuration commands. All software changes over time. The version of SDM that you are installing might be different. If this is the case, what you see on your screen might differ from the following figures.

On the host, start up SDM to configure R1. The SDM home page will appear, as shown in Figure 5-10. At the menu bar at the top of the window, click **Edit**, and then choose **Preferences**.

Figure 5-10   SDM Home Screen

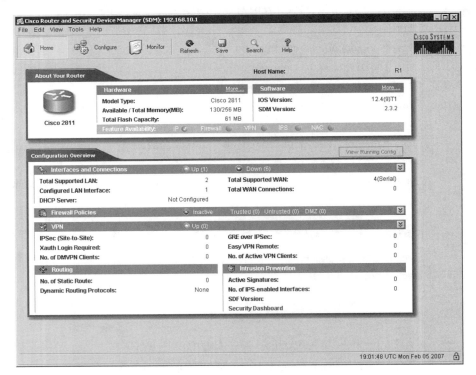

Make sure **Preview commands before delivering to router** is checked, and then click **OK**, as shown in Figure 5-11. From now on, you can preview exactly what configuration lines the SDM delivers to the router.

Figure 5-11   SDM User Preferences

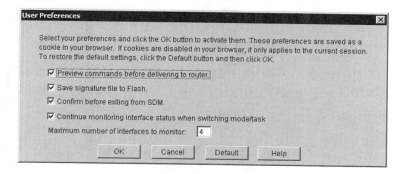

On the SDM home screen, click the **Configure** icon, as shown in Figure 5-12. Then, on the Tasks toolbar, click the **Security Audit** icon.

Click the **One-Step Lockdown** button to begin the process.

Figure 5-12   SDM Security Audit Screen

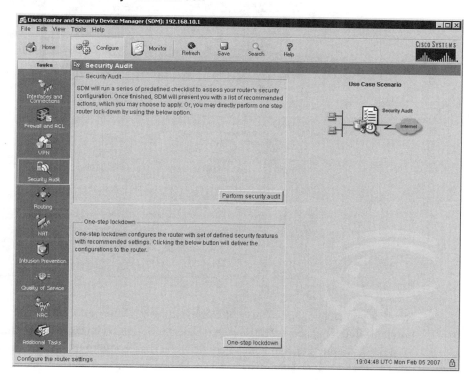

Click **Yes** to begin, as shown in Figure 5-13.

Figure 5-13   SDM One-Step Lockdown Warning

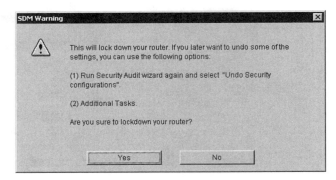

After analysis, SDM generates a list of changes to be made to your router's configuration. Click the **Deliver** button to have SDM add them to the router, as shown in Figure 5-14.

Figure 5-14   One-Step Lockdown Configuration Tasks

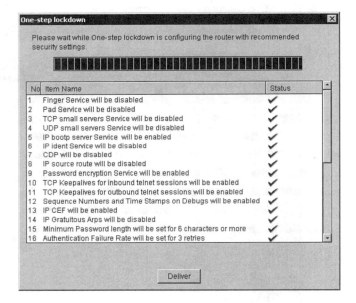

Because you enabled the display of commands to be delivered to the router at the outset of this step, a preview window appears that shows you the configuration changes SDM One-Step Lockdown intends to make. Examine the commands here or in the final configuration to see what security changes SDM makes. Click **Deliver** again when you finish reviewing, as shown in Figure 5-15.

Figure 5-15   One-Step Lockdown Command Preview

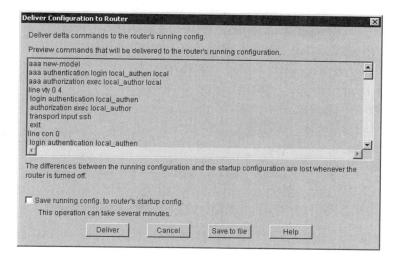

Click **OK** after the commands are delivered, as shown in Figure 5-16.

Figure 5-16   SDM Command Delivery Status

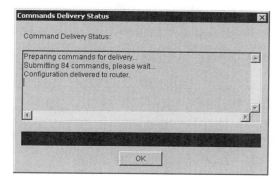

Close SDM when the operation completes.

Step 6: Use Nmap to See Changes

Run Nmap again to see that the router closed the Telnet port (because of One-Step Lockdown). However, the router can still be accessed through SSH. Your output might vary depending on what version of Nmap and what version of Windows you use:

```
Microsoft Windows [Version 5.2.3790]
(C) Copyright 1985-2003 Microsoft Corp.


C:\Documents and Settings\Administrator> cd ..


C:\Documents and Settings> cd ..


C:\> cd Program Files


C:\Program Files> cd Nmap
```

```
C:\Program Files\Nmap> nmap 192.168.10.1

Starting Nmap 4.20 ( http://insecure.org ) at 2007-02-05 13:58 Eastern Standard
  Time
Interesting ports on 192.168.10.1:
Not shown: 1694 closed ports
PORT     STATE SERVICE
22/tcp   open  ssh
80/tcp   open  http
443/tcp  open  https
MAC Address: 00:19:06:23:43:80 (Cisco Systems)
Nmap finished: 1 IP address (1 host up) scanned in 6.047 seconds
```

For what reason does One-Step Lockdown disable access via the Telnet protocol?

_____

_____

Conclusion

Identify and explain the logic of one configuration change in each of the following categories:

1. System services

   _____

2. Authentication options

   _____

3. Secure protocols (HTTPS, SSH, and so forth)

   _____

   _____

   _____

4. Terminal access

   _____

   _____

5. Interface protocols

   _____

   _____

   _____

6. Logging

   _____

If you are unfamiliar with particular protocols or services, use the product documentation available online at http://www.cisco.com/univercd/.

Lab 5-2: Securing a Router with Cisco AutoSecure (5.12.2)

The objective of this lab is to implement Cisco AutoSecure on a router.

Figure 5-17 illustrates the topology that is used for this lab.

Figure 5-17   Topology Diagram

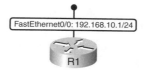

Scenario

In this scenario, you configure Cisco AutoSecure on a router. AutoSecure is a built-in tool in the Cisco IOS that uses a predefined set of commands for securing the router based on questions answered by the network administrator. The AutoSecure command set resembles some of the commands implemented by Cisco Security Device Manager (SDM) One-Step Lockdown in Lab 5-1. Before starting this lab, make sure that all previous configurations are deleted and the router reloaded.

Step 1: Configure the Physical Interface

Configure the R1 physical interface by using the IP address shown in Figure 5-17. You can force the interface into an "always up" state by using the interface-level **no keepalive** command. Then, use the **no shutdown** command to bring the interface up. Because you disabled keepalives, the interface status displays as link state (Layer 1) and line protocols state (Layer 2) up, even if it is not connected to an external device:

```
R1(config)# interface fastethernet0/0
R1(config-if)# ip address 192.168.10.1 255.255.255.0
R1(config-if)# no keepalive
R1(config-if)# no shutdown
```

Normally, you would not use the **no keepalive** command on a routed interface.

Step 2: Configure AutoSecure

At the privileged EXEC prompt, issue the **auto secure** command to start AutoSecure. You might notice that this command is hidden from the Cisco IOS inline help system. It is hidden because AutoSecure can lock out network administrators if it's executed by a user who gains unauthorized access to a router. AutoSecure is a command-line wizard that enables a set of features in the router's configuration. Its function is similar to SDM One-Step Lockdown; however, its functionality is text-based and more interactive:

```
R1# auto secure

          --- AutoSecure Configuration ---
```

```
*** AutoSecure configuration enhances the security of
the router, but it will not make it absolutely resistant
to all security attacks ***

AutoSecure will modify the configuration of your device.
All configuration changes will be shown. For a detailed
explanation of how the configuration changes enhance security
and any possible side effects, please refer to Cisco.com for
Autosecure documentation.
At any prompt you may enter '?' for help.
Use ctrl-c to abort this session at any prompt.

Gathering information about the router for AutoSecure
```

Use the default of **no** to answer the question, "Is this router connected to Internet?" To enter a default (the value in the square brackets), press **Enter** on your keyboard. After you press **Enter**, AutoSecure executes some prepackaged security precaution commands. These commands disable services that are typically not needed. AutoSecure also enables several security features:

```
Is this router connected to internet? [no]: no


Securing Management plane services...


Disabling service finger
Disabling service pad
Disabling udp & tcp small servers
Enabling service password encryption
Enabling service tcp-keepalives-in
Enabling service tcp-keepalives-out
Disabling the cdp protocol

Disabling the bootp server
Disabling the http server
Disabling the finger service
Disabling source routing
Disabling gratuitous arp
```

What is the function of each of the following system services and IP servers?

    1. Finger. _____

    2. TCP small servers. _____

    3. UDP small servers. _____

    4. Password encryption. _____

    5. TCP keepalives. _____

           _____

           _____

6. CDP. _____
   _____

7. BOOTP server. _____

8. HTTP server. _____
   _____

9. Gratuitous ARP. _____
   _____

The following prompt appears, requesting that you create a security banner:

```
Here is a sample Security Banner to be shown
at every access to device. Modify it to suit your
enterprise requirements.

Authorized Access only
  This system is the property of So-&-So-Enterprise.
  UNAUTHORIZED ACCESS TO THIS DEVICE IS PROHIBITED.
  You must have explicit permission to access this
  device. All activities performed on this device
  are logged. Any violations of access policy will result
  in disciplinary action.

Enter the security banner {Put the banner between
k and k, where k is any character}:
~CCNP Router
UNAUTHORIZED ACCESS PROHIBITED~
```

What should your security banner emphasize? Why?

_____
_____
_____
_____

To create a security banner, you need to enter a delimiting character, followed by your message, followed by the delimiting character. The character must be a character that your message will not contain. After this character is found again in the field, the message context will terminate. In the following example, the tilde character (~) is the delimiter.

If you have not previously configured enable passwords and enable secrets, or if both the enable pass and the enable secret password are the same, AutoSecure forces you to create them. AutoSecure also enforces a six-character minimum length on passwords, so create them based on that requirement. This lab uses password for the enable password and secret for the enable secret to meet the minimum length practices:

```
Enable secret is either not configured or
 is the same as enable password
Enter the new enable secret: secret
```

```
Confirm the enable secret : secret
Enter the new enable password: password
Confirm the enable password: password
```

Create a new user in the local user database, because AutoSecure enables authentication, authorization, and accounting (AAA) and uses local authentication. Use a username and password of ciscouser:

```
Configuration of local user database
Enter the username: ciscouser
Enter the password: ciscouser
Confirm the password: ciscouser
Configuring AAA local authentication
Configuring Console, Aux and VTY lines for
local authentication, exec-timeout, and transport
```

The router also enables some login enhancements, for which it needs some parameters. Use a blocking period of 10 seconds, a maximum failure number of 5, and a maximum time period for crossing failed login attempts of 10:

```
Securing device against Login Attacks
Configure the following parameters

Blocking Period when Login Attack detected: 10

Maximum Login failures with the device: 5

Maximum time period for crossing the failed login attempts: 10
```

The router configures a Secure Shell (SSH) server, which requires a domain name. Use cisco.com as the domain name:

```
Configure SSH server? [yes]: yes
Enter the domain-name: cisco.com
```

Why does AutoSecure enable SSH?

_____

_____

AutoSecure disables some unneeded or potentially vulnerable services on each physical interface. You are prompted to enable Context-Based Access Control (CBAC) and TCP intercept. For this lab, type **no** to not configure these services:

```
Configuring interface specific AutoSecure services
Disabling the following ip services on all interfaces:

 no ip redirects
 no ip proxy-arp
 no ip unreachables
 no ip directed-broadcast
 no ip mask-reply
```

```
Disabling mop on Ethernet interfaces


Securing Forwarding plane services...


Enabling CEF (This might impact the memory requirements for your platform)
Enabling unicast rpf on all interfaces connected
to internet


Configure CBAC Firewall feature? [yes/no]: no
Tcp intercept feature is used prevent tcp syn attack
on the servers in the network. Create autosec_tcp_intercept_list
to form the list of servers to which the tcp traffic is to
be observed



Enable tcp intercept feature? [yes/no]: no
```

From your reading, what function does "[e]nabling unicast rpf on all interfaces connected to the internet" serve?

The last step AutoSecure does is verify the configuration that it is going to add. After AutoSecure shows you the running configuration it has generated, AutoSecure asks you to verify that you want to apply the running configuration. Use the default of **yes**:

```
This is the configuration generated:


no service finger
no service pad
no service udp-small-servers
no service tcp-small-servers
service password-encryption
```

```
service tcp-keepalives-in
service tcp-keepalives-out
no cdp run
no ip bootp server
no ip http server
no ip finger
no ip source-route
no ip gratuitous-arps
no ip identd
banner motd ^CCCNP Router
UNAUTHORIZED ACCESS PROHIBITED^C
security passwords min-length 6
security authentication failure rate 10 log
enable secret 5 $1$d7wX$kb5JYyFOQmSRWVpW8iitA.
enable password 7 095C4F1A0A1218000F
username ciscouser password 7 02050D4808091A32495C
aaa new-model
aaa authentication login local_auth local
line con 0
 login authentication local_auth
 exec-timeout 5 0
 transport output telnet
line aux 0
 login authentication local_auth
 exec-timeout 10 0
 transport output telnet
line vty 0 4
 login authentication local_auth
 transport input telnet
line tty 1
 login authentication local_auth
 exec-timeout 15 0
login block-for 10 attempts 5 within 10
ip domain-name cisco.com
crypto key generate rsa general-keys modulus 1024
ip ssh time-out 60
ip ssh authentication-retries 2
line vty 0 4
  transport input ssh telnet
service timestamps debug datetime msec localtime show-timezone
service timestamps log datetime msec localtime show-timezone
logging facility local2
logging trap debugging
service sequence-numbers
```

```
logging console critical
logging buffered
interface FastEthernet0/0
 no ip redirects
 no ip proxy-arp
 no ip unreachables
 no ip directed-broadcast
 no ip mask-reply
 no mop enabled
interface FastEthernet0/1
 no ip redirects
 no ip proxy-arp
 no ip unreachables
 no ip directed-broadcast
 no ip mask-reply
 no mop enabled
interface Serial0/0/0
 no ip redirects
 no ip proxy-arp
 no ip unreachables
 no ip directed-broadcast
 no ip mask-reply
interface Serial0/0/1
 no ip redirects
 no ip proxy-arp
 no ip unreachables
 no ip directed-broadcast
 no ip mask-reply
interface Serial0/1/0
 no ip redirects
 no ip proxy-arp
 no ip unreachables
 no ip directed-broadcast
 no ip mask-reply
interface Serial0/1/1
 no ip redirects
 no ip proxy-arp
 no ip unreachables
 no ip directed-broadcast
 no ip mask-reply
ip cef
access-list 100 permit udp any any eq bootpc
!
end
```

When the router asks you to accept this configuration so that it can be applied to the router, answer **yes**:

```
Apply this configuration to running-config? [yes]: yes

Applying the config generated to running-config
The name for the keys will be: R1.cisco.com

% The key modulus size is 1024 bits
% Generating 1024 bit RSA keys, keys will be non-exportable...[OK]

*Feb  6 01:03:52.694: %SSH-5-ENABLED: SSH 1.99 has been enabled
*Feb  6 01:03:57.250 UTC: %AUTOSEC-1-MODIFIED: AutoSecure configuration has been
Modified on this device
```

How does the router generate the name for the public crypto keys shown in the preceding configuration text?

_____

_____

Lab 5-3: Disabling Unneeded Services (5.12.3)

The objectives of this lab are as follows:

- Identify and disable unneeded and insecure services on a router.

- Enable TCP keepalives.

Figure 5-18 illustrates the topology that is used for this lab.

Figure 5-18   Topology Diagram

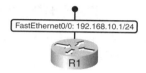

Scenario

In this lab, you disable unneeded services on a router. SDM One-Step Lockdown or AutoSecure disables many of the same services. This lab requires only one router. Make sure that all router configurations from previous labs are deleted and the router reloaded.

Step 1: Configure the Physical Interface

Because this lab uses only one router, you simulate an active FastEthernet connection by activating the interface and applying the **no keepalive** command to initiate an "always up" state, regardless of the existence of a device at the remote end. Normally, you would not use the **no keepalive** command on a routed interface, except in special circumstances. In this lab, you only use it for simulation purposes.

Configure the R1 physical interface by using the IP address shown in Figure 5-18. Use the **no keepalive** command in interface configuration mode, and then use the **no shutdown** command to activate the interface. Because you disabled keepalives, the interface status displays as link state (Layer 1) and line protocols state (Layer 2) up, even if it is not connected to an external device:

```
R1(config)# interface fastethernet0/0
R1(config-if)# ip address 192.168.10.1 255.255.255.0
R1(config-if)# no keepalive
R1(config-if)# no shutdown
```

Step 2: Ensure Services Are Disabled

Some services are disabled by default on more recent Cisco IOS releases, so you do not necessarily have to disable them. However, it is helpful to know the commands in case they are enabled and affect security. These commands are especially useful if you use older versions of the IOS.

The **no ip finger** command replaces the **no service finger** command. Both disable the finger service, which allows remote users or systems to identify users connected to the local router's terminal lines or who have active running processes:

```
R1(config)# no ip finger
```

How could the enabling of the finger service pose a security risk?

_____

_____

_____

The **no service udp-small-servers** and **no service tcp-small-servers** commands disable UDP and TCP small servers, such as echo and discard. The small servers are not needed in most environments:

```
R1(config)# no service udp-small-servers
R1(config)# no service tcp-small-servers
```

The TCP and UDP small servers are enabled by default on Cisco IOS Release 11.2 and earlier. They are disabled by default on Cisco IOS Release 11.3 and later.

It is recommended that you do not enable these services unless it is absolutely necessary. These services could be exploited indirectly to gain information about the target system or exploited directly with a fraggle attack, which uses UDP echo (see http://www.cisco.com/en/US/tech/tk59/technologies_tech_note09186a0080149ad6.shtml#topic5). Also, if a sender transmits a volume of fake requests for UDP diagnostic services on the router, the requests could consume all CPU resources.

Step 3: Manage Router Access

Name two popular TCP protocols that network administrators use to manage network devices.

_____

Recall that management applications, such as Telnet and SSH, connect to the vty port on a router. A Cisco router has five vtys configured by default, numbered 0 through 4, to which users connect to access the command-line interface (CLI). When one vty is in use, the next vty port is used. If all vty ports are being used, other users cannot connect to the device in this way.

Describe how individuals with malicious intent could exploit vty port functionality.

_____

_____

_____

_____

Describe at least two ways to prevent this type of attack.

_____

_____

_____

_____

_____

Enabling TCP keepalives causes the router to generate periodic keepalive messages, letting it detect and drop broken Telnet connections. This frees up hung Telnet sessions. This functionality also has the additional benefit of making the router more secure by preventing a hacker from exploiting a hung

Telnet session. To enable TCP keepalive packets on idle connections, use the **service tcp-keepalives-in** and **service tcp-keepalives-out** commands in global configuration mode:

```
R1(config)# service tcp-keepalives-in
R1(config)# service tcp-keepalives-out
```

Step 4: Disable CDP

Cisco Discovery Protocol (CDP) is a great troubleshooting tool, especially on poorly documented networks. However, it can also leave your network susceptible to reconnaissance attacks.

CDP is used for some network-management functions, but it is dangerous because CDP allows any system on a directly connected segment to learn that the router is a Cisco device and to determine the model number and the Cisco IOS Software version being run. This reconnaissance information can be used to design attacks against the router.

To globally disable the CDP service, use the **no cdp run** command in global configuration mode. To disable CDP on a per-interface basis, issue the **no cdp enable** command in interface configuration mode:

```
R1(config)# no cdp run
```

Step 5: Disable Other Unused Services

Disable the packet assembler/disassembler (PAD) on the router by using the **no service pad** command in global configuration mode. PAD translates between packets and character streams in legacy networks. You should not need this service in most current IP networks:

```
R1(config)# no service pad
```

The BOOTP service is used in networks that have a centralized Cisco IOS Software deployment: One router can be used by other routers to load its operating system (OS). However, the BOOTP service is seldom used, and it gives a hacker an opportunity to steal a Cisco IOS image. Therefore, in most situations, disable it by using the following command:

```
R1(config)# no ip bootp server
```

The most recent Cisco IOS Software releases issue the Hypertext Transfer Protocol (HTTP) to support remote configuration and monitoring. In general, HTTP access is equivalent to interactive access to the router. The authentication protocol used for HTTP is equivalent to sending a clear-text password across the network. Unfortunately, there is no effective provision in HTTP for challenge-based or one-time passwords. This makes HTTP a relatively risky choice for router management across the public Internet.

If you choose to use HTTP for router management, use the **ip http access-class** command to restrict access to IP addresses. You should also use the **ip http authentication** *method* command to configure authentication. As with interactive logins, the best choice for HTTP authentication is to issue a TACACS+ or RADIUS server.[1]

In the following example, you choose not to use the IOS web interface. Disable the Cisco IOS HTTP server with the **no ip http server** command in global configuration mode:

```
R1(config)# no ip http server
```

The IP protocol supports source-routing options that allow the sender of an IP datagram to control the route that a datagram takes toward its ultimate destination, and generally the route that any reply takes. These options are rarely used for legitimate purposes in real networks. Some older IP implementations do not process source-routed packets properly, and it is possible to send them datagrams with source-routing options to crash machines that run these implementations. The **no ip source-route** command discards packets that contain source-routing information. You can disable this if a network is not using source-routing information:

```
R1(config)# no ip source-route
```

Gratuitous Address Resolution Protocols (ARP) are unsolicited ARP requests and replies that can be generated for several reasons, such as when detecting IP address conflicts or updating ARP tables after an address change. However, attackers can use these packets to spoof a valid network device; for example, an attacker could send out a packet that claims to be the default router. If you choose to do so, you can disable Gratuitous ARP with the global configuration command **no ip gratuitous-arps**:

```
R1(config)# no ip gratuitous-arps
```

Step 6: Disabling Unneeded Interface Services

Some commands are used on a per-interface basis to mitigate certain types of hacker attacks or reconnaissance. Issue the following commands to the R1 FastEthernet0/0 interface.

The **no ip redirects** command disables IP redirects so that the router does not send out ICMP redirect messages. These messages occur when a router routes a packet out the interface that it came in on. The contents of the message tell the packet sender to send it directly to where the router would have sent it:

```
R1(config)# interface fastethernet0/0
R1(config-if)# no ip redirects
```

The **no ip proxy-arp** command disables proxy ARPs from the router, which means that a router can respond to an ARP request for an address on a remote subnet (with its own MAC address) and take responsibility for the packets getting to their destination:

```
R1(config-if)# no ip proxy-arp
```

The **no ip unreachables** command prevents the router from sending Internet Control Message Protocol (ICMP) unreachable messages when it has not learned a route to a destination. Normally, these messages are helpful for troubleshooting, but they can be involved in reconnaissance or DoS attacks:

```
R1(config-if)# no ip unreachables
```

Similarly, directed broadcasts can be used in reconnaissance and DoS attacks. You can prevent this by using the **no ip directed-broadcast** command. Although directed broadcasts are disabled by default in recent Cisco IOS releases, this command is included in this lab because it is a significant security point. This command makes the router discard packets with a destination address that is the broadcast address for a specific network. This packet can be used in a DoS attack. If a hacker located at 192.168.1.1 wants to attack a host at 192.168.2.2, he can ping 192.168.3.255, which is sourced from 192.168.2.2. Every host in the 192.168.3.0 /24 subnet responds to that ICMP echo request and directs the response to the spoofed source. In the given case, the spoofed source is the victim of the attack:

```
R1(config-if)# no ip directed-broadcast
```

Unnecessary ICMP messages can be sent in response to ICMP mask-request messages. Use the **no ip mask-reply** command to disable ICMP mask-reply messages:

```
R1(config-if)# no ip mask-reply
```

Maintenance Operation Protocol (MOP) is an old DECnet protocol that is not needed on most current IP networks. To disable it, issue the **no mop enabled** command. This is enabled by default on Ethernet interfaces only:

```
R1(config-if)# no mop enabled
```

Lab 5-4: Enhancing Router Security (5.12.4)

The objectives of this lab are as follows:

- Implement Cisco IOS login enhancements.
- Enforce a minimum password length.
- Modify command privilege levels.
- Configure a banner.
- Configure a router to use SSH.
- Enable password encryption.

Figure 5-19 illustrates the topology used for this lab.

Figure 5-19   Topology Diagram

VLAN 1:
192.168.10.0/24

Scenario

In previous labs in this module, you automatically configured numerous security features on routers using One-Step Lockdown and AutoSecure. This lab provides details on manual security configuration. Before you begin this lab, delete all previous configurations on routers and reload.

In this scenario, your corporation's CIO has a new security policy that must be rolled out across the network. The policy has strict rules regarding security banners, privilege levels, login security, password lengths, and password storage. Additionally, you must only allow SSH access to the vty lines on routers in the network.

In this lab, you configure your routers to conform to the following security policies:

- Enforce a minimum password length of eight characters.
- Display a security banner stating that unauthorized use is prohibited and prosecutable, and that the use of this device is monitored and used as evidence.
- Permit only secure management methods. No management passwords must be sent or stored as clear text. Antireplay measures must be taken.
- Login procedures must be guarded against DoS attacks.

R2 acts as a host whose only function is to access R1. You do most of the configuration on R1.

Step 1: Configure the Physical Interfaces

Configure the R1 and R2 physical interfaces by using the IP address shown in Figure 5-19, and activate the interfaces with the **no shutdown** command:

```
R1(config)# interface fastethernet0/0
R1(config-if)# ip address 192.168.10.1 255.255.255.0
R1(config-if)# no shutdown
```

```
R2(config)# interface fastethernet0/0
R2(config-if)# ip address 192.168.10.2 255.255.255.0
R2(config-if)# no shutdown
```

If you use a switch to connect the Fast Ethernet interfaces on your routers, erase the configuration in nonvolatile RAM with the **erase start** command and reload the switch. All ports default to VLAN 1, which provides connectivity between the Fast Ethernet interfaces on R1 and R2.

Step 2: Telnet to R1

On R2, issue the **telnet** *host* command from an EXEC prompt, where *host* is the R1 IP address:

```
R2# telnet 192.168.10.1
Trying 192.168.10.1 ... Open


Password required, but none set


[Connection to 192.168.10.1 closed by foreign host]
R2#
```

In troubleshooting, what does the previous output help you determine?

_____

_____

_____

_____

Notice that R1 accepts the Telnet connection, but then it terminates the connection because no line password is set. This can be easily fixed on R1 by setting up line authentication. For this lab, use the local username database. Another option is to configure communication to a RADIUS or TACACS+ server for AAA services.

Create a user account on the router with the username and password of cisco by using the **username** *name* **password** *password* command in global configuration mode:

```
R1(config)# username cisco password cisco
```

To configure the vty lines, enter the **line vty** *low* [*high*] command in global configuration mode. The *low* and *high* keywords refer to the bounds of the lines you are configuring. On a router, you simultaneously configure the five terminal lines in most scenarios, so the low number would be 0—the first line—and the high number would be 4—the last line. At the line-configuration prompt, enter the **login local** command to enable local authentication:

```
R1(config)# line vty 0 4
R1(config-line)# login local
```

Now, connect to R1 from R2:

```
R2# telnet 192.168.10.1
Trying 192.168.10.1 ... Open
```

```
User Access Verification
```

```
Username: cisco
Password: cisco
```

This time, the router allows your Telnet connection. Attempt to enter privileged EXEC mode on R1 through the Telnet session:

```
R1> enable
% No password set
R1> exit

[Connection to 192.168.10.1 closed by foreign host]
R2#
```

To fix the closed connection, configure an enable password with the **enable secret** *password* command on R1. Make the enable password cisco:

```
R1(config)# enable secret cisco
```

From R2, again connect to R1 via Telnet:

```
R2# telnet 192.168.10.1
Trying 192.168.10.1 ... Open


User Access Verification

Username: cisco
Password: cisco
R1> enable
Password: cisco
R1# exit

[Connection to 192.168.10.1 closed by foreign host]
R2#
```

Why does Cisco IOS not allow Telnet connections or remotely entering privileged mode unless the proper passwords are set up?

_____

_____

_____

Step 3: Configure Cisco IOS Login Enhancements

What happens when you repeatedly fail Telnet authentication on R1?

_____

_____

Test your answer by attempting to telnet from R2 to R1 using incorrect usernames and/or passwords:

```
R2# telnet 192.168.10.1
Trying 192.168.10.1 ... Open

User Access Verification

Username: cisco
Password: wrongpass
% Login invalid

Username: cisco
Password: guesspass
% Login invalid

Username: baduser
Password: badpass
% Login invalid

[Connection to 192.168.10.1 closed by foreign host]
R2#
```

The router disconnects the Telnet session after three failed tries, but it does not employ any further security beyond this. This router is still vulnerable to a dictionary attack, which is a hacker running a program that continually tries new passwords.

Fortunately, Cisco recently enhanced login security features to mitigate dictionary attacks. To view which login features are configured, use the **show login** command. Each of the following output lines corresponds to one of the new login features:

```
R1# show login
      No login delay has been applied.
      No Quiet-Mode access list has been configured.


      Router NOT enabled to watch for login Attacks
```

The **login block-for** *seconds* **attempts** *tries* **within** *seconds* command, issued in global configuration mode, allows the activation of all the other login security features. The first *seconds* parameter specifies the amount of time that login is not allowed after a violation occurs. The *tries* parameter represents the number of failed login attempts permitted during a configurable amount of time. The final *seconds* argument represents the time period over which the number of failed attempts must occur for the user to be locked out of the device. Configure R1 using the following, which blocks all login attempts for 30 seconds if there are two failed login attempts within a 15-second time period:

```
R1(config)# login block-for 30 attempts 2 within 15
```

Test this configuration by attempting to telnet to R1 from R2. Intentionally fail authentication twice and, when kicked off, attempt to telnet again. Look at the messages logged on R1 and their timestamps:

```
R2# telnet 192.168.10.1
Trying 192.168.10.1 ... Open

User Access Verification

Username: test
Password: test
% Login invalid

Username: guess
Password: guess
% Login invalid

[Connection to 192.168.10.1 closed by foreign host]
R2# telnet 192.168.10.1
Trying 192.168.10.1 ...
% Connection refused by remote host

R2#
```

```
R1#
*Feb  7 08:27:01.259: %SEC_LOGIN-1-QUIET_MODE_ON: Still timeleft for watching
  failures is 11 secs, [user: guess] [Source: 192.168.10.2] [localport: 23] [Reason:
  Login Authentication Failed - BadUser] [ACL: sl_def_acl] at 08:27:01 UTC Wed Feb 7
  2007
*Feb  7 08:27:31.259: %SEC_LOGIN-5-QUIET_MODE_OFF: Quiet Mode is OFF, because block
  period timed out at 08:27:31 UTC Wed Feb 7 2007
R1#
```

When the router reaches the login limit specified by the **login block-for** command, it enters Quiet Mode. Normally, access attempts are blocked during Quiet Mode, as shown in the previous output. However, you can set up an access list that permits trusted hosts to access the router, even in Quiet Mode. Issue the **login quiet-mode access-class** *acl* command in global configuration mode on R1. The access list specifies the source of trusted connections. The following allows hosts on network 192.168.20.0/24 to access the vtys on R1:

```
R1(config)# login quiet-mode access-class 1
R1(config)# access-list 1 permit 192.168.20.0 0.0.0.255
```

You can also configure the delay between login attempts. The default is 1 second when **login block-for** is enabled. Change the delay to 3 seconds by using the **login delay** *seconds* command in global configuration mode. Also, issue the **login on-failure log** command to have the router log failures:

```
R1(config)# login delay 3
R1(config)# login on-failure log
```

Verify the configuration by failing login to R1. Notice the delay between attempts on R2. Verify the login configuration with the **show login** command on R1:

```
R2# telnet 192.168.10.1
Trying 192.168.10.1 ... Open

User Access Verification

Username: test
Password: test
% Login invalid

Username: this
Password: isatest
% Login invalid

[Connection to 192.168.10.1 closed by foreign host]
R2#
```

```
R1# show login
     A login delay of 3 seconds is applied.
     Quiet-Mode access list 1 is applied.
     All failed login is logged.

     Router enabled to watch for login Attacks.
     If more than 2 login failures occur in 15 seconds or less,
     logins will be disabled for 30 seconds.

     Router presently in Normal-Mode.
     Current Watch Window
         Time remaining: 2 seconds.
         Login failures for current window: 0.
     Total login failures: 10.


R1#
*Feb  7 08:43:28.239: %SEC_LOGIN-4-LOGIN_FAILED: Login failed [user: test] [Source:
192.168.10.2] [localport: 23] [Reason: Login Authentication Failed - BadUser] at
08:43:28 UTC Wed Feb 7 2007


*Feb  7 08:43:34.475: %SEC_LOGIN-4-LOGIN_FAILED: Login failed [user: this] [Source:
192.168.10.2] [localport: 23] [Reason: Login Authentication Failed - BadUser] at
08:43:34 UTC Wed Feb 7 2007


*Feb  7 08:43:34.475: %SEC_LOGIN-1-QUIET_MODE_ON: Still timeleft for watching
failures is 1 secs, [user: this] [Source: 192.168.10.2] [localport: 23] [Reason:
Login Authentication Failed - BadUser] [ACL: 1] at 08:43:34 UTC Wed Feb 7 2007


R1# show login
     A login delay of 3 seconds is applied.
```

```
        Quiet-Mode access list 1 is applied.
        All failed login is logged.


        Router enabled to watch for login Attacks.
        If more than 2 login failures occur in 15 seconds or less,
        logins will be disabled for 30 seconds.


        Router presently in Quiet-Mode.
        Will remain in Quiet-Mode for 26 seconds.
        Restricted logins filtered by applied ACL 1.


    R1#


*Feb  7 08:44:04.475: %SEC_LOGIN-5-QUIET_MODE_OFF: Quiet Mode is OFF, because block
period timed out at 08:44:04 UTC Wed Feb 7 2007


    R1# show login
        A login delay of 3 seconds is applied.
        Quiet-Mode access list 1 is applied.
        All failed login is logged.


        Router enabled to watch for login Attacks.
        If more than 2 login failures occur in 15 seconds or less,
        logins will be disabled for 30 seconds.


        Router presently in Normal-Mode.
        Current Watch Window
            Time remaining: 11 seconds.
            Login failures for current window: 0.
        Total login failures: 12.
```

Step 4: Enforce a Minimum Password Length

Many companies require that passwords have a minimum length or use certain character combinations. You can configure a minimum password length on a router with the global configuration command **security passwords min-length** *size*.

Configure R1 to enforce a minimum password length of eight characters. Then, attempt to add a user with a password length that is less than eight characters. Then, add the user by lengthening the password to eight characters. Remove the user when you finish.

Note that in a production environment, you probably would want a password length that is at least eight characters:

```
R1(config)# security passwords min-length 8
R1(config)# username cisco2 password cis
```

```
% Password too short - must be at least 8 characters. Password configuration failed
R1(config)# username cisco2 password ciscocisco
R1(config)# no username cisco2 password ciscocisco
R1(config)# no security passwords min-length 8
```

Step 5: Modify Command Privilege Levels

By default, the user EXEC prompt on a router is privilege level 1. When you type the **enable** command, the CLI promotes the user's command privileges to user level 15. You can verify this with the **show privilege** command. To return to the user EXEC prompt, use the **disable** command:

```
R1> show privilege
Current privilege level is 1


R1> enable
Password: cisco


R1# show privilege
Current privilege level is 15
```

By default, commands are either privilege level 1 or 15, depending on how secure the command needs to be. Many commands, such as **show ip route**, can be performed at privilege level 1. Others, such as **show running-configuration** and **clear ip route ***, can be maliciously used, so they are restricted to privilege level 15. The privilege level includes all commands at that privilege level, plus every level below it. Try to perform a **clear ip route** at both privilege level 1 and 15:

```
R1> clear ip route *
        ^
% Invalid input detected at '^' marker.


R1> enable
Password: cisco
R1# clear ip route *
```

When you enter the **enable** command, the CLI prompts you for an enable password. Enter **enable ?**, and then try enabling privilege level 5:

```
R1> enable ?
  <0-15>  Enable level
  view    Set into the existing view
  <cr>


R1> enable 5
% No password set
R1>
```

You can set different privilege level passwords by using the **enable secret level** *level password* command in global configuration mode. Set the password for privilege level 5 to cisco5. Then, issue **enable 5** to get to privilege level 5:

```
R1(config)# enable secret level 5 cisco5


R1> enable 5
Password: cisco555



R1# show privilege
Current privilege level is 5
```

In some situations, you might want to give different access privileges to different users. This would be applicable, for example, at an Internet service provider (ISP), where technical support users have different access privileges.

You can change command privilege levels for specific command sequences with the **privilege** *prompt* **level** *privilege command* command in global configuration mode. The *prompt* argument is the prompt at which that command must be entered, such as EXEC, global configuration, or a particular submode. The *privilege* parameter is the minimum privilege level for this command, and *command* is the command that is modified.

For example, to allow privilege level 5 to shut down an interface, you must change privileges on several commands. Think about the steps that someone must go through to deactivate an interface, starting at the EXEC prompt. The user must first be in configuration mode, and then go to interface configuration mode. Finally, the user issues the **shutdown** command on the interface.

Set the minimum privilege level for each of these commands to 5, as follows:

```
R1(config)# privilege exec level 5 configure terminal
R1(config)# privilege configure level 5 interface
R1(config)# privilege interface level 5 shutdown
```

Write down all the commands necessary for this final command to be executed:

```
configure terminal
interface interface-type interface-number
shutdown
```

Using either the **enable** *level* command from the user EXEC prompt or the **disable** *level* command from the privileged EXEC prompt, change your user privilege level to 5 and attempt to deactivate the interface:

```
R1# disable 5
R1# configure terminal
Enter configuration commands, one per line.  End with CNTL/Z.
R1(config)# ?
Configure commands:
  atm       Enable ATM SLM Statistics
  beep      Configure BEEP (Blocks Extensible Exchange Protocol)
  call      Configure Call parameters
  default   Set a command to its defaults
```

```
   dss       Configure dss parameters
   end       Exit from configure mode
   exit      Exit from configure mode
   help      Description of the interactive help system
   interface Select an interface to configure
   netconf   Configure NETCONF
   no        Negate a command or set its defaults
   oer       Optimized Exit Routing configuration submodes
   sasl      Configure SASL
```

```
R1(config)# interface fastethernet0/0
R1(config-if)# ?
Interface configuration commands:
   default   Set a command to its defaults
   exit      Exit from interface configuration mode
   help      Description of the interactive help system
   no        Negate a command or set its defaults
   shutdown  Shutdown the selected interface
```

```
R1(config-if)# shutdown
*Feb  8 06:24:19.791: %LINK-5-CHANGED: Interface FastEthernet0/0, changed state to
   administratively down
*Feb  8 06:24:20.791: %LINEPROTO-5-UPDOWN: Line protocol on Interface
   FastEthernet0/0, changed state to down
R1(config-if)# no shutdown
*Feb  8 06:24:25.735: %LINK-3-UPDOWN: Interface FastEthernet0/0, changed state to up
*Feb  8 06:24:26.735: %LINEPROTO-5-UPDOWN: Line protocol on Interface
   FastEthernet0/0, changed state to up
```

Notice the limited available command set with the **?** command. Also, note that the **no shutdown** command is available when the **shutdown** command is available.

Go back to privilege level 15 and view the privilege level 5 commands that have been configured:

```
R1# show running-config | include privilege
privilege interface level 5 shutdown
privilege configure level 5 interface
privilege exec level 5 configure terminal
privilege exec level 5 configure
```

The reason there is an extra command beyond what was configured is because of the way the CLI parser receives input. With a command that has multiple keywords, such as **configure terminal**, each keyword in the sequence must be allowed. This is why there is an entry for both **configure** and **configure terminal**.

Would a user at privilege level 5 currently be able to use the **configure memory** command?

Step 6: Create a Banner

You can create a banner for users connecting to the router with the **banner** *character* command in global configuration mode. The *character* parameter is any delimiting character that you select to inform the router that the banner is complete. In the following example, a tilde (~) is used:

```
R1(config)# banner ~
Enter TEXT message.  End with the character '~'.
CCNP Lab Router
UNAUTHORIZED ACCESS PROHIBITED

Unauthorized users who attempt to connect to and perform unauthorized
operations will be prosecuted. Your actions are being monitored. The
monitoring information retrieved will be used against you in court.
~
```

Try connecting to R1 from R2:

```
R2# telnet 192.168.10.1
Trying 192.168.10.1 ... Open


CCNP Lab Router
UNAUTHORIZED ACCESS PROHIBITED

Unauthorized users who attempt to connect to and perform unauthorized
operations will be prosecuted. Your actions are being monitored. The
monitoring information retrieved will be used against you in court.


User Access Verification

Username:
```

In a production environment, the banner reflects a company's security policy.

Step 7: Enable SSH

Secure Shell (SSH) is a terminal connection protocol that is similar to an encrypted version of Telnet. Because SSH is encrypted with configurable encryption methods, it is not vulnerable to packet sniffing, like plain-text traffic.

This step requires a Cisco IOS image that includes the encryption suite CRYPTO. SSH includes public-key encryption methods similar to those used in IPsec virtual private networks (VPN).

First, set the domain name for the router by using the **ip domain-name** *name* command in global configuration mode. In this case, set the R1 domain name to cisco.com:

```
R1(config)# ip domain-name cisco.com
```

Next, generate RSA encryption keys with the **crypto key generate rsa** command in global configuration mode. When prompted for the number of bits in the modulus, enter **1024**. Notice that the name of the keys is the hostname of the router concatenated with the domain name you configured:

```
R1(config)# crypto key generate rsa
The name for the keys will be: R1.cisco.com
Choose the size of the key modulus in the range of 360 to 2048 for your
  General Purpose Keys. Choosing a key modulus greater than 512 may take
  a few minutes.

How many bits in the modulus [512]: 1024
% Generating 1024 bit RSA keys, keys will be non-exportable...[OK]

R1(config)#
*Feb  8 07:10:14.027: %SSH-5-ENABLED: SSH 1.99 has been enabled
```

After you generate the RSA keys, SSH is enabled automatically. On R1, you can view the crypto keys generated with the **show crypto key mypubkey rsa** command:

```
R1# show crypto key mypubkey rsa
% Key pair was generated at: 07:10:14 UTC Feb 8 2007
Key name: R1.cisco.com
 Storage Device: not specified
 Usage: General Purpose Key
 Key is not exportable.
 Key Data:
  30819F30 0D06092A 864886F7 0D010101 05000381 8D003081 89028181 00B88087
<OUTPUT OMITTED>
```

By default, all vtys allow connections using all available connection protocols, such as Telnet, SSH, rlogin, and so on. For enhanced security, force the vtys to accept only SSH traffic by using the **transport input** *type* command in line-configuration mode. The *type* parameter lists the incoming and outgoing connection types allowed:

```
R1(config)# line vty 0 4
R1(config-line)# transport input ssh
```

On R2, you can try to connect to R1 with SSH by using the **ssh –l** *username hostname* command. Use the username configured in the local username database on R1:

```
R2# ssh -l cisco 192.168.10.1

Password: cisco

CCNP Lab Router
UNAUTHORIZED ACCESS PROHIBITED

Unauthorized users who attempt to connect to and perform unauthorized
operations will be prosecuted. Your actions are being monitored. The
monitoring information retrieved will be used against you in court.

R1>exit
```

```
[Connection to 192.168.10.1 closed by foreign host]
R2#
```

Step 8: Encrypt Passwords

The **show running-config** command displays unencrypted usernames and passwords. Other types of passwords, such as line passwords, also show up as unencrypted. Secret passwords do not show up unencrypted, because they already have the message digest algorithm 5 (MD5) algorithm performed on them:

```
R1# show running-config | include username
username cisco password 0 cisco
```

To secure your router from access attacks in which a user sees an unencrypted password and uses it to raise his privilege level to something higher than the user should have, issue the **service password-encryption** command in global configuration mode. Display the username entries in the running configuration:

```
R1(config)# service password-encryption
```

```
R1# show running-config | include username
username cisco password 7 070C285F4D06
```

The passwords in the running configuration that were previously unencrypted now display in encrypted form. This encrypted form is easily reversible and is not the same as the MD5 hash used for secret passwords. It is only intended to prevent shoulder surfing, which is learning passwords from eavesdropping on someone else's workstation. Because it is reversible, do not send out configurations with passwords encrypted in this form; after someone has a hard copy of the encrypted password, they can easily retrieve the plain-text version.

To see how easy it is to decode a Cisco level 7 password, go to Google.com and enter **cisco level 7 password**. Several sites have the capability to decode Cisco level 7 passwords. Copy the level 7 password just given into this URL: http://www.securitystats.com/tools/ciscocrack.php. You see that the weakly encrypted password is easily decoded to yield the plain-text password **cisco**.

Lab 5-5: Configuring Logging (5.12.5)

The objectives of this lab are as follows:

- Configure a router to log to a syslog server.
- Use Kiwi Syslog Daemon as a syslog server.
- Configure local buffering on a router.

Figure 5-20 illustrates the topology that is used for this lab.

Figure 5-20   Topology Diagram

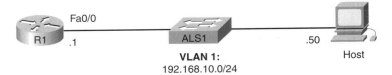

Scenario

In this lab, you configure a router to log system messages and notifications to a syslog server. You also view the logs on the syslog server.

Step 1: Configure the Interface

Configure the router interface shown in Figure 5-20:

```
R1(config)# interface fastethernet0/0
R1(config-if)# ip address 192.168.10.1 255.255.255.0
R1(config-if)# no shutdown
```

Apply the IP address shown in Figure 5-20 to the host. If you do not know how to set up an IP address on a host, see Lab 3-1: Configuring SDM on a Router.

Verify that you have connectivity between R1 and the host by using the **ping** command:

```
R1# ping 192.168.10.1

Type escape sequence to abort.
Sending 5, 100-byte ICMP Echos to 192.168.10.1, timeout is 2 seconds:
!!!!!
Success rate is 100 percent (5/5), round-trip min/avg/max = 1/1/4 ms
```

Step 2: Install the Kiwi Syslog Daemon

This lab uses the Kiwi Syslog Daemon, which is a free syslog server for use with Microsoft Windows. If it is not currently installed on the host, download the installer from http://www.kiwisyslog.com. If it is installed, go to Step 3.

As of the time of this writing, two versions of this software exist: a free version and a licensed version. This lab only uses the features found in the free version. When prompted to install the program as a service or application, you can choose whether you want the syslog daemon started automatically as a system service or triggered by user action, such as a normal Windows application. This lab was written using the service installation.

Step 3: Run the Kiwi Syslog Service Manager

Open the Kiwi Syslog Daemon Manager, which can be accessed either by the icon on the host's desktop labeled **Kiwi Syslog Daemon** or by clicking the **Start** button and choosing **Programs > Kiwi Enterprises > Kiwi Syslog Daemon > Kiwi Syslog Daemon** (see Figure 5-21).

Figure 5-21   Kiwi Syslog Daemon Manager Main Window

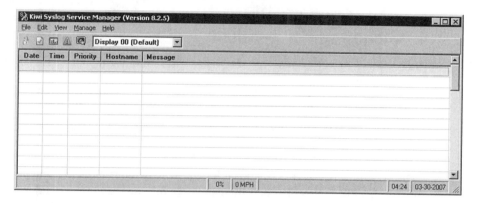

If this is your first time running the program after installing it, choose **Manage > Install the Syslogd service**. You need to start the service if you just installed it, or if you are not sure the service is running. Start the service with **Manage > Start the Syslogd service**. You can check if the service is running by selecting **Manage > Ping the Syslogd service**.

Step 4: Configure the Router for Logging

Configuring a router to use a syslog server is a relatively simple process and requires only a few commands in global configuration mode.

First, configure the IP address of a syslog server with the **logging host** *hostname* command. In this lab, use an IP address instead of a hostname:

```
R1(config)# logging host 192.168.10.50
```

Set the syslog severity level with the global configuration command **logging trap** *level*. You can specify the severity level by either using a keyword or an integer from 0 to 7:

```
R1(config)# logging trap ?
  <0-7>          Logging severity level
  alerts         Immediate action needed      (severity=1)
  critical       Critical conditions          (severity=2)
  debugging      Debugging messages           (severity=7)
  emergencies    System is unusable           (severity=0)
  errors         Error conditions             (severity=3)
  informational  Informational messages       (severity=6)
  notifications  Normal but significant conditions (severity=5)
  warnings       Warning conditions           (severity=4)
  <cr>
```

In order, the severity levels are as follows:

- Emergencies: 0

- Alerts: 1

- Critical: 2

- Errors: 3

- Warnings: 4

- Notifications: 5

- Informational: 6 (default)

- Debugging: 7

Each severity level includes the severity levels with lower numbers. This might seem counter-intuitive, so predict what will happen in this example.

Predict which severity levels of messages would be logged if you issued the following command:

```
Router(config)# logging trap critical
```

The default level is 6 (informational logging). To demonstrate the command, set the logging trap level to informational. Note that the command does not show up in the running configuration, because it is the default:

```
R1(config)# logging trap informational
```

Generate some logging messages for your log server by configuring your device to log users entering and exiting privileged mode with the **logging userinfo** command. When you finish entering commands, enter the **end** command to exit configuration mode. This user action generates a syslog message that the router was just configured. There might also be another syslog message stating that logging to the host just started:

```
R1(config)# logging userinfo
R1(config)# end
R1#
```

```
*Mar 30 08:39:23.458: %SYS-5-CONFIG_I: Configured from console by console
*Mar 30 08:39:24.458: %SYS-6-LOGGINGHOST_STARTSTOP: Logging to host 192.168.10.50
  started - CLI initiated
```

You might also want to verify logging settings with the **show logging** command:

```
R1# show logging
Syslog logging: enabled (11 messages dropped, 1 messages rate-limited,
                0 flushes, 0 overruns, xml disabled, filtering disabled)
    Console logging: level debugging, 46 messages logged, xml disabled,
                     filtering disabled
    Monitor logging: level debugging, 0 messages logged, xml disabled,
                     filtering disabled
```

```
    Buffer logging: disabled, xml disabled,
                    filtering disabled
    Logging Exception size (4096 bytes)
    Count and timestamp logging messages: disabled


No active filter modules.


    Trap logging: level informational, 50 message lines logged
        Logging to 192.168.10.50(global) (udp port 514, audit disabled, link up), 2
            message lines logged, xml disabled,
                    filtering disabled
```

Step 5: Verify Logging

On the host, look at the Kiwi Syslog Daemon Manager. The log messages that were just created are displayed, as shown in Figure 5-22.

Figure 5-22   Informational Log Messages from R1

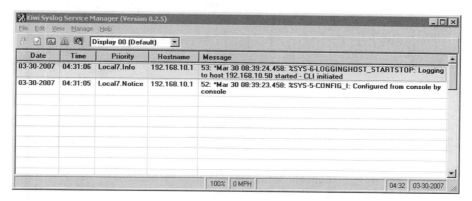

On the router, exit privileged EXEC mode, and then reenter it by using the **enable** command.

Log messages appear on the router and in the Kiwi Syslog Daemon Manager (see Figure 5-23). The reason log messages are generated is because of the **logging userinfo** command you issued earlier:

```
R1# disable

*Mar 30 08:42:26.474: %SYS-5-PRIV_AUTH_PASS: Privilege level set to 1 by unknown on
  console

R1> enable

*Mar 30 08:42:29.686: %SYS-5-PRIV_AUTH_PASS: Privilege level set to 15 by unknown on
  console

R1#
```

Figure 5-23 User Information Log Messages from R1

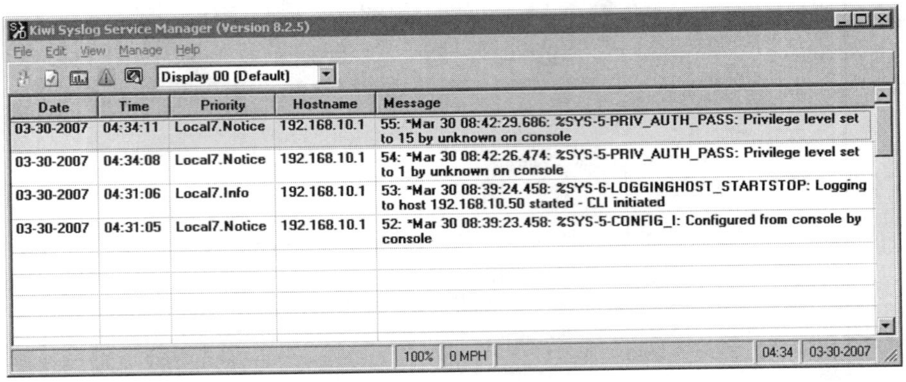

Why it is better to have centralized logging servers rather than only have the routers log locally?

_____

_____

_____

Step 6: Configure Buffered Logging

In cases where you have a small network and do not have a centralized logging server, you might consider buffering logs to a local memory buffer. The commands coincide with those used for the syslog server.

Issue the **logging buffered** [*bytes*] [*severity-level*] command on R1 to begin buffering to the local buffer. Use the informational level and set the buffer size to 32 KB. Exit global configuration mode, which generates a log message:

```
R1(config)# logging buffered 32768 informational
R1(config)# exit
R1#


*Mar 30 14:44:56.968: %SYS-5-CONFIG_I: Configured from console by console
```

Issue the **show logging** command to get general information about the buffer and view the buffer log:

```
R1# show logging
Syslog logging: enabled (11 messages dropped, 1 messages rate-limited,
               0 flushes, 0 overruns, xml disabled, filtering disabled)
    Console logging: level debugging, 54 messages logged, xml disabled,
                     filtering disabled
    Monitor logging: level debugging, 0 messages logged, xml disabled,
                     filtering disabled
    Buffer logging: level informational, 1 messages logged, xml disabled,
                    filtering disabled
    Logging Exception size (4096 bytes)
    Count and timestamp logging messages: disabled
```

```
No active filter modules.


     Trap logging: level informational, 58 message lines logged
         Logging to 192.168.10.50(global) (udp port 514, audit disabled, link up), 6
         message lines logged, xml disabled,

             filtering disabled


Log Buffer (32768 bytes):


*Mar 30 14:44:56.968: %SYS-5-CONFIG_I: Configured from console by console
```

Exit privileged EXEC mode and then reenter it. This generates some user information messages that are saved to the memory buffer:

```
R1# disable


*Mar 30 14:45:22.272: %SYS-5-PRIV_AUTH_PASS: Privilege level set to 1 by unknown on
  console


R1> enable
R1#
*Mar 30 14:45:23.200: %SYS-5-PRIV_AUTH_PASS: Privilege level set to 15 by unknown on
  console
```

Display the contents of the internal buffer again with the **show logging** command:

```
R1# show logging
Syslog logging: enabled (11 messages dropped, 1 messages rate-limited,
                0 flushes, 0 overruns, xml disabled, filtering disabled)
   Console logging: level debugging, 56 messages logged, xml disabled,
                filtering disabled
   Monitor logging: level debugging, 0 messages logged, xml disabled,
                filtering disabled
   Buffer logging: level informational, 3 messages logged, xml disabled,
                filtering disabled
   Logging Exception size (4096 bytes)
   Count and timestamp logging messages: disabled


No active filter modules.


     Trap logging: level informational, 60 message lines logged
         Logging to 192.168.10.50(global) (udp port 514, audit disabled, link up), 8
         message lines logged, xml disabled,

             filtering disabled


Log Buffer (32768 bytes):
```

```
*Mar 30 14:44:56.968: %SYS-5-CONFIG_I: Configured from console by console

*Mar 30 14:45:22.272: %SYS-5-PRIV_AUTH_PASS: Privilege level set to 1 by unknown on
  console

*Mar 30 14:45:23.200: %SYS-5-PRIV_AUTH_PASS: Privilege level set to 15 by unknown on
  console
```

Lab 5-6a: Configuring AAA and TACACS+ (5.12.6a)

The objectives of this lab are as follows:

- Install CiscoSecure ACS.

- Configure CiscoSecure ACS as a TACACS+ server.

- Enable AAA on a router using a remote TACACS+ server.

Figure 5-24 illustrates the topology that is used for this lab.

Figure 5-24   Topology Diagram

VLAN 1:
192.168.10.0/24

Scenario

In this lab, you set up CiscoSecure Access Control Server (ACS) as a TACACS+ server. You also set up R1 to use authentication, authorization, and accounting (AAA) services for line authentication.

Step 1: Configure the Interface

Configure the router interface shown in Figure 5-24:

```
R1(config)# interface fastethernet0/0
R1(config-if)# ip address 192.168.10.1 255.255.255.0
R1(config-if)# no shutdown
```

Configure the IP address of 192.168.10.50/24 on the host.

Verify that you have connectivity between R1 and the host with the **ping** command:

```
R1# ping 192.168.10.1

Type escape sequence to abort.
Sending 5, 100-byte ICMP Echos to 192.168.10.1, timeout is 2 seconds:
!!!!!
Success rate is 100 percent (5/5), round-trip min/avg/max = 1/1/4 ms
```

Step 2: Install CiscoSecure ACS

If you already installed CiscoSecure ACS, go to Step 3.

This step guides you through installing the 90-day trial version of CiscoSecure ACS (see Figure 5-25). After you download the trial and extract it, run Setup.exe.

Note: At the time of this writing, CiscoSecure ACS runs only on Microsoft Windows Server Editions. You cannot run CiscoSecure ACS on Microsoft Windows XP.

Figure 5-25   CiscoSecure ACS Splash Screen

After reading the terms of the license agreement, click **ACCEPT**, as shown in Figure 5-26.

Figure 5-26   CiscoSecure ACS License Agreement

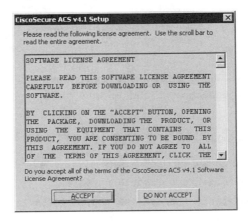

Click **Next** to continue the installation process, as shown in Figure 5-27.

Figure 5-27   CiscoSecure ACS Installation Wizard

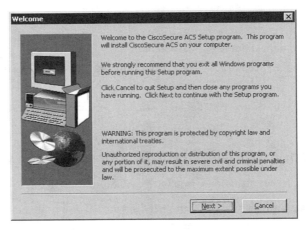

Verify that all the requirements in the checklist are satisfied and check all the options before clicking **Next**, as shown in Figure 5-28.

Figure 5-28   CiscoSecure ACS Preinstallation Checklist

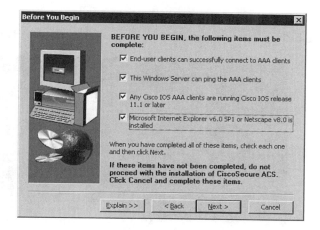

Use the default installation folder and click **Next**, as shown in Figure 5-29.

Figure 5-29   CiscoSecure ACS Installation Location

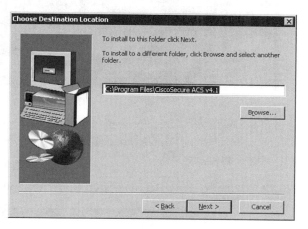

CiscoSecure has the capability to check the Windows User Database. However, for this lab, choose to authenticate using the internal database only. Click **Next**, as shown in Figure 5-30.

Figure 5-30   CiscoSecure ACS Authentication Database Options

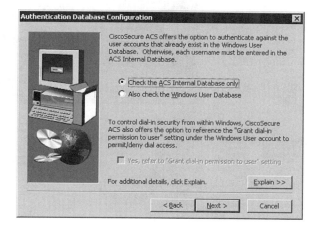

The installer begins copying files and registry keys. This process might take a few minutes, as shown in Figure 5-31.

Figure 5-31   CiscoSecure ACS Installation Progress Indicator

At the end of the installer, you are prompted whether you want to see any advanced configuration options in the user interface. You do not need to select any of these. Click **Next** after reviewing the options, as shown in Figure 5-32.

Figure 5-32   CiscoSecure ACS Advanced Configuration Options

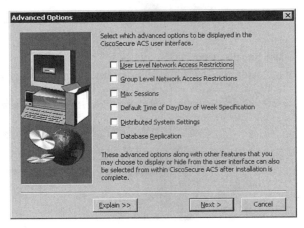

Keep the default settings in the next step of the installation wizard and click **Next**, as shown in Figure 5-33.

Figure 5-33   CiscoSecure ACS Log-In

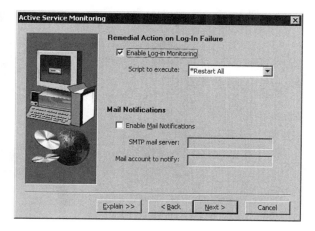

You must create a password for ACS internal database encryption. It must be at least eight characters and contain both letters and numbers. In the following example, ciscoacs4 is the password. After configuring the password, click **Next**, as shown in Figure 5-34.

Figure 5-34   CiscoSecure ACS Password Configuration

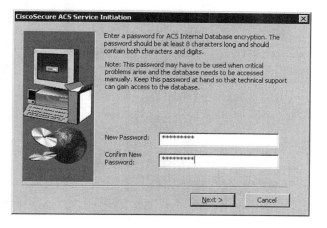

Choose to start the ACS service on the host now. You should also select the option to start the administration window after the installer ends to verify the installation. Click **Next** after selecting the options, as shown in Figure 5-35.

Figure 5-35   CiscoSecure ACS Service Configuration

Read the instructions and click **Finish**, as shown in Figure 5-36. Also, make sure your computer is compliant with all ACS access requirements, complying with the supported versions of Internet Explorer and the Java Runtime Environment.

Figure 5-36   CiscoSecure ACS Installation Complete Window

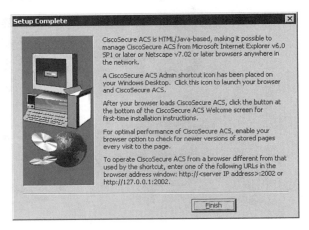

If the CiscoSecure ACS administrative screen comes up when the installer ends, it was successfully installed.

Step 3: Configure Users in CiscoSecure ACS

If CiscoSecure ACS is not open, start it by clicking the **Start** button and choosing **Programs > CiscoSecure ACS v4.1 Trial > ACS Admin**. The ACS home page will appear as shown in Figure 5-37.

Figure 5-37   ACS Home Page

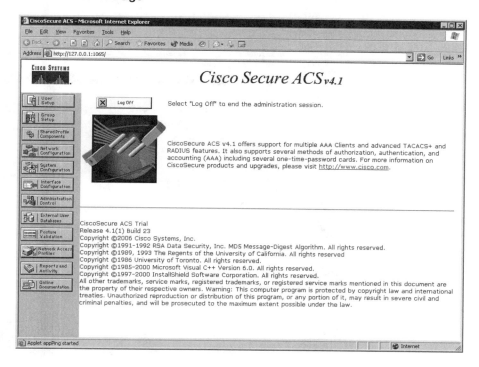

Click the **Network Configuration** button on the left side, as shown in Figure 5-38. On this screen, you can directly configure AAA clients. Click **Add Entry** under the heading AAA Clients.

Figure 5-38   ACS Network Configuration Page

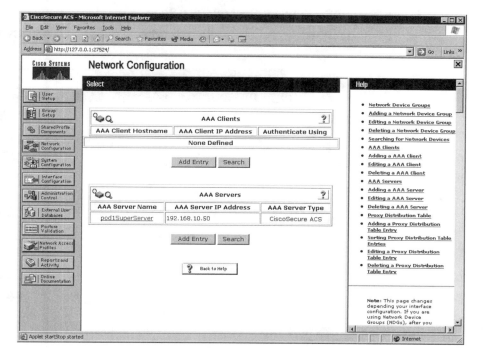

Configure R1 as a TACACS+ client, and then click **Submit + Apply**, as shown in Figure 5-39.

Figure 5-39   ACS AAA Client Configuration

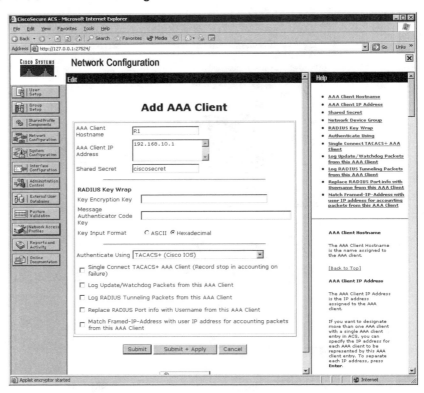

You should now see R1 listed as a AAA client on the network configuration screen (see Figure 5-40).

Figure 5-40   ACS Network Configuration Page, with Changes Applied

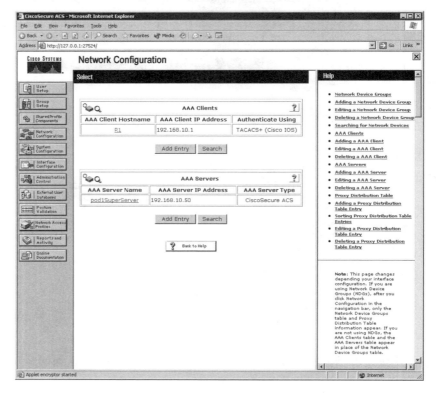

Click the **User Setup** button on the left side. Add a user named cisco, and then click **Add/Edit**, as shown in Figure 5-41.

Figure 5-41   ACS User Configuration Page

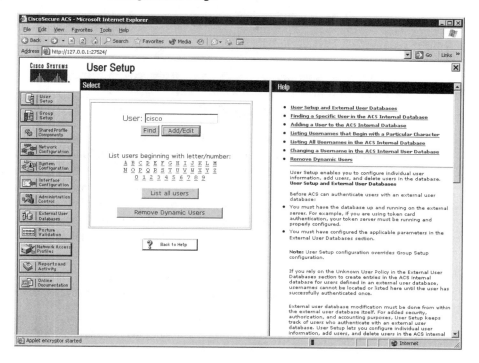

Assign the real name to be your own name, and set the password to cisco. Click **Submit**, as shown in Figure 5-42.

Figure 5-42   ACS Add New User Page

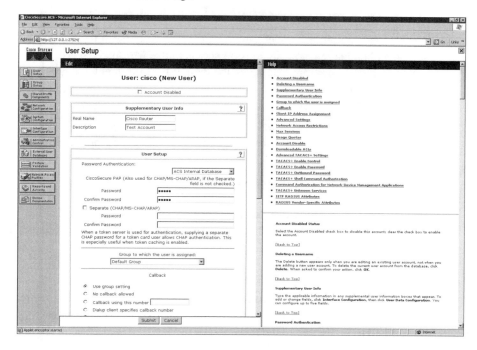

Why would a company want to use a centralized authentication server rather than configuring users and passwords on each individual router?

_____

_____

_____

_____

Step 4: Configure AAA Services on R1

On R1, enable AAA with the **aaa new-model** command in global configuration mode. Then, set up the default login authentication list with the **aaa authentication login default** *method1* [*method2*] [*method3*] command. You can create a list of authentication methods. Configure the list to first use TACACS+ for the authentication service, and then enter the **none** keyword. If no TACACS+ server can be reached and authentication cannot be performed, the router globally allows access without authentication. This is a safeguard measure in case the router starts up without connectivity to an active TACACS+ server. Alternatively, you could configure local authentication as the backup authentication method:

```
R1(config)# aaa new-model
R1(config)# aaa authentication login default group tacacs+ none
```

Caution: If you do not set up a default login authentication list, you could get locked out of the router and need to use the password recovery procedure for your specific router.

Specify a TACACS+ server by using the **tacacs-server host** *hostname* **key** *key* command. The *hostname* parameter accepts either a hostname or an IP address. *key* is a secret password shared between the TACACS+ server and the AAA client; it encrypts the TCP connection between the authenticator and the TACACS+ authentication server:

```
R1(config)# tacacs-server host 192.168.10.50 key ciscosecret
```

Next, create a unique authentication list for Telnet access to the router. This does not have the fallback of no authentication, so if there is no access to the TACACS+ server, Telnet access is disabled. To create an authentication list that is not the default list, use the global configuration command **aaa authentication login** *name method1* [*method2*] [*method3*]. Name the authentication method list telnet_lines. To apply the list to vtys on the router, issue the **login authentication** *name* command in line-configuration mode:

```
R1(config)# aaa authentication login telnet_lines group tacacs+
R1(config)# line vty 0 4
R1(config-line)# login authentication telnet_lines
```

Given the configuration just described, if you enter a username and password pair stored in the ACS authentication database, and the router can reach and use the authentication methods available through TACACS+, would the user be permitted to access the router?

_____

If you enter a username and password pair not stored in the ACS authentication database and the router can reach and use the authentication methods available through TACACS+, would the user be permitted to access the router?

_____

If you entered a username and password pair stored in the ACS authentication database, but the router could not reach a TACACS+ server, would the user be permitted to access the router?

_____

_____

You can test your configuration by opening a Telnet session from the host to R1 (see Figure 5-43). Click the **Start** button and choose **Run**. Enter the **cmd** command in the Run dialog box, and click **OK**. At the command prompt, issue the **telnet** *host* command. At the login prompt (shown in Figure 5-44), use the login credentials created earlier: The username and password are both cisco.

Figure 5-43   Host Telnets to R1

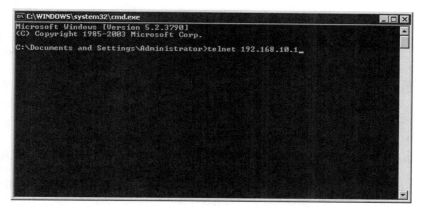

Figure 5-44   Test AAA Authentication Using Telnet

If your session with the router console port times out, you might have to log in using the default authentication list.

Which authentication database does the current default authentication list query?

_____

_____

Why is it advisable to assign redundant authentication methods when using AAA?

_____

Lab 5-6b: Configuring AAA and RADIUS (5.12.6b)

The objectives of this lab are as follows:

- Install CiscoSecure ACS.

- Configure CiscoSecure ACS as a RADIUS server.

- Enable AAA on a router using a remote RADIUS server.

Figure 5-45 illustrates the topology that is used for this lab.

Figure 5-45   Topology Diagram

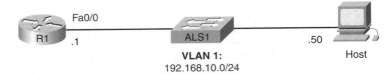

Scenario

In this lab, you set up CiscoSecure ACS as a RADIUS server. You also set up R1 to use AAA with reference to the RADIUS server. Because RADIUS is an open, standards-based protocol, many implementations are available. This lab shows how to configure CiscoSecure ACS. However, you could use a different RADIUS software solution. If you use another RADIUS solution, configure the server similarly to the configuration used for ACS. The router configuration is the same regardless of the software server used.

Step 1: Configure the Interface

Configure the router interface shown in Figure 5-45:

```
R1(config)# interface fastethernet0/0
R1(config-if)# ip address 192.168.10.1 255.255.255.0
R1(config-if)# no shutdown
```

Configure the IP address of 192.168.10.50/24 on the host.

Verify that you have connectivity between R1 and the host by using the **ping** command:

```
R1# ping 192.168.10.1

Type escape sequence to abort.
Sending 5, 100-byte ICMP Echos to 192.168.10.1, timeout is 2 seconds:
!!!!!
Success rate is 100 percent (5/5), round-trip min/avg/max = 1/1/4 ms
```

Step 2: Install CiscoSecure ACS

If you already installed CiscoSecure ACS, go to Step 3.

This step guides you through installing the 90-day trial version of CiscoSecure ACS (see Figure 5-46). After you download the trial and extract it, run Setup.exe.

Note: At the time of this writing, CiscoSecure ACS runs only on Microsoft Windows Server Editions. You cannot run CiscoSecure ACS on Microsoft Windows XP.

Figure 5-46   CiscoSecure ACS Splash Screen

After reading the terms of the license agreement, click **ACCEPT**, as shown in Figure 5-47.

Figure 5-47   CiscoSecure ACS License Agreement

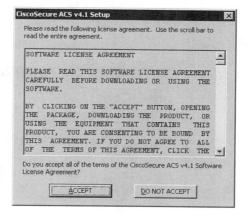

Click **Next** to continue the installation process, as shown in Figure 5-48.

Figure 5-48   CiscoSecure ACS Installation Wizard

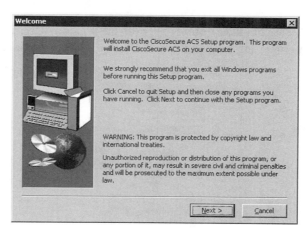

Verify that all the requirements in the checklist are satisfied and check all the options before clicking **Next**, as shown in Figure 5-49.

Figure 5-49   CiscoSecure ACS Preinstallation Checklist

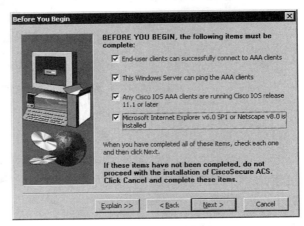

Use the default installation folder and click **Next**, as shown in Figure 5-50.

Figure 5-50   CiscoSecure ACS Installation Location

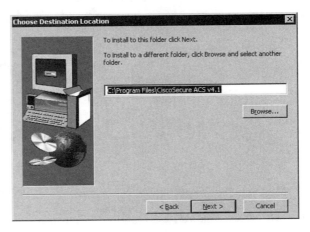

CiscoSecure has the capability to check the Windows User Database. However, for this lab, choose to authenticate using only the internal database. Click **Next**, as shown in Figure 5-51.

Figure 5-51   CiscoSecure ACS Authentication Database Options

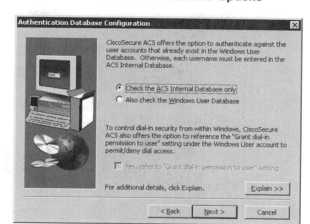

The installer begins copying files and registry keys. This process might take a few minutes (see Figure 5-52).

Figure 5-52   CiscoSecure ACS Installation Progress Indicator

At the end of the installer, you are prompted whether you want to see any advanced configuration options in the user interface. You do not need to select any of these. Click **Next** after reviewing the options, as shown in Figure 5-53.

Figure 5-53   CiscoSecure ACS Advanced Configuration Options

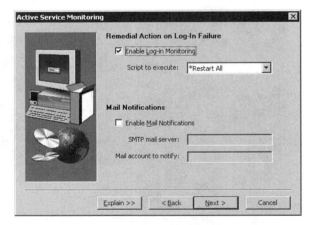

Keep the default settings in the next step of the installation wizard and click **Next**, as shown in Figure 5-54.

Figure 5-54   CiscoSecure ACS Login

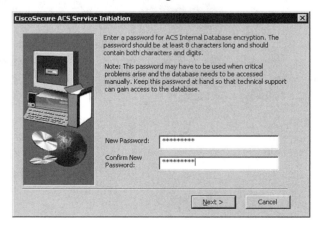

You must create a password for ACS internal database encryption. It must be at least eight characters and contain both letters and numbers. In the following example, ciscoacs4 is the password. After configuring the password, click **Next**, as shown in Figure 5-55.

Figure 5-55   CiscoSecure ACS Password Configuration

Choose to start the ACS service on the host now. You should also select the option to start the administration window after the installer ends to verify the installation. Click **Next** after selecting the options, as shown in Figure 5-56.

Figure 5-56   CiscoSecure ACS Service Configuration

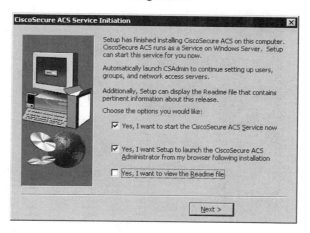

Read the instructions and click **Finish**, as shown in Figure 5-57. Also, make sure your computer is compliant with all ACS access requirements, complying with the supported versions of Internet Explorer and the Java Runtime Environment.

Figure 5-57   CiscoSecure ACS Installation Complete Window

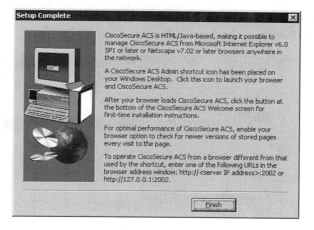

If the CiscoSecure ACS administrative screen comes up when the installer ends, it was successfully installed.

Step 3: Configure Users in CiscoSecure ACS

If the CiscoSecure ACS application is not open, start it by clicking the **Start** button and choosing **Programs > CiscoSecure ACS v4.1 Trial > ACS Admin**. The ACS home page will appear as shown in Figure 5-58.

Figure 5-58   ACS Home Page

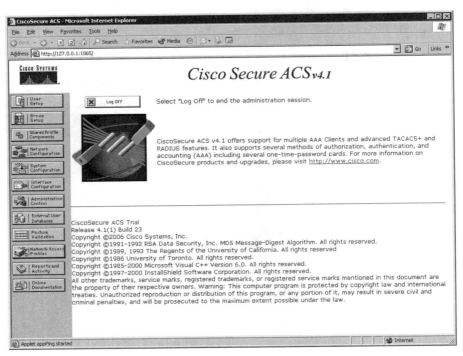

Click the **Network Configuration** button on the left side. On this screen, you can directly configure AAA clients. Click **Add Entry** under the heading AAA Clients, as shown in Figure 5-59.

Figure 5-59   ACS Network Configuration Page

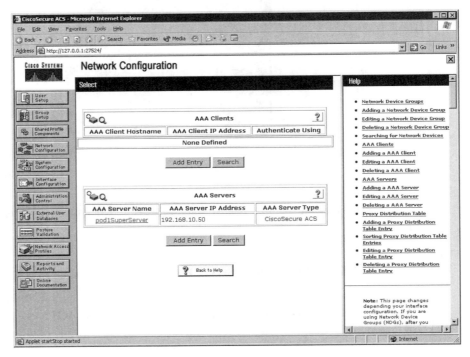

Configure R1 as a RADIUS client, and then click **Submit + Apply**, as shown in Figure 5-60.

Figure 5-60   ACS AAA Client Configuration

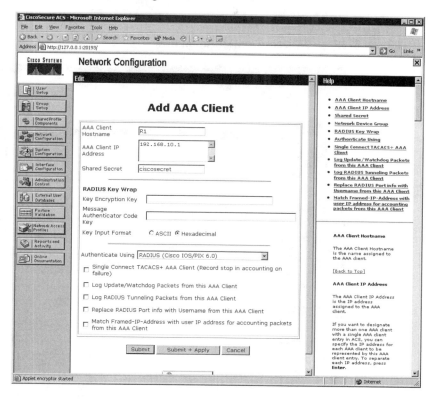

You should now see R1 listed as a AAA client on the network configuration screen, as shown in Figure 5-61.

Figure 5-61   ACS Network Configuration Page, with Changes Applied

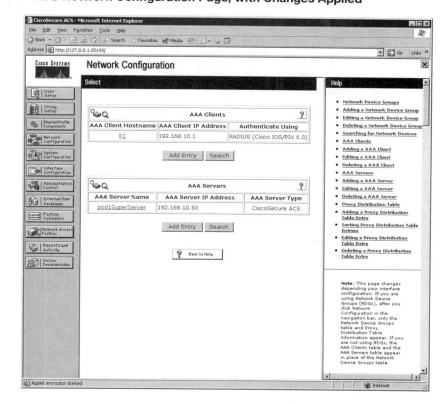

Click the **User Setup** button on the left side. Add a user named cisco, and then click **Add/Edit**, as shown in Figure 5-62.

Figure 5-62 ACS User Configuration Page

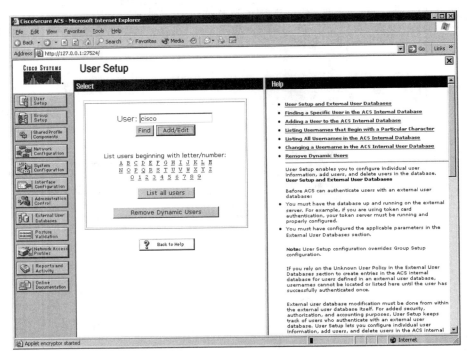

Assign the real name to be your own name, and set the password to cisco. Click **Submit**, as shown in Figure 5-63.

Figure 5-63 ACS Add New User Page

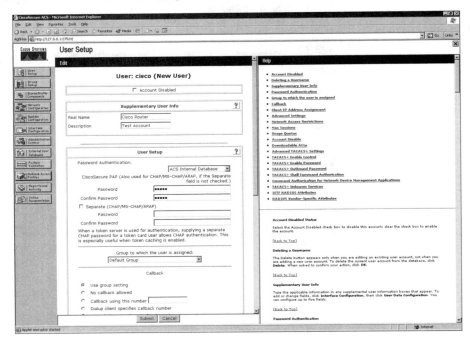

Why would a company want to use a centralized authentication server rather than configuring users and passwords on each individual router?

_____

_____

_____

Step 4: Configure AAA Services on R1

On R1, enable AAA with the **aaa new-model** command in global configuration mode. Then, set up the default login authentication list with the **aaa authentication login default** *method1* [*method2*] [*method3*] command. You can create a list of authentication methods. Configure the list to first use RADIUS for the authentication service, and then enter the **none** keyword. If no RADIUS server can be reached and authentication cannot be performed, the router globally allows access without authentication. This is a safeguard measure in case the router starts up without connectivity to an active RADIUS server. Alternatively, you could configure local authentication as the backup authentication method:

```
R1(config)# aaa new-modelR1(config)# aaa authentication login default group radius
  none
```

Caution: If you do not set up a default login authentication list, you could get locked out of the router and need to use the password recovery procedure for your specific router.

Specify a RADIUS server by using the **radius-server host** *hostname* **key** *key* command. The *hostname* parameter accepts either a hostname or an IP address. *key* is a secret password shared between the RADIUS server and the AAA client; it authenticates the connection between the router and the server before the user authentication process takes place:

```
R1(config)# radius-server host 192.168.10.50 key ciscosecret
```

Next, create a unique authentication list for Telnet access to the router. This does not have the fallback of no authentication, so if there is no access to the RADIUS server, Telnet access is disabled. To create an authentication list that is not the default list, use the global configuration command **aaa authentication login** *name method1* [*method2*] [*method3*]. Name the authentication method list telnet_lines. To apply the list to vtys on the router, issue the **login authentication** *name* command in line-configuration mode:

```
R1(config)# aaa authentication login telnet_lines group radius
R1(config)# line vty 0 4
R1(config-line)# login authentication telnet_lines
```

Given the configuration just described, if you enter a username and password pair stored in the ACS authentication database, and the router can reach and use the authentication methods available through RADIUS, would the user be permitted to access the router?

If you enter a username and password pair not stored in the ACS authentication database and the router can reach and use the authentication methods available through RADIUS, would the user be permitted to access the router?

If you entered a username and password pair stored in the ACS authentication database, but the router could not reach a RADIUS server, would the user be permitted to access the router?

_____

_____

You can test your configuration by opening a Telnet session from the host to R1 (see Figure 5-64). Click the **Start** button and choose **Run**. Enter the **cmd** command in the Run dialog box, and click **OK**. At the command prompt, issue the **telnet** *host* command. At the login prompt (shown in Figure 5-65), use the login credentials created earlier: The username and password are both cisco.

Figure 5-64   Host Telnets to R1

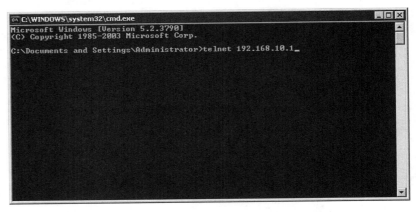

Figure 5-65   Test AAA Authentication Using Telnet

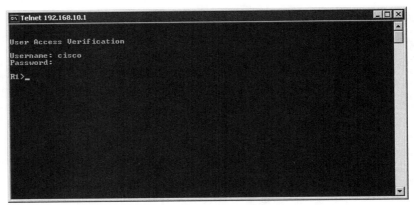

If your session with the router console port times out, you might have to log in using the default authentication list.

Which authentication database does the current default authentication list query?

_____

_____

Why is it advisable to assign redundant authentication methods when using AAA?

_____

Lab 5-6c: Configuring AAA Using Local Authentication (5.12.6c)

The objectives of this lab are as follows:

- Create a local user database on a router.

- Configure AAA on a router.

Figure 5-66 illustrates the topology that is used for this lab.

Figure 5-66   Topology Diagram

Step 1: Configure the Interface

Configure the physical interface on R1 and R2 with the IP addresses shown in Figure 5-66. Issue the **no shutdown** command to activate the interface:

```
R1(config)# interface fastethernet0/0
R1(config-if)# ip address 192.168.10.1 255.255.255.0
R1(config-if)# no shutdown
```
```
R2(config)# interface fastethernet0/0
R2(config-if)# ip address 192.168.10.2 255.255.255.0
R2(config-if)# no shutdown
```

Step 2: Configure the Local User Database

On R1, configure a user account in the local user database with the username and password of cisco using the **username** *username* **password** *password* command in global configuration mode:

```
R1(config)# username cisco password cisco
```

Step 3: Implement AAA Services

On R1, enable AAA services with the global configuration command **aaa new-model**. Because you're implementing local authentication, use local authentication as the first method and no authentication as the secondary method. Create the default login authentication list by issuing the **aaa authentication login default** *methods* command with a method list using the **local** and **none** keywords.

If you were using an authentication method with a remote server, such as TACACS+ or RADIUS, you would configure a secondary authentication method for fallback if the server is unreachable. Normally, the secondary method would be the local database. In this case, if no usernames are configured in the local database, the router allows all users login access to the device:

```
R1(config)# aaa new-model
R1(config)# aaa authentication login default local none
```

Caution: If you do not set up a default login authentication list, you could get locked out of the router and be forced to use the password recovery procedure for your specific router.

Next, create a unique authentication list for Telnet access to the router. This does not have the fallback of no authentication, so if there are no usernames in the local database, Telnet access is disabled. To create an authentication list that is not the default list, use the **aaa authentication login** *name method1* [*method2*] [*method3*] command. Name the authentication method list telnet_lines. To apply the authentication list to vtys, use the **login authentication** *name* command in line-configuration mode:

```
R1(config)# aaa authentication login telnet_lines local
R1(config)# line vty 0 4
R1(config-line)# login authentication telnet_lines
```

Verify that this authentication list is used by opening a Telnet session from R2 to R1:

```
R2# telnet 192.168.10.1
Trying 192.168.10.1 ... Open


User Access Verification


Username: cisco
Password: cisco


R1> exit


[Connection to 192.168.10.1 closed by foreign host]
R2#
```

If you can log in to the router, your user account was verified against the local database on the router.

If your session with the console port of the router times out, you might have to log in using the default authentication list.

If no user accounts are configured in the local database, which users are permitted to access the device?

Lab 5-7: Configuring Role-Based CLI Views (5.12.7)

The objectives of this lab are as follows:

- Configure prerequisites to role-based views.

- Enable AAA on a router.

- Change views on a router.

- Create views and superviews.

Figure 5-67 illustrates the topology that is used for this lab.

Figure 5-67   Topology Diagram

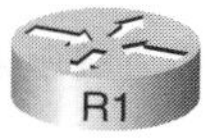

Scenario

In Lab 5-4: Enhancing Router Security, you assigned privilege levels to specific commands entered at the command-line interface (CLI) prompt. Users receive authorization for different command sets by authenticating with a password.

In this lab, you configure role-based CLI views, which is a newer method of controlling the Cisco IOS commands a user can execute. To complete this lab, you need to run version 12.4 of IOS with an AdvancedIPServices image.

Step 1: Configure an Enable Secret Password

Set the R1 enable secret password to **cisco**:

```
R1(config)# enable secret cisco
```

Step 2: Enable AAA

One of the requirements for configuring role-based CLI views is enabling authentication, authorization, and accounting (AAA) services. To begin, create a user account in the local database with the username and password cisco. The local database should be the only login authentication method in use. If you do not set a default login method list when enabling AAA, you might get locked out of the router if your EXEC session on the console line terminates. For more information on configuring AAA with a local database, see Lab 5-6c: Configuring AAA Using Local Authentication.

```
R1(config)# username cisco password cisco
R1(config)# aaa new-model
R1(config)# aaa authentication login default local
```

When are you prompted to enter a username and password?

_____

_____

If no user accounts are configured in the local database, are users able to log in?

_____

Describe the concept of authentication in terms of networking and standard authentication types.

_____

_____

_____

_____

Describe the concept of authorization in terms of networking and common items in need of authorization.

_____

_____

Step 3: Change to the Root View

Role-based CLI views constitute a system of configuring individual roles on a router. Each role has access to a specific group of commands. Configuring roles to control command usage is more granular than configuring privilege levels, because giving more commands to a single user does not necessarily mean that the user is authorized to access commands at a lower privilege commands. This method of configuring command usage is newer—introduced in the Cisco IOS 12.3T software train. As of the time of this writing, you might configure up to 15 views on a router, not including the root view.

To show the current view, use the **show parser view** command. Compare this output to that of the **show privilege** command:

```
R1# show privilege
Current privilege level is 15


R1# show parser view
No view is active ! Currently in Privilege Level Context
```

Available command sets are determined by either privilege level or by the view being used, but not both simultaneously.

To configure the views feature, you must first access the root view, which is not the same as being privilege level 15. Like the root user on a UNIX system, the root view has full authorization to all CLI commands. Issue the **enable view** name command using the **root** keyword in the name field.

Take special note that the root view password is the same as the enable password. Notice that a message is logged when the view is changed. After entering the root view, display the privilege level and view:

```
R1# enable view root
Password: cisco


R1#


*Feb 12 05:09:06.442: %PARSER-6-VIEW_SWITCH: successfully set to view 'root'.


R1# show privilege
Currently in View Context with view 'root'
R1# show parser view
Current view is 'root'
```

Why must command authorization be managed by *either* views or privilege levels?

_____

_____

Step 4: Create Views

The role-based view feature is fairly simple to implement. To create a view, issue the **parser view** *name* command in global configuration mode. An informational message that a new view has been created is logged to the console.

Create a view named INTVIEW, which has monitoring capabilities for physical and logical interfaces. Before defining the view's command set, you must set a password for the view by using the view configuration **secret** *password* command. The password is stored as an message digest algorithm 5 (MD5) hash value. Use iv as the password. Choose commands for the view by using the **commands** *prompt* **include** *command-sequence* command. Assign this view access to two commands, **show interface** and **clear counters**:

```
R1(config)# parser view INTVIEW
R1(config-view)#
*Feb 12 05:12:32.954: %PARSER-6-VIEW_CREATED: view 'INTVIEW' successfully created.
R1(config-view)# secret iv
R1(config-view)# commands exec include show interface
R1(config-view)# commands exec include clear counters
```

Before logging into the new view, display the commands that were just added:

```
R1# show run | section view
parser view INTVIEW
 secret 5 $1$CPI4$HIAH8aEqPztTPW0VLBYT60
 commands exec include show interfaces
 commands exec include show
 commands exec include clear counters
 commands exec include clear
```

When you assign a privilege level to a command sequence, each keyword in the sequence must have a corresponding **privilege** command in the configuration. Similarly, role-based view command sequences must also explicitly allow sequenced keywords in CLI commands, because of the manner in which the parser handles commands.

Log in to the INTVIEW view with the **enable view** *name* command using the iv password, and then enter **?** to view the available command set:

```
R1# enable view INTVIEW
Password: iv

R1#

*Feb 12 05:32:31.106: %PARSER-6-VIEW_SWITCH: successfully set to view 'INTVIEW'.

R1# ?
Exec commands:
```

```
  clear   Reset functions
  enable  Turn on privileged commands
  exit    Exit from the EXEC
  show    Show running system information
```

R1# **show ?**
```
  flash:      display information about flash: file system
  interfaces  Interface status and configuration
  parser      Display parser information
```

R1# **show interfaces**
```
FastEthernet0/0 is administratively down, line protocol is down
  Hardware is MV96340 Ethernet, address is 0019.0623.4380 (bia 0019.0623.4380)
  MTU 1500 bytes, BW 100000 Kbit, DLY 100 usec,
     reliability 255/255, txload 1/255, rxload 1/255
<OUTPUT OMITTED>
```

R1# **clear ?**
```
  counters  Clear counters on one or all interfaces
```

R1# **clear counters**
```
Clear "show interface" counters on all interfaces [confirm]
R1#
```

```
*Feb 12 05:32:55.318: %CLEAR-5-COUNTERS: Clear counter on all interfaces by console
```

Log out of the INTVIEW view and log in to the root view before proceeding:

R1# **enable view root**
Password: **cisco**

```
R1#
*Feb 12 05:35:25.174: %PARSER-6-VIEW_SWITCH: successfully set to view 'root'.
```

Create another view named INTSHUT, and assign this view access to the **shutdown** and **no shutdown** commands for the Fast Ethernet interfaces and the menus necessary to configure these commands. Make the password for this view "is." If your router has different ports, use any two existing ports on the router.

Which commands do you have to add to this view to allow the access just defined?

_____

_____

Enter these commands as follows:

```
R1(config)# parser view INTSHUT
R1(config-view)#

*Feb 12 05:36:37.738: %PARSER-6-VIEW_CREATED: view 'INTSHUT' successfully created.

R1(config-view)# secret is
R1(config-view)# commands exec include configure terminal
R1(config-view)# commands configure include interface
R1(config-view)# commands configure include interface fastethernet0/0
R1(config-view)# commands configure include interface fastethernet0/1
R1(config-view)# commands interface include shutdown
R1(config-view)# commands interface include no shutdown
```

Enter this new view to test out its privileges. Again, use ? to view the available command set:

```
R1# configure terminal
Enter configuration commands, one per line.  End with CNTL/Z.
R1(config)# ?
Configure commands:
  do        To run exec commands in config mode
  exit      Exit from configure mode
  interface Select an interface to configure

R1(config)# interface fastethernet0/0
R1(config-if)# ?
Interface configuration commands:
  exit      Exit from interface configuration mode
  no        Negate a command or set its defaults
  shutdown  Shutdown the selected interface

R1(config-if)# no shutdown
R1(config-if)#

*Feb 12 06:28:36.394: %LINK-3-UPDOWN: Interface FastEthernet0/0, changed state to up
*Feb 12 06:28:37.394: %LINEPROTO-5-UPDOWN: Line protocol on Interface
   FastEthernet0/0, changed state to up

R1(config-if)#shutdown
```

Return to the root view:

```
R1# enable view root
Password: cisco

R1#
```

Step 5: Create a Superview

A superview is the union of one or more regular views. It is created like a regular view, but you use the superview keyword to define it. Name this superview INTADMIN with the password ia. Finally, add the two existing views to this superview by using the **view** *name* command:

```
R1(config)# parser view INTADMIN superview
R1(config-view)#


*Feb 12 06:35:06.566: %PARSER-6-SUPER_VIEW_CREATED: super view 'INTADMIN'
  successfully created.


R1(config-view)# secret ia
R1(config-view)# view INTVIEW


*Feb 12 06:35:21.086: %PARSER-6-SUPER_VIEW_EDIT_ADD: view INTVIEW added to superview
  INTADMIN.


R1(config-view)# view INTSHUT


*Feb 12 06:35:29.594: %PARSER-6-SUPER_VIEW_EDIT_ADD: view INTSHUT added to superview
  INTADMIN.
```

While still in the root view, display the available parser views and superviews with the **show parser view all** command:

```
R1# show parser view all
Views/SuperViews Present in System:
 INTVIEW
 INTSHUT
 INTADMIN *
-------(*) represent superview-------
R1#
```

Enter this view and see the available executable commands:

```
R1# enable view INTADMIN
Password:


R1#
*Feb 12 06:36:31.774: %PARSER-6-VIEW_SWITCH: successfully set to view 'INTADMIN'.
R1# ?
Exec commands:
  clear      Reset functions
  configure  Enter configuration mode
  enable     Turn on privileged commands
  exit       Exit from the EXEC
  show       Show running system information'
```

Lab 5-8: Configuring NTP (5.12.8)

The objectives of this lab are as follows:

- Configure a router as an NTP master server.

- Configure an NTP server on a router.

- Configure an NTP peer.

- Implement NTP authentication.

Figure 5-68 illustrates the topology that is used for this lab.

Figure 5-68   Topology Diagram

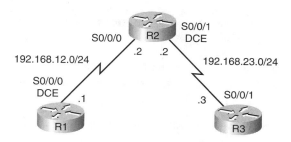

Scenario

In this lab, you configure Network Time Protocol (NTP) in a small topology. NTP is essential in a large network, because it reduces administrative overhead and allows for consistent times throughout the network for logging and other time-related features, such as crypto certificate lifetimes.

Step 1: Configure the Physical Interfaces

Configure the loopback interfaces with the addresses shown in Figure 5-68. Also, configure the serial interfaces shown in the figure. Set the clock rate on the appropriate interface, and issue the **no shutdown** command on all serial connections. Verify that you have connectivity across the local subnet by using the **ping** command:

```
R1(config)# interface serial0/0/0
R1(config-if)# ip address 192.168.12.1 255.255.255.0
R1(config-if)# clockrate 64000
R1(config-if)# no shutdown
```
```
R2(config)# interface serial0/0/0
R2(config-if)# ip address 192.168.12.2 255.255.255.0
R2(config-if)# no shutdown
R2(config-if)# interface serial0/0/1
R2(config-if)# ip address 192.168.23.2 255.255.255.0
R2(config-if)# clockrate 64000
R2(config-if)# no shutdown
```
```
R3(config)# interface serial0/0/1
R3(config-if)# ip address 192.168.23.3 255.255.255.0
R3(config-if)# no shutdown
```

Step 2: Set Up the NTP Master

R1 is the master NTP server in this lab. All other routers learn their time from it, either directly or indirectly. For this reason, you must first ensure that R1 has the correct Coordinated Universal Time set.

Display the current time set on the router by using the **show clock** command. To set the time on the router, use the **clock set** *time* command:

```
R1# show clock
*07:20:19.267 UTC Mon Feb 12 2007


R1# clock set 07:20:30 feb 12 2007
R1#
*Feb 12 07:20:30.000: %SYS-6-CLOCKUPDATE: System clock has been updated from 07:20:39
  UTC Mon Feb 12 2007 to 07:20:30 UTC Mon Feb 12 2007, configured from
  console by console.
```

Configure R1 as the NTP master by using the **ntp master** *stratum* command in global configuration mode. The stratum number indicates the distance from the original source. For this lab, use a stratum number of 5 on R1.

When a device learns the time from an NTP source, its stratum number becomes one greater than its source's stratum number:

```
R1(config)# ntp master 5
```

Step 3: Configure an NTP Client

R2 becomes an NTP client of R1. To configure R2, use the global configuration command **ntp server** *hostname*. The hostname can also be an IP address:

```
R2(config)# ntp server 192.168.12.1
```

After a while, verify that R2 has made an association with R1 with the **show ntp association** command. You can also use the more verbose version of the command by adding the **detail** argument. It might take some time for the NTP association to form:

```
R2# show ntp associations

    address         ref clock     st  when  poll reach  delay  offset   disp
*~192.168.12.1   127.127.7.1       5    24    64  377   23.1    0.72    0.5
 * master (synced), # master (unsynced), + selected, - candidate, ~ configured


R2# show ntp associations detail
192.168.12.1 configured, our_master, sane, valid, stratum 5
ref ID 127.127.7.1, time C97A9634.A5E51ED1 (07:31:00.648 UTC Mon Feb 12 2007)
our mode client, peer mode server, our poll intvl 64, peer poll intvl 64
root delay 0.00 msec, root disp 0.03, reach 377, sync dist 12.039
delay 23.09 msec, offset 0.7242 msec, dispersion 0.47
precision 2**18, version 3
org time C97A9643.CF0A3D1F (07:31:15.808 UTC Mon Feb 12 2007)
rcv time C97A9643.D1CFC661 (07:31:15.819 UTC Mon Feb 12 2007)
xmt time C97A9643.CBE4198B (07:31:15.796 UTC Mon Feb 12 2007)
```

```
filtdelay =    23.09  23.28  23.13  23.24  23.16  23.22  23.35  23.28
filtoffset =    0.72   0.44   0.07   0.06   0.04   0.06   0.05  -0.01
filterror =     0.02   0.99   1.97   1.98   2.00   2.01   2.03   2.04
```

Step 4: Configure NTP Peers with MD5 Authentication

In addition to the client-server model, NTP can also function with routers in a peer relationship in which each router synchronizes against its peers. For this scenario, R2 and R3 maintain a peering relationship.

Which security risks can either of these relationships pose?

_____

_____

_____

To avoid a spoofing problem, configure MD5 authentication between the two NTP peers, R2 and R3. Usually, when NTP authentication is configured in a client-server model, the client authenticates the server, but not vice versa. Thus, NTP authentication is *source* authentication; clients do not need to be authenticated because they cannot manipulate the clock on the server.

However, because there is a peering relationship in which each peer might act as a corrector to the other device, each device must be configured as an authenticated NTP source. First, enable NTP authentication with the **ntp authenticate** command in global configuration mode. Next, add an NTP authentication key to the router with the **ntp authentication-key** *number* **md5** *key-string* command. Apply a key number of 1 for the key cisco. Finally, apply the authentication configuration by specifying NTP key number 1 as a trusted NTP source key with the **ntp trusted-key** *number* command:

```
R2(config)# ntp authenticate
R2(config)# ntp authentication-key 1 md5 cisco
R2(config)# ntp trusted-key 1
R3(config)# ntp authenticate
R3(config)# ntp authentication-key 1 md5 cisco
R3(config)# ntp trusted-key 1
```

Configure the NTP peer on R3. NTP peers have a passive side and an active side. You only have to configure the active side (in this case, R3). R2 is listening on the NTP port and forms a peer relationship through this. Do not configure peers on both sides of the peer relationship, or it will not work. One of the devices in the peer relationship must be in active mode and the other device must be in passive mode for proper peer synchronization to occur:

```
R3(config)# ntp peer 192.168.23.2
```

It might take a few moments for the relationship to establish. On each of the three routers, verify NTP status and associations by using the **show ntp status**, **show ntp associations**, and **show ntp associations detail** commands. Notice how the stratum level increases at each hop. Verify that their clocks are indeed synchronized with the **show clock** command:

```
R1# show ntp status
Clock is synchronized, stratum 5, reference is 127.127.7.1
nominal freq is 250.0000 Hz, actual freq is 250.0000 Hz, precision is 2**18
reference time is C97A9B74.A5DF14AD (07:53:24.647 UTC Mon Feb 12 2007)
```

```
clock offset is 0.0000 msec, root delay is 0.00 msec
root dispersion is 0.02 msec, peer dispersion is 0.02 msec
```

R1# **show ntp associations**

address	ref clock	st	when	poll	reach	delay	offset	disp
*~127.127.7.1	127.127.7.1	4	55	64	377	0.0	0.00	0.0

```
 * master (synced), # master (unsynced), + selected, - candidate, ~ configured
```

R1# **show ntp associations detail**

```
127.127.7.1 configured, our_master, sane, valid, stratum 4
ref ID 127.127.7.1, time C97A9B74.A5DF14AD (07:53:24.647 UTC Mon Feb 12 2007)
our mode active, peer mode passive, our poll intvl 64, peer poll intvl 64
root delay 0.00 msec, root disp 0.00, reach 377, sync dist 0.015
delay 0.00 msec, offset 0.0000 msec, dispersion 0.02
precision 2**18, version 3
org time C97A9B74.A5DF14AD (07:53:24.647 UTC Mon Feb 12 2007)
rcv time C97A9B74.A5DF14AD (07:53:24.647 UTC Mon Feb 12 2007)
xmt time C97A9B74.A5DE90AF (07:53:24.647 UTC Mon Feb 12 2007)
filtdelay =     0.00    0.00    0.00    0.00    0.00    0.00    0.00    0.00
filtoffset =    0.00    0.00    0.00    0.00    0.00    0.00    0.00    0.00
filterror =     0.02    0.99    1.97    2.94    3.92    4.90    5.87    6.85
Reference clock status:  Running normally
Timecode:
```

R2# **show ntp status**

```
Clock is synchronized, stratum 6, reference is 192.168.12.1
nominal freq is 250.0000 Hz, actual freq is 249.9998 Hz, precision is 2**18
reference time is C97A9BC3.D3820015 (07:54:43.826 UTC Mon Feb 12 2007)
clock offset is 1.9937 msec, root delay is 23.32 msec
root dispersion is 2.04 msec, peer dispersion is 0.03 msec
```

R2# **show ntp associations**

address	ref clock	st	when	poll	reach	delay	offset	disp
*~192.168.12.1	127.127.7.1	5	14	64	377	23.3	1.99	0.0

```
 * master (synced), # master (unsynced), + selected, - candidate, ~ configured
```

R2# **show ntp associations detail**

```
192.168.12.1 configured, our_master, sane, valid, stratum 5
ref ID 127.127.7.1, time C97A9BB4.A5DEE42C (07:54:28.647 UTC Mon Feb 12 2007)
our mode client, peer mode server, our poll intvl 64, peer poll intvl 64
root delay 0.00 msec, root disp 0.03, reach 377, sync dist 11.902
delay 23.32 msec, offset 1.9937 msec, dispersion 0.03
precision 2**18, version 3
org time C97A9BC3.D1082A4F (07:54:43.816 UTC Mon Feb 12 2007)
```

```
rcv time C97A9BC3.D3820015 (07:54:43.826 UTC Mon Feb 12 2007)
xmt time C97A9BC3.CD87599E (07:54:43.802 UTC Mon Feb 12 2007)
filtdelay =    23.32   23.38   23.21   23.25   23.07   23.18   23.25   23.22
filtoffset =    1.99    1.95    1.99    1.98    1.93    1.98    1.96    1.94
filterror =     0.02    0.99    1.97    2.94    3.92    4.90    5.87    6.85
R3# show ntp status
Clock is synchronized, stratum 7, reference is 192.168.23.2
nominal freq is 250.0000 Hz, actual freq is 250.0000 Hz, precision is 2**18
reference time is C97A9BCF.B82D5269 (07:54:55.719 UTC Mon Feb 12 2007)
clock offset is -1.3696 msec, root delay is 25.59 msec
root dispersion is 3.92 msec, peer dispersion is 0.49 msec

R3# show ntp associations

      address         ref clock      st  when  poll reach  delay  offset    disp
*~192.168.23.2     192.168.12.1       6   27    64   377    2.3   -1.37     0.5
  * master (synced), # master (unsynced), + selected, - candidate, ~ configured

R3# show ntp associations detail
192.168.23.2 configured, our_master, sane, valid, stratum 6
ref ID 192.168.12.1, time C97A9BC3.D3820015 (07:54:43.826 UTC Mon Feb 12 2007)
our mode active, peer mode passive, our poll intvl 64, peer poll intvl 64
root delay 23.32 msec, root disp 2.06, reach 377, sync dist 15.335
delay 2.27 msec, offset -1.3696 msec, dispersion 0.49
precision 2**18, version 3
org time C97A9BCF.B788986A (07:54:55.716 UTC Mon Feb 12 2007)
rcv time C97A9BCF.B82D5269 (07:54:55.719 UTC Mon Feb 12 2007)
xmt time C97A9BCF.B7903BF8 (07:54:55.717 UTC Mon Feb 12 2007)
filtdelay =    2.27    2.26    2.29    2.30    2.29    2.27    2.29    2.26
filtoffset =  -1.37   -1.16   -0.90   -0.49   -0.10   -0.10   -0.09   -0.08
filterror =    0.02    0.99    1.97    2.94    3.92    3.94    3.95    3.97
```

Why would it be good to have routers peering equally rather than a client-server relationship?

CHAPTER 6

Cisco IOS Threat Defense Features

Lab 6-1: Configuring a Cisco IOS Firewall Using SDM (6.6.1)

The objectives of this lab are as follows:

- Use SDM to configure a router as a firewall.

- Understand basic firewall operation.

- Configure basic routing through a firewall.

- Verify firewall parameters using SDM.

Figure 6-1 illustrates the topology that is used for this lab.

Figure 6-1   Topology Diagram

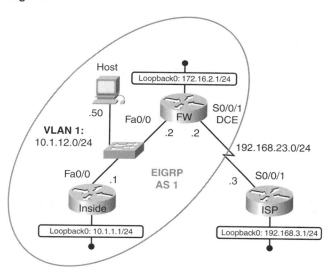

Scenario

In this lab, you configure a perimeter router for International Travel Agency (ITA) using Cisco Security Device Manager (SDM). The SDM firewall wizard allows you to create a relatively strong firewall configuration in a few simple configuration steps.

Each router represents a router in a large corporate network scenario. The ISP router is an ISP edge router connected to the ITA corporate firewall, and the ISP's loopback is a remote Internet network. FW is a corporate firewall router, and its loopback interface is a demilitarized zone (DMZ) where Internet-facing servers reside. INSIDE is an internal corporate router, and its loopback is a subnet within the internal corporate domain.

These labs were written using 2811 routers running the AdvancedIPServices image, version 12.4(10). You should be able to complete these labs using any 12.4 AdvancedIPServices image. You must run a version of IOS that supports the security subset of commands; otherwise, your router will not support the commands in these labs.

Step 1: Configure Loopbacks and Physical Interfaces

Configure the loopback interfaces with the addresses shown in Figure 6-1. Also, configure the serial interfaces. Set the clock rate on the appropriate interface and issue the **no shutdown** command on all serial connections. Verify that you have connectivity across the local subnet by using the **ping** command:

```
INSIDE(config)# interface loopback0
INSIDE(config-if)# ip address 10.1.1.1 255.255.255.0
INSIDE(config-if)# interface fastethernet0/0
INSIDE(config-if)# ip address 10.1.12.1 255.255.255.0
INSIDE(config-if)# no shutdown
```

```
FW(config)# interface loopback0
FW(config-if)# ip address 172.16.2.1 255.255.255.0
FW(config-if)# interface fastethernet0/0
FW(config-if)# ip address 10.1.12.2 255.255.255.0
FW(config-if)# no shutdown
FW(config-if)# interface serial0/0/1
FW(config-if)# ip address 192.168.23.2 255.255.255.0
FW(config-if)# clockrate 64000
FW(config-if)# no shutdown
```

```
ISP(config)# interface loopback0
ISP(config-if)# ip address 192.168.3.1 255.255.255.0
ISP(config-if)# interface serial0/0/1
ISP(config-if)# ip address 192.168.23.3 255.255.255.0
ISP(config-if)# no shutdown
```

Step 2: Configure Routing Protocols

Because this scenario is limited to three routers, be sure that you clearly understand what each major network shown in Figure 6-1 represents.

The 10.0.0.0/8 address space represents the internal network owned and administered by your corporation. Per your security policy, no traffic should enter the internal network from the ISP unless the connection was initiated from inside the firewall.

The connection between FW and ISP is a globally routable subnet in the public address space. Although RFC 1918 defines the 192.168.0.0/16 network as private, consider it as a global address space for the purposes of this lab.

The loopback interface on the FW router is an interface in the DMZ. A DMZ is often used to host web servers and other servers for which users from outside your network can access certain content without authentication or authorization.

Configure Enhanced Interior Gateway Routing Protocol (EIGRP) for AS1 on INSIDE and FW. Advertise the entire 10.0.0.0/8 major network and disable automatic summarization. Also, add the 172.16.0.0 network on FW to advertise it, but categorize the loopback interface as a passive interface, because this is simply a DMZ for servers, not routers. ISP does not participate in this routing process:

```
INSIDE(config)# router eigrp 1
INSIDE(config-router)# no auto-summary
INSIDE(config-router)# network 10.0.0.0
FW(config)# router eigrp 1
FW(config-router)# no auto-summary
FW(config-router)# network 10.0.0.0
FW(config-router)# network 172.16.0.0
FW(config-router)# passive-interface loopback0
```

Define the purpose and operation of a firewall.

_____

_____

_____

_____

Define some basic firewall rules about how traffic should be permitted through a network.

_____

_____

_____

_____

_____

_____

_____

Step 3: Configure Static Routes to Reach the Internet

Because ISP connects to the Internet, send all traffic to networks not in the corporate routing tables to the ISP via a default route. This route can be statically created on FW, but it must be redistributed into EIGRP so that routers on the inside of the firewall can learn the default route:

```
FW(config)# ip route 0.0.0.0 0.0.0.0 192.168.23.3
FW(config)# router eigrp 1
FW(config-router)# redistribute static
```

On ISP, create static routes for the major corporate destination networks. Remember that the 172.16.0.0 network is the company's DMZ, and 10.0.0.0 is its internal network:

```
ISP(config)# ip route 10.0.0.0 255.0.0.0 192.168.23.2
ISP(config)# ip route 172.16.0.0 255.255.0.0 192.168.23.2
```

At this point, you have full IP connectivity between all networks in Figure 6-1. After the FW router is fully configured, there is only partial IP connectivity as a result of implementing security policies:

```
ISP# ping 10.1.1.1

Type escape sequence to abort.
Sending 5, 100-byte ICMP Echos to 10.1.1.1, timeout is 2 seconds:
!!!!!
Success rate is 100 percent (5/5), round-trip min/avg/max = 112/112/112 ms
```

Step 4: Connect to FW Using SDM

Configure the 10.1.12.50/24 IP address on the host by using the FW Fast Ethernet interface as its default gateway. If you do not know how to set the IP address on a host or connect to a router using SDM, see Lab 3-1: Configuring SDM on a Router.

Prepare FW for access via SDM. Remember that SDM uses Secure Shell (SSH) and secure HTTP (HTTPS) technology and must authenticate with the router before configuration can begin:

```
FW(config)# username ciscosdm privilege 15 password ciscosdm
FW(config)# ip http secure-server
FW(config)# ip http authentication local
FW(config)# line vty 0 4
FW(config-line)# transport input telnet ssh
```

Connect to FW by using SDM. After you are connected, your screen displays something similar to Figure 6-2.

Figure 6-2   Cisco SDM Home Screen

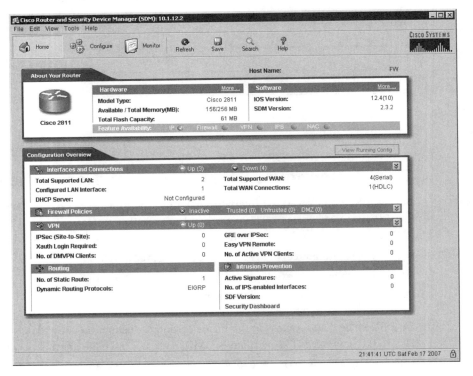

Select **Edit > Preferences**. Make sure that **Preview commands before delivering to router** is checked before continuing, as shown in Figure 6-3. Click **OK** when you finish configuring the preferences.

Figure 6-3   SDM User Preferences

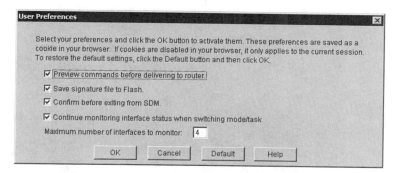

Step 5: Use the SDM Advanced Firewall Wizard

In SDM, start the Advanced Firewall Wizard by clicking **Configure** on the top toolbar and then clicking **Firewall and ACL** on the left-hand toolbar, as shown in Figure 6-4.

On the Create Firewall tab, choose **Advanced Firewall**, and then click **Launch the selected task**.

You do not configure the basic firewall in this lab because it is a less robust version of the advanced firewall. If you can successfully configure the advanced firewall, you will have no problem configuring a basic firewall. The difference is that you have less control with a basic firewall and there is no DMZ support.

Figure 6-4   SDM Create Firewall Tab

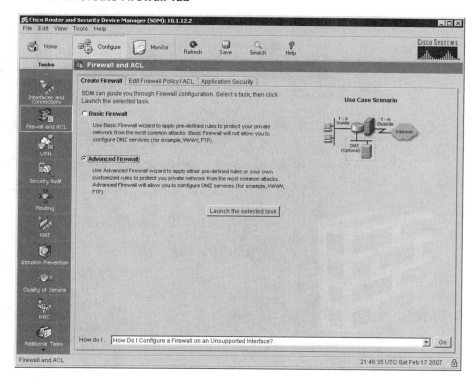

Read the information for the Advanced Firewall Configuration Wizard and click **Next**, as shown in Figure 6-5.

Figure 6-5   SDM Advanced Firewall Configuration Wizard

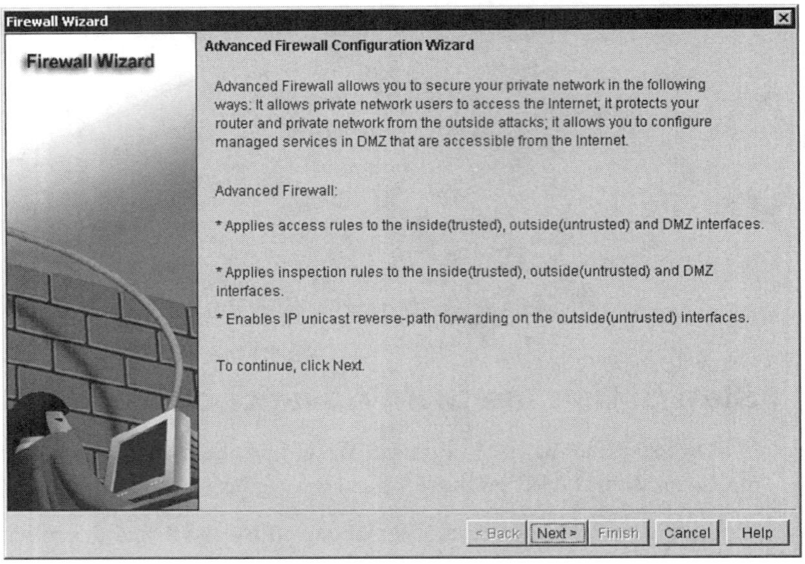

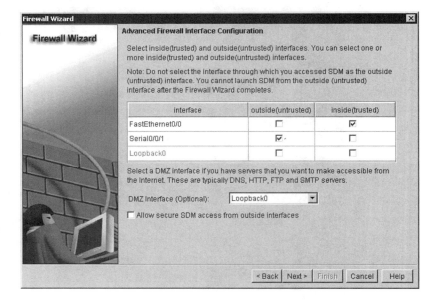

Choose the ISP-facing interface to be the outside untrusted interface, and the interface that faces the INSIDE router as the inside trusted interface.

Do not check either the inside or outside boxes for the loopback interface. However, select the loopback interface as the DMZ interface. You do not need to allow secure SDM access from the outside interfaces. After you correctly configure all interfaces, click **Next**, as shown in Figure 6-6.

Figure 6-6   SDM Firewall Wizard Interface Selection

Because you did not check the option at the bottom, SDM warns you that you cannot configure the router using SDM from the outside interface. Because you are using SDM through the inside interface of FW, this is acceptable. Click **OK** to continue, as shown in Figure 6-7.

Figure 6-7   SDM Connectivity Warning

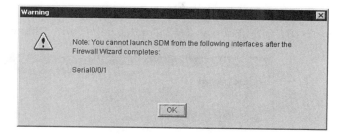

Now add DMZ services, by clicking the **Add** button, as shown in Figure 6-8.

Figure 6-8   SDM Firewall DMZ Configuration

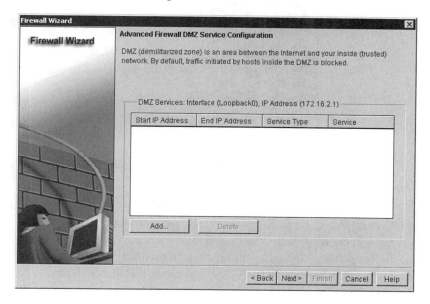

Add a range of web servers with addresses from 172.16.2.10 to 172.16.2.20. Configure the service as www, which is a keyword that the router identifies with TCP port 80 (the standard HTTP port). Click **OK** when your configuration is complete, as shown in Figure 6-9.

Figure 6-9   SDM DMZ Service Configuration

Review the added servers in the list of DMZ services, and then click **Next**, as shown in Figure 6-10.

Figure 6-10   SDM Firewall DMZ Configuration, with Changes Applied

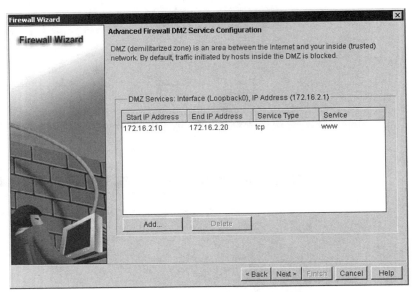

The configuration of interfaces as inside, outside, and DMZ interfaces applies access control lists to interfaces, creating firewall traffic boundaries.

Therefore, you might want to create permissions through the firewall for specific applications. Context-Based Access Control (CBAC) lists can examine the TCP and UDP layers of packets passing through the firewall to create per-flow holes in the firewall. CBAC watches generic transport protocols—such as TCP and UDP—and tracks connections, permitting incoming untrusted traffic only if it is return traffic for a TCP or UDP connection initiated from the inside. For some well-known protocols, CBAC also examines certain application layer data to make sure that the packets are correctly following those application protocols. For more information on CBAC, see Lab 6-2: Configuring CBAC.

For this lab, you do not use a default application security policy, but you create your own. Click **Use a custom Application Security Policy**, and then click **Create a new policy** in the drop-down box, as shown in Figure 6-11.

Figure 6-11   SDM Firewall Security Policy Configuration

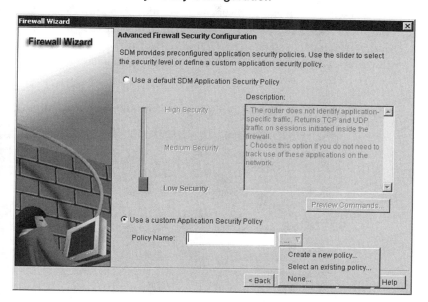

As shown in Figure 6-12, on the left side, click **HTTP**, and then check **Enable HTTP inspection** on the right to have CBAC ensure that the HTTP packets received are valid.

Figure 6-12   SDM CBAC Configuration Window, HTTP Options

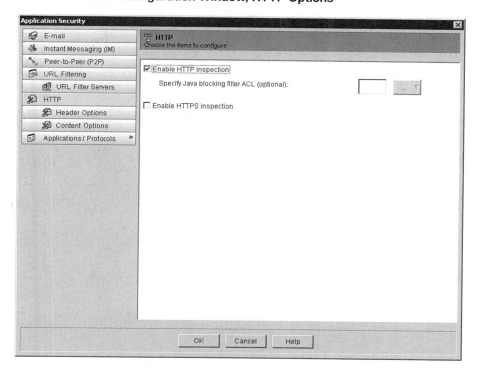

As shown in Figure 6-13, click **Applications/Protocols** on the left to expand it. In the tree, select **General** and the **tcp** and **udp** subentries to allow generic TCP and UDP inspection. For TCP connections, it monitors the TCP state of each connection initiated from the inside, and only allows return traffic matching that state. For UDP traffic, which is connectionless—and therefore stateless—it only allows return traffic matching source and destination addresses and UDP ports within a timeout period. Click **OK** to save this new policy.

Figure 6-13   SDM CBAC Configuration Window, General Options

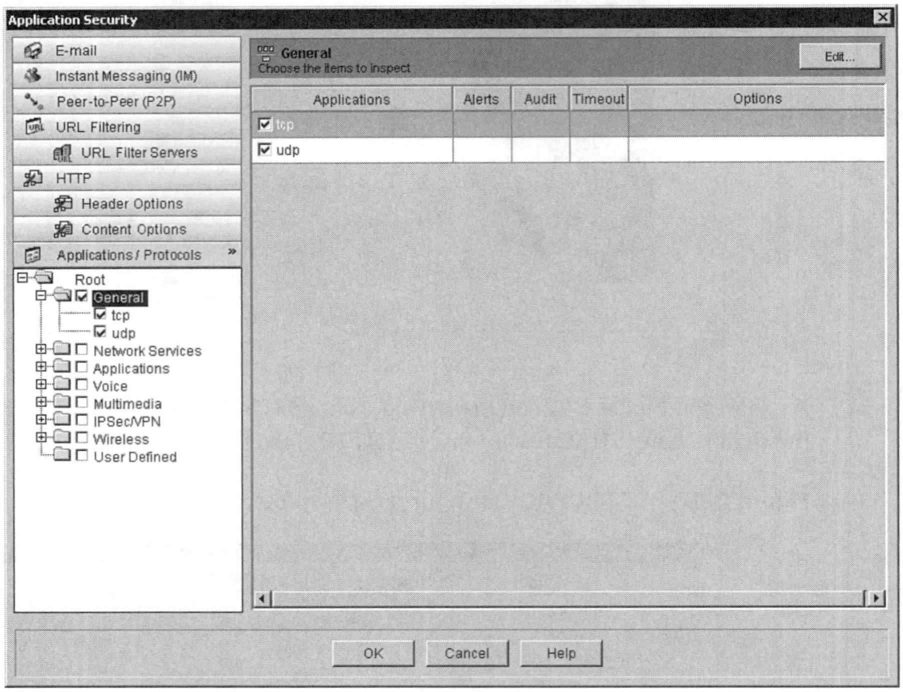

Why is it important to keep track of connection states, especially with TCP connections?

_____

_____

_____

The new policy appears in the text box. Click **Next** to continue, as shown in Figure 6-14.

Figure 6-14   Applying New Custom Security Policy with SDM

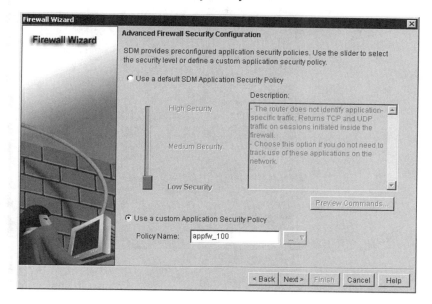

Verify the configuration summary and click **Finish**, as shown in Figure 6-15.

Figure 6-15   SDM Firewall Configuration Summary

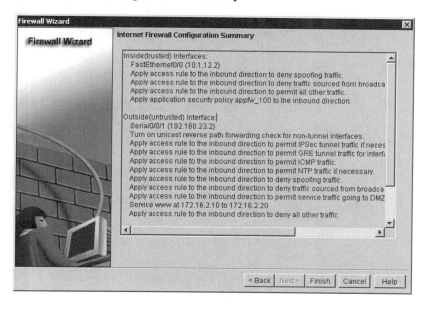

Preview the configuration commands that SDM will apply on the router, and then click **Deliver** to deliver the commands to the router, as shown in Figure 6-16.

Figure 6-16   SDM Firewall Configuration Delivery Notification

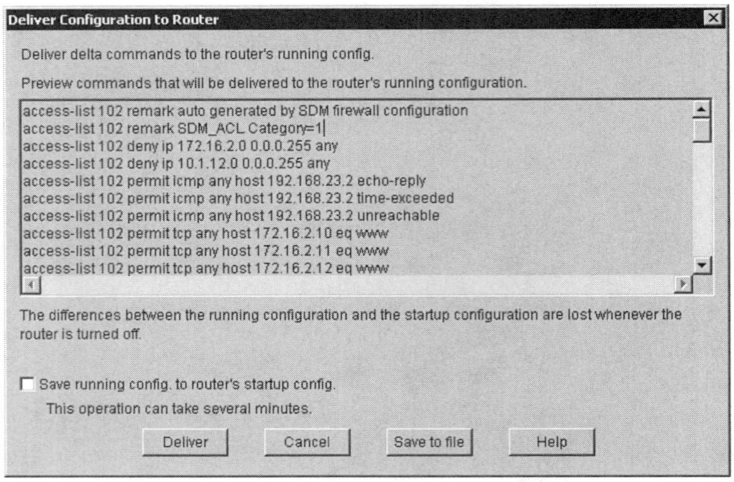

Click **OK** after the commands are delivered to the router, as shown in Figure 6-17.

Figure 6-17   SDM Firewall Configuration Delivery Progress Indicator

A dialog box informs you that the firewall configuration was successful. Click **OK**. The SDM success message appears, as shown in Figure 6-18.

Figure 6-18   SDM Successful Configuration Notification

Click **OK**, and you return to the **Edit Firewall Policy/ACL** tab in SDM, as shown in Figure 6-19.

Figure 6-19   SDM Firewall Policy Summary for Originating Traffic

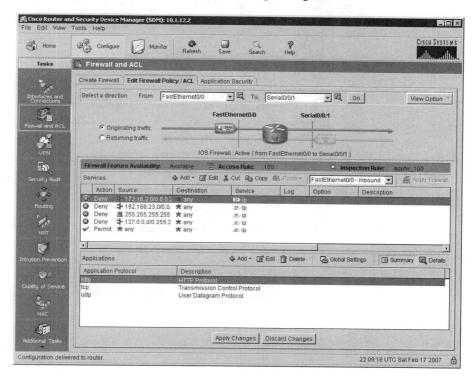

Step 6: Modify the Firewall Configuration

In which direction and to which interface were most of the access rules applied in the previous step?

_____

_____

As shown in Figure 6-20, select **Returning Traffic** in the upper part of the tab to view the access rules configured for returning traffic passing through the router from the outside interface to the inside interface.

Figure 6-20   SDM Firewall Policy Summary for Returning Traffic

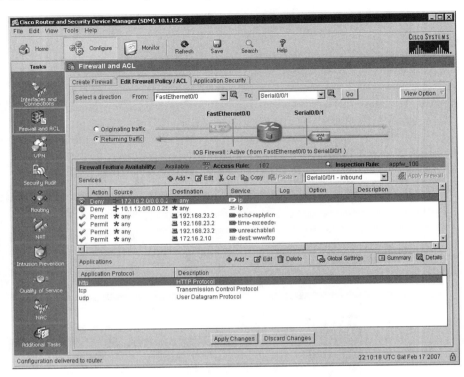

As shown in Figure 6-21, scroll down the access list to the deny statement for the 192.168.0.0/16 networks.

Why is this statement incompatible for this scenario?

_____

_____

Based on other elements in the access list, why do you think that this statement was added?

_____

_____

_____

Figure 6-21   Deny Statement in ACL 102 for 192.168.0.0/16

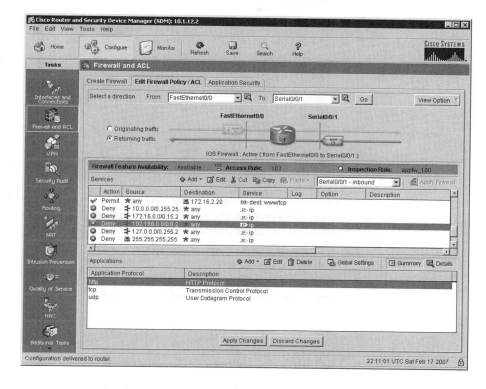

Select the 192.168.0.0/16 access rule statement and click **Cut** to remove it. Verify that the statement is removed, and then click **Apply Changes**, as shown in Figure 6-22.

Figure 6-22   ACL 102 After Deleting the Deny Statement for 192.168.0.0/16

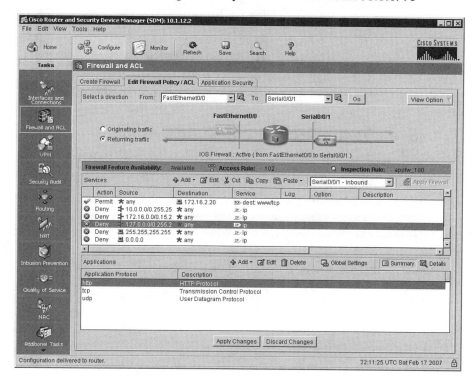

Preview the commands that SDM will send to the router, and then click **Deliver**, as shown in Figure 6-23.

Figure 6-23   SDM Firewall Configuration Delivery Notification

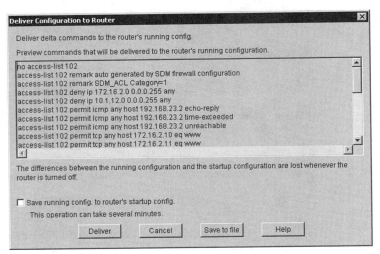

Click **OK** after the commands are delivered, as shown in Figure 6-24.

Figure 6-24   SDM Firewall Configuration Delivery Progress Indicator

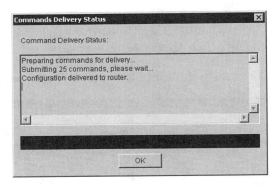

Step 7: Monitor Firewall Activity

On the ISP router, add the password cisco to the vtys to allow an authenticated Telnet session to the router:

```
ISP(config)# line vty 0 4
ISP(config-line)# password cisco
ISP(config-line)# login
```

On the INSIDE router, establish a Telnet session to the ISP's loopback interface:

```
INSIDE# telnet 192.168.3.1
Trying 192.168.3.1 ... Open

User Access Verification
```

```
Password:
ISP>
```

While the Telnet session is active, click the SDM **Monitor** tab, and then click **Firewall Status** on the left side, as shown in Figure 6-25. Click **Update** to get the latest firewall statistics. You should see the active Telnet session in the list.

Figure 6-25   SDM Firewall Monitor

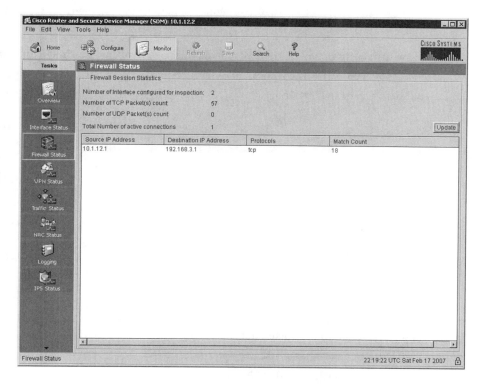

After displaying the parameters of the Telnet session through the SDM monitor, close the session by issuing the **exit** command:

```
ISP> exit

[Connection to 192.168.3.1 closed by foreign host]
INSIDE#
```

From the ISP router, initiate a Telnet session with the INSIDE loopback interface. Do not set up a line password. We want the Telnet session to fail:

```
ISP# telnet 10.1.1.1
Trying 10.1.1.1 ...
% Destination unreachable; gateway or host down

ISP#
```

Why does this Telnet session fail?

_____

_____

On the FW router, a log message appears, which indicates that a Telnet session was denied. The log message appears because the **log** keyword was used in the access list applied to the outside interface:

```
FW#
*Feb 17 22:21:01.085: %SEC-6-IPACCESSLOGP: list 102 denied tcp 192.168.23.3(20650) ->
  10.1.1.1(23), 1 packet
```

View the configuration on the FW outside interface by using the **show run** command:

```
FW# show run interface serial0/0/1
Building configuration...

Current configuration : 168 bytes
!
interface Serial0/0/1
 description $FW_OUTSIDE$
 ip address 192.168.23.2 255.255.255.0
 ip access-group 102 in
 ip verify unicast reverse-path
 clock rate 64000
end
```

From the **show access-lists** _number_ command, you can see that the **log** part of the access list is applied inbound to the outside interface:

```
FW# show access-lists 102
Extended IP access list 102
    10 deny ip 172.16.2.0 0.0.0.255 any
    20 deny ip 10.1.12.0 0.0.0.255 any
    30 permit icmp any host 192.168.23.2 echo-reply
    40 permit icmp any host 192.168.23.2 time-exceeded
    50 permit icmp any host 192.168.23.2 unreachable
    60 permit tcp any host 172.16.2.10 eq www
    70 permit tcp any host 172.16.2.11 eq www
    80 permit tcp any host 172.16.2.12 eq www
    90 permit tcp any host 172.16.2.13 eq www
    100 permit tcp any host 172.16.2.14 eq www
    110 permit tcp any host 172.16.2.15 eq www
    120 permit tcp any host 172.16.2.16 eq www
    130 permit tcp any host 172.16.2.17 eq www
    140 permit tcp any host 172.16.2.18 eq www
    150 permit tcp any host 172.16.2.19 eq www
    160 permit tcp any host 172.16.2.20 eq www
    170 deny ip 10.0.0.0 0.255.255.255 any
    180 deny ip 172.16.0.0 0.15.255.255 any
```

```
190 deny ip 127.0.0.0 0.255.255.255 any
200 deny ip host 255.255.255.255 any
210 deny ip host 0.0.0.0 any
220 deny ip any any log (1 match)
```

What are access control entries with sequence numbers 170–190 intended to prevent?

_____

_____

What other command applied in the SDM firewall configuration prevents the same type of attack?

_____

Conclusion

Given the previous ACL configuration, predict what will happen in the following scenarios and explain the reason for each:

ISP pings 10.1.1.1. _____

ISP pings 172.16.23.2. _____

ISP pings 172.16.2.1. _____

Imagine that ISP pings an existing web server at 172.16.2.10. _____

Imagine that a network connected to ISP initiates an HTTP session with a web server at 172.16.2.10.

_____

Lab 6-2: Configuring CBAC (6.6.2)

The objectives of this lab are as follows:

- Configure CBAC rules on a router.

- Apply CBAC rules on a router.

Figure 6-26 illustrates the topology that is used for this lab.

Figure 6-26   Topology Diagram

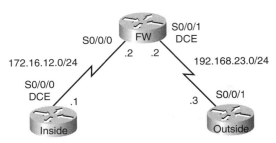

Scenario

Context-Based Access Control (CBAC) is a powerful tool in the Cisco IOS Firewall feature set. It allows stateful packet inspection of certain types of attacks. In this lab, INSIDE represents an inside corporate router, OUTSIDE represents an outside Internet or Internet service provider (ISP) router, and FW represents the corporate firewall. CBAC alone is not enough to make a router into a secure Internet firewall, but in addition to other security features, it can be a powerful defense.

Step 1: Configure the Physical Interfaces

Configure the loopback interfaces with the addresses shown in Figure 6-26. Also, configure the serial interfaces shown in the figure. Set the clock rate on the appropriate interface and issue the **no shutdown** command on all serial connections. Verify that you have connectivity across the local subnet by using the **ping** command:

```
INSIDE(config)# interface serial0/0/0

INSIDE(config-if)# ip address 172.16.12.1 255.255.255.0

INSIDE(config-if)# clockrate 64000

INSIDE(config-if)# no shutdown
```

```
FW(config)# interface serial0/0/0

FW(config-if)# ip address 172.16.12.2 255.255.255.0

FW(config-if)# no shutdown

FW(config-if)# interface serial0/0/1

FW(config-if)# ip address 192.168.23.2 255.255.255.0

FW(config-if)# clockrate 64000

FW(config-if)# no shutdown
```

```
OUTSIDE(config)# interface serial0/0/1

OUTSIDE(config-if)# ip address 192.168.23.3 255.255.255.0

OUTSIDE(config-if)# no shutdown
```

Step 2: Configure Static Default Routes

On the INSIDE and OUTSIDE routers, configure static default routes directing traffic to unknown destinations to be forwarded to the FW router. FW does not need any routes because it has interfaces directly connected to both networks (as shown in Figure 6-26):

```
INSIDE(config)# ip route 0.0.0.0 0.0.0.0 172.16.12.2
```

```
OUTSIDE(config)# ip route 0.0.0.0 0.0.0.0 192.168.23.2
```

At this point, your network should have full IP connectivity. If it does not have full connectivity, troubleshoot.

Normally, a single-homed company might use Network Address Translation (NAT) at its corporate edge to protect its network and allow private addressing within the bounds of its network. In that case, the OUTSIDE router—normally a provider edge router—would have a static route directing traffic to the address owned by the customer out one of its interfaces. In this scenario, you do not configure NAT, and you use a default route for simplicity.

Step 3: Enable Telnet Access

Use the Telnet protocol to test connectivity in this scenario. To enable Telnet access on a router beginning with its default configuration, simply apply the **password** *string* command on the virtual terminal lines.

Apply this configuration change on the INSIDE and OUTSIDE routers. Use cisco as the line password. This is used later for verification purposes:

```
INSIDE(config)# line vty 0 4
```

```
INSIDE(config-line)# password cisco
```

```
INSIDE(config-line)# login
```

```
OUTSIDE(config)# line vty 0 4
```

```
OUTSIDE(config-line)# password cisco
```

```
OUTSIDE(config-line)# login
```

Step 4: Create IP Inspect Rules

CBAC operates by statefully inspecting some protocols and tracking TCP connections and UDP flows. CBAC examines the protocols to determine if incoming, untrusted (outside) traffic is return traffic for an inside-initiated connection or the result of arbitrarily spoofed packets. For some well-known protocols, CBAC can also examine particular application layer fields to make sure that the packets are correctly following the protocols of those specific applications. Any traffic that is not accepted by CBAC is treated appropriately according to the rules indicated by the access list on the interface. This is done by explicitly blocking untrusted traffic (which we configure later), except when allowed by CBAC.

Why is it important to keep track of connection states, especially with TCP connections?

_____

_____

The critical part of configuring CBAC involves creating rules to track connections and flows. Create rules to track TCP and UDP flows by using the **ip inspect name** *name protocol* command. Use the name myrules and apply the CBAC rule to the Serial0/0/0 interface in the inbound direction. To see the available protocols (most of the protocols listed are application layer protocols), enter the **ip inspect name** *name* command followed by the **?** character. Newer IOS versions have more protocols listed:

```
FW(config)# ip inspect name myrules ?
  802-11-iapp       IEEE 802.11 WLANs WG IAPP
  ace-svr           ACE Server/Propagation
  aol               America-Online
  appfw             Application Firewall
  appleqtc          Apple QuickTime
  bgp               Border Gateway Protocol
  <OUTPUT OMITTED>
```

```
FW(config)# ip inspect name myrules tcp
FW(config)# ip inspect name myrules udp
```

You can also set CBAC timeouts for various protocols. To change the amount of time that should pass before a UDP flow times out, use the **ip inspect udp idle-time** *timeout* command in global configuration mode. The default UDP idle timeout is 30 seconds. Change the UDP timeout to 60 seconds:

```
FW(config)# ip inspect udp idle-time 60
```

Why is this particularly important for UDP protocols?

_____

_____

_____

_____

On a per-protocol basis, there are other adjustable settings. For example, you can manipulate CBAC to trigger logging messages based on the matched protocol. This is important for security accounting and debugging purposes. View the options available on a per-protocol basis by using the **?** character:

```
FW(config)# ip inspect name myrules tcp ?
  alert             Turn on/off alert
  audit-trail       Turn on/off audit trail
  router-traffic    Enable inspection of sessions to/from the router
  timeout           Specify the inactivity timeout time
  <cr>
```

In a secure network, you would likely set up a syslog server to monitor security information, including communication to external networks. Alert and audit trail messages allow holes in the firewall created by CBAC to be monitored and logged for later use. By default, CBAC logs alert messages to the console, which can be configured on a per-protocol basis to override the global settings for the alert messages (as previously shown). To change the global setting for alerts, use the command **ip inspect alert-off**. By default, alerts are on. To enable audit-trail messages, use the global command **ip inspect audit-trail**. By default, audit-trail messages are off. The **timeout** argument specifies a per-protocol connection timeout period. Add in Internet Control Message Protocol (ICMP) with a timeout time of 5 seconds, HTTP inspection without alerting, and FTP inspection with an audit-trail. ICMP inspection might not work on older IOS releases:

```
FW(config)# ip inspect name myrules icmp timeout 5
FW(config)# ip inspect name myrules http alert off
FW(config)# ip inspect name myrules ftp audit-trail on
```

To apply the rule set to an interface, use the interface level command **ip inspect** *name direction*. Apply myrules to the inside interface on FW with an inbound direction. This means that any traffic initiated from the inside interface going through the router will have IP inspection performed on it:

```
FW(config)# interface serial0/0/0
FW(config-if)# ip inspect myrules in
```

In this scenario, you could also apply it outbound on the outside interface to achieve the same effect. When would this not apply?

_____

_____

_____

Step 5: Block Unwanted Outside Traffic

Configure an extended access list to deny any traffic coming in the outside interface. The access list must be extended because CBAC needs to open up temporary holes in it for return traffic and cannot do this with standard access lists. Also, have the **deny** portion of the access list log packets that are blocked. Apply this access list to be inbound on the outside interface on the firewall.

Note that if you use an older IOS release that did not accept ICMP inspection earlier, you might want to add the statement **access-list 100 permit icmp any any** before the **deny** statement in this access list to allow all ICMP traffic to go through (because it is not inspected by CBAC):

```
FW(config)# access-list 100 deny ip any any log
FW(config)# interface serial0/0/1
FW(config-if)# ip access-group 100 in
```

Step 6: Verify CBAC Operation

Telnet from OUTSIDE to INSIDE. This should fail:

```
OUTSIDE# telnet 172.16.12.1
Trying 172.16.12.1 ...
% Destination unreachable; gateway or host down

OUTSIDE#
```

In addition, you should see a log message appear on FW. This log message is not from CBAC but from the access list denying the packet:

```
FW#
*Feb 18 02:11:11.823: %SEC-6-IPACCESSLOGP: list 100 denied tcp 192.168.23.3(0) ->
  172.16.12.1(0), 1 packet
```

Now, attempt to telnet from INSIDE to OUTSIDE. Leave the Telnet session open so you can verify the connection on FW:

```
INSIDE# telnet 192.168.23.3
Trying 192.168.23.3 ... Open

User Access Verification

Password:
OUTSIDE>
```

On FW, issue the **show ip inspect all** command to see the configuration and operation of CBAC. Notice that the inspected TCP connection between INSIDE and OUTSIDE is listed at the end:

```
FW# show ip inspect all
Session audit trail is disabled
Session alert is enabled
one-minute (sampling period) thresholds are [400:500] connections
max-incomplete sessions thresholds are [400:500]
max-incomplete tcp connections per host is 50. Block-time 0 minute.
tcp synwait-time is 30 sec -- tcp finwait-time is 5 sec
tcp idle-time is 3600 sec -- udp idle-time is 30 sec
dns-timeout is 5 sec
Inspection Rule Configuration
 Inspection name myrules
    tcp alert is on audit-trail is off timeout 3600
    udp alert is on audit-trail is off timeout 30
    icmp alert is on audit-trail is off timeout 5
    http alert is off audit-trail is off timeout 3600
    ftp alert is on audit-trail is on timeout 3600

Interface Configuration
 Interface Serial0/0/0
  Inbound inspection rule is myrules
    tcp alert is on audit-trail is off timeout 3600
    udp alert is on audit-trail is off timeout 30
    icmp alert is on audit-trail is off timeout 5
    http alert is off audit-trail is off timeout 3600
    ftp alert is on audit-trail is on timeout 3600
  Outgoing inspection rule is not set
  Inbound access list is not set
  Outgoing access list is not set

Established Sessions
 Session 458348C4 (172.16.12.1:54736)=>(192.168.23.3:23) tcp SIS_OPEN
```

View detailed session information by issuing the **show ip inspect detail** command on FW:

```
FW# show ip inspect sessions detail
Established Sessions
```

```
Session 458348C4 (172.16.12.1:54736)=>(192.168.23.3:23) tcp SIS_OPEN
 Created 00:03:25, Last heard 00:03:23
 Bytes sent (initiator:responder) [37:79]
 In  SID 192.168.23.3[23:23]=>172.16.12.1[54736:54736] on ACL 100  (11 matches)
```

Close the Telnet connection when you finish verifying CBAC operation:

```
OUTSIDE> exit

[Connection to 192.168.23.3 closed by foreign host]
INSIDE#
```

Note: If your Cisco IOS release does not support ICMP inspection, skip the following verification step because ICMP traffic is not inspected.

Enable debugging of IP inspection for ICMP traffic by using the **debug ip inspect** *protocol* command.

Caution: In a production environment, debugging CBAC is not recommended because it can generate high amounts of output.

```
FW# debug ip inspect icmp
INSPECT ICMP Inspection debugging is on
```

From the INSIDE router, **ping** OUTSIDE. Note that this would not work if you try to ping the other way because it would be denied by the access list. If attempted, the denied packets from OUTSIDE to INSIDE would also be logged to FW's console line:

```
INSIDE# ping 192.168.23.3

Type escape sequence to abort.
Sending 5, 100-byte ICMP Echos to 192.168.23.3, timeout is 2 seconds:
!!!!!
Success rate is 100 percent (5/5), round-trip min/avg/max = 56/56/60 ms

FW#
*Feb 18 02:23:29.591: CBAC: ICMP Echo pkt 172.16.12.1 => 192.168.23.3
*Feb 18 02:23:29.591: CBAC: ICMP Echo pkt 172.16.12.1 => 192.168.23.3
*Feb 18 02:23:29.591: CBAC: ICMP Echo pkt 172.16.12.1 => 192.168.23.3
*Feb 18 02:23:29.619: CBAC: ICMP Echo Reply pkt 192.168.23.3 => 172.16.12.1
*Feb 18 02:23:29.647: CBAC: ICMP Echo pkt 172.16.12.1 => 192.168.23.3
*Feb 18 02:23:29.675: CBAC: ICMP Echo Reply pkt 192.168.23.3 => 172.16.12.1
*Feb 18 02:23:29.703: CBAC: ICMP Echo pkt 172.16.12.1 => 192.168.23.3
*Feb 18 02:23:29.735: CBAC: ICMP Echo Reply pkt 192.168.23.3 => 172.16.12.1
*Feb 18 02:23:29.763: CBAC: ICMP Echo pkt 172.16.12.1 => 192.168.23.3
*Feb 18 02:23:29.791: CBAC: ICMP Echo Reply pkt 192.168.23.3 => 172.16.12.1
*Feb 18 02:23:29.819: CBAC: ICMP Echo pkt 172.16.12.1 => 192.168.23.3
*Feb 18 02:23:29.847: CBAC: ICMP Echo Reply pkt 192.168.23.3 => 172.16.12.1
FW# undebug all
```

Lab 6-3: Configuring IPS with SDM (6.6.3)

The objectives of this lab are as follows:

- Configure IPS using the Cisco SDM IPS Wizard.

- Modify default IPS settings.

- Create an IPS signature.

Figure 6-27 illustrates the topology that is used for this lab.

Figure 6-27   Topology Diagram

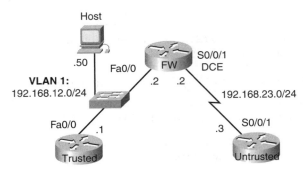

Scenario

In this lab, you configure the Cisco IOS Intrusion Prevention System (IPS), which is part of the Cisco IOS Firewall feature set. IPS examines certain attack patterns and alerts and/or mitigates when those patterns occur.

In this scenario, TRUSTED represents a trusted inside router, FW represents a router serving as an intrusion prevention router, and UNTRUSTED represents an untrusted outside router. Because UNTRUSTED is outside, FW examines packets inbound from it. IPS alone is not enough to make a router into a secure Internet firewall, but in addition to other security features, it can be a powerful defense.

Step 1: Configure the Physical Interfaces

Configure the interfaces with the addresses shown in Figure 6-27.

Set the clock rate on the appropriate interface and issue the **no shutdown** command on all connections. Verify that you have connectivity across the local subnet by using the **ping** command:

```
TRUSTED(config)# interface fastethernet0/0
TRUSTED(config-if)# ip address 192.168.12.1 255.255.255.0
TRUSTED(config-if)# no shutdown
```
```
FW(config)# interface fastethernet0/0
FW(config-if)# ip address 192.168.12.2 255.255.255.0
FW(config-if)# no shutdown
FW(config-if)# interface serial0/0/1
```

```
FW(config-if)# ip address 192.168.23.2 255.255.255.0
FW(config-if)# clockrate 64000
FW(config-if)# no shutdown
UNTRUSTED(config)# interface serial0/0/1
UNTRUSTED(config-if)# ip address 192.168.23.3 255.255.255.0
UNTRUSTED(config-if)# no shutdown
```

Step 2: Configure Static Default Routes

On the TRUSTED and UNTRUSTED routers, configure static default routes directing traffic to unknown destinations to be forwarded to the FW router. FW does not need any routes because it has interfaces that are directly connected to both networks:

```
TRUSTED(config)# ip route 0.0.0.0 0.0.0.0 192.168.12.2
UNTRUSTED(config)# ip route 0.0.0.0 0.0.0.0 192.168.23.2
```

At this point, your network should have full IP connectivity. If it does not have full connectivity, troubleshoot.

Normally, a single-homed company might use Network Address Translation (NAT) at its corporate edge to protect its network and allow private addressing within the bounds of its network. In that case, the UNTRUSTED router—normally a provider edge router—would have a static route directing traffic to the address owned by the customer out one of its interfaces. In this scenario, you do not configure NAT, and you use a default route for simplicity.

Step 3: Enable Telnet Access

On TRUSTED, enable Telnet access by setting a line password and enabling login on virtual terminal lines. Use cisco as a line password. These virtual terminal lines are used later to test the IPS:

```
TRUSTED(config)# line vty 0 4
TRUSTED(config-line)# password cisco
TRUSTED(config-line)# login
```

Step 4: Connect to FW Using SDM

Set up the host with the IP addressing shown in Figure 6-27. Set up FW for SDM access and connect to it by using the host. If you do not know how to set the IP address on a host or connect to a router using SDM, see Lab 3-1: Configuring SDM on a Router. The wizard in the next step requires that you use HTTPS to connect to the router with SDM, so make sure you check this option. When you are connected the SDM home screen will appear as shown in Figure 6-28.

Figure 6-28   Cisco Security Device Manager Home Screen

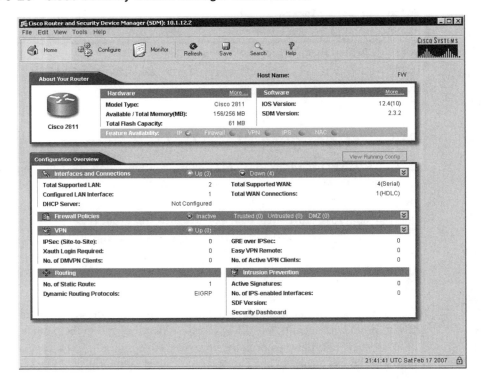

As shown in Figure 6-29, on the **Edit** menu, choose **Preferences**. Verify that the **Preview commands before delivering to router** option is checked before continuing. Click **OK** when you finish configuring the preferences.

Figure 6-29   SDM User Preferences

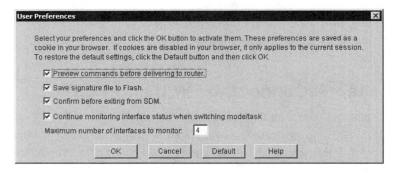

Step 5: Use the SDM IPS Rule Wizard

In SDM, to start the IPS Rule Wizard, click the **Configure** icon in the top menu bar (see Figure 6-30), click **Intrusion Prevention** on the Tasks toolbar, and then click the **Launch IPS Rule Wizard** button.

Figure 6-30   Launching the SDM IPS Wizard

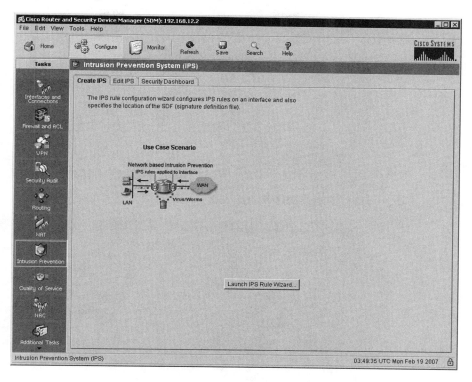

Some dialog boxes regarding SDEE notification appear. SDEE is a technology that reports security events and responses, and it is enabled when IPS is enabled on a router. Click **OK** in each dialog box, as shown in Figure 6-31 and Figure 6-32.

Figure 6-31   Notification of Enabling SDEE

Figure 6-32   Permission of Enabling SDEE

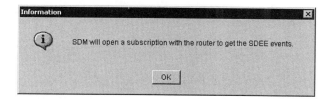

When prompted for a username and password, use the username and password you used to log in to SDM, as shown in Figure 6-33.

Figure 6-33   SDM Login to FW Router

Read the wizard's welcome page, and then click **Next**, as shown in Figure 6-34.

Figure 6-34   SDM IPS Wizard

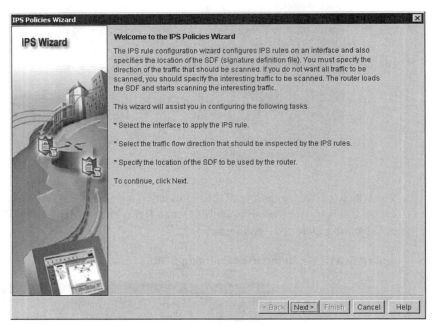

For inbound inspection, check the checkbox for the interface facing UNTRUSTED, and then click **Next**, as shown in Figure 6-35. Do not select any interfaces for outbound inspection.

Figure 6-35   IPS Interface Selection

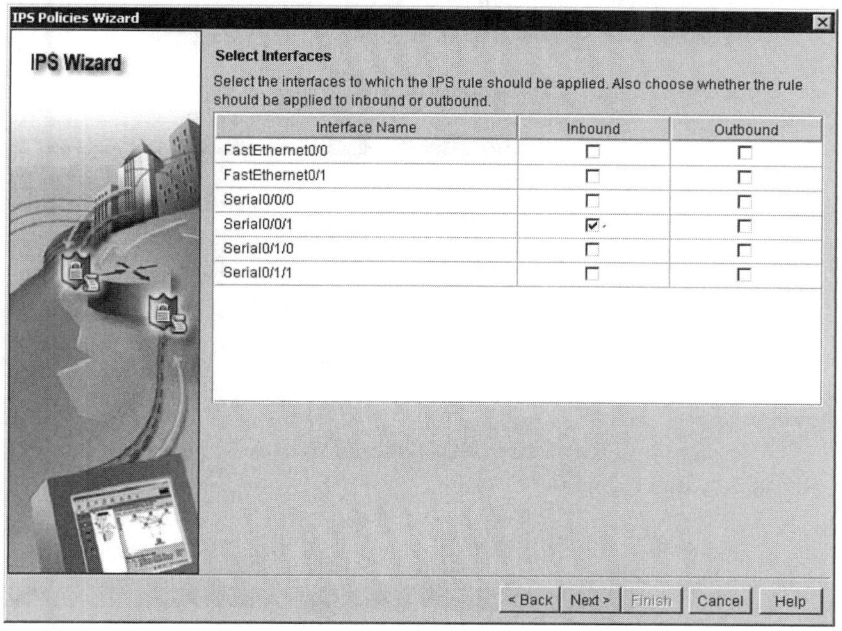

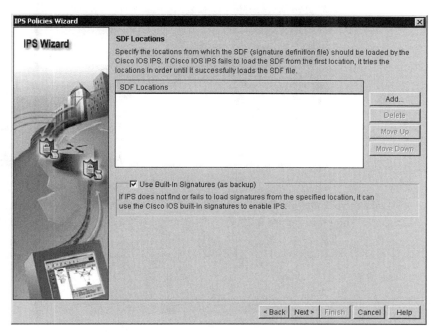

Signature definition files (SDF) are files that contain intrusion signature definitions. In a production environment, you would use the **Add** button to specify SDF locations. However, do not specify any SDF locations; instead, load basic signatures that are built into the Cisco IOS. Click **Next** on this page of the wizard, as shown in Figure 6-36.

Figure 6-36   SDF Locations

A warning dialog that is similar to the one shown in Figure 6-37 might appear if your router contains an SDF file in its flash memory. If you do receive the warning, click **No** to use the built-in signatures, as shown in Figure 6-37. Newer versions of SDM (version 4.21) do not give this warning.

Figure 6-37   SDF File Detection

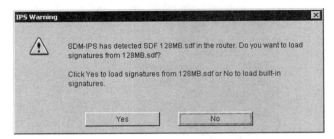

After verifying the changes SDM will make to the router, click **Finish** to begin applying the changes, as shown in Figure 6-38.

Figure 6-38   IPS Summary

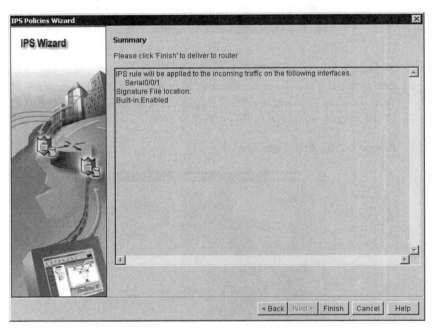

Verify the commands that SDM will use on the router, and then click **Deliver** to add the configuration, as shown in Figure 6-39.

Figure 6-39   IPS Configuration Summary

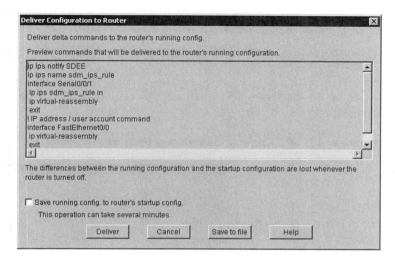

When the configuration is added, you might see many IPS engine messages logged on FW. Do not be alarmed; these are normal messages:

```
FW#
*Feb 19 04:19:52.375: %IPS-6-BUILTIN_SIGS: Configured to load builtin signatures
*Feb 19 04:19:52.511: %IPS-6-SDF_LOAD_SUCCESS: SDF loaded successfully from builtin
*Feb 19 04:19:52.519: %IPS-6-ENGINE_BUILDING: OTHER - 3 signatures - 1 of 15 engines
*Feb 19 04:19:52.519: %IPS-6-ENGINE_READY: OTHER - 0 ms - packets for this engine
 will be scanned
*Feb 19 04:19:52.519: %IPS-6-ENGINE_BUILDING: MULTI-STRING - 0 signatures - 2 of 15
 engines
*Feb 19 04:19:52.519: %IPS-6-ENGINE_BUILD_SKIPPED: MULTI-STRING - there are no new
 signature definitions for this engine
*Feb 19 04:19:52.519: %IPS-6-ENGINE_BUILDING: STRING.ICMP - 0 signatures - 3 of 15
 engines
*Feb 19 04:19:52.519: %IPS-6-ENGINE_BUILD_SKIPPED: STRING.ICMP - there are no new
 signature definitions for this engine
*Feb 19 04:19:52.519: %IPS-6-ENGINE_BUILDING: STRING.UDP - 1 signatures - 4 of 15
 engines
*Feb 19 04:19:52.531: %IPS-6-ENGINE_READY: STRING.UDP - 12 ms - packets for this
 engine will be scanned
*Feb 19 04:19:53.275: %IPS-6-ENGINE_READY: SERVICE.HTTP - 460 ms - packets for this
 engine will be scanned
*Feb 19 04:19:53.275: %IPS-6-ENGINE_BUILDING: ATOMIC.TCP - 6 signatures - 11 of 15
 engines
*Feb 19 04:19:53.279: %IPS-6-ENGINE_READY: ATOMIC.TCP - 4 ms - packets for this
 engine will be scanned
*Feb 19 04:19:53.279: %IPS-6-ENGINE_BUILDING: ATOMIC.UDP - 7 signatures - 12 of 15
 engines
*Feb 19 04:19:53.283: %IPS-6-ENGINE_READY: ATOMIC.UDP - 4 ms - packets for this
 engine will be scanned
*Feb 19 04:19:53.283: %IPS-6-ENGINE_BUILDING: ATOMIC.ICMP - 14 signatures - 13 of 15
 engines
*Feb 19 04:19:53.283: %IPS-7-UNSUPPORTED_PARAM: ATOMIC.ICMP 2000:0 IcmpType=0 - This
 parameter is not supported
```

```
*Feb 19 04:19:53.287: %IPS-6-ENGINE_READY: ATOMIC.ICMP - 4 ms - packets for this
  engine will be scanned
*Feb 19 04:19:53.287: %IPS-6-ENGINE_BUILDING: ATOMIC.IPOPTIONS - 7 signatures - 14 of
  15 engines
*Feb 19 04:19:53.287: %IPS-6-ENGINE_READY: ATOMIC.IPOPTIONS - 0 ms - packets for this
  engine will be scanned
```

After the commands are delivered, click **OK** to close the dialog box, as shown in Figure 6-40. Your output might vary if you use a newer version of SDM.

Figure 6-40   IPS Commands Delivery Progress Indicator

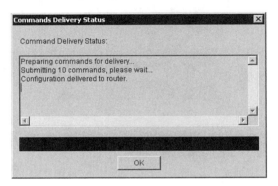

After clicking **OK** on the Commands Delivery Status dialog box, SDM displays the Edit IPS tab of SDM as a prompt, as shown in Figure 6-41.

Figure 6-41   SDM Edit IPS Tab

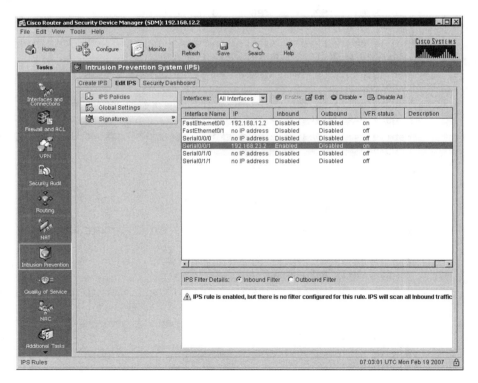

FW now examines each packet passing through it with an ingress interface of Serial 0/0/1. Note that no other packets are examined.

Step 6: Verify and Modify IPS Behavior

On UNTRUSTED, ping TRUSTED with a high repeat count:

```
UNTRUSTED# ping 192.168.12.1 repeat 100

Type escape sequence to abort.
Sending 100, 100-byte ICMP Echos to 192.168.12.1, timeout is 2 seconds:
!!!!!!!!!!!!!!!!!!!!!!!!!!!!!!!!!!!!!!!!!!!!!!!!!!!!!!!!!!!!!!!!!!!!!!!!!!!
!!!!!!!!!!!!!!!!!!!!!!!!!!!!!!!!!
Success rate is 100 percent (100/100), round-trip min/avg/max = 28/29/32 ms
```

View the messages logged to FW's console line. Initially, IPS logs each individual signature catch (which is triggered by each ICMP packet sent by the **ping** command), but it eventually stops logging each one individually. Finally, it shows a summary log message:

```
FW#
*Feb 19 06:55:05.603: %IPS-4-SIGNATURE: Sig:2004 Subsig:0 Sev:2 ICMP Echo Req
  [192.168.23.3:0 -> 192.168.12.1:0]

*Feb 19 06:55:05.635: %IPS-4-SIGNATURE: Sig:2004 Subsig:0 Sev:2 ICMP Echo Req
  [192.168.23.3:0 -> 192.168.12.1:0]

*Feb 19 06:55:05.663: %IPS-4-SIGNATURE: Sig:2004 Subsig:0 Sev:2 ICMP Echo Req
  [192.168.23.3:0 -> 192.168.12.1:0]

*Feb 19 06:55:05.695: %IPS-4-SIGNATURE: Sig:2004 Subsig:0 Sev:2 ICMP Echo Req
  [192.168.23.3:0 -> 192.168.12.1:0]

*Feb 19 06:55:05.723: %IPS-4-SIGNATURE: Sig:2004 Subsig:0 Sev:2 ICMP Echo Req
  [192.168.23.3:0 -> 192.168.12.1:0]

*Feb 19 06:55:05.751: %IPS-4-SIGNATURE: Sig:2004 Subsig:0 Sev:2 ICMP Echo Req
  [192.168.23.3:0 -> 192.168.12.1:0]

*Feb 19 06:55:05.783: %IPS-4-SIGNATURE: Sig:2004 Subsig:0 Sev:2 ICMP Echo Req
  [192.168.23.3:0 -> 192.168.12.1:0]

*Feb 19 06:55:05.811: %IPS-4-SIGNATURE: Sig:2004 Subsig:0 Sev:2 ICMP Echo Req
  [192.168.23.3:0 -> 192.168.12.1:0]

*Feb 19 06:55:05.843: %IPS-4-SIGNATURE: Sig:2004 Subsig:0 Sev:2 ICMP Echo Req
  [192.168.23.3:0 -> 192.168.12.1:0]

*Feb 19 06:55:05.871: %IPS-4-SIGNATURE: Sig:2004 Subsig:0 Sev:2 ICMP Echo Req
  [192.168.23.3:0 -> 192.168.12.1:0]

*Feb 19 06:55:05.899: %IPS-4-SIGNATURE: Sig:2004 Subsig:0 Sev:2 ICMP Echo Req
  [192.168.23.3:0 -> 192.168.12.1:0]

*Feb 19 06:55:05.931: %IPS-4-SIGNATURE: Sig:2004 Subsig:0 Sev:2 ICMP Echo Req
  [192.168.23.3:0 -> 192.168.12.1:0]

*Feb 19 06:55:05.959: %IPS-4-SIGNATURE: Sig:2004 Subsig:0 Sev:2 ICMP Echo Req
  [192.168.23.3:0 -> 192.168.12.1:0]

*Feb 19 06:55:05.991: %IPS-4-SIGNATURE: Sig:2004 Subsig:0 Sev:2 ICMP Echo Req
  [192.168.23.3:0 -> 192.168.12.1:0]

*Feb 19 06:55:06.019: %IPS-4-SIGNATURE: Sig:2004 Subsig:0 Sev:2 ICMP Echo Req
  [192.168.23.3:0 -> 192.168.12.1:0]

*Feb 19 06:55:06.047: %IPS-4-SIGNATURE: Sig:2004 Subsig:0 Sev:2 ICMP Echo Req
  [192.168.23.3:0 -> 192.168.12.1:0]

*Feb 19 06:55:06.079: %IPS-4-SIGNATURE: Sig:2004 Subsig:0 Sev:2 ICMP Echo Req
  [192.168.23.3:0 -> 192.168.12.1:0]
```

```
*Feb 19 06:55:06.107: %IPS-4-SIGNATURE: Sig:2004 Subsig:0 Sev:2 ICMP Echo Req
  [192.168.23.3:0 -> 192.168.12.1:0]

*Feb 19 06:55:06.139: %IPS-4-SIGNATURE: Sig:2004 Subsig:0 Sev:2 ICMP Echo Req
  [192.168.23.3:0 -> 192.168.12.1:0]

*Feb 19 06:55:06.167: %IPS-4-SIGNATURE: Sig:2004 Subsig:0 Sev:2 ICMP Echo Req
  [192.168.23.3:0 -> 192.168.12.1:0]

*Feb 19 06:55:06.907: %IPS-4-SIGNATURE: Sig:2004 Subsig:0 Sev:2 ICMP Echo Req
  [192.168.23.3:0 -> 192.168.12.1:0]

*Feb 19 06:55:06.935: %IPS-4-SIGNATURE: Sig:2004 Subsig:0 Sev:2 ICMP Echo Req
  [192.168.23.3:0 -> 192.168.12.1:0]

*Feb 19 06:55:06.967: %IPS-4-SIGNATURE: Sig:2004 Subsig:0 Sev:2 ICMP Echo Req
  [192.168.23.3:0 -> 192.168.12.1:0]

*Feb 19 06:55:06.995: %IPS-4-SIGNATURE: Sig:2004 Subsig:0 Sev:2 ICMP Echo Req
  [192.168.23.3:0 -> 192.168.12.1:0]

*Feb 19 06:55:07.023: %IPS-4-SIGNATURE: Sig:2004 Subsig:0 Sev:2 ICMP Echo Req
  [192.168.23.3:0 -> 192.168.12.1:0]

*Feb 19 06:55:07.055: %IPS-4-SIGNATURE: Sig:2004 Subsig:0 Sev:2 ICMP Echo Req
  [192.168.23.3:0 -> 192.168.12.1:0]

*Feb 19 06:55:07.083: %IPS-4-SIGNATURE: Sig:2004 Subsig:0 Sev:2 ICMP Echo Req
  [192.168.23.3:0 -> 192.168.12.1:0]

*Feb 19 06:55:07.115: %IPS-4-SIGNATURE: Sig:2004 Subsig:0 Sev:2 ICMP Echo Req
  [192.168.23.3:0 -> 192.168.12.1:0]

*Feb 19 06:55:07.143: %IPS-4-SIGNATURE: Sig:2004 Subsig:0 Sev:2 ICMP Echo Req
  [192.168.23.3:0 -> 192.168.12.1:0]

*Feb 19 06:55:07.171: %IPS-4-SIGNATURE: Sig:2004 Subsig:0 Sev:2 ICMP Echo Req
  [192.168.23.3:0 -> 192.168.12.1:0]

*Feb 19 06:55:07.883: %IPS-4-SIGNATURE: Sig:2004 Subsig:0 Sev:2 ICMP Echo Req
  [192.168.23.3:0 -> 192.168.12.1:0]

*Feb 19 06:55:07.915: %IPS-4-SIGNATURE: Sig:2004 Subsig:0 Sev:2 ICMP Echo Req
  [192.168.23.3:0 -> 192.168.12.1:0]

*Feb 19 06:55:07.943: %IPS-4-SIGNATURE: Sig:2004 Subsig:0 Sev:2 ICMP Echo Req
  [192.168.23.3:0 -> 192.168.12.1:0]

*Feb 19 06:55:07.971: %IPS-4-SIGNATURE: Sig:2004 Subsig:0 Sev:2 ICMP Echo Req
  [192.168.23.3:0 -> 192.168.12.1:0]

*Feb 19 06:55:08.003: %IPS-4-SIGNATURE: Sig:2004 Subsig:0 Sev:2 ICMP Echo Req
  [192.168.23.3:0 -> 192.168.12.1:0]

*Feb 19 06:55:08.031: %IPS-4-SIGNATURE: Sig:2004 Subsig:0 Sev:2 ICMP Echo Req
  [192.168.23.3:0 -> 192.168.12.1:0]

*Feb 19 06:55:08.063: %IPS-4-SIGNATURE: Sig:2004 Subsig:0 Sev:2 ICMP Echo Req
  [192.168.23.3:0 -> 192.168.12.1:0]

*Feb 19 06:55:08.091: %IPS-4-SIGNATURE: Sig:2004 Subsig:0 Sev:2 ICMP Echo Req
  [192.168.23.3:0 -> 192.168.12.1:0]

*Feb 19 06:55:08.119: %IPS-4-SIGNATURE: Sig:2004 Subsig:0 Sev:2 ICMP Echo Req
  [192.168.23.3:0 -> 192.168.12.1:0]

*Feb 19 06:55:08.151: %IPS-4-SIGNATURE: Sig:2004 Subsig:0 Sev:2 ICMP Echo Req
  [192.168.23.3:0 -> 192.168.12.1:0]

FW#

*Feb 19 06:55:35.603: %IPS-4-SIG_SUMMARY: Sig:2004 Subsig:0 Global Summary: 100
  alarms in this interval
```

Signature number 2004 detected the previous potential ICMP attack indicated in the previous output. For this lab, you disabled the signature numbered 2004, which was being set off by the **ping** command that was previously issued. Begin by clicking **Signatures** in the first pane of the tab, as shown in Figure 6-42. If you use version 4.21 of SDM, the options are **Other Services** > **General Services**.

Figure 6-42   Edit IPS Signatures Tab

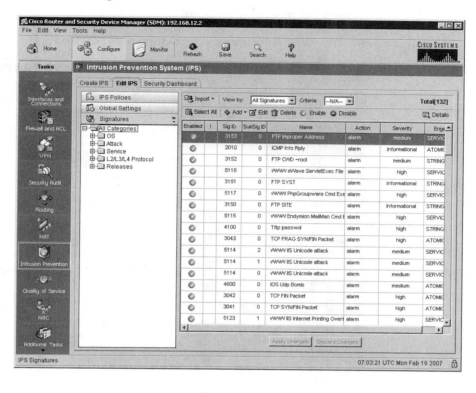

Choose **Service > General Service** on the Signature tree, as shown in Figure 6-43. Find signature 2004 in the list, and choose it. Then, disable the signature by clicking the **Disable** icon in the menu bar for the list.

Figure 6-43   IPS ICMP Echo Request Signature, Currently Enabled

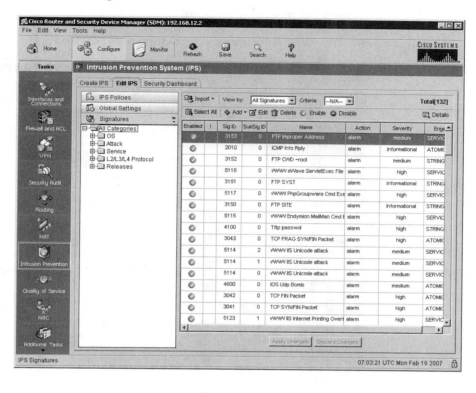

The **Enabled** column should change its icon to reflect that it is now disabled. Click the **Apply Changes** button to deliver the changes to the router, as shown in Figure 6-44.

Figure 6-44   IPS ICMP Echo Request Signature, Now Disabled

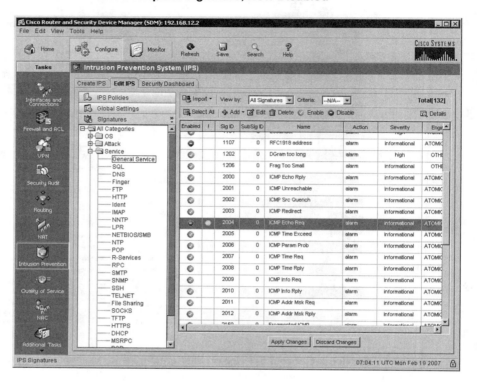

A new SDF is generated by SDM reflecting these changes, and it is delivered to the router from SDM. Figure 6-45 shows a sample delivery status.

Figure 6-45   IPS Signature Delivery Status

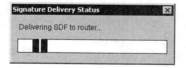

Note that, at the end of this lab, you will probably want to delete this SDF by using the privileged EXEC command **delete flash:sdmips.sdf**. Be careful not to delete any other files in the flash file system.

SDM also adds a configuration command to reflect the new SDF that it is adding and tells the IPS engine to load signatures from this file. After reviewing the configuration command, click **Deliver**, as shown in Figure 6-46.

Figure 6-46   IPS Configuration Command Delivery Notification

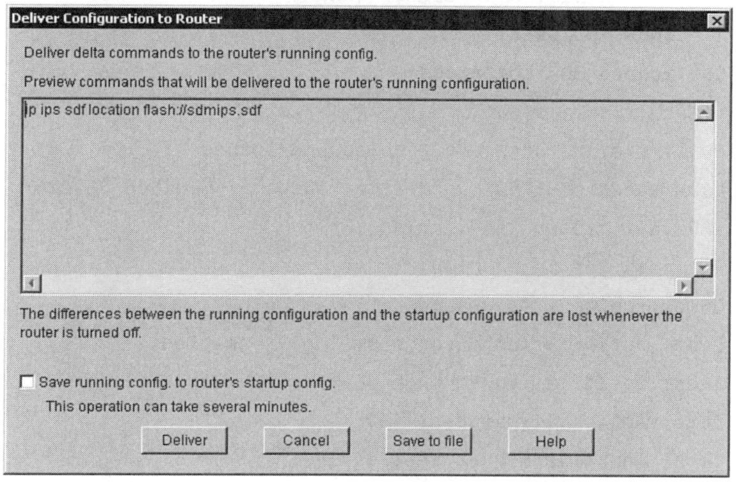

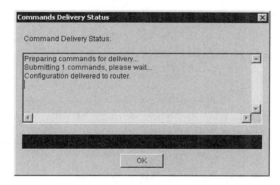

Click **OK** after the command is delivered, as shown in Figure 6-47. You might see some IPS engine log messages on FW.

Figure 6-47   Command Delivery Progress Indicator

When performing a ping from UNTRUSTED to TRUSTED, the log messages are not generated. Ping TRUSTED from UNTRUSTED:

```
UNTRUSTED# ping 192.168.12.1

Type escape sequence to abort.
Sending 5, 100-byte ICMP Echos to 192.168.12.1, timeout is 2 seconds:
!!!!!
Success rate is 100 percent (5/5), round-trip min/avg/max = 28/29/32 ms
```

Why would you want to disable IPS signatures?

On FW, execute **show ip ips all** to view various IPS configuration parameters. Notice that one of the signatures is disabled by default in addition to the signature we previously disabled:

```
FW# show ip ips all
Configured SDF Locations:
 flash://sdmips.sdf
Builtin signatures are enabled and loaded
Last successful SDF load time: 08:01:10 UTC Feb 19 2007
IPS fail closed is disabled
Fastpath ips is enabled
Quick run mode is enabled
Event notification through syslog is enabled
Event notification through SDEE is enabled
Total Active Signatures: 132
Total Inactive Signatures: 0
Signature 1107:0 disable
Signature 2004:0 disable
IPS Rule Configuration
 IPS name sdm_ips_rule
Interface Configuration
 Interface Serial0/0/1
  Inbound IPS rule is sdm_ips_rule
  Outgoing IPS rule is not set
FW#
```

Note: If you are ending the lab here, delete the SDF file that you created by using the **delete flash:sdmips.sdf** command in privileged EXEC mode.

Challenge: Add a Signature

Using SDM allows you to create custom IPS signatures. In this lab, you create a signature that detects a certain string in Telnet text and terminate the connection, if found.

Under the **All Categories** level of the Signature tree, filter the view by choosing **Engine** in the View By drop-down list. Also, choose **STRING.TCP** in the Engine drop-down list. After the two drop-down boxes are properly selected and the view is filtered to show only string-based TCP signatures, drag down on the **Add** icon to **Add New**, as shown in Figure 6-48.

Figure 6-48   IPS STRING.TCP Signatures

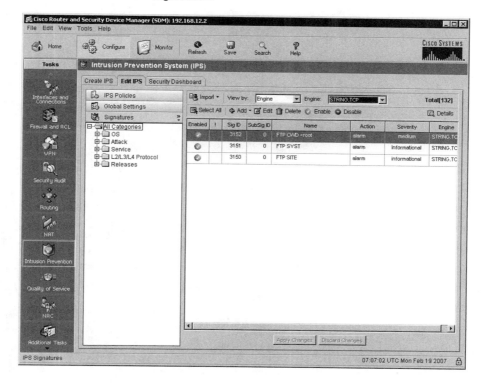

When creating or modifying signatures, to change the default values on certain fields, click the green square to the left of the field name. It changes to a red diamond, which means that the field will be changed from the default. This does not apply to all fields, only those with green squares.

As shown in Figure 6-49, leave the default signature ID number as 20000 for this new signature. Name the signature CCNP_ATTACK, because the attack string contains CCNP (as you will see subsequently). For EventAction, first click the default action of alarm, and then click reset. This means that when the signature is detected, a log message is generated and a TCP reset is sent to both sides of the connection, terminating the session. To select multiple actions, hold the **Ctrl** key on the keyboard while clicking each one with the mouse.

Figure 6-49   IPS Add Signature Configuration Dialog

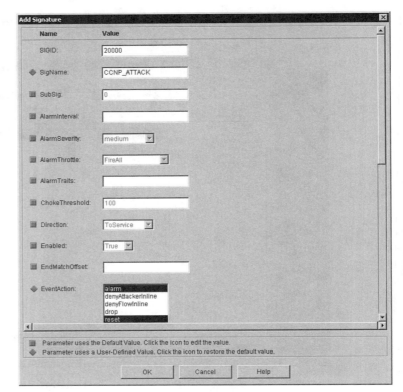

Toward the bottom of the Add Signature window, use a regular expression string of C+NP and a service port of 23. A regular expression is used to parse and search for certain strings. In this case, the + symbol indicates that there will be one or more of the characters before it in a string that matches. Regular expressions are case sensitive and must be matched exactly according to any regular expression symbols in it. In this case, TCP traffic matching the strings CNP, CCNP, CCCNP, and so forth, matches this signature. The service port simply tells the IPS engine to apply this signature to traffic on TCP port 23 (the Telnet port). Click **OK** when you finish, as shown in Figure 6-50.

For more information on regular expressions, consult the Cisco documentation.

Figure 6-50   IPS Add Signature Regular Expression

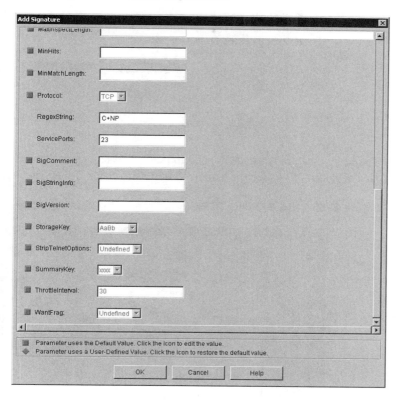

After the new signature appears in the signature list for the STRING.TCP engine, click **Apply Changes**, as shown in Figure 6-51.

Figure 6-51   IPS STRING.TCP Signatures, with New Signature

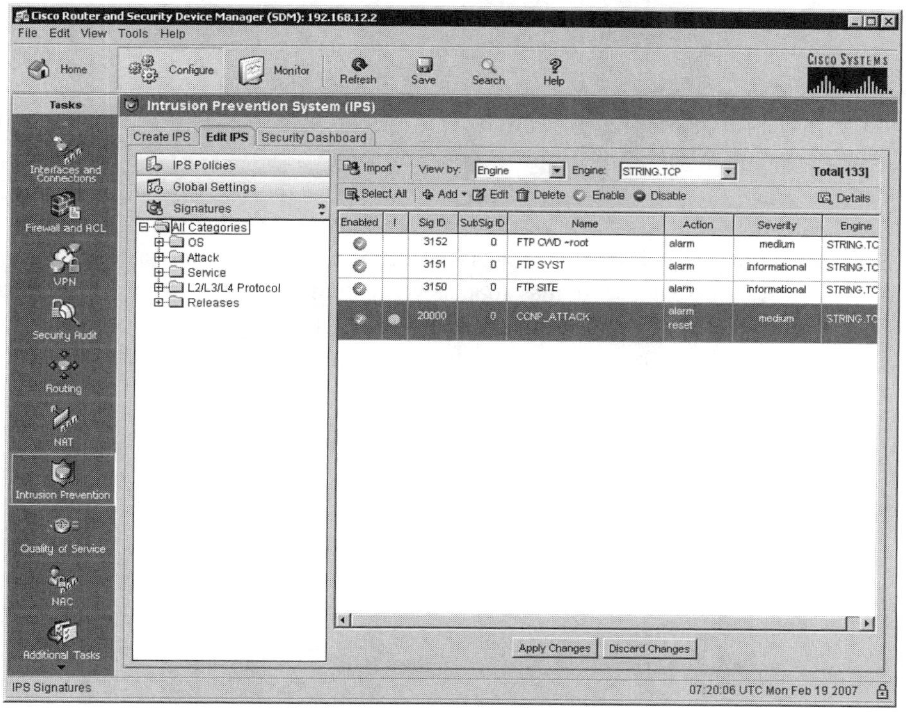

SDM updates the SDM it previously created with the new signature. Figure 6-52 shows an example of the signature delivery status.

Figure 6-52   IPS Signature Delivery Status

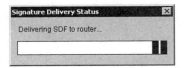

The new signature has been applied to the IPS, as shown in Figure 6-53. Packets with an ingress interface of Serial 0/0/1 are now examined by IPS to check if they also match the new signature.

Figure 6-53   IPS STRING.TCP Signatures, with Changes Applied

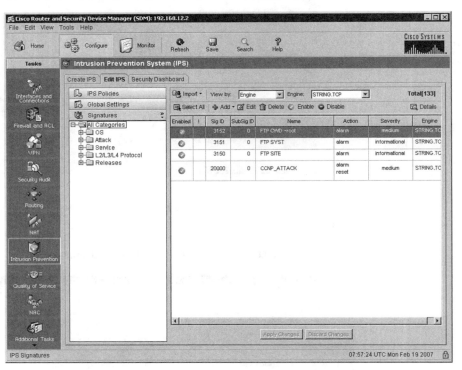

From UNTRUSTED, telnet to TRUSTED and enter **CCNP** (this is case sensitive). Notice that IPS closes the Telnet session as soon as you enter **P**. The P is not even echoed from TRUSTED because the IPS closes the Telnet session before it is echoed. You can try this multiple times with a different number of Cs, because the signature catches all strings for which there is more than one:

```
UNTRUSTED# telnet 192.168.12.1

Trying 192.168.12.1 ... Open


User Access Verification


Password:
TRUSTED> CCN
[Connection to 192.168.12.1 closed by foreign host]
```

```
UNTRUSTED# telnet 192.168.12.1
Trying 192.168.12.1 ... Open

User Access Verification

Password:
TRUSTED> CCCN
[Connection to 192.168.12.1 closed by foreign host]
UNTRUSTED#
```

The attempts are logged on FW.

```
FW#
*Feb 19 08:01:38.847: %IPS-4-SIGNATURE: Sig:20000 Subsig:0 Sev:4 CCNP_ATTACK
  [192.168.23.3:33186 -> 192.168.12.1:23]
FW#
*Feb 19 08:01:50.175: %IPS-4-SIGNATURE: Sig:20000 Subsig:0 Sev:4 CCNP_ATTACK
  [192.168.23.3:60904 -> 192.168.12.1:23]
```

Note: When you are done with the lab, delete the SDF file that you created by using the privileged EXEC command **delete flash:sdmips.sdf**.

Lab 6-4: Configuring IPS with CLI (6.6.4)

The objectives of this lab are as follows:

- Configure Cisco IOS IPS on an interface.

- Disable unwanted IPS signatures.

- Verify IPS settings.

Figure 6-54 illustrates the topology that is used for this lab.

Figure 6-54   Topology Diagram

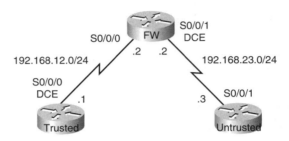

Scenario

In this lab, you configure the Cisco IOS Intrusion Prevention System (IPS), which is part of the Cisco IOS Firewall feature set. IPS examines certain attack patterns and alerts and/or mitigates when those patterns occur.

In this scenario, TRUSTED represents a trusted inside router, FW represents a router serving as an intrusion prevention router, and UNTRUSTED represents an untrusted outside router. Because UNTRUSTED is outside, FW examines packets inbound from it. IPS alone is not enough to make a router into a secure Internet firewall, but in addition to other security features, it can be a powerful defense.

Step 1: Configure Addressing

Configure the serial interfaces shown in Figure 6-54. Set the clock rate on the appropriate interface and issue the **no shutdown** command on all serial connections. Verify that you have connectivity across the local subnet by using the **ping** command:

```
TRUSTED(config)# interface serial0/0/0
TRUSTED(config-if)# ip address 192.168.12.1 255.255.255.0
TRUSTED(config-if)# clockrate 64000
TRUSTED(config-if)# no shutdown
```

```
FW(config)# interface serial0/0/0
FW(config-if)# ip address 192.168.12.2 255.255.255.0
FW(config-if)# no shutdown
FW(config-if)# interface serial0/0/1
FW(config-if)# ip address 192.168.23.2 255.255.255.0
```

```
FW(config-if)# clockrate 64000
FW(config-if)# no shutdown
UNTRUSTED(config)# interface serial0/0/1
UNTRUSTED(config-if)# ip address 192.168.23.3 255.255.255.0
UNTRUSTED(config-if)# no shutdown
```

Step 2: Configure Static Default Routes

On the TRUSTED and UNTRUSTED routers, configure static default routes directing traffic to unknown destinations to be forwarded to the FW router. FW does not need any routes because it has interfaces directly connected to both networks:

```
TRUSTED(config)# ip route 0.0.0.0 0.0.0.0 192.168.12.2
UNTRUSTED(config)# ip route 0.0.0.0 0.0.0.0 192.168.23.2
```

At this point, your network should have full IP connectivity. If it does not have full connectivity, troubleshoot.

Normally, a single-homed company might use Network Address Translation (NAT) at its corporate edge to protect its network and allow private addressing within the bounds of its network. In that case, the UNTRUSTED router—normally a provider edge router—would have a static route directing traffic to the address owned by the customer out one of its interfaces. In this scenario, you do not configure NAT, and you use a default route for simplicity.

Step 3: Create and Apply an IPS Rule

On FW, create an IPS rule by using the **ip ips name** *name* command in global configuration mode. Use the name myips for the IPS name. Although it won't be used in this lab, to create an IPS rule that operates only on certain traffic (specified with an access list), use the **ip ips name** *name* **list** *list* command in global configuration mode:

```
FW(config)# ip ips name myips
```

Note: This lab does not cover using signatures from a signature definition file (SDF). Instead, it uses the built-in signatures in the IOS Firewall software. In a production environment, you might want to specify an SDF file by using the **ip ips sdf location** *location* command in global configuration mode, where *location* is a relative location to the router, such as flash:128MB.sdf, which indicates that an SDF file in the router's flash memory named 128MB.sdf is used.

Apply the IPS rule to an interface with the **ip ips** *name direction* command in interface configuration mode. Apply the rule that you just created inbound on the interface facing UNTRUSTED. After you enable IPS, some log messages are sent to the console line, which indicates that the IPS engines are being initialized:

```
FW(config)# interface serial0/0/1
FW(config-if)# ip ips myips in
*Feb 19 09:16:09.923: %IPS-6-BUILTIN_SIGS: Configured to load builtin signatures
*Feb 19 09:16:10.067: %IPS-6-SDF_LOAD_SUCCESS: SDF loaded successfully from builtin
*Feb 19 09:16:10.075: %IPS-6-ENGINE_BUILDING: OTHER - 3 signatures - 1 of 15 engines
*Feb 19 09:16:10.075: %IPS-6-ENGINE_READY: OTHER - 0 ms - packets for this engine
  will be scanned
```

```
*Feb 19 09:16:10.075: %IPS-6-ENGINE_BUILDING: MULTI-STRING - 0 signatures - 2 of 15
  engines
*Feb 19 09:16:10.075: %IPS-6-ENGINE_BUILD_SKIPPED: MULTI-STRING - there are no new
  signature definitions for this engine
*Feb 19 09:16:10.075: %IPS-6-ENGINE_BUILDING: STRING.ICMP - 0 signatures - 3 of 15
  engines
*Feb 19 09:16:10.075: %IPS-6-ENGINE_BUILD_SKIPPED: STRING.ICMP - there are no new
  signature definitions for this engine
<OUTPUT OMITTED>
```

Step 4: Modify Default IPS Behavior

From UNTRUSTED, ping TRUSTED with a high repeat count:

```
UNTRUSTED# ping 192.168.12.1 repeat 100

Type escape sequence to abort.
Sending 100, 100-byte ICMP Echos to 192.168.12.1, timeout is 2 seconds:
!!!!!!!!!!!!!!!!!!!!!!!!!!!!!!!!!!!!!!!!!!!!!!!!!!!!!!!!!!!!!!!!!!!!!!!!!!!!
!!!!!!!!!!!!!!!!!!!!!!!!!!!!!!!!
Success rate is 100 percent (100/100), round-trip min/avg/max = 56/56/88 ms
```

Notice the log messages on FW. It starts off logging each signature match, but after 62 hits, IPS only reports a summary count without logging each match individually:

```
FW#
*Feb 19 09:30:41.823: %IPS-4-SIGNATURE: Sig:2004 Subsig:0 Sev:2 ICMP Echo Req
  [192.168.23.3:0 -> 192.168.12.1:0]
*Feb 19 09:30:41.879: %IPS-4-SIGNATURE: Sig:2004 Subsig:0 Sev:2 ICMP Echo Req
  [192.168.23.3:0 -> 192.168.12.1:0]
*Feb 19 09:30:41.935: %IPS-4-SIGNATURE: Sig:2004 Subsig:0 Sev:2 ICMP Echo Req
  [192.168.23.3:0 -> 192.168.12.1:0]
*Feb 19 09:30:41.991: %IPS-4-SIGNATURE: Sig:2004 Subsig:0 Sev:2 ICMP Echo Req
  [192.168.23.3:0 -> 192.168.12.1:0]
*Feb 19 09:30:42.051: %IPS-4-SIGNATURE: Sig:2004 Subsig:0 Sev:2 ICMP Echo Req
  [192.168.23.3:0 -> 192.168.12.1:0]
*Feb 19 09:30:42.107: %IPS-4-SIGNATURE: Sig:2004 Subsig:0 Sev:2 ICMP Echo Req
  [192.168.23.3:0 -> 192.168.12.1:0]
*Feb 19 09:30:42.163: %IPS-4-SIGNATURE: Sig:2004 Subsig:0 Sev:2 ICMP Echo Req
  [192.168.23.3:0 -> 192.168.12.1:0]
*Feb 19 09:30:42.219: %IPS-4-SIGNATURE: Sig:2004 Subsig:0 Sev:2 ICMP Echo Req
  [192.168.23.3:0 -> 192.168.12.1:0]
*Feb 19 09:30:42.275: %IPS-4-SIGNATURE: Sig:2004 Subsig:0 Sev:2 ICMP Echo Req
  [192.168.23.3:0 -> 192.168.12.1:0]
*Feb 19 09:30:42.335: %IPS-4-SIGNATURE: Sig:2004 Subsig:0 Sev:2 ICMP Echo Req
  [192.168.23.3:0 -> 192.168.12.1:0]
*Feb 19 09:30:42.391: %IPS-4-SIGNATURE: Sig:2004 Subsig:0 Sev:2 ICMP Echo Req
  [192.168.23.3:0 -> 192.168.12.1:0]
*Feb 19 09:30:42.447: %IPS-4-SIGNATURE: Sig:2004 Subsig:0 Sev:2 ICMP Echo Req
  [192.168.23.3:0 -> 192.168.12.1:0]
*Feb 19 09:30:42.903: %IPS-4-SIGNATURE: Sig:2004 Subsig:0 Sev:2 ICMP Echo Req
  [192.168.23.3:0 -> 192.168.12.1:0]
*Feb 19 09:30:42.959: %IPS-4-SIGNATURE: Sig:2004 Subsig:0 Sev:2 ICMP Echo Req
  [192.168.23.3:0 -> 192.168.12.1:0]
```

```
*Feb 19 09:30:43.019: %IPS-4-SIGNATURE: Sig:2004 Subsig:0 Sev:2 ICMP Echo Req
  [192.168.23.3:0 -> 192.168.12.1:0]

 *Feb 19 09:30:43.075: %IPS-4-SIGNATURE: Sig:2004 Subsig:0 Sev:2 ICMP Echo Req
  [192.168.23.3:0 -> 192.168.12.1:0]

 *Feb 19 09:30:43.131: %IPS-4-SIGNATURE: Sig:2004 Subsig:0 Sev:2 ICMP Echo Req
  [192.168.23.3:0 -> 192.168.12.1:0]

 *Feb 19 09:30:43.187: %IPS-4-SIGNATURE: Sig:2004 Subsig:0 Sev:2 ICMP Echo Req
  [192.168.23.3:0 -> 192.168.12.1:0]

 *Feb 19 09:30:43.247: %IPS-4-SIGNATURE: Sig:2004 Subsig:0 Sev:2 ICMP Echo Req
  [192.168.23.3:0 -> 192.168.12.1:0]

 *Feb 19 09:30:43.303: %IPS-4-SIGNATURE: Sig:2004 Subsig:0 Sev:2 ICMP Echo Req
  [192.168.23.3:0 -> 192.168.12.1:0]

 *Feb 19 09:30:43.359: %IPS-4-SIGNATURE: Sig:2004 Subsig:0 Sev:2 ICMP Echo Req
  [192.168.23.3:0 -> 192.168.12.1:0]

 *Feb 19 09:30:43.415: %IPS-4-SIGNATURE: Sig:2004 Subsig:0 Sev:2 ICMP Echo Req
  [192.168.23.3:0 -> 192.168.12.1:0]

 *Feb 19 09:30:43.927: %IPS-4-SIGNATURE: Sig:2004 Subsig:0 Sev:2 ICMP Echo Req
  [192.168.23.3:0 -> 192.168.12.1:0]

 *Feb 19 09:30:43.987: %IPS-4-SIGNATURE: Sig:2004 Subsig:0 Sev:2 ICMP Echo Req
  [192.168.23.3:0 -> 192.168.12.1:0]

 *Feb 19 09:30:44.043: %IPS-4-SIGNATURE: Sig:2004 Subsig:0 Sev:2 ICMP Echo Req
  [192.168.23.3:0 -> 192.168.12.1:0]

 *Feb 19 09:30:44.099: %IPS-4-SIGNATURE: Sig:2004 Subsig:0 Sev:2 ICMP Echo Req
  [192.168.23.3:0 -> 192.168.12.1:0]

 *Feb 19 09:30:44.159: %IPS-4-SIGNATURE: Sig:2004 Subsig:0 Sev:2 ICMP Echo Req
  [192.168.23.3:0 -> 192.168.12.1:0]

 *Feb 19 09:30:44.215: %IPS-4-SIGNATURE: Sig:2004 Subsig:0 Sev:2 ICMP Echo Req
  [192.168.23.3:0 -> 192.168.12.1:0]

 *Feb 19 09:30:44.271: %IPS-4-SIGNATURE: Sig:2004 Subsig:0 Sev:2 ICMP Echo Req
  [192.168.23.3:0 -> 192.168.12.1:0]

 *Feb 19 09:30:44.327: %IPS-4-SIGNATURE: Sig:2004 Subsig:0 Sev:2 ICMP Echo Req
  [192.168.23.3:0 -> 192.168.12.1:0]

 *Feb 19 09:30:44.387: %IPS-4-SIGNATURE: Sig:2004 Subsig:0 Sev:2 ICMP Echo Req
  [192.168.23.3:0 -> 192.168.12.1:0]

 *Feb 19 09:30:44.443: %IPS-4-SIGNATURE: Sig:2004 Subsig:0 Sev:2 ICMP Echo Req
  [192.168.23.3:0 -> 192.168.12.1:0]

 *Feb 19 09:30:44.899: %IPS-4-SIGNATURE: Sig:2004 Subsig:0 Sev:2 ICMP Echo Req
  [192.168.23.3:0 -> 192.168.12.1:0]

 *Feb 19 09:30:44.955: %IPS-4-SIGNATURE: Sig:2004 Subsig:0 Sev:2 ICMP Echo Req
  [192.168.23.3:0 -> 192.168.12.1:0]

 *Feb 19 09:30:45.011: %IPS-4-SIGNATURE: Sig:2004 Subsig:0 Sev:2 ICMP Echo Req
  [192.168.23.3:0 -> 192.168.12.1:0]

 *Feb 19 09:30:45.067: %IPS-4-SIGNATURE: Sig:2004 Subsig:0 Sev:2 ICMP Echo Req
  [192.168.23.3:0 -> 192.168.12.1:0]

 *Feb 19 09:30:45.127: %IPS-4-SIGNATURE: Sig:2004 Subsig:0 Sev:2 ICMP Echo Req
  [192.168.23.3:0 -> 192.168.12.1:0]

 *Feb 19 09:30:45.183: %IPS-4-SIGNATURE: Sig:2004 Subsig:0 Sev:2 ICMP Echo Req
  [192.168.23.3:0 -> 192.168.12.1:0]

 *Feb 19 09:30:45.239: %IPS-4-SIGNATURE: Sig:2004 Subsig:0 Sev:2 ICMP Echo Req
  [192.168.23.3:0 -> 192.168.12.1:0]

 *Feb 19 09:30:45.295: %IPS-4-SIGNATURE: Sig:2004 Subsig:0 Sev:2 ICMP Echo Req
  [192.168.23.3:0 -> 192.168.12.1:0]

 *Feb 19 09:30:45.355: %IPS-4-SIGNATURE: Sig:2004 Subsig:0 Sev:2 ICMP Echo Req
  [192.168.23.3:0 -> 192.168.12.1:0]
```

```
*Feb 19 09:30:45.411: %IPS-4-SIGNATURE: Sig:2004 Subsig:0 Sev:2 ICMP Echo Req
[192.168.23.3:0 -> 192.168.12.1:0]

*Feb 19 09:30:45.931: %IPS-4-SIGNATURE: Sig:2004 Subsig:0 Sev:2 ICMP Echo Req
[192.168.23.3:0 -> 192.168.12.1:0]

*Feb 19 09:30:45.987: %IPS-4-SIGNATURE: Sig:2004 Subsig:0 Sev:2 ICMP Echo Req
[192.168.23.3:0 -> 192.168.12.1:0]

*Feb 19 09:30:46.047: %IPS-4-SIGNATURE: Sig:2004 Subsig:0 Sev:2 ICMP Echo Req
[192.168.23.3:0 -> 192.168.12.1:0]

*Feb 19 09:30:46.103: %IPS-4-SIGNATURE: Sig:2004 Subsig:0 Sev:2 ICMP Echo Req
[192.168.23.3:0 -> 192.168.12.1:0]

*Feb 19 09:30:46.159: %IPS-4-SIGNATURE: Sig:2004 Subsig:0 Sev:2 ICMP Echo Req
[192.168.23.3:0 -> 192.168.12.1:0]

*Feb 19 09:30:46.215: %IPS-4-SIGNATURE: Sig:2004 Subsig:0 Sev:2 ICMP Echo Req
[192.168.23.3:0 -> 192.168.12.1:0]

*Feb 19 09:30:46.275: %IPS-4-SIGNATURE: Sig:2004 Subsig:0 Sev:2 ICMP Echo Req
[192.168.23.3:0 -> 192.168.12.1:0]

*Feb 19 09:30:46.331: %IPS-4-SIGNATURE: Sig:2004 Subsig:0 Sev:2 ICMP Echo Req
[192.168.23.3:0 -> 192.168.12.1:0]

*Feb 19 09:30:46.387: %IPS-4-SIGNATURE: Sig:2004 Subsig:0 Sev:2 ICMP Echo Req
[192.168.23.3:0 -> 192.168.12.1:0]

*Feb 19 09:30:46.443: %IPS-4-SIGNATURE: Sig:2004 Subsig:0 Sev:2 ICMP Echo Req
[192.168.23.3:0 -> 192.168.12.1:0]

*Feb 19 09:30:46.923: %IPS-4-SIGNATURE: Sig:2004 Subsig:0 Sev:2 ICMP Echo Req
[192.168.23.3:0 -> 192.168.12.1:0]

*Feb 19 09:30:46.979: %IPS-4-SIGNATURE: Sig:2004 Subsig:0 Sev:2 ICMP Echo Req
[192.168.23.3:0 -> 192.168.12.1:0]

*Feb 19 09:30:47.039: %IPS-4-SIGNATURE: Sig:2004 Subsig:0 Sev:2 ICMP Echo Req
[192.168.23.3:0 -> 192.168.12.1:0]

*Feb 19 09:30:47.095: %IPS-4-SIGNATURE: Sig:2004 Subsig:0 Sev:2 ICMP Echo Req
[192.168.23.3:0 -> 192.168.12.1:0]

*Feb 19 09:30:47.151: %IPS-4-SIGNATURE: Sig:2004 Subsig:0 Sev:2 ICMP Echo Req
[192.168.23.3:0 -> 192.168.12.1:0]

*Feb 19 09:30:47.207: %IPS-4-SIGNATURE: Sig:2004 Subsig:0 Sev:2 ICMP Echo Req
[192.168.23.3:0 -> 192.168.12.1:0]

*Feb 19 09:30:47.263: %IPS-4-SIGNATURE: Sig:2004 Subsig:0 Sev:2 ICMP Echo Req
[192.168.23.3:0 -> 192.168.12.1:0]

*Feb 19 09:30:47.323: %IPS-4-SIGNATURE: Sig:2004 Subsig:0 Sev:2 ICMP Echo Req
[192.168.23.3:0 -> 192.168.12.1:0]

*Feb 19 09:30:47.379: %IPS-4-SIGNATURE: Sig:2004 Subsig:0 Sev:2 ICMP Echo Req
[192.168.23.3:0 -> 192.168.12.1:0]

*Feb 19 09:30:47.435: %IPS-4-SIGNATURE: Sig:2004 Subsig:0 Sev:2 ICMP Echo Req
[192.168.23.3:0 -> 192.168.12.1:0]

*Feb 19 09:31:11.823: %IPS-4-SIG_SUMMARY: Sig:2004 Subsig:0 Global Summary: 100
alarms in this interval
```

To disable a signature on a router, use the **ip ips signature** *number* **disable** command in global configuration mode. Signature number 2004 detected the previous potential ICMP attack indicated in the previous output. Disable the signature numbered 2004, which was previously being set off by the ping:

```
FW(config)# ip ips signature 2004 disable
%IPS Signature 2004:0 is disabled
```

Try the ping again from UNTRUSTED to TRUSTED. You do not need a high repeat count because no summary messages exist (there are no matches to begin with):

```
UNTRUSTED# ping 192.168.12.1

Type escape sequence to abort.
Sending 5, 100-byte ICMP Echos to 192.168.12.1, timeout is 2 seconds:
!!!!!
Success rate is 100 percent (5/5), round-trip min/avg/max = 56/56/56 ms
```

Notice that no individual or summary IPS messages have been logged on the FW router.

Why would you want to disable IPS signatures?

_____

_____

You can also verify the current IPS configuration by using the command **show ip ips all**. Notice that in addition to the signature we just disabled, another signature was disabled by default:

```
FW# show ip ips all
Configured SDF Locations: none
Builtin signatures are enabled and loaded
Last successful SDF load time: 09:29:43 UTC Feb 19 2007
IPS fail closed is disabled
Fastpath ips is enabled
Quick run mode is enabled
Event notification through syslog is enabled
Event notification through SDEE is disabled
Total Active Signatures: 132
Total Inactive Signatures: 0
Signature 2004:0 disable
Signature 1107:0 disable
IPS Rule Configuration
 IPS name myips
Interface Configuration
 Interface Serial0/0/1
  Inbound IPS rule is myips
  Outgoing IPS rule is not set
```

Notice that you can use the syslog protocol to report detections and IPS actions to management stations. For the intrusion detection feature, the IPS router simply sends the notifications to the syslog server.

Case Studies

Case Study 1: CLI IPsec and Frame-Mode MPLS

The International Travel Agency needs parts of its network set up with IPsec and Multiprotocol Label Switching (MPLS), as shown in the topology in Figure 7-1, according to the following specifications:

- Configure all interfaces using the addressing scheme shown in Figure 7-1.

- Run EIGRP AS 1 in the entire International Travel Agency core network. All subnets should be included.

- Create an IPsec tunnel between R1 and R3 with an appropriate transform set and ISAKMP policy.

- This IPsec tunnel should only encrypt traffic between R1's loopback network and R4's loopback network.

- Use preshared keys for authentication in the ISAKMP policy.

- Do not create any new interfaces to achieve this task.

- Use any encryption algorithms desired for the tasks just listed that use the crypto suite of protocols.

- Configure MPLS on both ends of the link between R3 and R4.

- Configure R1 to send system logging messages at the error severity level to an imaginary host located at 172.16.2.200.

- Set up the correct time on R4 by using the **clock set** command. Use the inline IOS help system if you do not know this command's syntax.

- Configure R4 as an NTP master with stratum 5.

- Configure R3 as an NTP client of R4.

Implement the International Travel Agency network shown in Figure 7-1 by using the information provided. Implement the design on the lab set of routers. This case study should be completed by using the Cisco IOS command-line interface (CLI), without using the Cisco Security Device Manager (SDM). Verify that all configurations are operational and functioning according to the guidelines.

Figure 7-1   Topology Diagram

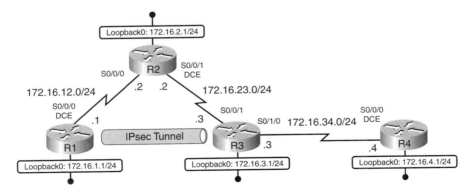

Questions

1. Will R3 or R4 send the NTP queries as MPLS frames? Explain.

_____

_____

_____

2. Will R3 or R4 send any packets destined to the other router as MPLS frames? Explain.

_____

_____

3. Will R3 or R4 send any packets as MPLS frames at all? Explain.

_____

_____

4. Differentiate among the algorithms by explaining which algorithms in your IPsec policy apply to encryption, which to authentication, and which to message integrity. According to your reading, which of the available algorithms in each category is most secure?

_____

_____

_____

5. How does NTP help prepare a network for system logging? Explain.

_____

_____

_____

Case Study 2: Device Hardening and VPNs

The International Travel Agency decided to extend its offices to a new branch location by using its existing network tunnel. The CIO has chosen to use a secure generic routing encapsulation (GRE) tunnel to connect the branch office to its headquarters (HQ). The tunnel terminates at the headquarters end on a Cisco router with the firewall feature set.

Implement the International Travel Agency network shown in the topology in Figure 7-2.

Figure 7-2   Topology Diagram

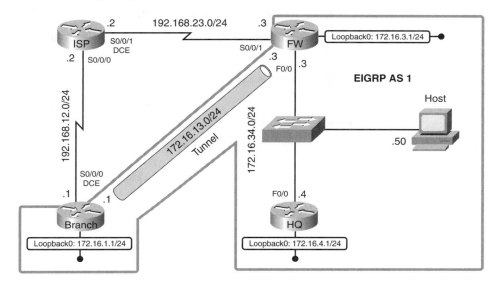

Demonstrate that this configuration allows routing between sites and secures intranet traffic as it traverses the service provider's domain. Implement the security policies defined next on both the FW and BRANCH routers.

Use the Cisco Security Device Manager (SDM) to configure the security tasks, except where noted in the following list:

Using the Cisco IOS CLI:

- Configure all interfaces by using the addressing scheme shown in Figure 7-2.

- Configure HQ, FW, and BRANCH to run Enhanced Interior Gateway Routing Protocol (EIGRP) in AS 1. (Until the tunnel is created, BRANCH does not have any EIGRP adjacencies.)

- Add the major 172.16.0.0 network to EIGRP and disable automatic summarization.

- Configure a static default route on FW toward ISP, and redistribute this into EIGRP.

- Configure a static default route on BRANCH toward ISP.

- Create a static route on ISP for 172.16.0.0/16 toward FW.

- After configuring the static routes, make sure that you can ping between FW and BRANCH.

- Configure the host with the IP address shown in Figure 7-2, and make FW its default gateway.

- Configure FW and BRANCH for SDM access from the host.

Using Cisco SDM:

- Create a secure GRE tunnel between FW and BRANCH by using IPsec.

- Use the addressing shown in Figure 7-2 for the tunnel addressing.

- Run EIGRP across the tunnel.

- Use the tunnel wizard to configure one end of the tunnel, and generate a mirror configuration using Cisco SDM for the other end. You can use the CLI to implement the mirror tunnel configuration on BRANCH.

- Apply any encryption algorithms desired for the secure GRE tunnel.

- Configure FW as a firewall using the basic firewall wizard. Assign the interface facing the ISP router to be the outside interface. Trust traffic from all other interfaces.

- If SDM does not automatically allow IPsec traffic through the firewall, explicitly allow it.

- Use the SDM IPS wizard to configure BRANCH to enable the Intrusion Prevention System (IPS) on the ingress interface facing the ISP router.

Verify that all configurations are operational and function according to the guidelines.